JONATHAN WILLIAMS
THE LORD OF ORCHARDS

EDITED BY JEFFERY BEAM AND RICHARD OWENS

WESTPORT AND NEW YORK

PROSPECTA PRESS

PROSPECTA PRESS
P. O. Box 3131
Westport, CT 06880
(203) 571-0781
www.prospectapress.com

Book design by Barbara Aronica-Buck
Front cover photograph by Guy Mendes, used with permission
Back cover image, *Poet's Silhouette* by Jonathan Williams, used by permission

Some of the works included here were originally published online as an issue of *Jacket* magazine #38 in 2009

This paperback and ebook edition published in September 2017

Paperback ISBN 978-1-63226-087-1
eBook ISBN 978-1-63226-088-8

Manufactured in the United States of America

FOR
ANN McGARRELL

CONTENTS

REVIEWING:

RECOLLECTING:

JEFFERY BEAM

TEACHING DAYLILIES TO READ—
INTRODUCTION TO THE PRINT EDITION

Matthew Fox once said about his dear friend M. C. Richards, Jonathan Williams' fellow Black Mountaineer, that to those around her she was "a way of knowing about the world." One recognizes Jonathan at hand. The slew of epithets used to describe Williams, his poetry, and Jargon over the decades—"the finest American poet of this century," "the Custodian of Snowflakes," "The Truffle-Hound of American Poetry," "our Johnny Appleseed," "of a kind, but of its kind it is unequalled in the whole of the English language," "a polytechnic institute," "america's largest openair museum," "the American Martial," "a magpie," "old Black Mountain-ear,"—should have served to prick the larger world into attention. It often didn't. More shame on them.

Richard Owens, a PhD candidate working in the Jargon archives at the Poetry Collection at SUNY-Buffalo, whom I had met at Williams' Skywinding Farm, near Scaly Mountain, North Carolina, first fielded the idea of some sort of memorial festschrift for Jonathan after his death—an idea that had already seeded in my own mind but with little thought of how to make it happen. Rich, however, did, and soon we were at work. Without Rich, then, this book might not exist. In the year after Jonathan's death I was numb with grief. My friend and teacher of 29 years was gone just at a moment that my work in the library at the University of North Carolina at Chapel Hill had taken a wearisome turn. As a result, Rich bore more than his share of conceptualizing the original online *Jacket* feature, in particular the technicalities involved. I was even in Italy, off the grid, during part of the time. So I thank Rich now for his extra efforts then, and for his support now.

Because the print book was so important to Jonathan, I promised myself, as we were producing the online festschrift, that one day the *Lord of Orchards* would be an expanded print book and more hybrid—festschrift and a first reflective look at Jonathan's legacy. Ann McGarrell—fellow Jargonaut and dear friend—and I frequently talked about it. I kept putting it on the back burner. Retirement came and its adjustments, a small handful of my own books and musical works by young composers inspired by my poems, filling my time. And I remained numb. Ann's passing in January 2016 reminded me of that promise to myself, to Jonathan, but most of all to her. Among all my Jargonaut friends, Ann and I shared our deep grief. Just weeks before her sudden illness in December 2015 we had spoken once again about the *Lord of Orchards*. Jonathan would have been 88 in March 2017. As of this book release, seven years have passed since the *Jacket* feature. Well, as Bronson Alcott said, "Time ripens the substance of a life as the seasons mellow and perfect its fruits. The best apples fall latest and keep longest."

And David Wilk stepped forward. A high salute to him. A barbaric yawp!

My life as a Jargonaut, as a Jonathan enthusiast, began with the arrival of a postcard in 1979, declaring surprise that there could be another nationally published *out* gay poet in North Carolina other than himself and Tom Meyer. Entering Jonathan's orbit, for anyone, was transformative. I was essentially a country boy dreaming to be part of a community like Black Mountain—of which I had heard so much from the very few adventurous high school teachers in Kannapolis, North Carolina—or being absorbed into a Blake, Yeats, Sitwell, Wilde, Eluard, Garcia Lorca, or Genet-like circle. I had only just stepped beyond my immersion in Surrealism, Symbolism, and the mystical poets and into an engagement with William Carlos Williams, Bly, Rich, and Merwin. Thus my intellectual and poetic life was rich, my knowledge fairly broad but zig-zaggy from my own wandering readings, and my experience little. I had never seen the ocean (being a mountain and Piedmont person) until I was 18. When I met Jonathan I had never been out of the state except to D.C. and New York a few times each, and to Philadelphia once. Europe not at all. My ground was fertile but not diversely seeded. I was HUNGRY. Some things Jonathan or Tom talked about, I knew of, I knew about, but I didn't KNOW. And suddenly a world heaved open. A desert bloomed. Jonathan scared, intimidated, and entranced me. He didn't blink.

Jonathan and Tom's friendship and the informal, and yet extensive, cultivation given to this raw creature before them, was life-changing. Jonathan was one of the four most important people in my development as a poet. Clearly THE most important, or at least equal to the grandmother who had allowed the poet space to grow. But she only knew how to turn the ground; Jonathan how to seed and fertilize it.

Jonathan's first inscription to me iterated Diaghilev's to Cocteau: "Astonish me!" I was wise (?), smart (?)—no, attuned (!) enough to understand that meant become my own person, my own poet. To absorb everything he and Tom had to offer; but not to copy. And to be responsible—as Jonathan was fond of repeating Robert Duncan's "Responsibility is to keep the ability to respond." I had already embraced Levertov's re-writing of one of Creeley's maxims: *Form is never more than a revelation of content* (Creeley: *extension of*). I was ready to eat. And for close to 30 years, eat keenly I did.

So many pleasant days and evenings. So many fine meals and wine, so much marvelous even staggering music, so many astounding and entertaining stories and rants, so many beautiful and odd places visited—most of all the people (the quick *and* the dead) met and befriended. Not a day goes by that something Jonathan said, or exposed Stanley and me to, or further illuminated upon, isn't remembered. And is USED.

I want to quote a letter here that Jonathan sent to me from Corn Close, his half-year English retreat, in response to a letter from me in which I must have complained about having to work 40 hours a week. Jonathan was fond of calling me "Miss Tick" or "Miss (S)tick":

[A photocopy image of Bunting in roundel appears at the top of the letter, with these words from Bunting surrounding: "Readers are not what one writes for after one's got rid of the cruder ambitions."]

June 17, 1991 Uncle Igor Straw-in-Sky

Dear Miss Tick,

Good biography to read is Alan Judd's on Ford Madox Ford. Old Fordie and Lord Gnang have a lot in common. One day FMF asked someone in amazement: "Why is this man attacking me? I have never once helped him to publish a book and I have never loaned him any money!" Ford wrote constantly, liked to live in houses with good views, and despised literary dullards and careerists. After writing 82 books he had no more money than when he started.

The times are squalid and most people in the arts are shits who think it's all sho-biz. The odd Mr. Eric Gill said all one could do was make a "cell of good living." Well, you and Stan the Man are doing that at Frog Level. What do you do in place of the jobs that now occupy and depress you? There's no way I can answer that. If [you] decide you want to try working at something in Highlands, we could offer you the use of the cottage until you could build something bigger on your own. That might be a help. A small nursery* [handwritten note at bottom: you could put it in the old orchard near the Richardsons'] offering garden work and design work just could be one answer. The demand is there and few seem to be meeting it.

Ah, time thou art fled. That's the rub, ain't it, mate? Who will take the time to read those funny little words we commit to paper? We all will take time to go to the mall, go to the movies, go see a ball-game, go out to dinner. Why not? But they all tend to come way ahead of reading a poem. Has ___ read more than 5 minutes by JW? Do ___ and ___ read more than 6 minutes of JW? There are many of one's friends who have read far less. We must teach daylilies how to read. We mustn't worry so much. To assist this process, I am on the water-wagon for some weeks or a month. My stomach gets too acid and my spirits plunge. Phooey. Fuck'em all and sleep till noon, as Wm Blake wld have said if he had the lingo.

It's going to be one of the coldest Junes on record. Haven't seen much of the sun for nearly two weeks and the winds are chill. The poppies refuse to be seen. The red ones I mean. The wild Welsh ones are all over the place.

Love,
Bent up Dent [handwritten]

It's Jonathan's generosity I remember the most. How subtly he chastises and thus instructs and embraces me—not, "You mustn't worry so much," but "we." That's the Jonathan who collected the world and offered it to anyone willing and capable of responding. I spoke with Jonathan the day before he died, and was able to tell him thank you and how much I (we) loved him. The *Lord of Orchards* is not only printed proof of that devotion and gratitude, but proof of fidelity and loyalty to his life's work and its unique and inestimable value. Further proof can be found especially in his poems, his photographic collection, *A Palpable Elysium*, the two books of published essays, *The Magpie's Bagpipe,* and *Blackbird Dust,* and on the horizon, a forthcoming volume of essays from this publisher, *Lord Nose's Gnosis*. Good supplements and insight into Jonathan's "circle" can be agreeably explored in the two birthday festschrifts: *JW/50* (*Truck* 21/Gnomon, 1979) and Reuben Cox's *Orpington Via Pratt's Bottom: JW at 75* (Brown Roux, 2004).

I should mention some of the rousing new additions to this book: a first time ever selection of letters between Jonathan and his first partner Ronald Johnson edited by Peter O'Leary, an article by budding British Jonathan/Jargon scholar Ross Hair, a recounting of the *White Trash Cooking* story by former Jargon lawyer Thorns Craven, an expanded bibliography of audio and visual recordings, and an extensive collection of transcriptions from two interview/filming sessions with North Carolina Emmy award-winning filmmaker Neal Hutcheson.

I look forward to the folk who in the near future, I trust, will step forward to write what has to be an absorbing Jonathan biography or comprehensive Jargon history. As Jonathan was certainly one of the best, most remarkable, and productive correspondents of the last century, there are volumes of letters to be published, and unpublished poems, and who knows what else, lurking in the antique spice cabinets of Corn Close and Skywinding.

Jonathan's [just shy of] eight decades and his work of more than half a century is such that no one activity or identity takes primacy over any other—seminal small press publisher of the Jargon Society; poet; book designer; editor; photographer; legendary correspondent; literary, art, and photography critic and collector; early collector and proselytizer of visionary folk art; cultural anthropologist and Juvenalian critic; curmudgeon; happy gardener; resolute walker; and keen and adroit raconteur and gourmand.

His refined decorum and speech, and his sartorial style, contrasted sharply, yet pleasingly, with his delight in the bawdy, with his incisive humor and social criticism, and his confidently experimental, masterful poems and prose. Lesser known for his extraordinary letters and essays, and his photography and art collecting, he is never only a poet or photographer, an essayist or publisher. This book of essays, images, and shouts aims to bring new eyes and contexts to his influence and talent as poet and publisher, but also heighten appreciation for the other facets of his life and art. One might call Jonathan's life a poetics of gathering, and this book a first harvest.

Thanksgiving, 2016
Golgonooza at Frog Level
Hillsborough, NC

DAVID WILK

Writing, especially poetry, is a combination of hard work and joy. Publishing even more so.

Jonathan Williams taught me that the work is the joy. And that you better keep a sense of humor about you at all times. Seriousness might best be cloaked with wit. The struggle is ongoing, but dammit, we will eat well along the way, and enjoy the pleasures of flesh and spirit too.

Where we go is critical, but how we get there matters as well. Driving is better than flying. Walking is best of all. As the great geographer Carl Sauer said: "locomotion should be slow, the slower the better."

Wakefulness does not occur by accident, but by conscious attention and dedication. Poetry can be beautiful, but is hard won, harvested from a garden well planted and tended: watered and weeded.

The books that matter require equal attention, and if there are only three hundred perfect readers for them, so be it.

Robert Duncan's ideal reader was an elderly woman, perhaps Emily Dickinson in her dotage. Jonathan's ideal reader was less specifically imagined and certainly more various. In fact, I am sure the Colonel wanted more than one. And he did have a few, didn't he?

They were a company, a battalion, a diverse troop of lovers and soldiers for books, for photography, for the joy of reading and discovery of the new and marvelous.

But it's the work itself that came first, and was always foremost for Lord Nose.

The poets and artists Jonathan loved most were the individualists, the true originals, solo practitioners, and eccentrics whose imaginations were not products of the traditional American education system.

The list of those he discovered, tended to, talked about, admired and published is pretty much incredible. It's a distinguished collection that includes Mina Loy, Lorine Niedecker, Alfred Starr Hamilton, Paul Metcalf, Ralph Eugene Meatyard, Denise Levertov, Joel Oppenheimer, Kenneth Patchen, Irving Layton, Gilbert Sorrentino, Lou Harrison, Doris Ulmann, Lyle Bongé, Russell Edson, Robert Duncan, Michael McClure, and so many more.

And that is not even to mention the list of Outsider Artists he celebrated, like Sister Gertrude, Howard Finster, and the wonderful St. EOM of Pasaquan.

Jonathan set high standards for himself and never wavered from his commitment to the transcendence of art in life. His sphere of influence was broad and not limited to the American experience, but was, like JW himself, quintessentially American.

Lord Nose was well read, listened to music (mostly classical and jazz), experienced art deeply, loved the (baseball) Braves, and could generally drink and talk anyone under any table anywhere, anytime. And he could walk farther and faster too.

How could any of us, who were along for the ride, keep up, or measure up? I am proud and grateful to have been his friend, and the publisher of some of his work, and to count him as one of the great influences in my life. And I miss him every day.

Here's to the Colonel. This book's for you, old friend.

David Wilk
September 2016

Poet's Silhouette, *(1951):* Looking forward to a Lifetime of Meditation on a Text by R. B. Kitaj, *Mixed media, 1978. By Jonathan Williams. Exhibited at the Cooper-Hewitt Museum, 1978.*

RICHARD OWENS AND JEFFERY BEAM

LORD OF ORCHARDS—JONATHAN WILLIAMS AT 80

[This introduction was published online in the original *Jacket* magazine feature published in 2009 a year after Williams' death at age 79, and remains unchanged in this volume.]

Birthdays were something Jonathan Williams insisted on attending to closely. In his private correspondence he often included the names of poets, artists and outsiders just below the date of composition, calling attention to the moment of their birth. Publicly he produced countless essays celebrating birthdays. In "Eighty of the Best," an essay celebrating Basil Bunting's birthday, Williams writes, "When a man reaches fourscore, it is assumed that he has outlived Wisdom; or is given to the curse of Old-Fartism; or has forgotten most of what he remembers." Unlike Bunting, Williams never made eighty. March 8, 2009, would have marked that moment. But as Williams approached fourscore, he like Bunting convincingly subverted these assumptions, willfully refusing to outlive Wisdom or forget the past. When he quoted Pound—as he quoted dozens if not hundreds of others from memory—he often appealed to Canto LXXXI:

What thou lovest well remains,
the rest is dross …

As his poetry, essays, photographs and the titles he published through Jargon remind us, Williams carefully appreciated, promoted, and preserved the things he loved, struggling to guarantee these remained—not only for himself but others. Recognizing this, Hugh Kenner hailed Jargon as "the Custodian of Snowflakes" and Williams as "the truffle-hound of American poetry." But in pursuing what one loves Williams warned against fetishizing big names and worked instead to nurture the nascent careers of hundreds of emerging or neglected poets, writers, artists, and photographers.

The work he produced for more than half a century is such that no one activity or identity takes primacy over any other. He is never only a poet or photographer, an essayist or publisher. What we find instead in the figure of Williams is a continuity that cuts across these practices—something we might call a poetics of gathering. All of his efforts are linked through an unswerving desire to collect and preserve, harvest and distribute. In the long poem *Mahler*—a work Guy Davenport insisted will mark "the introduction of Blake's Young Ancients to our shores"—Williams writes:

> The Lord of Orchards
> selects his fruit
> in the Firmament's
> breast

And it is from the breast—what nourishes—that Williams selected, constructing a constellation of cultural figures and objects that brings together in a single orbit the utterly unpolished and the cosmopolitan, the eccentric and the carefully measured, the odd and the familiar. A cursory but by no means exhaustive index of figures Williams supported through the years would easily include: American authors James Broughton, Robert Creeley, Guy Davenport, Robert Duncan, Russell Edson, Buckminster Fuller, Ronald Johnson, Denise Levertov, Paul Metcalf, Lorine Niedecker, Charles Olson, Joel Oppenheimer, and Louis Zukofsky; photographers Lyle Bongé, Elizabeth Matheson, John Menapace, Mark Steinmetz, and Doris Ullman; British poets Basil Bunting, Thomas A. Clark, Simon Cutts, Ian Hamilton Finlay, and Mina Loy; outsider artists Georgia Blizzard, St. EOM (Eddie Owens Martin), Howard Finster, James Harold Jennings, and Clarence Schmidt; bookmakers Jonathan Greene, Doyle Moore, and Keith Smith.

Celebrated as a Black Mountain poet, Williams' writing insists on the primary importance of imagination as a foil to ignorance and pinpoints ignorance (whether in the arts, civic, or personal realms) as the source of cultural blight. Informed like his other practices by the wide and varied breadth of his interests, his poetry has been described as a distillation of Martial, Socrates, Basho, Tu Fu, and Richard Pryor. Experimental and open in form, the symbiotic relationship between music and poetic composition and the possibilities found in the high and low, the ribald and the erudite, the metaphysical and the concrete, sets his writing apart as audaciously singular. Oftentimes expressed through word-play, found poems, paeans to pastoral significance, and rails against contemporary despoliation, his poems and essays draw on a range of subjects and themes as broad in scope as the range of figures he published and photographed. In his poems Mahler, Bruckner, Delius, Ives, Satie, Samuel Palmer, and William Blake commune with Mae West, Jelly Roll Morton, Thelonius Monk, Frederick Sommer, and Richard Diebenkorn.

As a correspondent his private epistles were commensurate with the transnational and cross-cultural scope of his interests. The number of people he regularly corresponded with was legion and his epistolary *noms de plume* were as rich and varied as the people and communities he brought together. Known variously through his missives as Lord Stodge, Big Enis, J. Jeeter Swampwater, Lord Crudvigil of Dentdale, Colonel Williams, Lord Gnang, and Lord Nose, for more than fifty years he crafted an average of fifty letters a week, struggling to live daily a statement by Duncan he was fond of quoting: "Responsibility is to keep the ability to respond."

As a gesture toward Williams' life-long commitment to this order of responsibility, we have drawn together a wide selection of contributions that address the scope of Williams' varied practices under the mantle of a single feature celebrating his life and work. Given the number of pieces included here we have, for the sake of convenience, arranged them in four sections.

In "Remembering," the first section, we have pooled together those works that remember, reminisce and respond to Williams with intimacy and affection. These pieces are situated in conversation with a gallery of photographs of Williams—from his early days at St. Albans School in Washington D. C., through his formative years at Black Mountain and into the present decade. While many of the essays and poems included in this section are new and previously unpublished, some of these pieces—such as Basil Bunting's comment on Williams in Cumbria and Ronald Johnson's prose meditation on his time with Williams in the mid-1960s—are presently out of print and reproduced here for the first time. Others like *Aperture* editor Diana Stoll's appreciation and poet-publisher Bob Arnold's comment are memorial essays published shortly after Williams' death. Williams himself was a prodigious writer of memorial essays and obituaries, attending to the passing of poets and artists with a sense of duty that makes the inclusion of these pieces an appropriate if not necessary gesture.

The second section, "Responding," brings into focus both new statements on Williams work by poets David Annwn, Jim Cory, and others as well as a host of previously published but presently out-of-print introductions and critical essays by contemporaries like Guy Davenport, Kenneth Irby, Ronald Johnson, and Eric Mottram. This section also contains prefaces by Charles Olson and Robert Duncan included in two early Williams titles—*Jammin' the Greek Scene* and *Elegies & Celebrations*—both of which have been out of circulation since their first appearances in these Jargon titles nearly half a century ago. A brief essay by Assistant Curator at the Buffalo Poetry and Rare Books Collection, Jim Maynard, contextualizes Duncan's preface and maps the shifting contours of the relationship between Duncan and Williams forward from their years at Black Mountain. Lastly, we have included in this section a facsimile reproduction of the typescript for Olson's 1953 poem "For a Man from Stuttgart," a work dedicated to Williams and included in Williams' *Elegies & Celebrations*. Here the typescript is juxtaposed against an image of the poem's first published appearance in *Elegies*.

The next section, "Reviewing," foregrounds Williams' work in photography. Despite the persistent circulation of his photographs within poetry communities, this section is paradoxically the shortest—yet the two essays contained in this section are rigorous in orientation. While poet-critic Richard Deming's essay investigates the way Williams' photographs gave shape to an emergent avant-garde community at Black Mountain and beyond, Vic Brand carefully considers the photographers Williams promoted and collaborated with, closing his essay with a photographic bibliography of the Jargon Society. These essays are complimented by a gallery of twenty-four photographs by Williams—several previously unpublished and many scanned directly from prints held in the Jargon Society Archive at the Buffalo Poetry and Rare Books Collection.

The fourth and final section, "Recollecting," is two-fold, addressing not only Williams as a collector committed to selecting his fruit from the Firmament but also the work involved in collecting Williams. An essay by friend, Williams' bibliographer and bookseller, James Jaffe begins this section, locating the Jargon Society in a broader fine press tradition while poet-critic and publisher Kyle Schlesinger reinforces this view of Jargon by historicizing the press, investigating several Jargon publications and calling attention to Williams' relationships with various typographers and designers. Critic Tom Patterson picks up on a different thread, focusing on Williams' interest in collecting Outsider art, a thread poet-critic Dale Smith also investigates with attention to Williams' deep affection for the strange. Next, in an interview conducted in June 2007, Williams speaks to his life and work himself and responds to a range of topics comparable to the scope of his interests. Finally the archive itself is addressed. Former curator of the Buffalo Poetry Collection Robert Bertholf points toward the centrality of Jargon Society to twentieth-century American poetry while Michael Basinski, the present curator, speaks directly to the present state of the archive, which he reminds us is "the largest single manuscript collection" at Buffalo. Two checklists are also included here, a bibliography of works by Jonathan Williams and a bibliography of Jargon Society publications from 1951 to 2008. Both of these checklists aspire to completeness, but given the number of ephemeral and otherwise uncatalogued items produced by Williams and published through his Jargon Society, neither pretend to be so.

Throughout his life in poetry and the arts Williams preferred active involvement with artists and the world at large over cloistered study or administrative labor: "I clearly did not want to become a Byzantinist in the basement of The Morgan Library; or an art critic for *The New Yorker*; nor did I want to live in the world of competitive business." His work in the arts thus demanded direct and persistent engagement with the world—a form of engagement that gave rise to both enduring friendships and irreconcilable conflicts. In his effort to "raise the common to grace" Williams often encountered resistance, yet it was precisely this resistance that signaled for him the importance of his work. As he remarks in an essay on the southern experience, "So, life is not the eyrie I would choose it to be, the poet living quietly, invisibly, making his poems as a peony bush makes peonies. There are demons about to chop through the poets and peonies, and other people too. One is *engaged*." If Williams maintained any commitment to Duncan's sense of responsibility this was a commitment that anticipated active engagement in advance in order to preserve for us the choice specimens he gathered across the span of a lifetime. And it is with this in mind that we hope you will engage the work gathered here in celebration of his commitment to selecting, harvesting, producing and preserving.

REMEMBERING

JONATHAN WILLIAMS—A LIFE IN PICTURES

JW at St. Albans, Washington D.C., ca 1941.

JW as Lucas Gerontes, Servant in the Highlands Playhouse production of Moliere's La Medecin Magre Lui, *August 1950. Photo Charles J. Wick II.*

JW by Francine du Plessix, Middle Creek Falls near Skywinding Farm, Summer 1951.

JW as a PFC in the Army Medical Corp at Hoelderlins Tower in Tübingen, Germany 1953. Photo by William Pease.

JW by Robert Creeley at Black Mountain College, 1955 using JW's Rolleiflex.

From right to left: Fielding Dawson, Emmanuel Navaretta, Bob Brown, and JW at Bob Brown's New York City apartment, 1958, for the group signing of 14 Poets, 1 Artist. *Photo by Robert Schiller.*

(opposite page) JW at Bob Brown's New York City apartment, 1958, for the group signing of 14 Poets, 1 Artist. *Photo by Robert Schiller.*

JW second from right in back row. Paul Goodman front row second from left.
Aspen Institute Volleyball Team, 1962.

*JW and Ronald Johnson,
ca 1965. Photographer
unknown.*

*JW at Corundum Hot
Springs, Aspen, Colorado,
1966. Photo by Willard
Midgette.*

JW at the Aspen Institute, ca 1966. Photo by Douglas Lewis.

JW in 1968 with a thrysus designed by Skip Taylor. Photo by Ralph Eugene Meatyard © The Estate of Ralph Eugene Meatyard, courtesy Fraenkel Gallery, San Francisco.

Thomas Meyer and JW, ca early 1970s. Photographer unknown.

JW, in Alex Gildzen's living room, Kent, Ohio, ca 1970s. Photo by Doug Moore.

Colonel Williams and Colonel Sanders at Corn Close, 1974. JW's sweater designed by Astrid Furnival features an image of Samuel Palmer. Photo by Joseph Anderson.

JW, Woodford County, Kentucky, 1974. Photo by Guy Mendes.

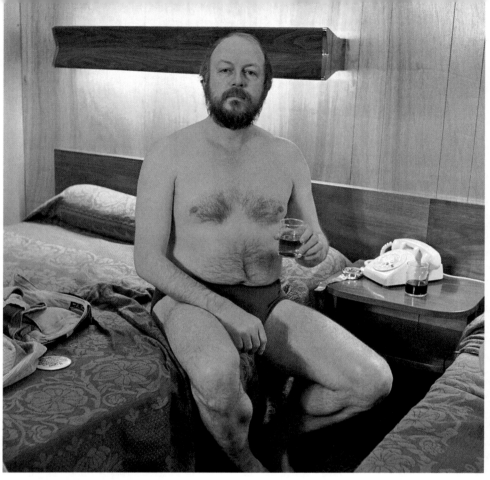

JW at Zoder's Best Western, Gatlinburg, Tennessee, 1974. Photo by Guy Mendes.

JW and Fielding Dawson searching for Dizzy Gillespie's birthplace, Cheraw, South Carolina, 1975. Photographer unknown.

From left to right: Joel Oppenheimer, Allen Ginsberg, Michael Rumaker, and JW at the 25th anniversary of Gotham Book Mart, February 14, 1976. Photo by Shelley M. Brown.

From left to right: Basil Bunting, JW, and Thomas Meyer at the back bar, Hotel Durham, during a November 18, 1977, Colpitts Reading Series event organized by Richard Caddel. Photo by David James.

JW near Corn Close, 1979.
Photo by Elizabeth Matheson.

JW and Thomas Meyer at Corn Close, August, 1981. Photo by Guy Mendes. (The camera appears to be a Mamiyaflex C330 – J.T.)

JW at Shakertown, Pleasant Hill, Kentucky, 1982. Photo by Guy Mendes.

JW at his desk, Corn Close, 1984. Photo by Mike Harding.

Thomas Meyer in front of Willard Midgette's portrait of JW, Corn Close, 1984. Photo by Mike Harding. Portrait ca 1967.

JW and Thomas Meyer, Library, Corn Close, 1984. Photo by Mike Harding.

JW conducting at Skywinding Farm, 1985. Photo by Jeffery Beam.

JW with folk artist Raymond Coins' hand to the left, ca 1986. Photo by Roger Manley.

JW bearing a thrysus by Harold Garrison of Madison County, NC, at James Harold Jennings', Pinnacle, North Carolina, 1989. Photo by Guy Mendes.

Fell End Clouds Walk, Dentdale, 1994. Photo by Dobree Adams.

JW at Moughton, Yorkshire Dales, ca 1997. Photo by Mike Harding.

JW at the entrance to his mountain home, Skywinding Farm, Scaly Mountain, North Carolina, 2003. Photo by Dobree Adams.

JW at Skywinding Farm, 2005. Photo by Reuben Cox.

BASIL BUNTING

COMMENT ON JONATHAN WILLIAMS

Basil Bunting, photo by Jonathan Williams.

The Clifford castles stood around once, at Brough and Skipton and Pendragon, like great crystals of salt in the mediaeval porridge, giving a savour of poetry and romance to all these dales, Dentdale amongst the rest; for Fair Rosamund, who founded their fortunes, had lived at Henry IInd's court amongst his troubadours and singers of lays and the men and women who invented the Round Table on a Welsh or Breton hint, and her relatives picked up the fashion; else why call their new fortress to guard the hawse between the Eden and Yoredale 'Pendragon', claiming a link with Arthur? If we thumb our noses at the scholars who want to transfer what seems like a Teesdale dialect to South Lancashire, we can fancy the author of 'Sir Gawain' bringing his poem over Stainmore to read it to the lord of Pendragon. By no means a land without literature then, and later, on Wordsworth's itineraries with and without Dorothy. What a pity the wars of the roses left no Clifford to welcome the American Martial when he pitched his handsome pavilion at Corn Close, like a great crystal of salt in our twentieth century porridge.

Perhaps it was one of my suggestions, though no doubt I told Jonathan that North Tynedale was even lovelier, besides chance—since cottages are not often empty in such a landscape—that fixed him here to the great advantage of Dent and Sedbergh, overlooking the extravagant meanderings of the Dee and patterns of bracken on the fellside opposite, without close neighbours unless you count the natty red weasel that lives at the side of his waterfall or a score or so of monosyllabic sheep. What better neighbours could a laconic poet wish for?

Good talk, good food, good wine and good sense cluster at Corn Close with accurate information about many things and active kindness all around like a garden. The width of the lane deters coach tours and may give unprepared drivers an unetymological notion of the origin of the name dent-dale, but visitors get through the obstacles in numbers sufficient to keep the talk varying and encourage the cook, a poet too with an assured future. Jonathan's VW knows its way around corners and is used to backing half a mile if it meets the milk tanker while it carries its master and his guests to every pub in driving distance turn and turn about, or to Burnley for the football or to Leeds for the test.

Thomas Meyer, Jonathan Williams, Basil Bunting, Briggflatts, early 1980s.

There is always some disc humming at Corn Close, with the typewriter tapping out a descant, unless Jonathan is tramping the fells, treading out tracks on the Howgills, where you must watch your step in a fog because of the crags. Half the farmers know him and all the barmaids. And he has become a solid buttress for the Friends Meeting House at Briggflatts.

Basil Bunting, photo by Jonathan Williams.

Basil Bunting, photo by Jonathan Williams.

Basil Bunting, Beside the Rawthey, Cumbria, 1980. Photo by Jonathan Williams.

ERICA VAN HORN

DEAR JW

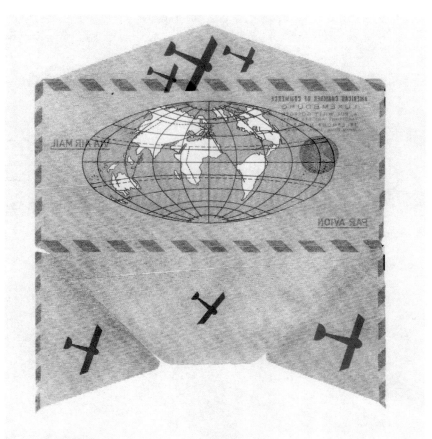

Air Mail envelope.

12 February 2009
Ballybeg, cold & bright with
a lot of snowdrops in
bloom

Dear Jonathan,

This from one letter-writer to another : We are dinosaurs.

Your letters have been a joy and a pleasure. It is
not just that you have been doing something so
diligently and so well. Mostly it is that you
have done it at all. There have been long letters
and there have been short letters. There has always
been the birthday of at least one famous person noted
beneath the day's date. There might be comments on
food, on weather, on music, on some drink, a note
about something you have been reading, or a note
about something you have been writing, gossip and
news of friends (and foes), and responses to
whatever I had written in my last letter. You
have been a truly consistent correspondent.

I always enjoyed seeing you at your morning
letter writing duties at Corn Close. It was not an
~~greater~~ occasional job, it was an everyday job.
It was a job as important as any job that needs

to be done daily. I liked knowing that someone was going to receive those very morning letters which I heard being typed. I wonder if you made carbons of your letters? Does anyone still use carbon paper?

Now everyone can e-mail everything that they might be thinking to anyone and everyone else. We all sit down and Do Our E-Mails in the morning, perhaps with a similar diligence as that with which you've typed your letters. In the early days of my computer use, I was reprimanded for writing e-mails as if they were letters. Apparently my inappropriate formality and my inappropriate use of the medium put horrific pressure on the recipient. No one will respond in kind, & they are too busy to really read all that chat. You have kept your e-mails letter-like. I wonder did you ever get reprimanded for it?

I still think of my long-distance contact with you as one committed to paper. Opening each envelope was to find your voice, and to continue the conversation.

With love, as always —
Erica. XX

JAMES McGARRELL

MOUNTAINSIDE READER—FOR JW

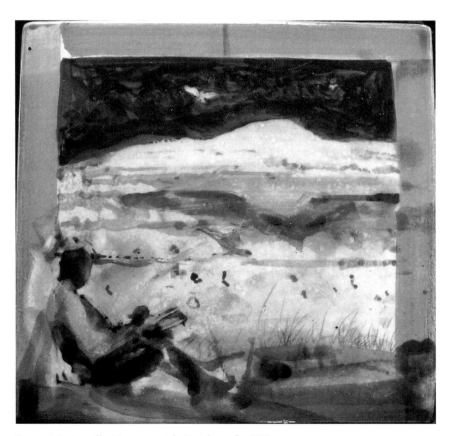

James McGarrell: Mountainside Reader—for JW.

Mountainside Reader—for JW, was artist James McGarrell's last birthday gift to JW. Tom Meyer carried it to the hospital for JW to see, and of course, JW was pleased by the homage. This is one of two of his last evocative portraits of his magpie friend, the other piece the cover of JW's memorial chapbook, *A Hornet's Nest*. JW and James became friends in 1952, having met in New Orleans at the first recording of a street marching band, the Eureka, by their friends, Alden Ashforth and David Wyckoff. In ensuing decades JW and Tom were occasional visitors of Jim and Ann's at their homes in Bloomington, Indiana; Polgeto di Umbertide; St. Louis; and Newbury, Vermont. Art, jazz, travel, baseball, high and low cuisine and good whiskey were common threads to their friendship. McGarrell contributed to numerous Jargon publications, as well as creating a couple of evocative images of his magpie friend, Jonathan.

ANN McGARRELL

À MON CHER STODGE

Bloodroot and grosbeaks
starry blooms,
shy lipstick lumage
so tame one comes to your hand

There still was snow in the shade
sun behind us
for once also benign
your arm warm through the chambray

extragalactic ginger
big kitty
twitching his tail
(he was trained by a comet)
amber eyes fixed on bird

oh isn't it time to exult about
something?
—the words and the music
in summer the whippoorwill
never varies his discourse
one string to his bow
pitiless, pitiful
unlike the blackbird
whose riffling all through
the variorum edition
change it, change it

sweet
change it
trills and runs rippling.
write it down write it down

Your hands tamp dark soil
cradling the roots
each one a red lifeline
attendrissements et
évanouissements
—they ought to be Satie titles
but you know they never are.
It was you, it was you.

ANNE MIDGETTE

ON WITH IT

"Compose aloud: poetry is sound." The words are by Basil Bunting, the neglected friend of Ezra Pound and author of *Briggflatts*, one of the great modern epic poems. Jonathan Williams, a poet who never neglected a friend's poetry, took Bunting's directive (the words are the start of an encomium to young poets headed "I SUGGEST") and printed it on a post-card, because finding words and savoring them and printing them and showing them to other people and making sure they paid attention was what Jonathan Williams did.

Sometimes he printed the words he found as poems of his own, like found objects: now irreverent or bawdy, now slightly diffident about their own beauty. Sometimes he printed the poems and writings and photographs of others (the neglected, the under-read), offering their work in beautiful volumes through his Jargon Society (founded in 1951, while he was at Black Mountain College), which published more than 100 titles by Charles Olson, Robert Creeley, Denise Levertov, Louis Zukofsky, Guy Davenport, Lorine Niedecker, Thomas Meyer, and on and on. Jonathan liked lists (one of his poems is simply a list of remarkable names from the phone book in the area around his home in Highlands, North Carolina) and most writings about him involve long lists of the names of the people whom he sought out and befriended and to whom he pounded out letters on his massive electric typewriter while Ravel or Delius or Arnold Bax played on the stereo behind him.

If poetry is a sound, Jonathan made it. For years, he drove across America in a battered Volkswagen [Editors' note: See footnote 5 in Tom Patterson's "If You Can Kill a Snake With It" in this volume for a more ful-some history of what automobiles Williams drove across the country], its trunk full of boxes of books, and spread poetry: "our Johnny Appleseed,"

Buckminster Fuller called him. When he stood up to read—tall, imposing, masking shyness with a forbidding sternness the poems became sound, rolling out with the rich savor of whisky and cigar smoke that colored his voice, and gradually sweeping away the reservations of listeners who, braced for Great Thoughts, found instead humor and homespun truths and even gleeful obscenity, delighted at its own naughtiness. You never knew what was coming. It might be

Leconte High-Top

under the rondelay
the sun

into the wind and rain a
winter wren

again, again—

its song needling the pines

And it might be

Spring Thaw at the Old Goodman Place
(for Paul)

THE MORE YOU COME
THE MORE YOU CAN!

"Some people … find the poems vulgar," he wrote. "I no more write for 'nice' people than I do for 'common' ones. I make poems for the people who want them."

Jonathan collected a lot of things the way he collected words. He approached the world with the attitude that there were many great things in it that not enough people knew about, and set about finding them with a tenacity that earned him the epithet, from Hugh Kenner, "the truffle hound of poetry." First, he collected poets and artists, living and dead, capturing portraits and gravestones with his Rolleiflex and Polaroid (some of them gathered in the beautiful eclectic book *A Palpable Elysium: Portraits of Genius and Solitude*). Other quests included outsider artists long before "outsider art" was a term; hikes in beautiful landscapes such as the Yorkshire Dales, where he spent half of each year in a seventeenth-century stone cottage; all manner of recorded music; and gourmet food (often thanks to Tom Meyer, his partner of forty years, whose own poems—collected in *At Dusk Iridescent* twine through the Jargon oeuvre with balletic grace).

He wanted to share all this bounty. When you visited, he would present you with great stacks of books (Kilvert's diaries, Mervyn Peake, the latest Stephen King), or sit you down, after another stunning dinner, for single-malt scotch and a recording of Messaien's *Turangalila Symphony*, whether or not that was what the assembled company really wanted. He felt keenly that not enough people wanted what he had to offer. ("Only about 83 people read poetry," he would grouse, in his favorite pose of alienated curmudgeon.) But he was allergic to anything that smacked of the establishment. Jargon's one commercial success (which finally had to be sold to another publisher who could handle the demand) was *White Trash Cooking* by Ernest Matthew Mickler, which was quintessential Jonathan: seen as being in poor taste by many people; focusing on an overlooked, marginalized population; and including some seriously good food.

Many of his poems (collected in 2004 in *Jubilant Thicket*) and essays (sampled in the exuberant *Blackbird Dust*) are memorials, valedictories, obituaries: a last chance to let people know about somebody they should have heard of, long past (the painter Samuel Palmer) or recent (the photographer Ray Moore). For Bunting, who led him to the Dales, Jonathan erected a postcard memorial that, like many of his poems, sneaks around so-called literary standards and into the consciousness, where it lies like a found beach pebble, smooth and solid and reassuring in the palm of one's hand. It stands, now, for him as well. *At Briggflatts Burial Ground.*

Dear Basil,

Eighteen months after you left us,
poetry (that abused & discredited substance;
that refuge of untalented snobs, yobs, and bores)
sinks nearer the bottom of the whirling world.

For the rest, you there in the earth
hear the crunch of small bones
as owl and mouse, priest and weasel,
stone and cardoon, oceans and gentlemen
get on with it …

BOB ARNOLD

SWEPT IN WITH THE RAIN

I sadly read many fine blogs and appreciations after the death of Jonathan Williams. I love seeing poets come to bat for their pals, and I can only live with myself and mankind if I likewise see it happening for the poets while they are still alive. Otherwise, what are we doing?

Williams was a class act at speaking up for and supporting the outsider, the backward but bird-fluted voice, art and lullabies and poetries of all sorts of stripes. He'd done it with his Jargon press since college age and he passed away, royally even, as an old man. His books were always published, even if only the choir read them, but the quality was lasting stuff. He's going to stick around, and so is Jargon because Black Mountain isn't going to topple quite yet, nor all those names, or the buddies he made, and the enriched ingredients of how the man was formed himself. Mud and wattle. A thatch hut, a long gone walking trail, good books and good humor and so good memories of the guy.

We never met but we spoke on the phone once upon a time about Lorine Niedecker and a book I published he wanted in quantities to give as gifts to his friends. See what I mean—thinking of others, even if he did sometimes come across in print as a crank. His photographs are marvelous and personal. His poetry swept in with the rain.

When I was on the phone with Williams it gave me the opportunity to tell him how I wrote him once in the late 1960s when I was a boy about my enthusiasm for discovering Kenneth Patchen and all the wholesome work he did for that poet. He wrote me back a full page letter about Patchen, beautifully typed and enthused. It was the first letter I ever received from another writer. It was so important and respectful, and conscientious, that I bet it'll stay in me and become my last.

CHARLES LAMBERT

ACTS OF KINDNESS

I first met Jonathan Williams when he came to Cambridge to read for Blue Room, a poetry society founded by John Wilkinson and run by John, his old school-friend Charlie Bulbeck, and the more recently co-opted me. I had the grand title of Blue Room Secretary and was responsible for, among other things, booking rooms in my college for the reading and the guest poet. On this occasion we had two guest poets because Jonathan came with his partner, Tom Meyer.

I don't remember if we were unaware of this and booked, as usual, a single room, or were aware of it but thought, as young people tend to do, that one small bed would be enough for the two of them. It may even have been the case that the college didn't offer a double room on the grounds that women weren't allowed to sleep within its walls. Jonathan took one look at the bed and said to Tom: "Well, you'll have to find somewhere else to sleep tonight," in a tone that struck me as playful but, thrillingly for me, not ironic.

Tom was no taller than I was, bottle-blond (though I didn't know this then), finely built and featured, a fragile adjunct to the solider, bearded, avuncular figure of Jonathan. They'd arrived the morning before the reading and had offered to drive us to a restaurant outside Cambridge for an early dinner that evening. I don't know whose idea it was to take them to eat kebabs for lunch at the Gardenia, a basement café just off Trinity Lane that's recently been saved from closure by, among others, Stephen Fry, but it wasn't a success. I remember Jonathan peering into his pita with a forlorn expression and muttering, "Hmm, street food."

Later that day, Jonathan and Tom drove John and me—Charlie having bunked off by this point—out of Cambridge to a pub that was famous at the time for its irascible owner, his taste for Wagner played loud, and his

accommodating, brow-beaten German boyfriend. We drank Adnam's ale—
we had no choice. This was followed by a hotel restaurant that Jonathan
had heard, or read, about and wanted to try. Jonathan cared about food in
a way that's utterly normal now but, in late 1973, seemed both luxuriously
decadent and pedantic, an attractive though somewhat forbidding mix. I
have no memory of what we ate. What I remember is the rather meandering
ride home and the way I managed to slump against Tom in the back of the
car, my thigh idly—would-be indifferently—pushed against his.

The reading was attended by the usual small group of enthusiasts, but
I was too taken by the physical memory of Tom's leg against mine to be
more than summarily aware of what was read; I was also drunk. At the inter-
val, it being my job to make coffee, I darted from the room to fill my kettle
and bumped into a friend—Paul Johnstone, now dead—who asked me how
the event was going. I think I'm sleeping with Tom tonight, I told him,
unaware that every word was heard in the room behind me, where the poets
and their audience were seated. John told me later, the following day, that
Jonathan had raised an eyebrow but was otherwise pokerfaced. I have no
idea how Tom reacted.

The post-reading party was in my room. By this time, I'd been told
about my gaffe but, stubborn and optimistic with alcohol, remained unde-
terred. Half an hour into the party, when Jonathan left, I was sitting in my
armchair, with Tom on the floor in front of me, his shoulders between my
knees. "I'll see you boys tomorrow," Jonathan said, and I imagine Tom nod-
ded and smiled, perhaps wryly, as I did not, not believing my luck. To
understand how much in love I was with the man whose head was almost,
almost against my groin, you would have to factor in so much that isn't
needed here, where what I want to do above all is to talk about Jonathan's
generosity. The rest of the party faded away quite rapidly after Jonathan's
departure and suddenly Tom and I were alone. "Shall I make some coffee?"
I said, and Tom said: "Coffee?" in a way that made me feel both foolish and
desired. Five minutes later, he was twisting peach-coloured toilet paper
around his contact lenses while I, like a bride, prepared for bed.

They left the next day. We walked with them to the brand-new multi-
storey car-park where they'd left the car, talking about Joseph Needham and
China, or Ronald Johnson, or Thomas A. Clark, a friend of John's who'd
recently been published by Jargon. Jonathan gave us their address, invited

us to visit them in their cottage in Cumbria. As the car pulled off I felt that the end of some essential organ in my body had been attached to their bumper and was slowly, smoothly unspooling. I didn't know who I was, nor where; with what was left to wave goodbye or with what had been drawn out, away, and gathered up, like wool, by what had happened. Thirty-six hours later, having made up my mind that I could never just go on with my life as it was, which now seemed as false and hollow as I'd become, I was on the road for Dentdale.

There was snow, and the last lift dropped me some way from the house. I must have called from a rural phone-box because Jonathan came in his car to collect me. I can't remember now if I'd let them know that I was coming or, fearful of rejection, had simply presented myself as near as damn-it to the house, giving them no choice other than to take me in.

Tom had a cold. He didn't seem pleased to see me, or not pleased; I wasn't certain he knew who I was, although that, surely, was impossible after only two days. More than anything, I imagine now, he must have been uncomfortable, perhaps even peeved. He'd had no idea what he'd mean to me when he chose the easy option of my room, more for Jonathan's comfort than for his own, as if I were the by-product of his own generosity towards his partner. He'd never considered that I might think I'd fallen in love with him, his New York past, his neck. He cooked for us while Jonathan showed me round, my head a whirl of names: Kitaj, Ginsberg, Hockney, Bunting, but soon after eating he went to bed. Alone with Jonathan, in the part of the house they worked in, filled with books and records, each desk with its own electric typewriter, I wondered what would happen. Jonathan asked if I'd ever had a sauna. I hadn't.

In the sauna, outside the house, we talked about my life, my future. It hadn't occurred to me until we were both naked and aching with the heat that I might want to have sex with Jonathan—I was, after all, in love with Tom!—but it seemed entirely natural, and right, that after the sauna and a glass or two of single malt we should go to my bedroom, a small room with walls painted burnt orange next to the room in which Jonathan and Tom normally slept. It hadn't occurred to me, either, how scared I was of what I'd done, and was about to do, until I was lying on top of Jonathan and snivelling into the hairs of his chest. Jonathan stroked my back, then scratched it gently. "You like that, don't you?" he whispered. "Yes," I said. "You're a brave boy," he said. "Am I?" I said.

The next day Jonathan called the City Lights bookstore in San Francisco and arranged a job for me. I can't afford the fare, I told him, but Jonathan smiled and said that didn't matter; he'd pay for my ticket. That evening, Tom still in bed with flu, he drove me down to the local pub. Jonathan was a local celebrity—I imagine he was always that – and the people he introduced me to, bank managers, store owners, family doctors, treated me with a mixture of respect and contempt I'd never experienced before; respect for Jonathan tinged with contempt for me. It was understood that I'd become a protégé. Someone, cattily, wanted to know where Tom was. By the time we were back at the cottage and it was clear that, this evening, I'd sleep alone, I knew that I didn't want to go to San Francisco at all. I wanted to pick up my own life once again and make it fit. Jonathan, to his credit, understood.

We wrote to each other a number of times afterwards and only lost touch when I really did leave Cambridge, at the appropriate time, with a degree, but I never saw Jonathan—or Tom—again. In his letters, Jonathan gently upbraided me for what he must have seen as a failure of will, hoping that I'd found my "Firbankian" pleasures on the banks of the Cam. I've never felt Firbankian in my life, but I was certainly as ill-equipped for life as Firbank had been, and it's to Jonathan's credit that he gave me the chance to risk a little and then retreat. He was generous with his time, and his body, a difficult man, superb in the Italian sense of not brooking mediocrity, with that pinch of arrogance that all snobs need to survive. I've never regretted my weekend at Dentdale. My only regret is that it was never repeated, and now, that it never will be.

DIANA C. STOLL

JONATHAN WILLIAMS—MORE MOUTH ON THAT MAN

Poet, essayist, photographer, and visionary—not words to be tossed about casually—Jonathan Williams may have been best known as the founder and fifty-year drive behind the Jargon Society, the small press that published in that half-century some hundred books of avant-garde writings, art, and photography.

Williams died in Highlands, North Carolina, within a hundred miles of his birthplace in Asheville, but the trajectory of his life was anything but simple. He grew up in Washington, D.C., and after a short stint at Princeton (which he later blasted as "an Ivy League chain gang") he encountered Harry Callahan at Chicago's Institute of Design. It was on Callahan's suggestion that Williams applied to Black Mountain College in Western North Carolina (incidentally near his family's summer house at Scaly Mountain—the homeplace that would be his base in years to come). In the ferment of Black Mountain in the early 1950s, Williams found himself in a mix of teachers and students that included photographers Callahan and Aaron Siskind, artists Robert Rauschenberg, Cy Twombly, Robert Motherwell, writers Francine du Plessix, Joel Oppenheimer, Robert Creeley, and a litany of others. Perhaps most galvanizing, he came in contact with the poet Charles Olson, then the college's rector, who helped to shape Williams into a writer and hired him to run the school's press. (One of Jargon's earliest endeavors was the publication of Olson's *Maximus Poems* in 1953.) In subsequent years, Jargon Press would champion writers (among them Louis Zukofsky, Paul Metcalf, Lorine Niedecker, Mina Loy) and photographers and artists (including Ralph Eugene Meatyard, Harry Callahan, Doris Ulmann, R. B. Kitaj). The books are beautiful, crafted with meticulous, human care—and yet only one Jargon title ever leapt off the bookshop shelves: *White Trash Cooking*, with photographs by Ernest Matthew

Mickler; royalties from that 1986 book are still rolling in.

As a poet and essayist, Williams had a powerful, fluid, wonderfully idiosyncratic voice. As a photographer, he was modest (he wrote in the foreword to *A Palpable Elysium*, his 2002 book of photographic portraits: "One hopes that 'professionals' will simply allow me to be a literary gent who takes the odd tolerable picture"). But his take on photography was adventurous and consuming, and it was perhaps inevitable that he would find his way early on to *Aperture*, where his writings would appear intermittently over the course of forty years. Williams' 1961 essay "The Eyes of 3 Phantasts" focused on Wynn Bullock, Frederick Sommer, and Clarence John Laughlin; his words interacted with the work of these wild masters with a troublesome, provoking beauty that was somehow just the right counterpoint. He was a contributing editor to *Aperture* for nearly two decades, beginning in the mid-1970s, and published writings, both in the magazine and in Aperture books, on Callahan, Laughlin, Art Sinsabaugh, "new Southern Photography," and more.

I was encouraged by friends to look Jonathan Williams up when I moved south from New York with my family about a decade and a half ago. This was to be one of the more meaningful encounters of our new Southern life. Visits to Skywinding Farm, the home that Jonathan shared with his partner Thomas Meyer, were extraordinary events that always included culinary phenomena (*jambon en gelée* on our first visit, vividly recalled) and a level of conversation that is not encountered every day: a fast-paced meander among friends and acquaintances such as Guy Davenport, Basil Bunting, Thomas Merton, James Broughton, Stevie Smith, Howard Finster, James Laughlin. Unexpurgated gossip and the deeper exploration of ideas intertwined nicely. (When the topic moved to the movies—as somehow it always does—Jonathan would grow irascible and look around for escape. He was an infamous curmudgeon, whose welcome mat bore the terse suggestion "GO AWAY.")

I had a couple of occasions—happily, no more than a couple—to conduct semi-"official" interviews with Jonathan. Ordinarily plenty gregarious and hugely generous with his thoughts and ideas, when the conversation threatened to be circumscribed in some boring way, he clammed up, recalcitrant: such discussions were a complete wash. Once I was nervously gearing up for an interview with Henri Cartier-Bresson, and knowing Jonathan was a great fan, I asked him rather lamely: "If you could ask HC-B anything, what would it be?" No pause: "I'd just ask him how he got to be so damn *good*" (here channeling some laconic mountain man). Jonathan was better approached more obliquely, without preconceived agenda. This because, like any mighty animal, his mind needed to be able to move in any direction at any point. Reading his essays you find a disarming combination of Higher Thought, fantastically wayward references, and hilarious raunch: tough pokeberry and Cumbrian plum, eaten with a raised eyebrow. His poems often grab snatches of local language in which Jonathan discovered cadences interesting enough to isolate—"The Colossal Maw from War-Woman Dell, Georgia" a title that almost outweighs its poem:

> more mouth on
> that woman
> than ass
> on a goose.

Despite Jargon's hundred titles, and the many books of Jonathan's work published by other houses, the theme of under-recognition—and the concomitant need for funds—was ever present. Of course, only hardheaded individuals run small presses for fifty-year stretches. But also, as Jonathan surely knew, he operated between audiences, or rather his audience was a most rarified group of illuminati. He was a self-proclaimed "bourgeois bourgeoisophobe." He asserted of his work that "the Great Unwashed will not dig this stuff at all," following up: "However, I do not write for the Great Unwashed. I write for them that wants it." Them that wants had better be both quick and smart, and their tastes may have to run tangent to at least one of Jonathan's—but that could mean anything from Catullus to Mingus, Montaigne to Mae West, Charles Ives to Uncle Iv. The field was so wide, and always fertile.

GARY CARDEN

THE BARD OF SCALY MOUNTAIN

While I was surfing the Internet last week, I stumbled on this: "Jonathan Williams, poet, dead at 79." For a moment, I sat attempting to absorb the fact that tall, courtly Jonathan, was gone. Then, I immediately recalled my most cherished memory of the Bard of Scaly Mountain.

Over a decade and a half ago when I was bemoaning the approach of my 64th birthday, two of my friends asked me what I wanted to celebrate my "natal day." At the time, I was reading *An Ear in Bartram's Tree*, and I quipped, "Jonathan Williams." My friends laughed and I went back to my book.

However, a few days later when I drove to Mirror Lake Road in Highlands for my "birthday dinner," I was ushered into a dining room, lit by candles. There were only two chairs at the table. In a few moments, there was a soft knock at the door and Jonathan Williams entered. I remember that he was all rumpled tweed and tousled hair and that he smiled and said, "Happy Birthday, Gary." I gawked like a fool and my friends said, "Jonathan can only stay for two hours."

Then, they departed, leaving me with a great deal of food, several bottles of wine and Jonathan Williams.

And so we talked … or rather, Jonathan talked and I listened. I asked about Black Mountain College; his friendship with Henry Miller; his awesome folk/outsider art collection; his publishing press (the Jargon Society); and his efforts to save Pasaquan, the fantastic "one-man paradise" of Eddie Owens Martin in Buena Vista, Ga. He told wonderful anecdotes about his trips down the back roads of America to find the multitudes of untrained artists who paint on cardboard, rusty tin and masonite, people who whittle, carve or make whirly-gigs—all compelled to create a personal vision that Jonathan found as deeply moving as a Degas or a Cezanne.

Jonathan also loved baseball and the recipes in *White Trash Cooking* (published by Jargon Press). He was a discerning collector of blues recordings and the works of unknown photographers, such as Ralph Eugene Meatyard.

During our conversation, I noticed that Jonathan had a small notebook in his vest pocket, and that he occasionally made notes in it. When I asked about it, he said that he collected things other people said, and that he liked my comment about falling in love with the folksinger Hedy West because "she had hairy legs." Of course, I knew that he sometimes converted a chance remark that he had heard in a barber shop or a garage: "Your points is blue / and your timing's / a week off."

Several years after our conversation, I heard Jonathan read his poems in Asheville and was flattered to find a note that I had once written him transformed into a poem. As best as I remember, it went something like this:

Report from Gary Carden at the Coffee Shop in Sylva

A friend approached while I sat reading.
What you reading, Gary?
"Jonathan Williams," I responded, holding up the book.
"Oh, that funny feller."
"No, you're thinking about Winters."
"Damn straight. It was down to 20 last night."

After that night on Mirror Lake Road, we maintained an uncertain correspondence. Jonathan seemed resigned to both his own obscurity and the decline of all that was fine and good in America. He despised most modern poetry and felt that theatre had died with Tennessee Williams.

Although he continued to publish his own poetry, he seemed to devote the majority of his efforts to calling attention to the works of others. Occasionally, he would venture out for a reading and he often acted as a commentator for exhibits of his folk art collection. As for the recent popularity of folk art, he noted that the field had been taken over by money-grubbing opportunists and fakes.

However, each time he found himself making grim observations about a world where bad food and deranged politicians held sway (Jesse Helms seemed to epitomize the worst in Southern culture), Jonathan would suddenly change the subject and, retreating behind his shield of humor, laugh, quote a bit of doggerel and sing a song. As many of his later works attest, he was fond of addressing his dead friends, saying things like, "If there is a flight out of the Elysium Fields tonight, old friend, I'll pick you up at the airport."

Over the years, I have often searched for a fitting icon or symbol for Jonathan Williams. Aside from the undeniable merits of his poetry, his greatest gift was his amazing knack for perceiving talent in others. Whether it was Edgar Tolson, the carver in Compton, Ky., Vollis Simpson and his wind machines in Lucama, N.C., or artists like James Harold Jennings down in Stokes County, Jonathan always saw what the rest of us missed. That includes the art critics who often made belated acknowledgements of his unerring judgment. Finally, I can pick my icon.

Jonathan is a magpie!

I have watched a magpie stalking through a landfill and I'm thinking of his discerning eye. In the midst of all that plastic and Styrofoam, he will halt, peer into the debris and extract something ... a colored stone, a bauble or an earring. Then, taking flight, he will carry his discovery home to his nest where he will give it a choice setting, a niche that displays its merits. Jonathan did that. He waded through the wreckage of our culture, indifferent to the gaudy fakes. Yet, he sometimes saw it (the real thing!) glinting down there under the debris, and when he saw it he lifted it up and said, "Look what I have found."

Ave, to the Bard of Scaly Mountain.

HARRY GILONIS

FROM PLINY: *NATURALIS HISTORIA* XXVII. XVI 58
(done for Corn Close, October 1987)

Democritus disapproved of sex;
it's just the way one human
comes from another; and,
by Hercules, the less of that
the better.

   Athletes, however,
when they are sluggish, are refreshed
thereby; and the voice, when it has
lost its lustre and gone husky,
can also be restored.

   Sex is the cure for pains
in the groin, unsoundness of mind,
dull vision & melancholia.

JOHN MITZEL

JONATHAN WILLIAMS—AN APPRECIATION

I had known Jonathan Williams since the 1980s. During his visits to Boston, he'd occasionally visit at the bookshop; we'd go for a drink and have a long chat. Jonathan knew the majority of creative people of his generation. He was born in North Carolina, an only child. Later the family moved to Washington, D.C. He attended St. Alban's school; he was a freshman there when Gore Vidal was a senior. He attended Princeton for one year before dropping out. After college, he did independent studies in book design, photography, painting and the graphic arts. These, among others, remained the passions for the rest of his life.

He did a stint at the Chicago Institute of Design and followed that with studies at Black Mountain College where, like John Wieners and others, he came under the influence of Charles Olson. While at Black Mountain, he established Jargon Society Press. As Jeffery Beam noted in his recollection of Williams, "Ultimately Jargon—along with New Directions, Grove and City Lights—became one of the four most famous small presses of a burgeoning 1960s movement that continues not only on the printed page, but today, even on the Internet."

Poets and photographers published by Jargon read like a Who's Who of alternative and/or avant-garde talent. Williams, himself, was author of over one hundred titles,

Williams was a big guy, over six feet, and sported a distinguished look. He had, when he wanted, a stentorian voice. He didn't like fakery in the arts. He had the gift to cover all the bases, a man who could be the perfectly refined gentleman, while maintaining an appreciation of life's bawdy side. Being of the South, Williams knew its history and did so much to celebrate its bright spots. Williams, according to Jeffery Beam, was drawn to the rural, the offbeat, something not-New York, and made his commitment "more and more away from the High Art of the city." Beam has even a more dramatic quote: "Known for his irascibility and opinions, [Williams] once stated (quoting Henry Miller paraphrasing Celine) 'One of the things Jargon is devoted to is an attack on urban culture. We piss on it all from a considerable height.'"

It was not easy work. Keeping a small press alive takes energy and cleverness. Williams got his various grants over the years, but still had to rattle the cup. Jargon's list, though smart, beautifully done, and terribly important, was a hard sell. Williams would get in his compact car, loaded up with product and hand-sell them to booksellers. It sounds romantic, but it ain't.

His obits recount the famous story wherein Allen Ginsberg offered Jargon the rights to print *Howl*. Jonathan turned him down. His line: if Jargon had published it, *Howl* would have only sold five hundred copies and, thus, been swept into the poetry graveyard, a vast expanse. Instead, *Howl* went to City Lights, and *Howl* has sold hundreds of thousands of copies over these 50 years. With the right alignment of stars, you can get that brass ring.

Jargon did have its moment of media celebrity. Williams, true to his pursuit of the off-beat, signed Ernest Mickler to a contract. The book came out under the title *White Trash Cooking*. Mickler had shopped his book around New York publishers. They all declined unless Mickler changed his title to something more genteel. Mickler stuck by his guns. Williams had no problem with the title. The book was one odd item. It featured recipes from Mickler's table: cooter pie, okra, and other delicacies. My favorites included potato chip sandwiches and pork-fried beef. Like any good cookbook, the title featured gorgeous photos of the delicacies presented. The press went crazy over the book and it became a hit, even winding up on the *New York Times* bestseller list, imagine that. Williams quickly sold the reprint rights.

Jonathan Williams was in Boston one night in the 1970s, starring at a poetry reading, organized by the Good Gay Poets, at the late and lamented Charles Street Meeting House. It was a slim crowd, as usually happens with such events. I was not in attendance that night, but my dear friend Charley Shively was and he recounted the event for me. Just as Williams was beginning to read, this big, butch number, dressed in leathers, noisily came into the temple and sat down. Jonathan read and carried on a bit, and the leather number finally figured out the milieu, and stood up and screamed: "What you all are doing is a sin in the eyes of God!"

Williams didn't miss a beat. He said: "Honey, to quote Mae West, if your cock is as big as your mouth, meet me after the show!" The leather evangel fled. And Williams carried on and on. He was a great engine. I miss him.[1]

---

[1] Editors' note: Compare Mitzel's version of this story with Charley Shively's first-hand report, "Toiling in the Bullpen: The Blues of Colonel Williams," later in this volume. Editor Jeffery Beam queried Tom as to the true story. His reply: "I was reading. Khaki was the heckler's attire. But he was at the back of the sanctuary, cute or not, can't attest. The crowd almost immediately hounded him out of the building, and the voice clearest among them was Bill Corbett's. Although the Mae West quote appears in both 'tellings,' it's nothing I remember and could well have been a remark Jonathan made later when he had the podium—or was it pulpit?" And a day later Tom added: "What has come to mind (hesitate to say memory) about the Boston Legend was that the 'heckler' asked me if the love poem I'd just read was about another man. I said yes and then he made the remark about sin etc."

MICHAEL RUMAKER

LAST LETTER TO JONATHAN WILLIAMS

193 North Franklin Street
Nyack New York 10960
Friday, March 14, 2008

Dearest Jonathan,

Belated March 8th birthday greetings. Am most distressed to hear that you're laid up in the hospital—what a rotten place to welcome in your 79th year. Hope your illness turns round in this turning of the season and you will be back with Tom in dear old Highlands in that beloved home the 2 of you have made there together over many a year now since first meeting at Bard. Just the thought of those gorgeous surrounding mountains going that heartbreakingly smoky green in the commonplace miracle of spring is something I sure hope you're at home again to see, you who have brought that same sense of miracle into the enchanting and delightful freewheeling handsprings of your many years of writing and singing out loud your "pomes," as Whitman called his (and, were he around to hear them, would I betcha' give the nod to yours hands down).

Well, I had my 76th on March 5th, which makes us fellow Pisceans ("the old souls," as Olson might've said), the poets and the dreamers, the visionaries—Not sure I can claim much of that for myself, but evidence of that is certainly in your work, both in its written form and in all the work you've done for so many decades, keeping the word alive and sprightly in all its authentic nooks and crannies, in all the equally authentic overlooked spirits hidden in plain sight throughout the piedmont and hills of North Carolina, throughout the Southland and wherever your feet and that old station wagon took you roaming and looking. And the *books*—yes, those superb and beautiful books you made: what a grand treasure for all our eyes.

Michael Rumaker, Sausalito,
California. 1956. Photo by JW.

What a grand treasure and illumination your life has been in these benighted States, in these benighted times.

Well, old fellow Black Mountaineer—old Black Mountain-*ear*—wasn't that a gift and pleasure, despite the hardships, to have been there, to have found our feet on that lively (sacred?) ground. Sure were lucky. And among so many that I met and cherished there, whose memory I've kept in my heart all these years, including your own, since we all scattered out into world after Black Mountain closed, well, those memories have and still are riches beyond riches.

This is mainly to say, dear Jonathan, I hope you'll be up and about soon. Are you planning to be at the Black Mountain College celebration at Lenoir-Rhyne College in Hickory in September? I sure do hope so. It'll be more than wonderful to see you again, you and Tom, together as it should be, so we can chew over old Black Mountain days and speculate on what's the latest, the newest, ahead on the road.

Much love always,
Mike Rumaker

Editors'note: This letter was sent to co-editor Jeffery Beam two days after Williams' death. Jeffery and Michael had been introduced by Jonathan, of course. After some correspondence they first met at the one and only Black Mountain College Reunion in October 1995 at the old Lake Eden campus near Black Mountain, where their friendship deepened, and Michael joined the mentors that Jonathan bigheartedly bestowed upon Jeffery. Although Michael believed Jonathan did not read this letter, Tom Meyer had carried it to the hospital and read it to Jonathan. Michael attached this hand-written note to the photocopied letter he sent to Beam:

March 18, 2008

Jeffery dear, the loss of Jonathan saddens us all, but I know it saddens you especially, you and Stan, because you loved him as if he were family. What a wonderfully lovely tribute to Jonathan, to his life and work, your NY Times obituary is—I can't imagine Jonathan not being mightily pleased. I was very sorry my March 14th letter to him arrived too late for him to read, but I wanted you to have this copy, in our shared love and deep admiration for a man who gave us so much.

Love always to you and Stan,
Michael

Editors' note: *The New York Times* did not use Beam's obituary, they supplied their own writer, although Beam's was used in many other publications in print and online.

ROBERT KELLY

COLONEL GENEROSITY—SAYING THANK YOU TO JONATHAN WILLIAMS

I miss the elegance of the man, the energy of the poet, and above all the generosity that made sure publishing was publick-ing, and that brought to the commonwealth (as he might call it), the shivering needy children we are, news that concerned us and made us better—or at least (often) made us laugh.

The first publisher of Buckminster Fuller, Guy Davenport, Charles Olson—yes, of course they had other little books, but Jargon, with the always beautiful big format, lucid printing, visual sense of importance, endurance—Williams put their names and work out where the hungry poets and readers of the late '50s and early '60s could find it, did find it. We were sick to death of the gentrified poesy of that era, and the books Jonathan made us read (made the Eighth Street Bookshop stock, display) cured us, gave us a fresh wave to ride.

I first met him when I was a frantic reader buying on credit (they kept tally for such ravenous ones) and he was working in Ted and Eli Wilentz's stockroom—a tall slender not very articulate young man, much callower (for all the work he'd done, his travels, his Black Mountain days, his publishing) than the upright gent I'd meet a decade later, when he came to read at Bard College. Or maybe he just didn't like me then.

What am I to do with his death? Same month as Robert Owen Callahan, the San Francisco poet whose own publications reminded me a little bit of Jonathan's, and reminds me too that the great publishers are not those who print and distribute great books but those who create a great new zone of intersection of idea, image, music, and history—a new zone in which books can be read, and our minds can be made known, shared and renewed. That's what Jargon did, and Barney Rossett's famous Grove Press, and Dalkey Archive, and McSweeney's, and Black Sparrow, and some few more.

Jonathan knew and revered Mahler and Elgar way back when nobody played them, when academic composers dismissed them as pompous romantics. Long before the recent fashion of rediscovering tonality, Jonathan was humming Mr. Delius to me on the phone, or reminding me of anecdotes in Bruckner's sad little life around his immense music.

What am I to do with the death of any friend? Any one? I have to understand that the last gift a friend gives is his death. The death is a gift. Not in the narrow, cynical sense of leaving stuff for his heirs, or leaving space for his competitors, crowing room for his rivals. Not at all—those aren't gifts, they're obligations or commitments or curses. No, what is a gift about the friend's death is that he has, now, at last, given himself completely to you, in peace and thoroughness. He is yours now, to hold in mind, to be reminded by, to talk to and, who knows, be answered by. Death takes away the alterity of the friend, and brings him to you, me, in the place of sameness, where we know ourselves. And where our own death is waiting.

The grief I feel for him is for a man who was a friend for forty years, a voice in poetry and public discourse grandly and often dizzyingly different from anyone else in his time. The grief I propose the community of poets should feel, though, is for the loss of one of those rare writers who somehow are able to include within their own work the propagation, care, and feeding of the work of other artists. Names come to mind: Harry Crosby, Robert McAlmon, Lawrence Ferlinghetti, perhaps Cid Corman more than any— they were poets who perceived no gap—much less created one—between their own poetic productions and promoting the work of others. Not just their friends—dozens of the writers Corman brought into the world never met him, never did a thing for him, except let him bring them forward as part of the large, subtle project of his own poetics.

So it was with Jonathan Williams. This is the thing that's so remarkable about him—how he embraced publishing as publicking, and what is writing in the first place but the publicking of speech? What he himself wrote, and what he published in the six decades of Jargon, the press he founded, form a kind of indissoluble figure, an ideograph of the kind Pound made us lust for and try to construct.

I need to state a simple gratefulness to Williams, for all he published of the great ones of the last half century—Zukofsky, Olson, and all the rest—and also, personally, for his own work. It was his *Empire Finals at*

Verona that showed me in the late 1950s, for the very first time, that the sparse, ironic, vernacular of what would soon come to be called the New American Poetry was capable of subtle resonance, quiet rehearsals of ancient beauty, shocking clarity. Those poems of his, setting Catullus to new measures at once historically challenging and linguistically (that is, politically) consequential, showed it could be done. There was a freshness, playfulness, and sniggerless sexiness that did speak Catullus. Some years later, his *In England's Green & (A Garland and a Clyster)* allowed the old stuff to show through, the Blake whose own mighty ironies awakened British pastoral into visionary energy and transpersonal love.

This was the same Williams who would, clear-eared and wicked-witted, make lyrical conundrums out of signs along the highway and hasty scrawls in public places—all the while listening to Elgar and Mahler. I once watched him attending to Elgar's *Second*—his whole body moved to the music, stately, arms swaying, as if to some celestial, slow-motion bluegrass. Maybe Williams let the world take him too much as that wry teasing commentator, maybe he was too shy, finally, to assume the vatic role his lyric gift entitled him to swagger about in. Too much a gentleman.

He never failed to recognize and promote those gifts in others. In the dozens of artists he proposed to the commonwealth through Jargon publications, the famous and the obscure are in balance. Charles Olson's *Maximus* in its first outing or Louis Zukofsky's *Some Time* (surely one of the most beautiful books ever printed) share the bookshelf with the unknown poems of Alfred Starr Hamilton, the unlikely epic by Buckminster Fuller, the eerie photos of Lyle Bongé.

Williams reckoned it a privilege to discover and promote the under-attended-to, and he had his own distinct notions of what made a poet or photographer worth his efforts. None of the books made money, or only a few did, so the whole of what Jargon accomplished was to manifest an early and very handsome instance of what had by the mid-1900s become a new art form: the small press, which has now metamorphosed into the moneyless transactions of blog, zine, Web site, file-sharing, and all the other forms of free love we hasten to embrace. In Taoist measure, being small and being heard. Being small and making a difference.

Above all my heart keeps coming back to the generosity of Williams and how he made promoting the work of others into an ordinary and everyday part of his own work, all toward a sense of enriching the community of poets—a community that artists need as much as the commonwealth needs them: a quiet, desperate hunger often recognized only when it has been filled and those who filled it are taken away.

As they say in the newspapers, Jonathan is survived by the poet Thomas Meyer. They met in my house on that visit to Bard in 1969, fell in love, and lived together ever since, mostly in North Carolina (where Jonathan was born and died, hard by Black Mountain College, of which he was one of the most distinguished alumni) and in Dentdale in Cumbria. Thomas Meyer is, in my opinion, the strongest, strangest, richest poet of his generation, and has contented himself with the quiet, the mysterious domestic peace that nestles inside the wild gay life of London and New York in which they also moved. In that quiet (as Schiller famously remarked), his talent ripened.

Jonathan is survived too by their heart-son, Reuben Cox, the photographer. And that is apt. Williams made thousands of photos, the real things, 2 x 2 glass slides, of poets and poets' graves and gloomy places that make us glad. And into the great zone of meaningfulness that his writing and publishing both declared, he drew also American photographers—Meatyard, and Laughlin, and Lyle Bongé—who were creating a new *vulgaris eloquentia* for us, the images of our condition.

For forty years, Jonathan Williams lived with the poet Thomas Meyer—two poets living together, sharing and abetting each other's work. Considering how viperish poets can be, that ordinary domestic creative continuity seems itself a marvel and a demonstration of the kind of generosity I'm talking about. Meyer, who entered into that relation when he was fresh out of college, has been quietly creating an astonishing body of poetry and translations; for me, he is one of the preeminent poets of our time. It seems to me that as different as Meyer's work is from the work of his life companion, it reflects, on an intimate but telling level, the generosity of this grand seigneur we have lost.

Williams and Meyer, Meyer and Williams, wise critics in days to come will analyze what I can only intuit, or foreshadow: each enriched the other's freedom to investigate areas of extreme poetics. To study their work—which always abstained from any trace of the collaborative—would be profoundly important for a study of the psychology of the writer. (Their surface image was appealing but misleading: the portly Henry James keeping house with an even more angelic Arthur Rimbaud.)

They supported one another, these two poets, their work radically different, Jonathan moving steadily into the gaffes and grandeurs of American talk, roadside signs and malaprop miracles; his work moved over the years from complex music towards wise, witty, foolish one-liners, if sometimes into Deep Whimsy where I dared not follow.

RONALD JOHNSON

A MICROSCOPIC/TELESCOPIC COLLAGE OF
THE EMPIRE FINALS AT VERONA

Adjust the focus to fifteen years or so ago, and the glass frames, at a flick, an unshaven Fielding Dawson saying "Jay Zoos, man!"—with a beer can fast in his left hand, a scrap of *The Times* held out for all to see in the other. The long table at which he sits is piled with several dozen empties beyond which a window extends square out over the roofs of Staten Island in the air, in and out through several dozen gulls, for an instant clear to the closed window of Louis Zukofsky's apartment, and Marianne Moore astroll— just—behind a mist that is Brooklyn.

When you look into your head what you see is collage with what is remembered. (Past as paste.) Which was/is:

Fee had had I remember the drawings completed. But the collages needed something more in the order of a jam session with *The Empire Finals* text. At the time he lived mostly third booth from the back, right side, The Cedar Bar: Franz Kline's booth. After several months drinking to the occasion, J.W. and I finally decided to steal him intact, one night, direct to the Ferry. Pick up a couple cases of Bud and some glue. Then keep him at it in the quiet—I can't imagine now why—of Staten Island.

Back at the table. Jonathan's and my flat was rented from an eminent (though necessarily nameless) literary critic who drank a gallon of Virginia Dare sherry a day and towards afternoon fancied he was the Pope. We lived on the third floor and even before Fee had his eyes open from the night before The Critic would ascend the stair announcing "Cock! Tail hour … " He tended to trip on his long black cape as he carried a pontifical staff in one bony hand and a glass of sherry in the other. The climax of this daily process would be a *scene* in which he would, "my deah," as he proclaimed in a voice he supposed approximate to late Henry James, "spit! on the

Church." It was all sadly more apoplectic, and the discharge was liable to spray only completed ink drawings.

Add to the side of the collage: The Critic lived with an ageing "young man of delicate Athenian sensibility"—T.C.'s Firbankian euphemism for gay. (Once in Washington D.C. where J.W. and I both met him, he encouraged one of his students—a peroxide blond youth from Texas with an alarmingly peppermint pink convertible Cadillac—to skip through Jonathan's rooms with nothing but crepe paper streamers up his ass.) There were somewhere in the number of 23 cats downstairs and the kitchen as well as dining room were uninhabitable, at the moment, because of the smell. I was later to sock him, giggle, Henry James, and glass of Virginia Dare, all, clear through a French door into an assortment of yowling fur. Jonathan and I were exiled from The Presence thereafter, without a place to stay and about $75.00 between us. It snowed a hell of a lot that winter, and the painters' lofts were cold.

Zero into the first collage of the actual, the book, the last of the American Empire as Catullus might have viewed it. There we are. "Just the news," as Jonathan was later to state. Jazz, The Bird, The Bomb, Black Mountain blasted, sports (the memory of Fee in his barefoot Rimbaud days playing softball like Franz before a canvas), love, hate, heroes, language. After Black Mountain how do you put it together with where we were? "We are wary? Where are we?"

The poems had been based on the riffs and strokes of jazz and Abstract Expressionism. The tune to play sound around is often a quotation—as if Miles improvising Ives. The first, the Catullus poems, were written with Louis Zukofsky: Louis was to translate the sound, and Jonathan was to do em jazz. After, we bat from Walt Whitman to Stan Musial. The records stacked (Jonathan to this day keeps the record player hot, I'm sure, all day) were:

> Miles (muted on standards, open on
> originals):
> then Couperin le Grand and
> Stravinsky: *Symphony in C*

The light from that window falls, exact through the beer cans, on poems written before New York—between and beyond Washington D.C., and Highlands, N.C. There is there a love letter from Michael McClure, and one to Robert Duncan (it is itself a collage of "utterly unquiet" distillations that stirs still whatever air beneath this magnification). There are as well three or four written to me in letters at the time J.W. and I were first separated: "the renewal of mystery, out of which one feeds and lives" I read now as it is pulled from the file. March 1958. One of these is *The Grounds* written at the time Edward Dahlberg had been advising J.W. to put "loam, ordinary dirt, foliage, moss, and even the dead carcasses of birds" into a book.

Collage. *Autopsy* was lifted whole from newspapers of Whitman's time, and *The Sounds* suspends Poe in the crystal air of Ono no Komachi. Others invent themselves out of their sound: "the ear fears for its sound-barriers" while the last bombs fall "and burst the livers of great whales." "O!" the book ends. Williams and Dawson putting together the last ball game of the empire—batting balls against the void.

The Critic was, as always everyone else, magnetized to Fee's helter-skelter energy, and the black cape swirls an inch closer, as we see it telescoped, toward the eye of the storm of newsprint. I would, I remember, return from a day studying at Columbia to find havoc in progress and the ageing young man on the trapeze of delicate Athenian sensibility sent out for another jug of sherry.

The only words I pick up from this distance—San Francisco, 1973—are those of Fielding staring down on the completed collage of Kevin McCarthy arching his eyebrow at a bar in front of Ed Begley and some forgotten starlet, announcing in miraculous anguish: "My God it looks like me."

PETER O'LEARY

AM SPARKED TO WRITE AGAIN—A SELECTION OF LETTERS FROM RONALD JOHNSON TO JONATHAN WILLIAMS 1958 TO 1979

Ronald Johnson died in Topeka, Kansas on March 4, 1998. Not long after, Jonathan Williams wrote an obituary and remembrance that ran in *The Independent*. There, he writes,

> I met Ronald Johnson in Washington, D. C., at the beginning of 1958. I was using the proceeds of a Guggenheim Foundation grant to read in the Library of Congress for six months, and to publish two early Jargon Society books: *Letters*, by Robert Duncan, and *Overland to the Islands*, by Denise Levertov. One evening I went with the literary critic Marius Bewley to visit a pianist friend who lived on R Street, Northwest, in the house of Mrs. King-Smith, a notable hostess of the time, when the young of the well-to-do were taught dancing and deportment. Another roomer in the house was RJ. He was handsome, red-haired, feisty, ebullient, and clearly very bright. The friendship was immediate…. We joined forces. And I became a mentor, just enough older for that relationship to work.[1]

Together, for a decade, they were companions, living together in New York while Johnson completed his Bachelors degree at Columbia University, and then setting out, legendarily, in 1961 to cover the nearly 1500 miles of the Appalachian Trail on foot, to be followed by two extensive walking tours of England out of which Johnson's *Book of the Green Man*, published by Norton in 1967 (and republished in 2015 in the UK by Uniformbooks), emerged. In 1966, they traveled together to Austria and Central Europe, where Williams gave readings sponsored by the U.S. Information Agency. Periodically, they lived in Aspen, Colorado, where Williams was a fellow at the Aspen Institute, first in 1962 and then once again in 1967. In the fall of 1967, while Williams was on tour in the U.S. promoting Jargon Society books, and while Johnson remained in Aspen working at a restaurant, they split up, Johnson heading to San Francisco, and Williams returning to Aspen to complete his fellowship. Writes Williams,

> In 1967 I was again at the Aspen Institute as a scholar-in-residence. RJ worked again at the *Copper Kettle*. Things were about to change. Our companionship of nearly a decade was always much more peripatetic than restricted and passionate. Roving legs meant roving eyes. When RJ realized I was tired of living in cities, he packed his bags one day and got a ride to San Francisco with some mysterious amoroso. He was 32 years old and wanted more space between himself and the perils of rustic living and Kansas, the Sunflower State.[2]

Initially, upon Johnson's departure, they remained in regular contact, exchanging letters with each other, despite being separated often by great distances, as when Williams began to spend part of each year living in England. Upon arriving in San Francisco, Williams' connections to poets and artists were valuable to Johnson, especially to Robert Duncan, who became one of his closest poetry allies. Johnson's letters often include updates on poetry friends and other acquaintances. They also include rehearsals of hurt feelings; their break up was not without acrimony. Nevertheless, the connection between them remained strong. Williams was Johnson's first publisher, issuing Johnson's *A Line of Poetry, a Row of Trees* with Jargon in 1964. Williams continued to act in this capacity, issuing Johnson's pamphlet of "Eccentric Translations from Two Eccentrics," entitled *The Spirit Walks, the Rocks Will Talk* as Jargon 72 in 1969, as well as *Eyes & Objects (Catalogue for an Exhibition: 1970–72)* as Jargon 84 in 1976.

As the years progressed, however, the relationship seems to have cooled, despite their literary involvements (Johnson, as described below, wrote the entry on Williams for the *Dictionary of Literary Biography*), and as a result the letters from Johnson to Williams thinned. The letters included in this selection were written by Johnson over the course of twenty years, from shortly after their first meeting to shortly before Johnson's book, *ARK: The Foundations*, was published by North Point Press in 1980, a span which includes their break up.

In the early letters included here, Johnson is shown as a young man in his early twenties discovering his poetic powers, ones that Williams decidedly shaped into being. This period includes Johnson's first success in being published, while still a student at Columbia. As the letters progress, Johnson comes into his own, adapting techniques and themes borrowed from Williams, and then testing new techniques as he feels his powers sharpen and expand. Finally, in the last letters, Johnson regards Williams as an old friend and ally, but independent from his former mentor, having fully established himself in San Francisco, where he was writing his masterpiece *ARK* and making his living writing cookbooks.

A NOTE ON THE LETTERS

Johnson's letters to Williams are included in the Jargon Society archives in the Poetry Collection at SUNY-Buffalo. Not until later in his life did Johnson include dates and places of composition in his letters. As a result, especially in the early letters, it's not always clear where and when these letters were written. The photocopies of the letters I have in my possession do not include envelopes, which would have postmarks, clearing up some confusion. Johnson's chronology during the years he was with Williams are not always clear either, often because—and despite their companionship—they lived apart from each other. After Johnson completed his service in the U.S. Army (from 1954 to 1956-7), he lived in Washington, D.C., where he was enrolled at George Washington University. This is why he was in D.C. when Williams and he met. Johnson transferred to Columbia University in the fall of 1958, attending for two years and graduating in 1960. (Before joining the Army, Johnson had attended the University of Kansas in Lawrence for a year.) From here, the chronology becomes unclear to me until the spring of 1961, when Johnson and Williams walked the Appalachian Trail for six months. For a period, if the context of Johnson's letters can be trusted, he appears to have been living in Washington, D.C., again, while Williams appears to have been elsewhere. The sequence of this selection of letters, as best I can tell, is chronological. The places where Johnson lived while writing them seems to have been: Washington, D.C., New York City, Washington D.C., Aspen, San Francisco.

A NOTE ON EDITING THE LETTERS

All of these letters were written on a typewriter. Throughout the letters, I have silently corrected typographical errors and spelling mistakes, as well as changing orthography where appropriate ("60s" for "60's," for instance). Otherwise, I have preserved as much of the quality of the letters as possible. In the early letters here, Johnson added a space between paragraphs. Later, when beginning a new paragraph, Johnson turned the paper in the roller of the typewriter while keeping the carriage in place, without returning it to the left margin, a habit he kept until the end.

Throughout, I've edited the content of the letters, removing portions, which I have indicated by an ellipsis inside of brackets [...]. Likewise, any content I have added is included inside brackets, including dates and places. Finally, I have provided some footnotes to add background information where it seems helpful.

3-28-58 [Washington D.C.]

A little fresh (though Cherry blossomless) spring air from the provinces you there—

O lost and hopelessly city-enchanted brother return to the perennially spring of 400 S. Capitol ...

[...]

Neck hurts. Washing done. Pipe numb. Mary vocal. Satie caressed. Don Q. waiting. 11:47 unshaven. Sleep soon. I. Sit here writing for you placed physically mentally and emotionally in time and space awfully dully—it must be the effect of that steady diet of naturalism in American Lit, ugh, like mashed potatoes morning, noon and night. And then Angry Young Men (God save us and Colin Wilson too) of which I have been gagging through tonight and of which a good cartoon is encl.

Duly received and perused yours of twentysomething March per Elder Pullets et itinerary for the day. Yo shuah is jes abewt th ichnist mahan ah evah did see. Suh to you too. And I'll have you know back or no back my feelings stop short at any length of 1/16" of MAH FINGAHNAILS! They collects dirt that-aways. Speaking of dirt. My Engl Teacher today was telling about a talk he had with some other students (when, if ever, he was a student) with Mr. Rbt-type Frost. A little half-baked-obscurantist-girl poet asked the Frost what "he thought of H.D." And he replied: "Oh yes, I remember her. She was the little girl with dirt under her fingernails!"

H.D. of all people.

Reading an essay by Mencken in which he states: "writing poetry ... is chiefly a function of intellectual immaturity." What's with this 'angry old man?'

Thinking of H.D. with dirty fingernails reminds me of my mother saying in her last letter that she was trying to get through "By Love Possessed" but kept knocking against the TIME magazine image of Cozzens "picking his nose" and it was hard, mighty hard!

Sam lies here flicking his tail through my pipes because he knows I don't like it. So I move his twitcher up an inch and he starts flicking it in my ash tray and around my little pig which I dislike even more. SAMUEL! Stop that! Cats, like people, I guess have bad habits and we have to learn to love them anyway. But Sam doesn't love me—look there, he's getting down from the desk because my pipe smoke is bothering him. Ah incompatibility!

No new collages—I've been working faithfully on studies, but hope to get some maybe done this weekend. Takes so long—you can spend a couple of hours just looking for one word. BUT forge ahead!

> N hey ther—yuh forge ay-head tooo,
> n cum own home. Ya hear?

[signed]
Moi

::

[no date][New York City]
     I know, no epistle in the pouch yesterday, but then neither have I and I was busy crocheting (as thou puttst 't, sirrah) for entry in Columbia's

BOARS HEAD CONTEST ... And, also I went to Bey's to see Calamity in Oscarville: Ye Gods! That last, grand, three-tiered, rouses of Theres no Biz like Sho Biz! And, Gigi, empty-sugar-plum, suppose they didn't make enough money on it? That, only, could explain the hoax.
Enclosed please find entry samples, which, in spite of being written by me might please you. At least one great line—"cold sea churns ... " and another that is pure Williamsiana: "Spawn, fawn— etc. &c & Just think, your first disciple? (I might hit you)! Anyway, you can have Cat., I'll take Hoar. — not a very good trade, but you got there, decidedly, first. I'm not sure whether this contest is a good idea or not, wot wit all the unplucked poultry on campus, and the decision of the academics—but. I was going to send poms to Rbt the Creeley, sans vous, but now that Blk Mt, is kaput. kaput.

Would they be too much for Louis, if I sent them, do you think?[3] He couldn't be any harder on me than thou. HM?

(...)

Let me know.
O Bear:

[signed]
Miss you—
Rom beaucoup unto beaucoup!
Moi, yeah!

::

10-16-57 ? (O.K. so I *dont* know what year it is!!) 8 [p.s., hand-written in the margin, "can't spell either!"] [New York City]

Gadzooks I just noticed I don't know what month it is either what with "Those fierce darts Despair at me doth throw"—but you knocking time awry, what use is it to reckon by months and years? Days distend, you away, filled with useless hours, hopeless for studying, reading or things having to be done. But,

I have been doing something to keep my mind occupied, engrossed—buried—Canada behind bars as it were: Iron Curtained from communication. I've been pasting wonderful poems armed with a razor, ruler, glue and newspapers, Crime, Astrology, True Love, Mechanics magazines and an Almanack. You started it all—the last letter where I pasted the picture of the monkey. I saw the article on Mamie and started without stopping since. I made three poems that night and now there are quite a few stacking up. The others (besides Mamie) are really GOOD**some anyway make it**even, gulp, I think you'll like 'em. Of course there are drawbacks to this sort of thing, the most obvious being the inability to ever reproduce them in printing. The other technical difficulty is relying too much at times on the Gimmick of blown up letter and the fresh positioning obtained from different print sources. But this is also an advantage because the very freshness and delight comes from obvious slogans and advertisements juxtaposed in a way to make a transformation into something different. The reinforcement of placing the words on the page more for the effect of a picture than a poem also makes an effect like Patchen's drawings. An example of all this is one (Japanese-type) which actually falls a little flat printing here, but on the page is wonderful. It has some simple little flowers strategically placed and a HUGE 2. It is entitled simply:

spring

TULIP
TOILET SEATS

2¢ ea

And then another, which is translated rather better, is a sort of Printers garbage. It fills practically the whole page—not in descending order like I have them here—but rather with the impression a garish page of advertisement leaping at you:

6118 Magic Little Tablet

2 Clean Bombs
Six people 60 to 80
8 Sanity Studies
75 FACTS
1 Noisy Radio
10 years younger

500,000 Letters to the Editor
1,000,000 grateful users
1 Rectal Itch
AND A
Big Tombstone
    fully guaranteed

Voila!

[...]

Well—I blush talking so much about the poems. But they are the only news not being out all weekend but two times and then only for a few minutes. And I hardly inhabit this room anymore, you filling it now. How odd it is to find that after living here for nearly six months, it is possible to feel a visitor in my own room. I don't belong here anymore. Home is in Canada. How can I tell you, communicate, "Words fail. In your name poems begin."

(Lotte singing: "Mein Gott, Johnny, und ich liebe dich so ... "

Mein Gott, Johnny,

::

[No date][1959, New York City]

Well, the SUMMER, 1959 ISSUE of THE COLUMBIA REVIEW, bless it' soul, be born dis week, and Lard, Lard, Ise a published poet! One would not credit them with that much courage. I think it is significant that the prize-winners, as well as the other poets represented, except yours truly, are, in some capacity or other, on the magazine staff! And The Editor-in-Chief, whose poetry is so bad that even a professor could tell, has a love example of four pages appr. all like this:

Who
ev
er
woo
all alone
soul alone
so lone so-
lo will sing
a lone soul
will alone
woo a lone
soul so so-
lo alone
soul alone
so ... ,

this amazing production is labeled: THE WALTZ OF THE RIVER. Like?
four pages! I went through that sound stage when I was pre-college! Another
memorable experience in, MOTHER.

I have a mother—
yellow wine hair
knees of pine that sting the tongue

she wonders when I cry

I have a mother—
whose ears are roses ...
whose belly is a bronze gong that harbors sleeping warriors
whose thighs rhyme
whose feet are never never heard

because they cannot hate.

All that, and more! His MOTHER, Jonathan! The second-prize winner
imitates Pound and the third imitates Eliot, which, you must admit, may

mean something for the academic mentality. Memorable title of Larde: SUFFERING THE MUSIC OF THE SPHERES. And such lines as:

> The dark-haired body on the rocks,
> Pale, was broken by the shocks
> Of wave on wave against the stone.
>
> A silver lady stood alone
> Above the waves and granite cliff
> And elegantly shed her grief.

The first-prize winner, is not really bad, in fact it almost might be a poem, but the nice things are hopelessly entangled on the way. I guess he is imitating Eliot too. Speaking about Eliot, studying him in Trilling's class, I finally discovered what you mean about the poetry. How really bad it is! Even when you want most to like it, there is that inevitable self-conscious awkwardness of the language.

Anyways they chose the least noxious of mine, and the one they could most easily make an excuse about it someone questioned their move: The Horace translation. The very last poem wedged in the issue like a plug in the dike. Luckily it doesn't get too soiled being the last.

Enclosed, a tid-bit for you, really more than a tid-bit, and means you can introduce me this summer, no longer as a "critic." This one is good.

Only two more weeks, mmmmmmmmm.

> chk chk scht
>   (scratching)
> sssssssssss!

[signed, in exaggerated letters]
Ronald Johnson, Esq.

::

[undated][D.C.?]

'Lo Busy One,

looks like what you needed all the time was to seethe in the hills awhile. God what lovely poems. The Familiars make it all the way in that (thank de good lord) more frequenter cosmic-chaotic vein of yours. & wow, that Christopher Smarty-pants ending. Mmmm—good as that other 'epithetic' scene. But look, bear, what is there to say about Cobwebbery? It makes it like the best of anybody I guess. What else? Damn dad you got everything working for you in that one—I tend to get carried away with it so much it really haunts me, but you must know how really fine it is. What we all gonna do now that you're the South's finest poet, huh? It really is the apotheosis of the Big Foot country with a capital S: from D.C. to New Orleans, it's all there & gets up & walks.

O.K.

Mad scenes here. Rbt. the Duncan in town for reading the 6th. Chez Rbt. Richmond, who testily handed me out a couple tickets. Taking Mel for great bard, etc. Saw him in the Saville yestidy, said ARE YOU THE ROBERT DUNCAN? Yes, dad, fixing me with both (how bout that?) eyes. & I heard tell of scenes in N.Y. & at Cornell, quote they're paying me enough this time sos I don't have to make a lot of little readings unquote. Well, we'll see. The Creeley & Rumaker arrived grubby but welcome. Nice to have them all, though out of the aegis of beardom they look a little rawrer & the new ones tireder toward the end. All the copies were snatched up immediately, because say, do you know ho has come to work chez Toad? Parker Hodges. Member him? Says he published you in the Carolina Quarterly or some such & has you considering a manuscript. Well Downs don't know it but the beat is infiltrating. He is really quite nice, though not all the Village has quite rubbed off him yet. Will have to have him over when you get to town, etc.

Well, got to get back to the slave quarters. Keep it all UP ...

liddle bear.

::

[undated] [D.C.?]

Big J,

Thanks for the Niedecker, it is lovely & the poems are so good one could hardly expect better. Better than Duncan in retrospect who was less pleasing that I thought he would be. Don't read so well, & he insisted on singing (have you ever heard that stuff?) in a voice no more true than his eyes. But he was very very nice to me—came by the shop three times & invited me to a party after the reading. Barbara Guest, that whole crowd. Just sold her the last Creeley, by the way, saved it for Mel who didn't want it (also just couldn't make it to the Duncan reading). What with him these days?

Yes damnit I have the flower book. Mosta them entries are mine too, dad, can't I have it awhile. Writing a series (a garland) of small song-type pomes now anyway about wildflowers for which I need it. And there is not, nor ever has been, as far as I know, a raincoat of yours here—can't remember seeing it with you since before the trail. Sleeping bags haven't been cleaned, by the way, but am taking them today, so surely they will be ready in time.

Not much continues to happen here. Ghastly season for cherry-blossoms, rain every day, etc. Looks like I'll never get to see them. And then when everyone expected that spring which usually really comes on in D.C., it turned cold. Brrr.

[...]

Hope you get here soon, the toad is getting more & more orc-like.

See you bear,

[signed]
Me—

::

[undated] [D.C.?]

'Lo Big B.:

Well, festivities over, & a colossal depression over all that over 'n well, New Year's Resolutions not made but what th' hell might as well keep them as if they were. So. Here am I.

Mainly depressed over all tham damn work, viz: 10:00 to 9:00 all during the week of Christmas, (no wonder it took a week to recoup) & of course all the free time was tekn up with family, including my little brother who was here for three days, & huge dinners chez Aunt Missile, & (much more pleasant) friendly gatherings here & elsewhere—everybody really damn sweet. Like, a painting of James Russell Lowell's grave which is really like a cross between Ray Johnson & Hartley from Don. Indiana, wow! A beautiful tigergold sweater from John, cravat from Arthur & various pots from Bob & Bill, caviar & socks (?!) from the Missiles an chillum, sweater & socks from home plus huge sweet-scene, etc. With my book credit from the old toad at the Savile I got the Artists & Writer's cook-book which I expected from any of various quarters & didn't get. Where, by the way, is ol D? Sent her a book, (you must read it, really wild) and high-class cracklins, but not even a card. & by the way called there New Year's Day for you in the midst of those Mordor-black clutches. No luck. Guess youz livin it up with the Bone. No call all season from you dad …

Well, mainly depressed over not being able to get any work done. Threw away the poem I sent you & started all over, & it is nearly completed, & did have one day which was productive (see enclosure). But so many things in the pot & no damn time to light the fire. I just relapse into a neurotic (let's just do nothin' stage, letter, the whole typewritten bit. That's mostly it. The more I think of it now, the greater California was last winter. Bears, beetle in the fog, fires in the fireplace, Salinger salads, Jew juice & jabberwocky. Time to 'be always on time,' etc.

I got a card from the Patchens, by the way, & want to write them. Don't have their address, however. Can you send it pronto? Also the Metcalfs sent their love & greetings so must send them current poultry, etc. Martin & Bay another matter—had given them up like you kept saying to do. & now you say write? Oh well. I grit my teeth every time I think of the Knout & Bone—got a card with their name printed on it. Wha? Fuckers. In the future they can sit & rot as far as I'm concerned.

Ugh! here I am getting vindictive again, just 'a little bit nervous' as they say. Come get me on an even keel bear—'love you. Love me?—what the hell, I need you all, evahthins lean without you.

See you later this month, talk more then, write before then, I will, you will, thanks for the soup du jour de jargon, & this may be the muddiest letter I've ever written.

Phew!

[A draft of Johnson's poem "Still Life," which appeared in *A Line of Poetry, a Row of Trees* (Jargon 42, 1964), concluded the letter.]

::

[Letterhead: American Society of the Loon/Poultry Division]

January 30th [1967][Aspen]

Dear Jargonaut—

This stationery is the only bright thing happen in HEAP much slush. The January thaw has set in, & about all I can see it's thawed is some more flu germs & the snow. Slush is much harder to mush through than ice. But it arrived (the stationery) (Lyle) from Peru, Indiana tother day address to Williams & Johnson. It is almost too lovely to use.

I descended from the Opera House Sunday after seeing TWO FOR THE ROAD, into the arms of a Pat Moore Fan Club & after hugging Erika who looked like Dr. Zhivago all in black fuuuuuuurs, Pat said we'll see you later. Later! I could have hit her: was I then going to a chick after-dinner drink at The Paragon? For a night-cap chez the P.M. Palazzo? She knew I had to trudge all the way home through what was at that moment a virtual blizzard. And then Saturday Leonie broke down on the way home and told me the story of her life: how [someone] she has been married to or loved turned out to be queer and she supposed I was to. Somehow instead of kind of breaking through to having someone I can talk to & be friends with, it was so hysterical & sad it simply made me more frantic & hysterical & sad. As Bette Davis sez in the movie—"What a DUMP."

The only thing I have seemed to get done was to finish the m.s. of

THE VALLEY OF THE MANY-COLORED GRASSES. Dedicated to

Jonathan Williams
who first found it

The ulcer pains continue & I've terrible arthritis pains in my knees so I have to very careful bending down or it is impossible to get back up. I simply can't can't can't get into that bag again for if I get a full fledged ulcer I won't be able to work at the Restaurant or do anything but sit home. It is bad enough as it is since the only place I ever go is to the movie Sunday night! I realized suddenly that I will just have to kick over the traces for awhile & get the hell out where there are friends & something happening. So after that first payment I've stopped paying Columbia, got royalties from Longman's, sold a silk-screen portfolio to the Andersons & have more than $400 saved up. I contacted a place in Denver that you get cars to transport for them, and after you get back I'm going to head for San Francisco & see if I can't get a job & stay for awhile & get all this hysteria out of me system. I called my parents & what I think I'll do is this. I asked for a car around February 14th, so I shall take the train to Denver on the 12th & go to Goodland, then have my mother drive me back to Denver (picking up some books & things at home) & pick up the car, then come here & pick of the rest of the things. A car seems a good idea not so much for the sake of money, though that is good too, but so I can carry some things.

I know this sounds horrid, & you'll be furious—but I think I just have to do it. I don't think I'm anymore cut out to endure year-long country stays, as nice as they might be for several months, & I long for some bloody city to percolate in. You'll only be here by yourself for a month—& if I can do it, so can you! And then off to the Carib Isles, etc., etc. And by that time I'll have tried my wings & have seen whether I can get a job & whether the grass not only grows somewhere, but perhaps is greener. As it is I could hardly restrain myself from fleeing there when you were in town, but I thought I should probably wait till yo got back & have you hit your own roof rather than Dave's. So I just sit here & call up Dave & Glenn or Doyle Moore, just to have someone to talk to for a change. Martha has 7! busboys at the moment, so it will be no strain on her if I quit, so I won't tell her till a couple of days before. Ugh, not going is impossible, & going is impossible. But what [else?]—getting an ulcer is not worth it.

Jaundice Johnson

::

November 2nd [1968?]
4566 18th St.
San Francisco, Calif. 94114

Dear Dr. (& Tom—)

Wot hoppen? Did you not receive me Airmail m.s.? Didn't hear from you so I didn't send your name in the Guggle Gaggle. But thought the Imaginary Menagerie has expanded twice the size since I sent it to you, and still will be (particularly the whole first section) changed considerably, still I think it's exciting enough to merit an encouraging word. (As the song goes.)

It's now shaping up to be akind of cosmology or Imago Mundi. And I've devised a way, I think, to end the book like a Mahler Adagio. That one puzzled me for a couple of weeks—but it came through suddenly.

There is a new tortoiseshell puss (with markings like marbled continents all over). Its name is Chaos and I am teaching it to dance. Though it seems incapable of [an electric?] gesture rather like the tedious Isodora.

> I have a cat named Chaos
> I teach to dance
> (crisscross, toss, and loss)
> across expanse.
>
> Chaos in the corner,
> Chaos on its head.
>
> Order out of Chaos—
> hanging by a thread.

Everything goes in the pot these days. Ian says you all made up, and Mel indicated you are ailing (or Guy, or someone). The jungle tom-toms speak of you anyway

as I sit under the Bam, under the Boo.

Just finished Big Ed's Confessions, which is, as Gus said, a funny book. Or Boke as the case might be. This month the huge Vuillard show arrives and I am expecting they will make G. Stein's Picassos look Gris with envy.

[signed]
Love, Ron
WRITE!
[at the top of the page]

p.s. Also saw Lou Harrison recently who says he might be coming to York-shire? As per Wilfred Mellers. His puppet opera of the life of Julius Caesar is being put on this month. And he asked for you address which I just sent.

::

February 20th [1969]
4566 18th Street

Dear J.W.—
And a most cosmic 40th to you iffen my present doesn't arrive: I have been awaiting copies of new Valleys, etc. but though they were sent a week ago nary a one has arrived. The insides should be ok, but con-sider the cookbook one shivers a little thinking what they might have done to the cover, Philip Van Aver and all. ... Anyway it would be most happy to have it there, dedication & all, on your birthday.
I think Doyle is—after over a year—going to do the covers to the BALLOONS [for Moonlit Nights]. At least he indicated he would send the booklets for me to sign and then bind when I had an order. So I'm getting everything together. He mentioned that he brought copies there for Phil Hanes & U. of N.C.—did they have booklets? I suppose not since they weren't signed. At any rate how do I find out, & how do I collect? I shall write also to J. Laughlin. Also—can you send me Mel's address, & Jim Lowell's? I have Henry Wenning's. So far with between you & Doyle, The Andersons and prospective copies for KU and the above—it comes to about 13-15 copies. That's good, and also the money would be blessed as I have finally finished paying off Columbia, am working part time starting first of March, Yea yea yea! Doctor says I'm full-fledged again, though no Kentucky Bourbon for months. It was actually not a bad thing since I got to read &

start writing a bit and got paid by the State of California nearly as much as I will be getting part time. (No great shakes.)

Speaking of writing, I am bemused to find that Saint Geraud who wrote the delightful (if rather less than immortal):

It must be true
That masturbation drives you crazy
Something has driven me crazy

is the white hope of the great unwashed/Rexroth/anti-academic razzmatazz as well as the academics now. In a current review in Poultry Ralph Mills writes "he can with this initial volume already keep company with the best of his relative contemporaries; I mean with James Wright, Gary Snyder, James Dickey, Louis Simpson, Donald Hall, Frank O'Hara, John Logan, Donald Justice, Robert Creeley, and a handful of others—"[4] Wow, poor pussy caught in between like jelly under juggernaut ... He's not too bad actually—but I don't think I understand quite all that fuss—do you? It makes one more & more long for Lorine and some laundered starched verse ... the whiteness of her ALL.[5]

Time has wound round toward the end of February without hearing from the Guggenheims, so I suppose the catalogue will arrive soon indicating my absence from, my fall from, grace, yet again.

I don't think I understand that cover to Jargon's Spring catalogue by La Van Aver. Isnt there some pussy in that picture? There is a huge Blakelock show here this month Glenn & I are going to this weekend. Wow. Will give a review of it in next letter.

YELLOW SUBMAROON has some rather tiresome monsters but on the whole it, with Barbarella, makes the 60s seem—if not worth it—at least acceptable.[6]

be happy,

[signed]
Love
Ron

::

[January 1970]
4566 18th Street
SF 94114

Dear Be-Cottaged one:

You may not have heard yet, there in the damp
bucolic counting the cuckoos in the 1st Symphony toward the first real one
in the larch grove outside, that Charles Olson died about three or four days
ago. He had cancer of the liver and by the time Creeley and Duncan
(among, one supposes, others) arrived they were not even able to see him.
He died of a heart attack, that abused, absurd, bear-like body: "and the
mind go forth to the end of the world … "[7]

[…]

Onward and upward, your unexpected
Mahler arrived, newly tightened and tuned and honed and expanded and
beautiful.[8] I know—Aspens are grafted on the 10th for me as well. A very
personal, direct, directed poem—that of Pussy Galore. The hills begin to
purr horribly. Yes …

I was inspired to go
back to my Song of the Earth translations I was doing for you, and have
spun off in delight the ewig and even "Dark is life, dark is death" which I
thought too loaded for concrete poems. I want to do the whole thing in
kinetic concrete squares.[9] Wow. Talk about limitations. Hopefully, strung
tight as lyres, though. And the idea came to me that since you and Guy and
I seem to be collaborating anyway, these years, why not all three try trans-
lations or whatever, in the manner of you and the Zuk with Catullus? I
have just written him, too, suggesting he might crazily translate the German
and the Chinese and see what he comes up with. There might even be others
interested. Maybe Robert & Jess?

[…]

No one is ready, I think, for the 70s,
but salubrious ones anyway …

[signed]
Ron

::

August 21ˢᵗ [1970?]
722 Arkansas

Dear 'Jonathan',

      It is discouraging, love, to see you settle even more firmly into that attitude of sourness I had hoped, among other things, to break somewhat by leaving. I won't quote your letter back at you (though it is all those things you accuse me of) but rather say remember always "volleyball, Thomas Jefferson, Catullus, William Bartram, Frederick Delius, Maker's Mark, Samuel Palmer, Charles Ives, Mount Le Conte, anemones, Archilochus, Basho, Anton Bruckner, winter wrens, and Wharfedale"—it is in these, not in quarreling with the world, you will grow and expand.

      I might have quoted flippantly from the shallow Umpqua, but it was in essence, too, what Guy Davenport has been sagely writing to you, and what the winter wren sings always. It was enjoy, enjoy. I love you as I said and will not let it turn to bitterness. You no longer seem to write to Guy, or to Kitaj, nor … ? But true friends and lovers are those who wish you well, no matter what you do. You wouldn't wish to cage the wren, and it is absurd to accuse it of vulgarity because it does not, cannot, become a canary.

      I love you, and you love me. Ten years is unshiftable, not shallow. But it would sadden me to lose your friendship. I will not quarrel, and will continue to write, and do whatever I can when you need it.

[…]

I know you too well, and love you too much, Jonathan, to have you provoke me.

[signed]
Ron

::

RJ: Jan 31ˢᵗ, 4041 18ᵗʰ Street, S.F. Calif. 94114 [1979]

Dear Jonathan & Tom,
            "Welcome back to the Winter Estate" a letter begins last
month. Dorothy it seems is looking for our birds (and Don Anderson)[10] in
Africa […]. Meanwhile the Winter Estate must be socked in.
                        ARK was finally shrugged off by Harpers, with
some nudging. I looked back at it and they are quite right—it is indeed
much too much for the city. Only Jess' new color collage has as many angles.
Robert's new Whitman poems are a revelation. Guy's Bicycles awaited.[11]
The poem for Louis in Paideuma has been selected for a New Directions
Best Poems of 1978, but sliced to its ending only because Jay has limited
space. I am plugging holes in ARK's Foundations as well as the diet of the
Nation. The cookbook had been laid aside during the long inquiry at
Harpers, but now must be polished. Has Tom got the new Marcella Hazan
MORE CLASSIC ITALIAN COOKING? I hope to have invented a cui-
sine as well. Slugging away at dumplings.[12]
                        I have a Xerox of Louis' last Flowers, and
am sparked to write again.
                        Galax,

                        [signed] R.J.
::

July 25, RJ, 4041 18ᵗʰ St., S.F. Ca. 94114

Dear Jonathan,
            Your essay is done as well as I can turn it, I think, though
it will have to marinate several days to make sure.[13] I'll write a more lengthy
epistle when I send it to you, but first I need an 8 x 10 Glossy, or some
such professional photo for the Dictionary in which you are to be included.
And to check one fact: In my recollection Empire Finals was actually written
after the 'trilogy' of Amen, Elegies & Jammin? Also I don't know what to
do with those scads of private editions, some printed, some not, but I'll
meet that when I come to it. I notice, by the way, that your early "Garbage
Litters, et c." has been whisked away from the list in rather a Soviet way—
something I'll respect as well.

As I say, more later. Have interrupted the cook-book for a week, as it is, and I'm trying to get it finished for the fall when everyone is back in N.Y. It stands at nearly 600 single space pages in first draft, so will be nearly 1000 when done. ARK went to press last week. Shoe-maker doing a posh new press ["North Point" hand-written in margin] which will debut with it, Guy's selected casual essays, and a couple of other largish tomes.[14] Jack Stauffacher is overseeing the printing and design, so it will be splendidly classic, and I didn't have to even fight when I said I wanted the cover white and shiny as a drugstore paperback.

Best to Tom,
[signed] RJ

[1] Jonathan Williams, "Ronald Johnson (November 25, 1935–March 4, 1998)," *Blackbird Dust* (New York: Turtle Point Press, 2000), p. 228.

[2] Ibid., p. 231. Johnson was born in Ashland, Kansas.

[3] Louis Zukofsky.

[4] Ralph J. Mills, Jr., "Critic of the Month," *Poetry* January 1969, p. 284. This quotation is in reference to *The Naomi Poems: Corpse and Beans*, by Saint Geraud, written by Bill Knott.

[5] Lorine Niedecker.

[6] The Beatles' *Yellow Submarine* was released in the U.K. during the summer of 1968.

[7] Charles Olson died on January 10, 1970.

[8] Jonathan Williams, *Mahler* (Cape Golliard Press/Grossman, 1970).

[9] In 1970, Johnson's concrete poetry settings of Mahler's "Das Lied von der Erde" was published as *Songs of the Earth* by Grabhorn-Hoyem.

[10] Dorothy Neal was a friend and sometime patron of RJ. Donald and Patricia Anderson were also friends and patrons. "The Foundations" section of *ARK* is dedicated to the Andersons; "ARK 38" is dedicated to Neal.

[11] *Da Vinci's Bicyle*, by Guy Davenport, was published by Johns Hopkins Press in 1979.

[12] *The American Table*, Johnson's cookbook of American regional cuisine, which he sometimes described as "the diet of the Tribe," was published by William Morrow & Co., in 1984.

[13] Johnson wrote the entry on Jonathan Williams for the Volume 5 of *Dictionary of Literary Biography*, published by Gale Research in 1980. See, Ronald Johnson, "Jonathan Williams (8 March 1929–)," *American Poets Since World War II*, Donald J. Greiner, ed., Vol. 5 (Detroit: Gale, 1980), pp. 406–409.

[14] *ARK: The Foundations* was published by North Point Press in 1980 as one of its first volumes. *The Geography of the Imagination*, by Guy Davenport, was published by North Point in 1981. Jonathan Williams' *The Magpie's Bagpipe* was published by North Point in 1982.

SIMON CUTTS

ANGLOPHONE DIGRESSIONS

Jonathan Williams approached England as he approached everything: with an erudite and eclectic Epicureanism. In the nineteen sixties he travelled the country from his base in Hampstead London in the company of Ronald Johnson in search of new innate qualities that would fit his vision of the place. It resulted in Ron's *Book of the Green Man* and Jonathan's *The Lucidities* (1967), among many other things.

Later, settling with Thomas Meyer at Corn Close in Dentdale, Cumbria, just west of the Pennines, he extended his fascination for what he came to see as a peculiar place. It remains enigmatic to many of us, even if we come from it. Where he chose to live is littered with footnotes from Bunting's *Briggflatts*, names and places on a journey across the north of England, from the Quaker Meeting House itself, near to Corn Close, through Teesdale to darkest Tyneside.

For myself this territory is somewhat bound-up with a circumspect view of the North, well beyond my parts in lowland Derbyshire. Erica and I once walked from my father's house there in Belper to Jonathan's in Dentdale, along the Pennine Way and then branched off towards Dent, over about ten days. It was a way of locating his open moorland while at the same time escaping the industrialised, over-populated and built-up Midlands.

A SWALE WALK

six poets, editors and artists arrive at

The Muker Literary Institute

Swaledale, North Yorkshire

on Tuesday June 21st 1994 at 7.30 pm

to read from their work

Simon Cutts, Thomas Meyer, Stuart Mills,
Erica Van Horn, Jonathan Williams,
accompanied by Greville Worthington

Photograph by Peter Fuller

Telephone 0748 812127   for further details   Fax 0748 811552

Jonathan was always looking for great pub food, but was often disappointed. Armed with *The Good Beer Guide, The Good Pub Guide,* and on occasion even *The Good Food Guide,* he thought he might find the true vernacular of English cooking. Instead, he was once served the blackened kidneys of a mixed grill at the High Force Hotel in Upper Teesdale in 1977, only to be drawn in charcoal by Ian Gardner for a retaliatory postcard. The Sun Inn in Dent was his local, but only for drinking. It was here that they thought Jonathan must be Canadian because he was such a nice chap! It was at times all very tweedy. He called himself The Squire and often dressed appropriately.

Tom would often cook in the vernacular of the American South. They had published *White Trash Cooking,* and it was with a recipe from that book that they came first in *The Independent* newspaper's cookery competition one year. *Rack of Spam* won them a bottle of extra virgin Tuscan olive oil.

Jonathan often remarked on the names of the owners of the Sharrow Bay Hotel and Restaurant at Windemere in the Lake District. Francis Coulson and Brian Sack were a rather Pythonesque couple, who, they claimed, had invented Sticky Toffee Pudding. Jonathan revelled in the names of all the odd dinners and puddings of English cooking: *Dead Baby, Babies Head, Spotted Dick, Blue Vinny, Wet Nelly, Sussex Pond Pudding, Toad in the Hole,* names he delighted in and celebrated in *Super-Duper Zuppa Inglese (and Other Trifles from the Land of Stodge.)* In these interests, there is more than a nod to Jane and Geoffrey Grigson, and their attempt to locate a certain Englishness.

He thought the beer from Faversham, Kent was called *Shepherd's Knee*, when in fact it was *Shepherd's Neame*, after the family who made it.

He delighted in the composer Frederick Delius, the composer being born in Bradford, and that his brother still had a garage there.

I once took all the bones out of a trout for him at the Tate Gallery Restaurant

We both thought later on that John Livingstone Learmonth's *Wines of the Northern Rhone* was a kind of bible.

I remember Jonathan first of all as the reluctant compere of Poetry 66 in Nottingham, hearing in advance of his legendary epicurean tastes, his 'wants' list, which as a young poet, I could never match or provide. Years later in Norfolk, when he asked for 100 oysters and the best Sancerre, I could.

Jonathan was one of the few Americans who could grasp the game of cricket. We were both great admirers of John Arlott, legendary commentator of the game, but also poet, policeman, expert and writer on Beaujolais ("I like to drink Beaujolais with my Beaujolais," he once said). His drôle, laconic voice, with perfect pace and pitch, still echoes down the years. I think I read that he died falling down the steps of his cellar.

Watching John Arlott on television, ca 1991.

My last visit to see him was to his Skywinding Farm, Scaly Mountain, North Carolina—Corn Close in a parallel universe, the way it is perched above the road and the turn up to it. We went to talk of his archive of photographs taken over the years. We brought with us, among other things, an astounding Grüner Veltliner—exactly his kind of wine, and with more than a touch of Bruckner about it. He only moved from his chair with great difficulty. The Weather Channel was still on as it had been during my last visit, and the video-loop of the fire was still burning in the hearth.

In May 2008 we made a last visit to Corn Close. It was strange to be there without him, and more than a little bleak, but it was such a beautiful day that the valley across the Dee was singing, a score propped-up in front of us. I did a rubbing of Jonathan's cigar-cutter left there on the desk, almost the ghost of itself, open and with the blade receded, as if he were just about to take the closed end off the day's cigar.

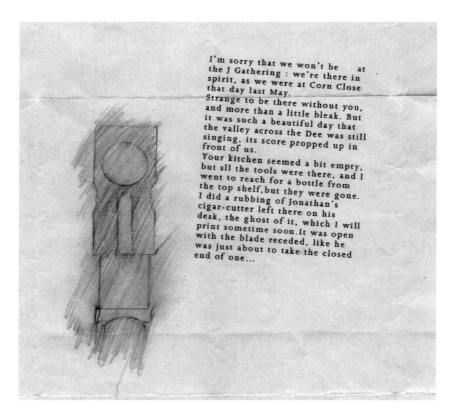

I'm sorry that we won't be   at the J Gathering : we're there in spirit, as we were at Corn Close that day last May.
Strange to be there without you, and more than a little bleak. But it was such a beautiful day that the valley across the Dee was still singing, its score propped up in front of us.
Your kitchen seemed a bit empty, but sll the tools were there, and I went to reach for a bottle from the top shelf, but they were gone. I did a rubbing of Jonathan's cigar-cutter left there on his desk, the ghost of it, which I will print sometime soon. It was open with the blade receded, like he was just about to take the closed end of one...

JW in Norfolk, England, Summer 1993, warming a Polaroid from his trusted SX70 Land Camera, whilst ice-cubes melt in his glass.

Jonathan Williams, Simon Cutts, 1979, Jonathan's birthday at Coracle, Camberwell, London.

THOMAS A. CLARK AND LAURIE CLARK

POEM AND FLOWER

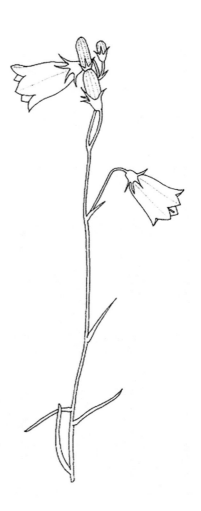

you won't hear it
  on the hill
you won't hear it
  in a hollow
the lost blue tintinnabulation
  of the harebell
you won't hear it

ALEX ALBRIGHT

WHAT JONATHAN WOULDN'T MIND (FOR BREAKFAST)

[This poem derives from Jonathan's wishes from the night before breakfast at Venter's Grill, Greenville, 19 January 1996. Wish I could remember what the breakfast was. Not possum.—Alex Albright]

Coffee
or tea.
Peanut
butter
smooth and
mayonnaise.

Something to put it on.

Juice
grape or
orange.

No possum
no cooter.

Maybe just
some toast
'n jam.

JOHN FURNIVAL

LETTERS TO THE GREAT DEAD—JONATHAN'S LAST WORDS

[John and Astrid Furnival's friendship with JW was rich and long. John and JW's collaborations include *St. Swithin's Swivet, Kinnikinnick Brand Kickapoo Joy-Juice*, and the on-going project they started in 1984, *Letters to the Great Dead*. This piece (2014) can be perceived as their last print of the series with JW collaborating from beyond the grave. The expansive text/image series uses letterpress, etching, silkscreen, and lithography.]

Jonathan's last words

His doctor wanted Jonathan
to spend some of his day upright
and asked me to help by talking him through the procedure.

Several able-bodied pairs of hands
were involved at this point.

When the pivitol moment came,
just as he was to be lifted
from bed to chair I said:

'Jonathan it's easy. Just put one foot down,
then the other foot right behind it'.

He looked me straight in the eye and said:

'Tom, this is
no time for Chinese philosophy!'

Jonathan Williams 1929-2008

THOMAS MEYER

KINTSUGI WITH A FOREWORD BY ROBERT KELLY

[*Kinstugi* has, since the *Jacket* feature publication, has been published in two editions (2011). Flood Editions published an edition with this elegy as the first part of a suite of poems in lament, grief, and wonder. And Coracle printed a limited edition letterpress of extractions from the texts, with four printed drawings by Erica Van Horn, entitled *mending*. Editor Richard Owens' Punch Press published the first edition of this elegy, also in limited letterpress, in 2009.]

SPEAKING TO THOMAS MEYER'S *KINTSUGI*

In that sad and famous way in which every photograph is, whatever else it is, somehow also about pastness—itself the quality that Wittgenstein felt epitomized by a certain passage, "As if from far away," in Schumann's *Dances for the David Brotherhood*—in some kindred way we can and perhaps should read every poem as an elegy.

In Homer grieving for the men of old who mourned for Linos, in Virgil's meaty grieving for the very substance or flesh he gazed at, fleeting as its perception, we read that sorrow which is the true ground of language. It is the reference that language, in its essence and by its presumed first purpose, *makes to what is not here*. Every object or relationship or feeling, ill-roused from its sleep by words, soon slips back into lostness, pastness, leaving the same sort of aftertaste that music does.

I don't think I ever felt this more keenly than when I read Tom Meyer's elegy for Jonathan, a text written in and through the very death it mourned—like a parallel text to that dying. The ancients used to speak of one who is in the very act of dying as being *in articulo mortis*, the limb of it, in the nick of death.

Tom calls the forty-eight threnodic pulses of his observation of Jonathan's dying, his own surviving, by a curious Japanese word, *kintsugi*, which he describes as the "practice of repairing ceramics with gold-laced lacquer to illuminate the breakage." So the very rupture is what is highlighted: the error becomes the meaning of the text. Tom's *presence to* the dying and the death and the after is the golden line that holds all this together. His love that is so worn and deep and thorough that it does not need to speak its usual endearments. When we are that close, so close that the whole of one's attention is given to that person who is going away, love means little more than paying attention. In a strange, almost selfish way, the reader (or this reader) feels embraced too a little in the amative circle of that attention, his own secret breaks and fissures healed by these lines sung at right angles to us, and straight at the dying man.

—Robert Kelly

KINTSUGI:

Japanese practice of repairing ceramics with gold laced lacquer to illuminate the breakage

All dogs bark his name.
He who has gone

there from here
past time's gap. Jumped.
Do we come back in our fathers' blood?
What happened a year ago gets pierced by today?

Where did I leave that book? In the car.
Those uncertain seconds are everything

when I can't put my hand on it
whatever it is. Or wherever.
A new moon. What is not there felt for.
In the dark. Get up, go out to the car.

Set the chair at the table and put
the loaf right there. No knife. Tear it.

Sit. Write. I drift. Books. In black and white
the honey here of a difficult pattern not
to shy from or even follow but let stand
until it sticks. Is that all there is? Some
lines going where.

A place the tongue finds. An afternoon.
Tasted. Said. All the world Maya

while here we are to wonder: Is this seen?
Or heard. Herd. Scene.

At the frilly edges of thinking. Such.
Thoughts.

Sit so you don't hurt the grass.
An impossible grace
everyday we
fall from.

To sit while outside a light but steady rain falls
while someone walks into the room
though he's not there if I look up. I won't.

What a luxury this loneliness is.
To sit in the sun on that flat spot
up behind the house
where the bloodroot still hasn't come
to tell me you are gone.

Once a river only a shudder
of sunlight and water is left

and a complete blank
when it comes to deserts.

Drought I've seen though
how the sight of no rain

looks remains, not a mystery,
but another cul-de-sac

talking about it leads us
down.

That shelter included shadow, surprises.
But why? Hidden under a bushel basket.
Stood in front of. Protection.

Each hand cupped and whatever it is
that needs this care slips like water
through the fingers but remains refreshment.

The key is here but not the room number.
Does that mean try all the locks?

Or wait? For what? I'm sure any angel
would agree: Who wants in when the time comes?
Not the time, but Time. Who, just who.

In a pool beside the sycamore
we see who hides in that tree

with a hand to cup cold water.
Who will come down when?

Careful of the stars when you pass
through the cloud. At the edge of town

I'm standing there. Then look up. See
you and me on a sled

in each other's arms sliding down
a slope. New snow.

What disturbs the air? Strikes the note
and breaks the cord? A match
struck in the dark, after it goes out,
after a few minutes the eye can see
full well.

You whom I never dream of I dream of
your tender final sleep
and think of
those kids lost in the woods
praying to a sonnet of angels
to protect them:

Go, my envoy, into
the month spring comes.

Gathered up and let go. Honeysuckle, wisteria.
A river of stars. Hold my hand.

Startled rust, black and white towhee on the gravel.
Slow long cool spring. Red fox
carries the gingerbread boy across the river. Run
for your life. Run.

My feet almost not there in the wet grass.
An evening, not cold yet spring.

It has come this.
My sitting here writing this
beside your sleep.

Pindar had it right:
Sing for those

who hear the song
and they …

what?
Last. Their souls

asleep, limbs
awake.   .

A thief in the night. Did I say that already?
But isn't everything in the dark stolen?
Day's other half the great burglar
of all we hold on to then let go of.

Gap you could drive a Mack truck through
or the whole vernacular.

Then what's left?
Apart from a personal indifference to pronouns.

All my life I've been waiting for something
and now here it is. Unapparent

like a wood in Germany. Not fog but a mist
for a moment obscures you.

An empty pair of shoes out in the middle of the room.
The thing about waiting. Take away anticipation
and that's all there is. Those words from Latin

"I" tries to avoid. A lesson I can't or it won't be
learned.

Talk with us. We too fear both fire and time
certain they are the same. What is left
when they are done? What is left to do
but move to Spain and live there life's cruelty.

Walk into a room.
Not know where I am.
Once it was Love
had me so distracted.
Now it's Death.

It won't be hours until this happens
what took seconds to transpire.

Moments in each other's arms
when time is a toy. Something simple.

Winds up. Runs down. Clatters.

The story itself isn't remarkable
though not all that believable:

a young man, apparently the gardener,
who tells the women to do something

they don't and then they ran away afraid.

It hardly matters. I've probably already heard it.
Or never will. Anticipation is the—what to call it?
Not the "answer," really.

There is a music
I've been waiting for

I want to say
all my life.
Some vast Russian novel in which I am packing
and unpacking belongings. Mine? I own? My Hindu friends
tell me I'm part of a long line of warriors but
in this life a writer under Sarasvati's blessing.

Flesh and grass. Brahms *Requiem*.
The women weep over the last lines.
The ones not written yet.

They carry a child.

Forty-some years ago
he would've been the Aeon. Today
he sells cars south of Chicago.

I often mistake the watering can for the cat.
For that matter any flux of shadow
seems to be him coming to find me.

"In the middle of the floor," I wanted to say.
Or meant, but it was an emptiness that swept
away that ground to include what else?
Windows? Chairs? A table. A "where,"
and a "we are ..."

Who must dream the dream
before we can dance it?
Honey in the difficult
pattern of dark and light.
That world we see
is music, music in a dream then.
It moves. Red sun. Green field.
Black Angus. Tree above.

Rain. Or night.
Ever careful of the stars.

Yellow river. In a distant haze klezmer music.
On those banks pamplemouse was invented.

No time for Chinese philosophy. One foot
in front of another. "Not being there."

For that they drew a branch to show
the bird had flown.

Put the ending on the table.
Better yet, in the drawer.

Forget beginning and middle.
They are lies. Neither has been

nor ever was. Where were they?
This is the happiness that wipes

the face clean and puts a smile
on it. Stars in your eyes.

Napoleon's men didn't want to
(or couldn't) restore the rose's petals
to the diadem of its stem.

Forever water falls. An ankle held between neck and shoulder.
Completely but easily. Someone walking in the hallway.
Morning details swept up. A damp sheet pulled out from under a
      hip.
Something. Or rather some place. Fingers discover.

Not quietude, but reticence. What does that mean? A net?
A tacit agreement. Again. Not saying. Not saying. Again.

A car though the leaves barely seen
except for sunlight on a wet
morning.

A fight to get rid of "like." Not even
"A car … " Movement. Something.
Color.

Then something else steps in:
"though the leaves barely seen
except."

For me the hardest and last things to do
have been the least.

To pick up your glasses and know
you will never look through them again.

La vita nuova. Where does it end.
Or begin when. The rain and wind were
only mice in the ceiling. Mice

in the silence. Lips parted, slight arch
of tongue. A bit of air.

There was a book there before I nodded off
my hand can't find nor is there enough light
to see just where I am. A place I know I knew
yet can't quite place right now.

The curtain lifts and the dead enter
while the living exit. This is what the world is.
A hand held out amidst noise and dust
whose touch is a wide-eyed lifetime.

No end to what is, and not water
or whatever else we know as stuff

all that comes from this. While everything
so to speak that comes also goes away

and
is gone

Damp sheet pulled out from under a hip.
Moon light, so much, not full, a quarter.
My hand in front of my face. Where to go?

In this room the sound of water, of breath.

In this dream you are you twenty years ago
getting up to pay for lunch

and I am me now thinking "My god,
what have I done?"

knowing
you will die in a day or two.

RESPONDING

GUY DAVENPORT

JONATHAN WILLIAMS, POET

[The following essay was first published in Williams' *An Ear in Bartram's Tree* and later brought out as a pamphlet by Jim Lowell's Asphodel Book Shop, March 8, 1969.]

Jonathan Williams, poet. He is an entertaining array of other things, too, but they are for the historian of publishing to talk about, the connoisseur of fine books, the biographer, the raconteur, the chronicler, if any ever comes forward, of the poets who in our new intellectual ecology have risked their stomachs, nerves, and reputations to read in colleges, YMCAs, high schools, YWCAs, filling stations (yes, filling stations), universities, YMHAs, churches, and even department stores. There is a reason for this goliardry, to which we shall return. It was R. Buckminster Fuller, on his way from Carbondale to Ghana (and deep in Kentucky at the time) who remarked of Jonathan Williams that "he is our Johnny Appleseed—we need him more than we know." He publishes poets, introduces poets to poets, poets to readers, professors to poets, poets (perilous business) to professors, and he photographs poets.

The color slide, descendent of the magic lantern, is still the most charming disseminator of culture, and Jonathan Williams is its master. He is the iconographer of poets in our time, and of the places and graves of poets gone on to Elysium. He is an ambassador for an enterprise that has neither center nor hierarchy but whose credentials are ancient and respected. He is also a traveler, hiker, botanist, antiquarian, epicure, and much else to engage our attention if we wish to look at the poet rather than the poetry. And so, quickly, before the poet gets in our line of sight, the poetry.

Its weightlessness is that of thistledown and like the thistle it bites. Its

Guy Davenport.
Photograph by
Jonathan Williams.

coherence is that of clockwork, at once obvious and admirable. Its beauty is that of the times: harsh, elegant, loud, sweet, abrupt all together. The poet in our time does what poets have always done, given a tongue to dumbness, celebrated wonderments, complained of the government, told tales, found sense where none was to be perceived, found nonsense where we thought there was sense; in short, made a world for the mind (and occasionally the body too) to inhabit. Beauty, poets have taught us, is the king's daughter and the milkmaid, the nightingale and the rose, the wind, a Greek urn, the autumn moon, the sea when it looks like wine. None of which appear often in the confusion of our world. Yet, perhaps all too rarely, poets keep to their traditional loyalties—

> dawn songs in the dews of young orange trees;
> and ranging orisons; and wordless longings
>
> sung in tranquility's waters sliding in sun's
> light;
>
> and benisons sung in these trees ...

That cello passage is Jonathan Williams meditating on Frederick Delius. The imagination of the poet converses with the imagination of the composer. The language for talking to Delius is Delius. And what if the poet wants to talk back to the TV set? It is there that he encounters of a morning rockets blasted toward a star his ancient craft has sung for two thousand years (and probably longer). He switches from cello to clarinet, piano, snare drum, and trombone:

Woke up this mornin'
Cape Canaveral can't get it up …
Woke up this mornin'
Cape Canaveral can't get it up …

But sent a cable to Great Venus—
told her, better watch her ass!

"Unravished bride of quietness,"
blasts off in my head …
"Unravished bride of quietness,"
blasts off in my head …

Liable to be a whole lot more people
than just John Keats dead!

Lonnie Johnson and Elmer Snowden, accomplished singers of the blues, were enlisted in this enterprise, for their tradition of eloquent dismay before a world independent of their will and opaque to their evaluation of life has been under refinement for three centuries, and their sly alignment of technology's troubles with a ribaldry both venerable and primitive is worthy of Brer Fox. The art of Méliès is there too—the poet is remembering *The Rocket to the Moon* in which Verne's astronauts smack the planet's outraged eye. And Keats' great ode. Poets are licensed idiots and can be counted on without fail to note the change when the silent moon—Sappho's wild-rose-fingered moon born from the violet sea, Vergil's friend of silence, Shakespeare's moist starre—becomes a junkyard.

Sketch of Jonathan
Williams by
Guy Davenport.

The poet, like the horse, is a mythological creature. The accoutrements of both are the same now as in the days of Hsiang Yü, Mimnermos, and Caedmon. Their duties are the same, their *numen*, their intractable identity and presence. They are, they have always been. The horse is as archaic as he is modern, forever the "neighing quadruped, used in war, and draught and carriage" that Johnson said he was, independent of time and fashion: which is why the poet Christopher Fry called him the last mythological beast. Eternity seems to have made a separate contract with him, and extended the same gracious codicil to the poet, who also is neither archaic nor modern, or rather is most modern when he is most archaic. For the work of the poet is continuous while all other modes of discourse—mathematics, physics, politics—are wildly discontinuous, repeating stupidities because they forgot the past, stopping and starting because of barbarians, rebellions, and simple loss of vision. The poet works his melodies into the very grain of existence.

An eidetic Ezra Pound, we learn from the poem "Some Southpaw Pitching" in this volume, once appeared to the poet Charles Olson to say, "*Let the song lie in the thing!*" Our other recorded appearance of Ezra Pound as "a familiar compound ghost" was to Air Raid Warden Eliot during the Blitz when he could be discerned "in the waning dusk," along with Dante and Mallarmé, saying

> … our concern was speech, and speech impelled us
> To purify the dialect of the tribe
> And urge the mind to aftersight and foresight

Eliot of course is here re-imagining Dante's encounter with his teacher Brunetto Latini—the meeting to which the title of Jonathan Williams' first book alludes in its elate way, *The Empire Finals at Verona* (1959).

> *Poi si rivolse, e parve di coloro*
> *che corrono a Verona il drappo verde*
> *per la campagna; e parve di costoro*
> *quelli che vince, non colui che perde.*

The ghost also said to Mr. Eliot: "… next year's words await another voice." Another master to whom Jonathan Williams has listened with care wrote: "No ideas but in things." That was William Carlos Williams (no kin), who appears in this volume saying (in *Dangerous Calamus Emotions*):

> him and that Jesuit, them with the variable feet—
> they changed it!

Walt Whitman, he means, and Gerard Manley Hopkins. What they changed is what Jonathan Williams (with help and in good company) is still changing: poetry. "Next year's words await another voice." By paying careful attention to William Carlos Williams, who insisted that the poet's business is to let the world speak for itself, Jonathan Williams learned to make such poems as this:

Mister Williams
lets youn me move
tother side the house

the woman
choppin woods
mite nigh the awkerdist thing
I seen

The title to this poem is a verbal gesture alerting us to cock our ears: *Uncle Iv Surveys His Domain from His Rocker of a Sunday Afternoon as Aunt Dory Starts to Chop Kindling.* The poem defines a culture. Edwin Markham was satisfied to let the man with the hoe remain as voiceless as the Barbizon painting in which he found him. That the world they have been so diligently describing might have a voice seems to be a late idea to American poets. James Joyce offered as the purpose of literature the simple but radically unassailable office of making the dumb to speak. And not in paraphrase. The poet locates himself between reality and the poem, and trains himself to be the medium through which reality flows into the poem.

I found the poems in the fields
and only wrote them down

That is John Clare as he speaks in Jonathan Williams' *What the Flowers in the Meadow Tell Me.* And there is a response:

John, *claritas* tells us the words are not idle,
the syllables are able
to turn plaintains into quatrains,
tune raceme to *cyme, panicle* and *umbel* to
form corollas in light clusters of tones ...

Sam Palmer hit it:
"Milton, by one epithet
draws an oak of the largest girth I ever saw,
'Pine and *monumental* oak':

I have been trying to draw a large one in
Lullingstone; but the poet's tree is huger than
Any in the park."

Muse in a meadow, compose in
a mind!

Any poem worth its salt is as transparently complex as air in a
hornet's nest.

over the water makes a
solid, six-sided music

Wherein every quality is mirrored in another (and an *aria* and a *horn*
are camouflaged into the richness); that the lines are typographically iso-
metric, seven-syllabled, and inwardly ornamental (-net's nest, solid/sided,
s, m, and *n* so placed as to make a bass line to the treble) is as native an
instinct to the poet as hornet's hexagonal architecture.

Native, to be certain, but only after much work. Man is the animal that
chooses its instincts through emulation, and all his learning has roots and
branches. Jonathan Williams' first masters would seem to be Charles Olson,
whose *Maximus* poems he later published and whose master was Ezra Pound.
We cannot draw a direct line of descent from Pound to Olson, however, for
there is an intervening generation. Louis Zukofsky and William Carlos
Williams are at its center, its Mallarmé and its Whitman. Their admonitions
to the young stressed objectivity, technique, honesty, clarity, realism. The
European poem was not to be continued in America; it was not republican.
Rhyme was feudal; recurring metrical patterns warped thought and natural
speech. Images must come not from books but the world. The poet must
therefore find a new shape for every poem, and liberty turned out to make
far harder demands than the sonnet. Hence Olson's heroic struggle with bal-
ance of phrasing, William Carlos Williams' plain carpentry and boyish hon-
esty, and Zukofsky's daredevil integrity and fierce control of rhythm and
design—a passionate mathematics engraved on steel with a diamond. Never
before had American poetry worked with such fine tools or insisted upon
such a craftsmanship. Professors of literature, ever conservative, cautious,

and lazy, will discover all this in their own sweet time.

The young poets who went to school to these hard masters—Robert Creeley, Robert Duncan, Jonathan Williams, Robert Kelly, Ronald Johnson—have by now each evolved a style of his own. The spare asceticism of their training remains, however, as an armature within. Jonathan Williams learned how to write a poem as trim and economical as a tree. And like a tree his poems have roots, exist against a background, and convert light into energy. And take their shape not only from inner design but also from the weather and their circumjacence.

Which brings us to the fact that the honey bee has a lethal sting. Were it not for a long and distinguished history of poets who have balanced a love affair and a feud with the world — Archilochos, Catullus, Horace, Villon, Pope, E.E. Cummings—Jonathan Williams' double-threat handiness with a lyric would seem charmingly schizoid. *Odi et amo*. A settled hatred for one's species (Little Harp's excuse for his *terreur*, and his last words) is traditionally counterpoised in the satirist by a rich sensuality before all that's innocent.

The satire has been there from the first; wit and sense do not exist apart from each other in Jonathan Williams' mind. Pathos must appear in comic socks or not at all. Incongruity seems to be the stuff of existence, and outrage may be our surest response to the universe. There is a moral discourse of some consequence in the poet's reply to political rhetoric:

Hush, L'il Guvnuh,
don't you fret ...

The genius of Jonathan Williams' satire is as old as tyranny. The slave learns to speak in riddles and sly enigmas; *The Blue-Tailed Fly*, homely folksong as it seemed, was in fact a song of emancipation. Look hard at the satires in this volume: their pungency and sass are not irresponsible, nor their wit flippant. In *Faubus Meets Mingus during the Latter's Dynasty* the particular politician and composer easily translate into the struggle between power and art anywhere. It is Jonathan Williams' surest instinct that poetry is not ideas or rhetoric. He locates meaning specifically. To the child's question,

what fer
thesehyar
animules
be,
Granny?

The reply is:

haint fer
to name! why Adam's
Off-Ox
is thishyar
Garden
haint got
no name
neither
yet
but the Lord's
liable to call
thishyar
tree
Arber
Vity
hit's got
thishyar
sarpint
in it

"And out of the ground the LORD GOD formed every beast of the field, and every foule of the aire, and brought them unto Adam, to see what he would call them: and whatsoever Adam called every living creature, that was the name thereof …" The child who inquired about the gingham and calico animals in the patchwork quilt will have heard these words in Sunday School and may never hear Milton's

The grassie Clods now Calv'd, now half appeered
The Tawnie Lion, pawing to get free
His hinder parts, then springs as broke from Bonds,
And Rampant shakes his Brinded main; the Ounce,
The Libbard, and the Tyger, as the Moale
Rising, the crumbl'd Earth above them threw
In Hillocks; the swift Stag from under ground
Bore up his branching head

Nor Jules Supervielle's

Sombres troupeaux des monts sauvages, étagés,
Faites attention, vous allez vous figer.
Ne pouvant vous laisser errer à votre guise
Je m'en vais vous donner d'éternelles assises.
Les chamois bondiront pour vous …

but has his vision all the same of the Garden, its Tree, and its Serpent.

As we read into this collection we become aware that whereas the satirist's predilections are as esoteric as the headlines in this morning's newspaper, the lyricist's predilections begin to display a wonderful strangeness. A pattern of artists emerge—Blake, Ives, Nielsen, Samuel Palmer, Bruckner—and (if we have our eyes open) a whole world. It is a world of English music, especially the Edwardian Impressionists and their German cousins Bruckner and Mahler, of artists oriented toward Blake and his circle but going off by centrifugal flight into wildest orbits, men like Fuseli, Calvert, and Mad Martin. The poet's admiration for Edith Sitwell will have had something to do with this exploration of English eccentricity, and the poet's Welsh temperament, and, most clearly, William Blake himself. The artist is aware of a heritage not only because, like the rest of us, he recognizes in it his origins and values, but because he is consciously adding to it. What Jonathan Williams found in England, Wales, and Scotland was not a second heritage (as it might seem to a casual glance) but the heritage in which he was raised from the beginning. When, for instance, he met the Scots poet Ian Hamilton Finlay, among whose work we can find (in the Glaswegian tongue):

hooch
a heilan coo
wis mair liker
it
    the hiker
s
hoo hoos
ferr feart
o ma
herr-do

he was, as perhaps only a citizen of Appalachia can know, solidly within his heritage. Finlay probably got his matter out of the air (the *heilan coo* can be found in his *Glasgow Beasts, an a Burd, Haw, an Inseks, an, Aw, a Fush*) without necessarily knowing that he was retelling a song that can be traced to Taliesin (the *Câd Goddeu*), is known in Spanish, Italian, Roumanian, Greek, and Serbian versions, and is sung in Jonathan Williams' neck of the woods as "She looked out o the winder as white as any milk."[1] Finlay has remarked of the Glaswegians that their dialect parodies itself, so that arch comic banter has become the preferred mode of discourse. The same observation describes Appalachia, the linguistic horizon that Jonathan Williams has never cared to stray very far from.

English eccentricity goes back to the Druids and beyond—the Sutton Hoo jewelry discovered in 1939 looks remarkably as if it were what Jonathan Williams calls Theosophical Celtic Art Nouveau. From Blake's Ancients (Samuel Palmer and Edward Calvert) stems a tradition. The Rossettis belonged to it; Browning paid it his respects; but for the most part it is a tangled and untraced path in and out of official literature and art. There's Charles Doughty whom entire departments of literature, university after university have not read, a state of affairs roughly analogous to a department of physics sublimely ignorant of Proteus Steinmetz. There's Stanley Spencer, J.R.R. Tolkein, Edith Sitwell. And Bruckner and Bax and John Ireland. And Odilon Redon and James McGarrell. And more—we await the historian of these visionaries. Literature, as Harry Levin is wont to say, is its own historian, and Jonathan Williams' honor to his spiritual forebears may be the beginning of a resuscitation. Meanwhile, we must recognize that they constitute a tradition, and that he has taken up their torch, and carries it to and fro in the United States. His *Mahler*, responses movement by movement to the ten symphonies, will mark (once the dust has settled) the introduction of Blake's Young Ancients to our shores, a hundred and forty years later. If Walt Whitman had married the Widow Gilchrist as she proposed, we should not have had to wait so long, perhaps. And that speculation makes it clear that I have wandered far enough into an unwritten history.

Poetry is always inviolably itself, and it is always something more. Jonathan Williams offers us in every poem a lyric line of suave clarity and a highly involved verbal harmony. The poem itself finds and articulates a single image or action. This is an art like pole vaulting: the center of gravity is outside the trajectory. Build-up and follow-through are not the poem, though the poem depends upon them; the one is in the poet's control, the other in yours. We are not surprised to learn that the poet is an athlete.

And the poet is a wanderer. If his poetry defines and extricates a tradition from his past, his wandering (as Buckminster Fuller points out) defines the curious transformation of the shape of American culture. There is no American capital; there never has been. We have a network instead. A French poet may plausibly know all other French poets by living in Paris. The smallest of American towns contain major poets, and all other kinds of artists. In no other country does such a distribution of mind appear. Milledgeville, Ga., contained Flannery O'Connor (and at one time Oliver Hardy); Milledgeville, Ga., contained Flannery O'Connor (and at one time Oliver Hardy); Jackson, Miss., Eudora Welty; Minerva, O., Ralph Hodgson; Rollinsville, Col., Stan Brakhage. If you know where Carl Ruggles lives, Ray Bradbury, Michael McClure, or Edward Dorn, you may count yourself a learned man indeed. For a decade now Jonathan Williams has made it his business to go from point to point on this network: there has been nothing like it since the medieval scholars who for want of any other means of communication wandered from university to university. His long zig-zag trips can easily be explained by noticing that he is a publisher of books unwelcome to commercial publishers (who are closer to the grocery business than to that founded by Gutenberg); by invitations from universities to read, show slides, lecture on book design, architecture, and poetry; and by the fact that to know artists and poets one has to go to Pocatello, Id., and Pippa Passes, Ky. The true significance of all this gadding about is this: the poet with his preternatural, prophetic sense knows that this is the way he must live. Buckminster Fuller, who has also been on the road for the same decade, knew why Jonathan Williams is there, too: for the simple fact that they are each in his own way doing the same thing. Each has perceived that all other lines of communication are overloaded. Anything worth knowing passes from one man to one man. The book is still a viable way of communicating, provided one has taught oneself to find the book one needs to read. It isn't easy. All the electronic media are a flood of noise. And no medium can replace what may be an essential need in the poet: an audience. Homer recited his poems to people who cheered and even gave prizes; at least they passed around wine. Chaucer read his poems in warm firelit rooms. Every line of Shakespeare was written to move a paying audience. The next time you read a slack, obscure, convoluted poem, reflect that it was written in an age when printing has replaced recitation, and that the poet cannot tell his good poems from his bad except by fortuitous criticism. Jonathan Williams' books have been published in fine editions, many of them collectors' items from the moment of their printing, and all of them by this time scarce. It is therefore not hyperbole to say that thousands of people have heard them at colleges and auditoriums (and at that one filling station) for every five who know them on the printed page. Their clarity to the ear and the inner eye has been tested in the classical weather of poetry, listening faces. This collection, chosen by himself, is the first to be offered to that charming fiction, the reading public.

[1] Ian Hamilton Finlay's little book is based on the transformation theme. The protagonist shifts shape from one animal to another for various reasons. See Buchan's *Ancient Ballads and Songs*, I, p. 24, and Child's *English and Scottish Ballads*, I, p. 244.

CHARLES OLSON

FOR A MAN GONE TO STUTTGART WHO LEFT AN AUTOMOBILE BEHIND HIM

The facsimile image below of the manuscript copy of Charles Olson's "For a Man Gone to Stuttgart Who Left an Automobile Behind Him" is one of three carbon copies produced by Olson in April 1953—two of which are maintained with the original typescript at the Thomas J. Dodd Research Center, Storrs, Connecticut. The third carbon, reproduced below, was in Jonathan Williams' possession and is presently maintained in the Jargon Society archive at the Poetry and Rare Books Collection, State University of New York at Buffalo.

The image below Olson's typescript is the poem as it first appeared in Williams' *Elegies and Celebrations* (Jargon 1962). In this instantiation of the poem the title is emended so that "Strasbourg" —where Olson believed Williams to have gone—becomes "Stuttgart," the city Williams was stationed at while serving in the US Army Medical Corps. The poem later appeared in Cape Goliard's 1970 selection of Olson poems *Archaeologist of Morning* and finally in *The Collected Poems of Charles Olson* edited by George Butterick. As Butterick points out in a footnote from his introduction to *The Collected Poems*, Olson did not directly approve the selections for *Archaeologist of Morning,* and so the instantiation of the poem appearing in the Cape Goliard edition retains a subtitle written by Williams for inclusion in his *Elegies & Celebrations*: "a Lost Poem by Charles Olson, for JW, to inaugurate the book." The subtitle does not appear in the typescript— which Olson produced nine years before the publication of *Elegies & Celebrations*—suggesting the editors of the Cape Goliard edition used Williams' *Elegies* as their copy text while Butterick appealed to the typescript when editing *The Collected Poems*, where the subtitle does not appear.

Composed the year Jargon brought out *The Maximus Poems/1–10* in Stuttgart, Olson's "For a Man" is not a blurb or foreword written expressly for Williams' *Elegies* but a gesture of friendship and gratitude. In editing the poem for Olson's *Collected*, Butterick clearly invests the typescript copy with greater authority than its first published appearance edited by Williams. He not only excises the subtitle given the poem but splits the poem into two discrete sections by restoring a "2" that appears in the typescript and not in *Elegies*. What Butterick does not restore from the typescript is the title—which he addresses in a textual note at the back of the collection—and the dedication at the bottom right of the typescript: "for j w / o."

—Richard Owens

For a man gone to Stuttgart
who left an automobile behind him

a Lost Poem by Charles Olson, for JW, to inaugurate the book

> the callacanthus
> out again (the golden fury seen
> thru those red candles
>
> not at all a dead car, curiously,
> even though it hasn't moved as what pushes out buds
> has
>
> not deadhead (as Grady's
> two were, all winter

Beyond, the grove of little dogwood (today's
entry

> But, by the heady red flowers (their smell
> will be heavy), the large dogwood (the single bush,
> back of the stone steps,
> glares
>
> and it came out this way (just after you had left,
> a year ago

suddenly the spring field is blue, of figwort
and the callacanthus smell is intercepted by that color
as the dogwood was by the green of my pleasure
that I slept under it, for an hour, and woke,
as they have, to the rising of
the forces

*Charles Olson, Black Mountain
College, 1953. Photo by JW.*

CHARLES OLSON

NOTA TO JAMMIN' THE GREEK SCENE

Charles Olson, Black Mountain College, 1953. Photo by JW.

NOTA:

Fluff it. Everything got treated as scalar for the 2500 years immediately preceding. And indeed the Gods

It will take a little time still before more know how serious we cards are

The risk now is the opposite of theirs. To be serious at all. Thus the real danger is the corruption of youth by hecticism. The false speed of the mere exercise of terminology. Cant. Anything for the phrase from the stance

What Brother Jonathan does in hyar is to keep up the velocity at the same time that the things are let be. Ganymedes, or Echo, or that one Io, get back, by vulgarism, their patent vector powers. In his lightness the spoof

Barbarism, neologism, vulgarism, these London better have her old car out for The soul sd Duns Scotus is on a rubber band runs out the mouth and if you wake a body tee quick

I'm sure we got askance from utter shyness. They made us shy, the whole thing fronted so. We winced. Now we's wincin' back. I mean, we's shy. Bro Jonathan, he shy   He's got these things where   We's bristletails and earwigs, most even at the feast

ROBERT DUNCAN

PREFACE TO JONATHAN WILLIAMS' *ELEGIES AND CELEBRATIONS*

Robert Duncan, Mission District, San Francisco, 1955. Photo by JW.

Prizefighters, winners, prizepainters, homeruns, everybody's homesick soldier boy. "Whip/whap, that's it" but "the eyes are the mirrors of the soul." "The man in our hearts stands" "stifling all repulsion." These poems come "across invisible mountains" ELEGIES & CELEBRATIONS; and declarations too then of occult allegiances.

The accomplished thing remains amazing: that this style permits busy effect, passionate utterance, cool and hot jive, right scattert insight, and nice discrimination to co-exist. Permits? demands. It is the demand that makes its path poetry. The collagist recognizes his sense of collage. I, who have searched for love thru poetry, find it here: painful as Truth is painful— "and with fact's stroke it came up swirling"; the "completely impossible" of the poem THE PROBLEM—and wish-full too "under lightning we lay" "suited to loneliness."

Such life in writing forces us, even as it touches us most intimately, to recognize that we share only here what is unique. There are "unrelieved facts" and sensualities. The smart enthusiasm and the cantus firmus: he insists. These poems outlive me as I read. They are not comfortable.

The assertion by which the dilettante true to his delecto moves into the passion of beauty is the strength that moves us.

—Robert Duncan 1956

JAMES MAYNARD

SOME NOTES ON JONATHAN WILLIAMS AND ROBERT DUNCAN

One of the scholarly luxuries of the Poetry Collection's holding of both the Jargon Society and Robert Duncan Collections is the ability to read both sides of the Jonathan Williams/Robert Duncan correspondence in their extant entirety. For Williams, what became a significant literary relationship began, innocently enough, with a letter he typed at Black Mountain College dated 6 October 1951. Having been assigned a paper on Duncan's writing by Charles Olson, JW wrote to Duncan asking for a list of his available publications. (What young student writing to a poet can ever know where such an overture will lead?) Earlier that summer, Williams had traveled to Black Mountain—where Duncan himself would later teach as Robert Creeley's replacement in the spring and summer of 1956—from the Institute of Design in Chicago to study photography with Aaron Siskind and Harry Callahan. As he recounts in a 1973 interview with Barry Alpert, prior to leaving for Asheville, NC, Williams had attempted to visit with Duncan during a trip to San Francisco in June of 1951, but the two did not connect. Although Williams' letters indicate that Duncan responded to his initial query, the first surviving letter from Duncan to JW is from the fall of 1953, in which Duncan describes his efforts to distribute and sell copies of Jargon's *Maximus* in Berkeley. In 1954 Williams returned to San Francisco where, in his own words, he "stayed … about 6 or 8 months, [and] became very close to Duncan." JW's photographs of Duncan and Jess, taken against an industrial background from the Mission District in the spring of 1955, were later published in *Blackbird Dust: Essays, Poems, and Photography* (Turtle Point Press, 2000) and *A Palpable Elysium: Portraits of Solitude and Genius* (David R. Godine, 2002).

For Williams' collection of poems entitled *Elegies and Celebrations*, published by Jargon in 1962, Duncan wrote a 1956 preface—reprinted here in this issue of *Jacket*—praising the writing for, among other things, its "smart enthusiasm." But just a year later, in a letter to Denise Levertov dated 12 February 1957, Duncan qualified his remarks by stating: "In my introductions to Jonathan's poems I think I anticipated the disabilities as well as the virtues. He has enthusiasms but not passions. He collects experience; don't undergo it." Truth be told, by this point in time the correspondence between Duncan and JW had become severely intense in both frequency and tone in the many months leading up to Jargon's 1958 publication of Duncan's *Letters: Poems 1953–1956*. In his letters Duncan grows increasingly upset with Williams over several frustrations pertaining to delays in the production process as well as Williams' marketing and pricing of the book. A few of these disagreements are mentioned by Robert J. Bertholf in his afterword to the Flood Editions reprint of the book (2003), which usefully provides transcribed excerpts from Duncan's detailed memos to Claude Fredericks, the printer chosen for the letterpress publication. At the height of his discontent, Duncan went so far as to confide to Levertov a decision "to strike Williams out of my world entirely." Nonetheless, the early letters back and forth between Duncan and Williams leading up to the completion of *Letters* present a remarkable record documenting a crucial period in the emergence of Duncan's poetics, the early history of Jargon, and the individual actions and communal interactions of the larger group of Black Mountain poets.

Although Duncan never quite cut out Williams "entirely," after 1960 his letters to JW became increasingly intermittent, with gaps of as many as three or four years in between the occasional short letter or Christmas greeting. Williams, however, continued to write Duncan with some regularity into the 1980s, sending him invitations to visit, reading announcements, Jargon newsletters, and brief updates and notes often bemoaning Duncan's relative silence. (How ironic, then, that Williams would appreciatively quote several times in print Duncan's statement that "Responsibility is to keep / the ability to respond.") And yet, Duncan did contribute a picture-poem entitled "Johnny's Thing" to *Truck* magazine's special twenty-first issue, "A 50th Birthday Celebration for Jonathan Williams" (1979). After Duncan's death on February 3, 1988, Williams published an obituary for him six days later in the British newspaper *The Independent* (reprinted in *Blackbird Dust*), in which, along with lamenting the fact that he hadn't seen him in twenty years, JW cited their "shared tastes on the margins of American culture" and praised Duncan as "the bard of gay domesticity" who "was the absolute master of the campy imagination." Surely one could make similar claims about Williams. In hindsight, such a longstanding distance between the two provides an additional layer of irony when reading the following poem dedicated to Duncan by JW, first published in *The Empire Finals at Verona: Poems 1956–1957* (Jargon, 1959) and subsequently collected in *An Ear in Bartram's Tree: Selected Poems, 1957–1967* (University of North Carolina Press, 1969) and *Jubilant Thicket: New & Selected Poems* (Copper Canyon Press, 2005):

A Vulnerary
(for Robert Duncan)

one comes to language from afar, the ear
fears for its sound-barriers—

but one 'comes', the language 'comes' for
The Beckoning Fair One

plant you now, dig you
later, the plaint stirs winter
earth …

air in a hornets' nest
over the water makes a
solid, six-sided music …

a few utterly quiet scenes, things
are very far away—'form
is emptiness'

comely, comely, love trembles
and the sweet-shrub

ROSS HAIR

"HEMI-DEMI-SEMI BARBARIC YAWPS" — JONATHAN WILLIAMS AND BLACK MOUNTAIN

> *I yearn for more accommodation, more generosity, more passion on the part of writers who take it upon themselves to publish others. I don't think poetry in the hands of little groups helps very much.*
> —Jonathan Williams, interview with Barry Alpert, 1973

Before enrolling at Black Mountain College, Jonathan Williams had experienced a number of different education institutions, which included studying art history at Princeton (for three semesters), "painting with Karl Knaths at the Phillips Memorial Gallery in Washington, etching and engraving with Stanley William Hayter at Atelier 17 in New York, and the whole range of arts at Chicago's Institute of Design" (Johnson, "Jonathan Williams," 406). It was this educational trail that eventually led Williams to Black Mountain College, where he enrolled in 1951 in order to study photography with Harry Callahan. Williams made the decision while studying typography and graphic art at the Institute of Design where Callahan was teaching, and where the potter and Black Mountain teacher M. C. Richards, in the spring of 1951, visited as part of a recruitment drive for the college. Richards was Williams' first exposure to Black Mountain. As he explains to Robert Dana, it was Callahan who encouraged him to sign up there:

> It never occurred to me to want to go there particularly. But Harry Callahan the photographer whom I wanted to study with, said one afternoon, "I'm going to be down in North Carolina this summer. Why don't you sign up at Black Mountain College?" "Well," I said, "I just heard about Black Mountain yesterday." "There's a terrific guy named Aaron Siskind, friend of mine from New York, who's going to come down too." So it sounded perfect. And I didn't know who

Charles Olson was. He just happened to be on the place, as I say, when I got there. (201–2)

Williams' first impression of Olson was of "a huge myopic man [...] shambling about the place" who would subsequently encourage Williams to pursue other creative avenues in addition to photography (*Magpie's Bagpipe* 83). Although, according to Duberman, "it was more a case of antagonism than love at first sight between Williams and Olson," the rector of the college still managed to influence both Williams' "poetic vision" and his "whole vision of life" (382):[1]

> The most persuasive teacher I ever had was Olson ... I really didn't have knowledge of or interest in the Carlos Williams/Pound line of descent. Olson opened that up for me. I found him an extremely enkindling sort of man, marvellously quick and responsive. You got a lot from him at all times. (383)

Equally important was Olson's influence on Williams' publishing activities. Although he had already published his own poem, "Garbage Litters the Iron Face of the Sun's Child," under the Jargon imprint, it was Olson, Williams claims, who spurred him on to continue publishing. "The reason, really, why Jargon started," Williams tells Dana, "was to publish Olson":

> Golden Goose published Robert Creeley's first book and were going to publish an Olson book, but then they went bust. And so [...] there was nobody, as far as we could determine, who was going to publish any Olson. Being new to the cause, as well as full of adolescent fervour, I decided I was going to do it. (192)

Williams went on to play a pivotal role in establishing the reputations of many of the poets closely associated with Black Mountain, and the "school" of poetry with which it became synonymous, by publishing their early work. Most significantly, perhaps, was Jargon's role in publishing Olson. In 1953, Jargon published the first edition of Olson's *The Maximus Poems/1–10* which, typographically, Williams remarked in 1989, "is the best thing Jargon has given us to date" (*Uncle Gus* 5). A second volume, *The Maximus Poems/11–22* followed in 1956. Four years later, in 1960, these two volumes were published, in conjunction with Corinth Books, as a single edition. During this period, roughly from the mid-1950s to 1960, Williams published other Black Mountaineers, including Victor Kalos and Joel Oppenheimer. The latter's first poem, *The Dancer*, was published in 1951 as a pamphlet, accompanied by the first printed work by another notable Black Mountain student, Robert Rauschenberg. Jargon published four titles by Creeley between 1953 and 1959 and in 1958 published Robert Duncan's *Letters: Poems 1953–1956* and Denise Levertov's *Overland to the Islands*. Along with Larry Eigner, who Jargon published in 1960, Levertov was a poet closely associated with Black Mountain despite never visiting the college. Together, this roster presents a comprehensive cross-section of what is generally perceived as the Black Mountain School of poetry. With the exception of Kalos, all of these poets, including Williams himself, were featured in Donald Allen's anthology *The New American Poetry* (1960) as representatives of what Allen categorised as Black Mountain poetry:

> The first group includes those poets who were originally closely identified with the two important magazines of the period, Origin and *Black Mountain Review*, which first published their mature work. Charles Olson, Robert Duncan, and Robert Creeley were on the staff of Black Mountain College in the early fifties, and Edward Dorn, Joel Oppenheimer, and Jonathan Williams studied there. Paul Blackburn, Paul Carroll, Larry Eigner, and Denise Levertov published work in both magazines but had no connection with the college. (xii)

After this group of poets appeared in *The New American Poetry*, Duberman notes, "the three measuring rods that categorizers have used to admit or deny a place in the school to given individuals" have been determined by a perception of "Black Mountain as a place, a review and a section in a history-making anthology" (388). "Diverse as those measurements are," Duberman stresses, "they seem downright uniform when set against the actual work of the individuals in question—for the differences in their styles are vast" (388).

This may be one of the reasons why Williams, despite his close and largely amicable links with several of the Black Mountain poets, and his keen promotion of their work, remained ambivalent about being associated with the college and the school of poetry it inadvertently sponsored. Williams has claimed to be "as little interested in coterie as I can possibly be": "Princeton was one club, and Black Mountain was another. I made distance from each as quickly as possible" (*Blackbird Dust* 119). Stressing similar aversions in an interview with Jim Cory, Williams claims: "I don't like labels. I don't like being called a Black Mountain poet. I don't feel comfortable with that. BMC is a place I studied at 40 years ago" (3). Williams elaborates on similar misgivings in an interview with Barry Alpert:

> I've always been wary and sensitive to "the exclusive." Particularly these days, whether it's true or not, Black Mountain has come to be a "way," and a group of people, rather embattled and rather isolated. And I, frankly, while I certainly derived a tremendous amount from it, at the time, I want no more to do with it. Obviously, at the time it was a place where I knew some very important people to me. It did a lot of things for me. I published some books for them and they did some things for me, but that's been over with now since about 1956. (59)

This essay examines the reasons behind Williams' ambivalent relationship with Black Mountain (both the college and the "school" of poetry) and elucidates the various ways in which Williams distanced himself from the label. However, as his numerous interviews, accounts, and essays attest, Williams remained gracious enough throughout his career to acknowledge the beneficial and formative influence that Black Mountain had on him as a poet and as a publisher. Indeed, as this essay will argue, Williams' relationship to Black Mountain is, ultimately, a paradoxical one. As Kyle Schlesinger, in his illuminating overview of Jargon's history, suggests, "The Jargon Society may forever be marked by Williams' stint as a student at BMC, what did not change (paraphrasing Olson) was the will to change" (para 5). While that "will to change" would eventually lead Williams to question and challenge the very ethos of Olson's Black Mountain, the lessons he took away from the college, as we shall see, opened his eyes and ears considerably as a writer and as a publisher. Indeed, contrary to Thomas F. Merrill, who believes that "the aims of Black Mountain and the aims of

Charles Olson are indistinguishable" and that "Black Mountain and Olson project one another" as "the hallmark of an attitude, a perspective, a 'stance' […] that literary 'school,' magazine, College, and man all share," Williams, by applying many of the lessons he learnt from Olson, puts considerable distance between himself and the "Black Mountain" label in order to acknowledge the more diverse achievements of the college's faculty and alumni that flourished beyond that prescriptive moniker.

OLSON'S BOYS

Whereas Williams saw Black Mountain College as simply a place where he had studied, Michael Davidson suggests that Black Mountain "was both a place and an ideology, a community and a set of legitimating practices and forms" (40). The latter certainly seems the case for the students that fell under Olson's influence at Black Mountain. According to Duberman, Olson "was impossible to ignore—not simply because of his mountainous size, but because of his largeness of manner, the way he disposed himself" which prompted reactions that ranged from "intense dislike to blind adulation" (369). Duberman's suggestion that these reactions tended to "cluster strongly on the side of admiration" is reiterated by Tom Clark who notes how Olson "won from most of his listeners a trust that included considerable suspension of disbelief" (Duberman 370; Clark 143). The relationship between Olson and his acolytes was a mutually dependent one, however, with the rector being "overprotective of his *boys* and overly reliant on their adoration" (Duberman 376).

Indeed, as Duberman emphasis implies, Olson's Black Mountain was predominantly a male affair "organized around a masculine heteronormative model" cemented via "fraternal bonds" that sidelined the college's female minority (Davidson 18, 16). Davidson's assessment is one shared by Williams. "Black Mountain's major disservice to many persons," he suggests, "was a *machismo* thing that revolved around Olson's stance: that men were the shakers and makers, and women cooked the cornbread and made children and kept quiet" ("Colonel" 77). Echoing Williams' observation, Davidson suggests that the female students "who attended Black Mountain were not exactly kept out of Olson's classes, but they had a difficult time learning under his autocratic pedagogy" (36). No doubt, this was due to what Clark calls "the standard Black Mountain 'straight' male view of women as alluring but largely vacuous creatures" (210). And with "many more unmarried men than women in the community during its last years," as Duberman suggests, "sexual tension and rivalry could be fierce," exacerbating "the decided *machismo* feel to the community" which, under Olson's influence, "measured masculinity against the specific qualities found in the males at the head of the pecking order: Olson, Creeley and Dan Rice" (397, 398). According to Duberman this established "a hierarchy based on talent, toughness, intelligence and honesty" which "could be as rigidly exclusive, as impassable to the uninitiated—and *more* male chauvinist—than anything found on a traditional university campus" (407).

Williams had experienced a traditional university campus as an undergraduate at Princeton. Disillusioned with the "arrogant, boring" and "anti-intellectual" students there, Williams left after three semesters: "There were a tremendous number of people who were sleeping their way through four years, including the faculty" (Dana 199). The highly charged masculine climate of Black Mountain, however, fostered similar indiscretions. "There were sexual thugs by the dozen on campus," he tells Ronald Johnson, and describes his fellow students as "he-men flaunting their hemi-demi-semi barbaric yawps in the sylvan air of Black Mountain" (229).

Alluding to Whitman in "Song of Myself"—"I too am not a bit tamed—I too am untranslatable / I sound my barbaric yawp over the roofs of the world"—Williams raises significant questions about the deeper impulses and implications of the chauvinistic thuggery at Black Mountain (87). As a poet who, as Robert K. Martin notes, "still continues to challenge our assessment of our sexuality and the ways we organize it," and who "refuses the tyranny of the family and compulsory heterosexuality," Williams' allusion to Whitman subtly queers the heteronormative model of Black Mountain by identifying the homoerotic dynamics and tensions simmering under the surface of its intensely straight male bonds and heteronormative model (xxi). Indeed, Whitman's "barbaric yawps" and the claims about "the manly love of comrades" he expresses throughout his poetry speaks eloquently for both hetero- and homosexual values (272). According to Ed Folsom and Kenneth M. Price, the imagery and the language that Whitman frequently uses in his poems "do not prohibit one from concluding that he engaged in genital sexuality with his male lover, but neither do they require that conclusion. The terms themselves retain an insistent mystery, a feature Whitman prized highly in love poetry" (65). The "insistent mystery" of Whitman's ambiguous language is also effective for highlighting what Rachel Blau DuPlessis considers a distinct "compact of hetero- and homosexual men in the formation of 1950s poetic manhood, no matter the possible homophobia of the straight men, or the exclusionary campiness of the gay men" (para 82).

The language and imagery in Whitman's poetry pertinently anticipates this ambiguous "compact" of sexualities that DuPlessis describes, with Whitman's espousal of "manly" virtues and relationships speaking plausibly for homoerotic and homosexual relationships while also anticipating the "accelerated exchange[s] of emotionally complex manhoods" that Williams recognised at Black Mountain (para 82). Indeed, the fact that a Whitman poem can "slip ambiguously between celebrations of same-sex and opposite-sex love" implies that the notion of manliness and "manly" relations does not so much reassert and reaffirm distinct notions of gender and sexuality but exposes their instability and ambiguity (Erkkila 144).

But, in invoking Whitman's "barbaric yawps," Williams also tacitly acknowledges how "straight" manhood at Black Mountain was expressed and performed through hyper-masculinised, feral expressions of self, "which meant, inevitably, a lot of noise—'pure messy noise,' as Francine du Plessix Gray has called it" (371). However, because it was such an intensely small and isolated community, there was, according to Duberman, "a great deal more 'self-expression' at Black Mountain than selves to express" (372). Such unfettered self-expression brought with it numerous casualties. Consequently, Williams "periodically had to take people to his family's summer home in nearby Highlands to protect them from, or nurse them through, a crack-up" brought on by the pressures and excesses of campus life (Duberman 395).

Thus, these self-expressive "barbaric yawps" were, to use Davidson's term, "legitimated" by Olson's pedagogic model. Olson "was dealing with a group of mostly late teen-agers/early adults, and in a highly charged, isolated community setting" (Duberman 371). This, Duberman suggests, "meant, inevitably, a lot of noise," which Olson actively encouraged "in the hope that something that might count would come out of it" (371–2).

OLSON AND SITWELL

Despite his charismatic teaching style, Olson also met resistance from some of the college's female students, as Williams explains:

> He was a real dazzler, and most people were there prepared to be dazzled. Not everybody. I remember Francine du Plessix [Gray] thought he was a total crock. "I don't feel I have to teach girls as ignorant as you. You shouldn't be in my class." [...] They were great antagonists. (Dana 207)

Williams found his own ways of resisting Olson's imposing autocracy, but he did so by utilising the experiences and lessons he learnt from the man himself. As he was for many of the students at Black Mountain, Olson was instrumental in Williams' development as a poet. "No blarney and no mush" and "a useful guide for any of us, now," is how Williams, in his essay "Am-O," describes the "marginal comments made scrupulously and magnanimously by Olson on piles of fledgling JW poems" (*Magpie's Bagpipe* 8). Such guidance, however, came with its own costs, as Williams has explained:

> The only problem was, Olson is almost enough to wipe you out … It took me a long time to get out from under Leviathan J. Olson. Of course some poets said that I would be stuck there. They didn't like him. Zukofsky thought I was being victimized. Rexroth thought so. Dahlberg still thinks so. He asks baleful questions like "Why do you imitate Olson? and Pound?" [Dahlberg has elsewhere referred to Olson as the Stuffed Cyclops of Gloucester.] I don't think I do, but I would say it took me ten years to achieve whatever the thing is they call "my own voice." (Duberman 383–4)

Williams eventually found his own voice by assimilating Olson's example with other models and influences. "Well, one of the first poems that seemed to me really did the job was a poem about Stan Musial, from 1958,"

Williams tells Cory, referring to "O For A Muse of Fire!" published in his 1959 collection, *The Empire Finals at Verona* (1). Despite the title's allusion to Shakespeare's *Henry V*, Williams' poem is concerned with baseball, one of the most popular sports at Black Mountain and which, according to Duberman, was integral to the Black Mountain "machismo:"

> There was, in fact, a decided machismo feel to the community in these years—like the costume parties where people came dressed as gangsters and acted as tough as they could; or the drunken binges (men only) where the palm went to those who could swig the home brew straight—and hold it down; or the "wild thrill" from defeating the championship local baseball team; or the fascination with—even the occasional appearance of—motorcycles (George Fick got fifteen stitches in the face after one crash). (398)

"O For A Muse of Fire!" inverts the implicit machismo of the sport by celebrating a legendary moment in baseball history when one of its most celebrated hitters, Stan Musial, on May 13, 1958, reached his 3000-hit milestone. "Only six major-league players in baseball history had hit safely 3000 times prior to this occasion," Williams adds in a footnote to the poem: "The density of the information surrounding the event continues to surprise me, rather belies Tocqueville's assertion than Americans cannot concentrate" (*Jubilant Thicket* 259).

After establishing some initial facts regarding the event—date, place, time, attendance, situation, public address—Williams adopts the idiomatic terminology and colloquialisms—including Musial's nickname, "Stan the Man"—and emulates the tone of the sports pundit:

The Muse muscles up; Stan the Man stands … and

O, Hosanna, Hosanna, Ozanna's boy, Moe Drabowsky comes

2 and 2
"a curve ball, outside corner, higher
than intended—
I figured he'd hit it in the ground"

("it felt fine!")

a line shot to left, down the line,
rolling deep for a double—

("it felt fine!")

Say, Stan, baby, how's it feel to hit 3000?

"Ugh, it feels fine" (*Jubilant Thicket* 259–260)

"If you look at that poem," Williams explains to Cory, "it's kind of a peculiar marriage of Edith Sitwell and Charles Olson. Which is an unholy marriage! Neither of course could possibly, would possibly, countenance the other" (1). Sitwell, an aristocratic and eccentric English poet, according to Clark, was one of the poets that Duncan introduced to the curriculum at Black Mountain as one of his "casual heretical recommendations of 'Indexed' works and authors (*Finnegans Wake*, Eliot, Stein, Zukofsky, H.D., even Edith Sitwell)," all of whom were anathema to Olson's canon (255). Just how much of a rebuke Sitwell is to Black Mountain machismo can be grasped in Duncan's claim that, "It's easier to announce that you are a homosexual than to say you read Edith Sitwell" (113). Williams' comment to Ronald Johnson regarding the "hemi-demi-semi barbaric yawps" of Black Mountain implies a similar consideration of Sitwell:

> Let's face it, Dame Edith Sitwell was too much, too much
> indeed, for all those he-men flaunting their hemi-demi-semi barbaric
> yawps in the sylvan air of Black Mountain. There were sexual thugs
> by the dozen on campus. A titled English woman like ES would be
> allowed to cut no ice. [...] Anyone stupid enough to say he or she
> hasn't much to learn from Edith Sitwell deserves to be a life-time cap-
> tive of the Soi-Disant Language Poets or the cult of Ally-Oopists on
> the West Coast. Her notebooks are wonderful. (229)

Duncan and Williams' esteem for Sitwell and her work rests partly on
her notoriety as "a provocative and controversial figure" who, like Olson,
provoked strong reactions from both her admirers and her critics: "It was
apparently not easy," John Ower claims, quoting Sitwell, "to be neutral
towards the Sibylline yet impish figure who neither in her art nor in her
life was afraid to be 'an unpopular electric eel in a pool of catfish'" (253).
The fact that Sitwell was "titled," as Williams points out, and that she cul-
tivated an air of eccentricity would, no doubt, have exacerbated these strong
reactions. Indeed, advocating this English eccentric is not only a subtle
reminder of Williams' own semi-aristocratic southern background but also
a notable contrast to Olson's working class origins.

It is also Sitwell's prosody that Williams finds instructive, particularly
the theories she outlines in her essay in her *Collected Poems*, "Some Notes
on My Own Poetry," as well as in *A Poet's Notebook*. In the latter, Sitwell
considers the "texture" and the "varying uses of consonants, vowels, labials,
and sibilants" for determining "rhythm and [...] variations in speed of the
poem" (18). These ideas are developed further in "Some Notes on My Own
Poetry" in which Sitwell proposes how "assonances and dissonances put at
different places within the lines and intermingled with equally skillfully
placed internal rhymes have an immense effect upon rhythm and speed"
(*Collected Poems* xvi). "For me," Ronald Johnson claims, "and poets like
Jonathan Williams and Robert Duncan, her theories of words' rhythm and
texture in the treatise *Some Notes on My Own Poetry* [...] were a text to
shove alongside Charles Olson's *Projective Verse* and Louis Zukofsky's anthol-
ogy *A Test of Poetry*" ("Six, Alas!" 27). It is for similar reasons of prosody
that Williams, as he explains to Cory, married Sitwell and Olson:

I was able to do something with Olson and with Edith Sitwell that became something new. Sitwell … because she's so interested in so many aspects of words. What color they are. If they leave shadows. How much they weigh. And Olson … what he really is is symphonic. There's a big, big symphonic expanse there, particularly in *The Maximus Poems.* (1)

Olson's influence on "O For A Muse of Fire!" is evident in what Eric Mottram describes as Williams' "speed of cadence (Olson's 'velocity') and controlled turns of phrase," which are reflected in the poem's counterpoising of long and short lines and the repeated refrain "it felt fine!" (104). As one of Williams' "masters of the exact curve," Musial also utilizes speed, control, and accuracy on the ball field. Williams implicitly conflates the batter's velocity with "the *kinetics*" of Olson's "Projective Verse," transposing "COMPOSITION BY FIELD" to the ball field where Olson's "LAW OF THE LINE" now suggests the foul and grass lines of the playing field (Mottram 104; Olson, *Collected Prose* 240, 242, 244). In this respect, "O For A Muse of Fire!" might be read as an acknowledgment of the holistic approach to education at Black Mountain, which occurred as much outside the classroom as within it. At Black Mountain, Williams recalls, "you could learn a lot about a man—and his art—from playing poker with him, or *Monopoly* to the death, or seeing him perform during the Sunday afternoon softball game" ("Colonel Colporteur's" 77).

However, "O For A Muse of Fire!" also undermines the implicit machismo of the sport and recreation at Black Mountain. Williams does this via the poem's richly alliterative phrases—such as "The Muse muscles up; Stan the Man stands"—and by utilizing a dense, compacted assonance, all of which recall the phonetic flamboyance of Sitwell's prosody in poems such as "Waltz" from *Façade,* in which music leads meaning:

> Our *élégantes* favouring bonnets of blond,
> The stars in their apiaries,
> Sylphs in their aviaries,
> Seeing them, spangle these, and the sylphs fond
> From their aviaries fanned
> With each long fluid hand
> The manteaux *espagnols*,
> Mimic the waterfalls
> Over the long and light summer land. (*Collected Poems* 145)

According to Sitwell, the poem's "movement" is achieved via "softening" and "trembling" assonances set against a "ground rhythm" based on the alliteration of "m," "p," and "b" sounds (*Collected Poems* xx). For Johnson, the effect is one of joy and gaiety: "the writing of *Façade* seems to have been done in a sense of fun, music spurring text" ("Six Alas!" 27).

Williams' own tendency for dense alliteration, digraphs, assonance, and compacted music—for example, "A-cephalous, off-key, Orpheus / floats out to sea, he // bleeds indefinitely // into the Egyptian scene, seen," from another poem with a nod to Olson in its title, "Always the Deathless Mu-Sick"—finds a precedent in Sitwell's densely wrought lexis which Johnson describes as being like "a stiff tapestry of over-embroidered and ever-recurring images, with here and there an incandescence" (Williams, *An Ear*; Johnson, "Six, Alas!" 29).

In taking these aspects of Sitwell's poetry and marrying them with Olson's poetics in "O For A Muse of Fire!" Williams subtly queers an otherwise straight-talking, straight-hitting "heroic" sporting moment into something more sexually suggestive. The phallic, erectile implications of the line, "The Muse muscles up; Stan the Man stands," along with the refrain "*it felt fine!*" and the allusion to Polish "Ozanna's boy, Moe Drabowsky" who "comes," suggest a homoerotic undertone in this blue collar sport. Sexualizing such a "manly" discourse in this way, Williams' poem more tacitly undermines the hyper-masculine he-man culture at Black Mountain and the sporting culture that bolstered it.

More tacitly, "O For A Muse of Fire!" also reflects Williams' ambivalence towards Olson as a patriarchal figure. According to Andrew Mossin, "one cannot easily stand outside the masculine context of Olson's poetry.

That is, a reader is either seduced by the language and enacted mythos of manliness or is likely to feel excluded by the exhortation of masculinity flowing out of the text" (19). Williams' own relation to Olson's language of manliness, however, is not quite so straightforward. As his warm accounts of Olson attest, Williams was not necessarily excluded by the underlying masculinity of Olson's stature as "a patriarch in poetry," yet he still felt the need to question it (DuPlessis para 78).

As "O For A Muse of Fire!" shows, Williams frequently adopts the "language and [...] mythos of manliness" in order to illuminate its latent homoerotic resonances. Thus, Williams essentially writes from within the discourses that he critiques. This is evident in Williams' poem "Funerary Ode for Charles Olson," included in *The Loco Logodaedelist In Situ: Selected Poems 1968–70* (1971). Notably, this poem occurs at the end of a suite of found-poems titled "Excavations from the Case Histories of Havelock Ellis." That Williams' "Funerary Ode" should immediately follow a series of candid poems acknowledging "Ellis's pioneer work in acquiring sexual information in the form of case histories"—particularly homosexual experiences—tacitly acknowledges Olson's ambivalent attitude toward sexuality and the body (*Loco*).

The sexual "caprice" presented in "History XXI," for example, with a description of "urine / over my body, / limbs // in my face!" adumbrates the carnality that Williams evokes in "Funerary Ode for Charles Olson" (*Loco*). Recalling his correspondence with Olson, Williams asks: "so what about that word *amorvor*, Charles, / or the way you used to write *am O?* – / *I love*; or, *I am Olson?*" (*Loco*). Williams later returns to Olson's neologism—"so, Charles, let us (and you as well as us) / take you at your word," he writes, demarcating Olson from an "us" that my be implicitly homosexual—charging it with a proprioceptive force that elaborates on Olson's claims about the body as "the data of depth sensibility" and "an object which spontaneously or of its own order produces experience" (*Loco*; Olson, *Collected Prose* 181):

let lust drag it off the word-list
down into the Bed Incarnate—

where heads have tongues up assholes,
and come's all over chests and fingers,
when your eyes finally tell the poem is no place
for polite usage only

it is only when the beloved's come, shit, and heated juices
receive the same sanctification as one's own substance
that a state of love may be said to exist—
what poets call sacramental relationships, what Freudians
call excremental visions (*Loco*)

Olson may have proclaimed that "the song is heat!" and proposed a proprioceptive, "corporeal poetics" very much centered on physiognomy, but in his own lifetime, Williams implies, Olson was "a cold man pretending to be hot" (Elder 341; *Loco*). "Sex is one form of heat; poetry another," Williams has claimed (Browning 285). To claim that Olson "lived cold" would therefore seem to suggest something about Olson's own frigid sexuality and, more generally, acknowledge the ambivalence toward "the sexual frankness and body consciousness of gay male poets," that, according to DuPlessis, was prevalent among the "counter-cultural poetries" of the 1950s (para 83).

Williams' own "body consciousness" is evident in the way that his poetry repeatedly demonstrates a "refusal to keep the flesh and the spirit separate" (Chambers 749). "Funerary Ode for Charles Olson" is no exception. By dragging the great platitude and abstraction, *love*, "down into the Bed Incarnate" Williams endeavors to make it flesh. Williams' "refusal" in this particular poem to abstract spirit from flesh also addresses the question of Olson's ambivalent, cold, "body consciousness." Williams does this by way of what, initially, appears as an innocuous comparison of Olson with Orpheus: "the severed head of Charles John Orpheus, Jr. / floats off Massachusetts" (*Loco*). While this recalls Olson's claim in *The Maximus Poems VI* that, "the mind go forth to the end of the world," this is actually a loaded term considering that Orpheus carries homosexual connotations in Williams' poetry (*Maximus* 290). For example, in "Always the Deathless Mu-Sick," the title of which derives from "Maximus to Gloucester: Letter 2," Williams claims that "Orf's *awfully* gay, / despite Eurydice ..." and describes Orpheus's decapitation: "A-cephalous, off key, Orpheus / floats out to sea" (*Maximus* 12; *An Ear*). While "gay" suggests happiness, such gayness is unequivocally sexual too.

In another poem, "The Electronic Lyre, Strung with Poets' Sinews," from *In England's Green &* (1962), Williams makes the same pun, but in a more overtly sexual context:

> Be polymorphous perverse,
> Orpheus!
>
> All orifices,
> Orpheus!
>
> "It's all good." (*An Ear*)

Williams attributes to Orpheus the bisexual urges that, according to Freud, are common during a child's sexual development. "The constitutional sexual predisposition of the child is more irregularly multifarious than one would expect, that it deserves to be called 'polymorphous-perverse,'" Freud writes in his *Selected Papers on Hysteria and other Psychoneuroses*, "and that from this predisposition the so-called normal behavior of the sexual functions results through a repression of certain components" (191). In perverting Olson's proprioceptive ideas in his "Funerary Ode" Williams shows how Olson's poetics unwittingly, or potentially, promote an "openness [...] to multiple avenues of cathexis" that transgress so-called "normal," "straight" sexual behaviour (Rothenberg 3).

Furthermore these "sacramental relationships" in Williams' poem transcend simple gender distinctions and sexual preferences, as the non-gender-specific "beloved's come, shit, and heated juices"—as well as the sexless "heads," "assholes," "chests and fingers"—indicate. This sexual ambiguity is very much in keeping with Williams' wider mistrust of, and resistance to, abstracting labels and categories. "I don't like these tiresome words *gay* and *straight*," he remarks in his *Gay Sunshine* interview, "but I am so disinterested with politics outside the house that I put up with them, like most of us have to" (Browning 283). Likewise, Williams has remarked:

> The words male and female must have been invented by the same crowd that talks about Truth and Beauty—abstractions that can be made to pay off commercially and politically when spoken out of the moola-side of the mouth. (282)

It is, Williams implies here, the phenomenon itself that demands attention not the concept that it is reduced to, be it one's sexuality, gender, or for that matter, one's affiliations in poetry.

The frequent allusions to "outlawed sexualities" in Williams' poetry not only "challenge the faked ignorance of the self-consciously respectable and up-tight," but they also propose "strategies for holding together the body's loves and sensuousness in language" (Mottram para 15). Williams' reading of Olson's proprioceptive "heat," therefore, is not simply a "queer" critique of Olson's "straight" approach to the subject, but also a way of indicating how Olson stops short in his "polite"—perhaps even repressed— claims about the physicality and carnality of cognition. Indeed, when Williams writes that, "when your eyes finally tell the poem is no place / for polite usage only," he draws attention to the possibility that Olson was blind to the wider sensual and corporeal implications of his own poetry.

BLACK MOUNTAIN ROOTS

"Funerary Ode for Charles Olson" also demonstrates Williams' discerning capacity for realizing the latent potential, the repressed content, and the felicitous contingencies inherent in other people's words and expressions. "Alert for eccentrics, roadside cafes with the accent over the *f*, stray-cat-scratched wisdoms of the urinal, foibles and follies, slips of the tongue, seers and doers, masters of schtick and spiel from sidewalk to bedroom and back," as Johnson writes, Williams "seldom errs with eye or ear" ("Williams" 407). As Thomas Meyer explains, it is in Williams' unerring attention for the linguistic and phonetic richness of the vernacular that he recognizes and realizes the rich sensuous possibilities of language most acutely:

> A man is most eloquent—Dante proclaimed in *La Vita Nuova*—who uses the speech of ordinary men. The secret, Dante knew and Jonathan Williams knows, of the vernacular, of the way we talk, is its openness, its alert sensual tones (its vowels actually). (para 29)

The "poetic marriage of Edith Sitwell and Charles Olson" that Williams promotes also informs this concern for an open, "sensual" language. In an early poem entitled "Found Poem Number One" Williams proposes "the world's first marriage of the poetics of Charles Olson and Dame Edith Sitwell" by way of a found vernacular that, like his Ellis excavations, derives from psychiatric experiences (*Jubilant Thicket* 207). "Found Poem Number One" dates to 1952–1953 when Williams' Black Mountain studies were interrupted by the draft. "As a conscientious objector," Tom Patterson writes, Williams "was exempted from combat training and service, and assigned to non-combatant work for the U.S. Army Medical Corps in Stuttgart, Germany" (9). Williams was placed in the locked ward of the Fifth General Hospital in Stuttgart, "working as a 'neuro-psychiatric technician,' subduing and pacifying malingerers and psychopaths and really mean folks" (Dana 209). It is one of these "folks" that provides the subject and language of "Found Poem Number One":

FOUND POEM NUMBER ONE:

(Fifth General Hospital, Bad Canstatt/ Stuttgart, 1953: the speaker, a bop
spade from Cleveland in a fugue state, making the world's first marriage
of the poetics of Charles Olson and Dame Edith Sitwell —and you are
there!)

<pre>
       man,
       i come from
       the 544
               motherfuckin'
                       double-clutchin'
                               cocksuckin'
                                       truckin' company!

                       U CALL—
                       WE HAUL
                       U ALL . . .

       we got
       2 plys
               4 plys
                       6 plys
                               8 plys, semi's—

       and them BIG motherfukers
       go

       CHEW!
       CHEW! (Jubilant Thicket 207)
</pre>

"Found Poem Number One" is concerned with the semi-conscious
ramblings of a soldier suffering a fugue state of mind. Indeed, as the con-
cluding phrase—"CHEW! CHEW!"—suggests this found poem is about
verbal trains of thought that create their own kind of musical fugue. An
initial reference to the soldier's military "company"—expressed in a "bop"

hipster idiom—morphs into commercial jargon advertising a logistics truck company ("U CALL— / WE HAUL / U ALL . . .") and a timber supplier ("ply"). The trucks these companies use ("them BIG motherfuckers") subsequently blur into trains, which go "CHEW! CHEW!" Indeed, when the meaning of the word "fugue" is recalled, this poem is very much about *loco* (mad, insane) *motion*. In psychiatric terms, a "fugue" denotes the flight from one's own identity, and often involves mental travel to some unconsciously desired locality, a point that Williams implies when, in the poem's subtitle, he writes, "and you are there!"

Despite its Stuttgart provenance, "Found Poem Number One" is also a product of Black Mountain. As well as drawing upon two very different poetic models he encountered at the college—either in person (Olson) or on Duncan's curriculum (Sitwell), the poem also demonstrates Williams' attentive ear for dialect. This aspect of his poetry emerges from his time at Black Mountain College and his renewed interest in his birthplace in nearby Asheville, Buncombe County. In his conversation with Dana, Williams explains that, "Most of my connection with Buncombe County, after getting born there, was coming back to go to Black Mountain College" (188). Studying at Black Mountain, Williams was not only exposed to the progressive, liberal, and avant-garde ideas of the college but he also reconnected with, and reassessed, the wider cultural environs of his nearby birthplace (Asheville, North Carolina), particularly the tradition of Southern dialect literature and the local mountain speech that he grew up with. "It must have had its effect," he tells Dana, "because, in my own way, I finally turned back and became very acutely interested in what southern mountain speech was all about" (189).

Dialect literature remains a contentious subject. As Joan Wylie Hall stresses, the Southern dialect literature, which became widely popular after the American Civil War, has been accused of reaffirming "the comforting mythology of the plantation South as a lost Eden whose kind and well-spoken masters and illiterate but loyal slaves nurtured each other in a pastoral landscape" (206). Both of the white Southern writers that Williams enjoyed as a child—John Charles McNeill, who wrote *Lyrics From Cotton Land* (1906) and Joel Chandler Harris, author of the popular book *Uncle Remus: His Songs and His Sayings* (1880)—who appropriated African-American dialect in idealised rural, plantation settings could be charged with such pastoralizing. Indeed, it is feasible to see both writers' work as examples of "a highbrow convention which employed exaggerated, humorous speech to camouflage a patronizing sentimentality and satire" (Jones 8).

While the avuncular sentiments of Harris' Uncle Remus certainly supports these assessments, Gavin Roger Jones suggests that "Ethnic dialect could provide writers with a voice for social commentary and political satire" and articulate a "cultural and aesthetic politics of difference" that "over turn[s] linguistic hegemony" (5, 2). It was for similar linguistic reasons that urbane modernists such as Eliot and Pound were attracted to Harris' *Uncle Remus* stories. The black dialect of those stories, Michael North writes, offered "a prototype of the literature that would break the hold of the iambic pentameter" and provide an incipient "example of visceral freedom triumphing over dead convention" with "black speech seem[ing] to Pound the most prominent challenge to the dominance of received linguistic forms" (78). In particular, the "unlikely example" of *Uncle Remus* implied "a cultural program," North suggests, "that would demolish the authority of the European languages and even the Roman alphabet":

> In this way Pound would carry the social and cultural dislocations of the modern period, dislocations of which he felt himself to be the deracinated product, to their logical conclusions in a new language. (North 99)

However, Williams' appropriation of a black vernacular in "Found Poem Number One" seems—uncomfortably so—to corroborate Matthew Hart's suggestion, via Michael North, that "the Anglo-American avant-garde conducted its formal experiments '*over* a third figure, a black one,'" which Williams, in "Found Poem Number One" describes problematically as "a bop spade" (27, emphasis added). Despite the poem's title, which positions Williams as an indifferent amanuensis for the dialect that he has found, "Found Poem Number One" treads awkward (one might argue, exploitative) ground by using a black idiolect that threatens to repeat a familiar caricature of the "furtive, jive-talking sociopath, the hipster [who] was supposedly only alert to his own whims and cravings for intense experiences" (Rosenthal 82).

Williams' explorative celebrations of the "linguistic difference and diversity" of local dialect are more successful in the context of the Appalachian "mountain speech" of his immediate neighbors in Highlands, North Carolina (Jones 2). These poems tend to shed subtle light on "the cultural and political issues surrounding questions of linguistic variety" because, as Herb Leibowitz stresses, they "make up an unofficial oral history in verse of the Southern Appalachian folk often vilified and dismissed as hillbillies" (n. pag).

Southern mountain speech forms a considerable part of Williams' book, *Blues & Roots/Rue & Bluets: A Garland for the Appalachians* (1971). According to Johnson, this book "should sit on our shelves alongside *Uncle Remus* (1880)," no doubt because of Williams' skill in capturing the rich linguistic and phonetic nuances of his Appalachian neighbors (409). These poems, overheard or found, implicate the poet as "an autochthonous mindless recording mechanism established ecologically within a mountain region" who is keen to note the singular qualities of Appalachia's cultural and natural histories (*Magpie's Bagpipe* 164). Thus, as the result of this "mindless recording mechanism" Williams claims that *Blues & Roots* represents "the best of what mountains and I have found out about each other, so far. And a little of the worst as well" (*Blackbird Dust* 122).

Blues & Roots also consolidates Williams' experiences at Black Mountain. Williams' return to Buncombe County to study at Black Mountain, and the interest in dialect and "mountain speech" that resulted from it, is a telling reminder that "radical" means to be progressive and innovative as well as *rooted*. The title, *Blues & Roots*, draws on both senses of the word by deriving from Charles Mingus' 1959 album of the same name in which the noted jazz musician and composer revisits his musical roots by reworking blues, gospel, and Dixieland into modern jazz forms. But, if the poems in *Blues & Roots* tacitly draw upon Williams' Black Mountain experiences, some of them also respond critically to his time there. "The Nostrums of the Black Mountain Publican," for example, reads like an Appalachian equivalent of Gary Snyder's "In Praise of Sick Women" which presents male superstitions and myths about menstruation. Williams' poem also entertains ignorant superstitions and concludes with a warning against cunnilingus:

but, boys, lemme
tell you;

DON'T EAT NO
HAIRPIE
ON FRIDAY!   (*An Ear*)

This overheard talk in a local Black Mountain bar suggests Ma Peak's Tavern, a "local" for Black Mountain teachers and students during Williams' time there. According to Williams, for "those fortunate of us to be in nether Buncombe County, North Carolina, then (Charles Olson, Dan Rice, Lou Harrison, Joel Oppenheimer, Fielding Dawson, Ben Shahn, Katherine Litz, Francine du Plessix Gray, to name a few) spent many a long evening down at Ma Peak's Tavern, three miles from the college" (*Magpie's Bagpipe* 92). These excursions would have also been one of the few opportunities where students came into contact with locals and where Williams could sharpen his ears on local speech. Indeed, for that very reason, Williams claims, "The beer joint in Hicksville, USA should never be underestimated" (*Magpie's Bagpipe* 92).

As much as it is about the locals, "The Nostrums of the Black Mountain Publican" also seems to be a wry critique of the college itself. The recipients of the publican's quack medical advice are exclusively men, as the colloquial "boys" suggests, implying a homosocial bar culture that mirrors Black Mountain's own fraternity. Indeed, Williams' poem is a good indication of why Williams might have felt uncomfortable being associated with an exclusive Black Mountain club, as the exclusively male culture the poem portrays—whether in a local tavern or a liberal college—seems to only compound small-mindedness. The word "nostrums" (from the Latin *noster*, meaning "our") compounds this further by highlighting the polarization that can occur in communities and the "us-versus-them" mentality that such divisions can encourage. However one reads the poem—as an instance of Black Mountain provincialism or as a slantwise critique of the campus life of the nearby college—in "The Nostrums of the Black Mountain Publican" Williams makes a similar assessment as Lorine Niedecker in her poem "In the great snowfall before the bomb" about "the folk from whom all poetry flows / and dreadfully much else" (142).

BLACK MOUNTAIN SEEDS

If Williams' efforts as a publisher helped put Black Mountain on the map, they have done so by promoting the achievements that occurred there that extend well beyond the "rather embattled and rather isolated" group of poets typically associated with that name. Thus, in addition to Olson and Creeley, for example, Williams has also published many more peripheral Black Mountaineers, including the composer Lou Harrison, the photographer Lyle Bongé (Williams' former roommate at Black Mountain) and R. Buckminster Fuller.

This "other" Black Mountain reflects the tensions that developed between Williams and Olson, with whom, Williams claims, he "came to grief after the publishing of the first three books of *The Maximus Poems*" and the two men "started playing Lazy Southerner and Imperious Yankee" respectively (*Magpie's Bagpipe* 6–7). Behind Williams' publishing decision, as Duberman implies, were wider issues concerning what Olson perceived as Williams' lack of commitment to his perception of Black Mountain:

> Williams' relations with Olson deteriorated, in part because of complications that developed between them over further publication of the Maximus poems; in part because Olson didn't approve of some of the other people Williams published—like Patchen, Bob Brown, Mina Loy, or Buckminster Fuller (the latter according to Williams, was "anathema" to Olson); and in part because Black Mountain was, as Williams said to me, "literally a place. The associations were very close and very constant. But if you suddenly are not all in one place, and there is no community in fact, then all the separations and distances and divergences seem to enter." Among the divergences was Olson's occasional tendency to treat Williams like a servant, to patronize his talents as a poet (Olson was more interested in Dorn, John Wieners, and later LeRoi Jones and Ed Sanders than in Williams), and to regard his publisher's "sins" in printing the likes of Mina Loy et al., as akin to a betrayal of the "movement." (383)

"The voluble dome guru," R. Buckminster Fuller, Clark claims, "provided [Olson's] main competition for students' attention" at Black Mountain and, according to Ralph Maud, a number of antagonisms and conflicts arose between Olson and Fuller as they competed for the leadership of the college (Clark 155; Maud 115–117). Bearing such tensions in mind, it is possible that Williams' decision to publish Fuller's *Untitled Epic Poem on the History of Industrialization* in 1962 was also a way of undermining Olson's imperiousness. To publish Fuller would have undoubtedly be seen as a willful insubordination on Williams' part, but such a decision shows how Williams' perception of Black Mountain recognized the importance of the achievements that occurred beyond Olson's curriculum.

In his poem "The Big House," Williams proposes to "cast celebration / like a seed!" (*An Ear*). Despite his misgivings about Black Mountain, this is exactly what Williams has done via the numerous titles that Jargon has published by various Black Mountaineers. As well as securing the college's legacy and reputation, Jargon's diverse catalogue also serves as a tacit reminder that Olson's presence in that legacy is but a part of a much larger and more complex story. In particular, Williams' eclecticism is very much in the spirit of another Black Mountaineer that he admired, M. C. Richards. In her book *Centering* Richards writes passionately about the college's ideals and lauds its endeavors "to bring elements into a whole which could move in a variety of ways without falling apart" and "integrate individual spirit and community spirit" (119). "When its spirit withdrew," Richards writes, "the college closed," but she is also keen to stress that, "It lives in all of us who were there initiated into a life that has an open end" (123).

As an inclusive "society," rather than an exclusive "club," Jargon shows a similar concern for integrating singular individual endeavors into a non-homogenizing community. This openness to, and celebration of, difference, diversity, and individuality affirms a level of autonomy that sets Williams' imprint from any singular aesthetic or school. As James Jaffe stresses, the books that Williams published through Jargon "were allowed to be as individual and independent as he was himself":

It wasn't about putting his stamp, his signature, on everything.

And as such the Jargon Society differed from other literary private presses in being radical and democratic, in giving each book its own identity, its own idiosyncratic form. (para 7)

Williams reaches a similar conclusion in his interview with Albert, when he explains that, "I didn't really design my press as an axe-grinding operation":

> I hope I didn't. I also hope that it wasn't "calculated" to try to dominate and make a position that was dominant or exclusive. I don't see how it can be so judged if I printed people as bizarrely disconnected as say Alfred Starr Hamilton and Charles Olson. (59)

Davenport captures the open, inclusive, non-positioning spirit of Jargon when he proposes Williams to be "an ambassador for an enterprise that has neither center nor hierarchy" (181). With similar connotations of capaciousness, Beam and Owens have described the Jargon ethos as "a poetics of gathering" which links together Williams' "unswerving desire to collect and preserve, harvest and distribute" a rich miscellany of writers, artists, and photographers (para 4).

Beam and Owens' choice of words, "harvesting" and "distributing" to describe Williams' activities are especially apt in the context of Black Mountain whose history has been expressed in similar terms of dissemination and propagation. Mervin Lane, in *Black Mountain: Sprouted Seeds*, for example, is interested "in how John Andrew Rice's seeds—planted back in 1933— sprouted, how they blossomed and what was remembered of the nurturing process" (4). Duberman couches his account of Black Mountain's closure in similar terms. For Olson, Duberman writes, "Black Mountain had merely dispersed, not ceased; it hadn't failed, it had stopped. [...] Or as Eric Weinberger has put it, 'the seeds live inside you'" (412). These seeds drifted— or, as Duberman suggests, "were scattered"—to a number of locations including the Beat milieu of the West Coast Bay Area and the Cedar Bar crowd of New York's Greenwich Village (412–13).

Echoes of this scattering and dissemination are evident in one of Williams' "found" poems that initially appeared in *Roots & Blues* titled,

"JOHN CHAPMAN PULLS OFF THE HIGHWAY TOWARDS KEN-
TUCKY AND CASTS A COLD EYE ON THE MOST ASTONISHING
SIGN IN RECENT AMERICAN LETTERS":[2]

> O'NAN'S
> AUTO
> SERVICE

(Jubilant Thicket 191)

A sign advertising an Irish car mechanics takes on biblical proportions
via an allusion to Onan, second son of Judah, who spilled his seed while
having sex with his sister-in-law, Tamar, so as not to impregnate her (Genesis
38:8-10). God may have killed Onan for his disobedience, but his name
endures in the word "onanism," a term for *coitus interruptus* and that pri-
mary act of "auto / service": masturbation.

Williams' poem also alludes to the American folklore hero John Chap-
man, better known as "Johnny Appleseed." Chapman earned the name
"Appleseed" because of his charitable activity of sewing apple-seeds in parts
of Ohio, Indiana, and Illinois in order to establish apple nurseries. Williams
puns on the Appleseed legend by conflating onanistic suggestions with
Chapman's arboreal disseminations. In doing so Williams—who claims that
"Jacking off remains (solitary or in company) one of the great releases"—
also evokes his own disseminating activities (Browning 281). Williams
earned himself the title of Johnny Appleseed for his similar peripatetic "do-
it-yourself" ethos. As Davenport points out, "It was R. Buckminster Fuller,
on his way from Carbondale to Ghana (and deep in Kentucky at the time)
who remarked of Jonathan Williams that 'he is our Johnny Appleseed—we
need him more than we know'" (180). Williams got this title due to how,
after Black Mountain's closure, he pursued a program of cultural propaga-
tion similar to Chapman's arboreal one:

> In North Carolina, Jonathan Williams loaded up his father's station
> wagon with Jargon, Golden Goose, City Lights, Grove Press and New
> Directions books and started his travels around the country, travels not yet
> ceased, peddling the books, reading the work of "The Black Mountain
> Poets," spreading their reputation and influence. (Duberman 413)

Just as Chapman's travels changed the landscape of the places he visited as a consequence of the seeds he sowed, Williams' peripatetic evangelism also helped change and influence America's cultural topographies. "If his poetry defines and extricates a tradition from his past," Davenport writes of Williams, "his wandering (as Buckminster Fuller points out) defines the curious transformation of the shape of American culture" (188). When the word's root sense of "careful" is recalled, it is evident how Black Mountain College remains a vital seed in these "curious" enduring transformations of American culture, as Beam suggests:

> The events that brought Black Mountain College to North Carolina, and Jonathan to Black Mountain, continue to bless our state and her arts, allowing each of us to confront the greater questions of attention, aesthetics, and exclusion. Black Mountain taught us that "the pure products of America" are often found beneath the stone walls, outside the city gates. (A Snowflake)

"There is no American capital," according to Davenport; "there never has been. We have a network instead" (188). For this reason, Williams' peripatetic disseminations have been, indeed, *seminal* in spreading Black Mountain's legacy and ensuring that it travels beyond "the city gates" of metropolises such as New York or California. Williams—quoting Edward Dahlberg, another former Black Mountain teacher—writes in his poem "Enthusiast" that "we flower in talk," and claims that "the way we ripen ourselves" is with "*literature*" (*Jubilant Thicket* 250). Black Mountain's legacy has flowered—and continues to flower—in a large part because of the attention Williams gave it in the talks, lectures, and poetry readings he gave across the United States as well as the literature he published associated with the college. True to his word, Williams cast celebration like seed and helped the legacy of Black Mountain College, as he saw and experienced it, take root in new, fecund soils.

ATTENTION AND EXCLUSION

Jeffery Beam's perceptive assessment of Williams' poetry as providing opportunities to "confront the greater questions of attention, aesthetics, and exclusion" accurately sums up Williams' own complex relationship with Black Mountain College. Attention, aesthetics, and a non-discriminatory acceptance (rather than discriminating exclusion) of things are, perhaps, the defining terms for Williams' poetry. According to Thomas Meyer, Williams, like "the true Epicurean, [...] embraces it *all* precisely because for him or her there is nothing else, absolutely, resolutely **nothing else**" (para 33). There is nothing else except for the immediate "panoply of detail and experience" which elicits "close attention," *care*, and *curious* regard (paras 39, 42):

> His attention when it focuses centers. There is no background, foreground, or middleground. There is only what is there—a kind of "in-your-face" phenomenology. (para 41)

The exclusions at Black Mountain College under Olson's influence and the prescriptive, oppressive attitudes they encouraged—particularly towards notions of gender and sexuality—are antithetical to this "kind of 'in-your-face' phenomenology." But by queering the pitch of the college's hyper-masculine culture and appropriating its machismo, Williams' poetry is a poignant reminder of a broader, more inclusive "tradition" that Black Mountain College should be remembered and celebrated for.

Williams has suggested that, "*Tradition* could be defined as (1) what you care to remember; or (2) what you simply cannot forget" ("Colonel" 79). He also believes that "*tradition* is what the making of poems is celebrating" ("Colonel" 79). In all these respects Black Mountain remains an integral and *indelible* part of the tradition that Williams celebrates in his work. But, as Jargon's substantial bibliography, as well as Williams' own reminiscences, reviews, and essays indicate, that tradition is not, despite Williams' debts to it, simply the Black Mountain of Olson and the poets he fostered there. Rather, the Black Mountain that Williams celebrates is the one that eludes such homogenizing group mentalities and labels, and

instead encompasses a more diverse and eclectic "gathering" of names—
Harry Callahan, Lyle Bongé, M. C. Richards, Hilda Morley, Lou Harrison,
to name but a few—who, *together*, show just how fluid, dynamic, and inclu-
sive the college was during its twenty-four years of existence and how far
its intellectual and creative seeds have travelled.

[1] Williams' initial response to Olson, as Duberman's comments indicate, was not
unusual: "Along with the fact that most of those who came into prolonged contact with
Olson ended up loving the man, I've been struck by a second fact: that even the most furious
of his detractors single out important gains for themselves for having known him" (371).

[2] In fact, this poem was not "found" by Williams but "passed onto" him by Guy Dav-
enport in 1966 (see Davenport and Williams, A Garden Carried in a Pocket 87).

WORKS CITED

Albert, Barry. "Jonathan Williams: An Interview (Washington D. C., June 14, 1973)." *VORT 4* (Fall 1973): 54–75.

Allen, Donald, ed. *The New American Poetry, 1945–1960*. Berkeley and Los Angeles: University of California Press, 1999.

Beam, Jeffery. "A Snowflake Orchard and What I Found There: The Jargon Society—One Village Idiot's Oh-So Personal Appraisal." <http://jargonbooks.com/snowflake1.html>

Browning, John. "Interviews Jonathan Williams and Thomas Meyer," in Winston Leyland, ed. *Gay Sunshine Interviews: Volume 2*. San Francisco, CA: Gay Sunshine Press, 1982: 281–88.

Chambers, Douglas. "Jonathan Williams," in Claude J. Summers, ed. *The Gay and Lesbian Literary Heritage*. New York Henry Holt and Company, 1995: 749–750.

Clark, Tom. *Charles Olson: The Allegory of a Poet's Life*. Berkeley: North Atlantic Books, 2000.

Cory, Jim. "High Art & Low Life: An Interview with Jonathan Williams." *The James White Review: A Gay Men's Literary Quarterly* 11. 1 (1992): 1, 3–4.

Dana, Robert. *Against The Grain: Interviews with Maverick American Publishers*. Iowa City: University of Iowa Press, 1986.

Davenport, Guy. *The Geography of the Imagination*. Boston: David R. Godine, 1997.

————. and Jonathan Williams. *A Garden Carried in a Pocket: Letters 1964–1968*. Ed. Thomas Meyer. Haverford, PA: Green Shade, 2004.

Davidson, Michael. *Guys Like Us: Citing Masculinity in Cold War Poetics*. Chicago and London: The University of Chicago Press, 2004.

Duberman, Martin. *Black Mountain: An Exploration in Community*. London: Wildwood House, 1974.

Duncan, Robert. "Interview with Michael Andre Bernstein and Burton Hatlen." *Sagetrieb* 4.2/3 (Fall & Winter 1985): 87–135.

DuPlessis, Rachel Blau. "Manhood and its Poetic Projects: The Construction of Masculinity in the Counter-cultural Poetry of the U.S. 1950s." *Jacket* 31 (October, 2006): <http://jacketmagazine.com/31/duplessis-manhood.html>

Elder, R. Bruce. *The Films of Stan Brakhage in the American Tradition of Ezra Pound, Gertrude Stein, and Charles Olson*. Waterloo, Ontario, Canada: Wilfrid Laurier University Press, 1998.

Erkkila, Betsy, ed. *Walt Whitman's Songs of Male Intimacy and Love: "Live Oak, with Moss" and "Calamus."* Iowa City: University of Iowa Press, 2011.

Folsom, Ed, and Kenneth M. Price. *Re-Scripting Whitman: An Introduction to His Life and Work*. Malden, MA: Blackwell Publishing, 2005.

Freud, Sigmund. *Selected Papers on Hysteria and other Psychoneuroses*. Trans. Abraham Arden Brill. New York: The Journal of Nervous and Mental Disease Publishing Company, 1912.

Hall, Joan Wylie. "Dialect Literature," in Joseph M. Flora and Lucinda H. MacKethan, eds. *The Companion to Southern Literature: Themes, Genres, Places, People, Movements, and Motifs*. Baton Rouge: Louisiana State University Press, 2002: 206–207.

Hart, Matthew. *Nations of Nothing But Poetry: Modernism, Transnationalism, and Synthetic Vernacular Writing*. New York: Oxford University Press, 2010.

Jaffe, James. "Jonathan Williams, Jargonaut." *Jacket* 38 (Late 2009): <http://jacketmagazine.com/38/jwd01-jaffe.shtml>

Johnson, Ronald. "Jonathan Williams," in Donald J. Greiner, ed. *American Poets since World War II: Dictionary of Literary Biography* Vol. 5. (Detroit: Gale Research, 1980), 406-409.

————. "Six, Alas!" *Chicago Review* 37.1 (Winter, 1990): 26–41.

————. and Jonathan Williams. "Nearly Twenty Questions." *Conjunctions* 7 (Spring 1985): 225–238.

Jones, Gavin Roger. *Strange Talk: The Politics of Dialect Literature in Gilded Age America*. Berkeley and Los Angeles: University of California Press, 1999.

Killingsworth, M. Jimmie. *The Cambridge Introduction to Walt Whitman*. Cambridge: Cambridge University Press, 2007.

Lane, Mervin, ed. *Black Mountain College: Sprouted Seeds: An Anthology of Personal Accounts*. Knoxville: University of Tennessee Press, 1991.

Martin, Robert K., ed. *The Continuing Presence of Walt Whitman: The Life After the Life*. Iowa City: University of Iowa Press, 1992.

Maud, Ralph. *What Does Not Change: The Significance of Charles Olson's "The Kingfishers."* Cranbury, NJ: Associated University Presses, 1998.

Merrill, Thomas F. *The Poetry of Charles Olson: A Primer*. Newark: University of Delaware Press, 1982.

Meyer, Thomas. "JW Gent & Epicurean." *Jacket* 38 (Late 2009): <http://jacketmagazine.com/38/jwb12-meyer-thomas.shtml>

Mossin, Andrew. "'In Thicket': Charles Olson, Frances Boldereff, Robert Creeley and the Crisis of Masculinity at Mid-Century.' *Journal of Modern Literature* 28. 4 (Summer 2005): 13-39.

Mottram, Eric. "An Introduction: 'Stay in Close and Use Both Hands.'" *Jacket* 38 (Late 2009): <http://jacketmagazine.com/38/jwb07-mottram.shtml>

———. "Jonathan Williams." *VORT 4* (Fall 1973): 102–111.

Niedecker, Lorine. *Collected Works*. Ed. Jenny Penberthy. Berkeley, Los Angeles, and London: University of California Press, 2002.

North, Michael. *The Dialect of Modernism: Race, Language and Twentieth-Century Literature*. New York and Oxford: Oxford University Press, 1994.

Olson, Charles. *Collected Prose*. Eds. Donald Allen and Benjamin Friedlander. Berkeley and Los Angeles, University of California Press, 1999.

———. *The Maximus Poems*. Ed. George F. Butterick. Berkeley and Los Angeles: University of California Press, 1984.

Owens, Richard and Jeffery Beam. "The Lord of Orchards: Jonathan Williams at 80." *Jacket 38* (2009): <http://jacketmagazine.com/38/jw-intro.shtml>

Ower, John. "Edith Sitwell: Metaphysical Medium and Metaphysical Message." *Twentieth Century Literature* 16. 4 (Oct., 1970): 253–267.

Patterson, Tom. "O For A Muse of Fire: The Iconoclasm of Jonathan Williams and the Jargon Society." *Afterimage* 23 (March/April 1996): 8–12.

Richards, M. C. *Centering in Pottery, Poetry, and the Person*. Middletown, Connecticut: University of Wesleyan Press, 1969.

Rosenthal, David H. *Hard Bop: Jazz and Black Music 1955–1965*. Oxford and New York: Oxford University Press, 1992.

Rothenberg, Molly Anne and Dennis A. Foster, "Beneath the Skin: Perversion and Social Analysis," in Molly Anne Rothenberg, Dennis A. Foster, and Slavoj Žižek, eds. *Perversion and the Social Relation*. Durham, NC: Duke University Press, 2003: 1–14.

Schlesinger, Kyle. "The Jargon Society." *Jacket 38* (2009): < http://jacket-magazine.com/38/jwd02-schlesinger.shtml>

Sitwell, Edith. *A Poet's Notebook*. London: Macmillan, 1944.

———. *Collected Poems*. London: Sinclair-Stevenson, 1993.

Whitman, Walt. *Poetry and Prose*. New York: Literary Classics of the United States, 1982.

Williams, Jonathan. *Blackbird Dust: Essays, Poems, and Photographs*. New York: Turtle Point Press, 2000.

———. *Blues & Roots/Rue & Bluets: A Garland for the Southern Appalachians*. Photographs by Nicolas Dean. New York: Grossman Publishers, 1971.

———. *Blues & Roots/Rue & Bluets: A Garland for the Southern Appalachians* (second edition). Durham, NC: Duke University Press, 1985.

———. "Colonel Colporteur's Winston-Salem Snake Oil." *VORT 4* (Fall 1973): 76-83.

———. *Jubilant Thicket: New and Selected Poems*. Washington: Copper Canyon Press, 2005.

———. *The Loco Logodaedalist In Situ: Selected Poems 1968–70*. London: Cape Goliard Press, 1971.

———. *The Magpie's Bagpipe: Selected Essays*. Ed. Thomas Meyer. San Francisco: North Point Press, 1982.

———. *Uncle Gus Flaubert Rates the Jargon Society In One Hundred One Laconic Présalé Sage Sentences*. Chapel Hill, NC: Hanes Foundation, 1989.

JED BIRMINGHAM

WILLIAM BURROUGHS AND JONATHAN WILLIAMS

As an obsessive collector who places great significance in every scrap of Burroughsiana, it delighted me to learn that in 1965 Jonathan Williams and Ronald Johnson invited William Burroughs and Buckminster Fuller to dinner. Williams and Johnson were living in a temporary flat in London, and Burroughs must have recently arrived in town after a nine-month stay in the United States. Williams reports that Burroughs and Fuller did not know each other. It is a bit of a mystery to me just how friendly Burroughs and Williams in fact were, but in the 1965/1966 timeframe, they appeared together in some obscure little magazines like *The Spero*, *Cleft*, and *Residu*.

This is not all that surprising given that William Burroughs seemingly published everywhere during the mimeo revolution. It is interesting to consider where Burroughs did not appear. The Cleveland scene of d. a. levy is one, and Williams' Jargon Society series is another. Burroughs' closest link to Williams as a publisher is not that close. Burroughs appeared in the legendary final issue of *Black Mountain Review* in 1957. A key appearance for Burroughs. Williams attended Black Mountain in the early 1950s and began his first forays into publishing there, but he was not involved with the *Black Mountain Review* as Robert Creeley was in charge of the editing and printing. Of course, Fuller taught at Black Mountain, and he attempted to construct his first geodesic dome there in 1948. So Burroughs had a tenuous link to the Black Mountain scene and was aware of the college. Maybe Williams, Johnson, Fuller and Burroughs talked of Black Mountain at their dinner.

This link in publishing history is indeed tenuous. Williams did not publish the Beats. He turned down *Howl* before City Lights stepped in after the Six Gallery Reading. Williams never felt bad about his decision. *Howl* would have only sold 300 copies if Jargon had published it he reasoned. Williams did not ask for much in the way of readers. He was happy with 50 dedicated eyes and ears.

There are similarities between Jonathan Williams and Burroughs. Both men had privileged backgrounds; both had a sophisticated, aristocratic air about them; both were gay; both lived as expatriates in England; both were jacks of all trades in all aspects of experimental literature and art. Yet I cannot think of two writers more different in their personality, lifestyle, creative work, and literary concerns. I think we can get to the heart of some of those differences by comparing the two men's relationship to England.

For Burroughs, England was simultaneously an escape and a prison. In the mid-1950s, Burroughs went there seeking a cure to his addiction to heroin with the help of Dr. Yerbery Dent. The apomorphine treatment temporarily freed Burroughs from staring at his shoe in Tangier and allowed him to pour himself into the process of writing *Naked Lunch*. Yet Burroughs also viewed England as a straitjacket: too buttoned up with university tie fixed on too tight; the royal crown screwed on too tight. In a sense, he hated England. I should stress that England for Burroughs was quite simply London. Anywhere else in the country was strictly Hicksville. Clearly, Burroughs found even London boring: the pubs closed too early as did the subway and restaurants, but in the late summer of 1965, Burroughs saw signs of life in the old slag. Burroughs moved to London just as Swinging London exploded into the global consciousness. Beatles London, Pop London, the Albert Hall Reading London, Mary Quant London, Indica Bookshop London. This was England for Burroughs. He lived at St. Duke Street, St. James from 1966, residing near Anthony Balch and Brion Gysin. The ties to film and art are important. London at the time was the center of international popular culture in music, film, fashion, and art. It was an international center on par with Paris and New York. Such locales were Burroughs' natural habitat. He was an urban creature, and his best work is urban in nature, even if his view of the city is not entirely positive. Burroughs' literary landscape and his characters are generally urban: Interzone, the drug underworld, corporate bureaucracy run amok. The cut-up is the urban experience par excellence. Reading the landscape out of a rushing subway, the flood of images and text at Times Square, the polyglot gibberish of an international marketplace, scanning a newspaper over somebody's shoulder at a street corner.

Jonathan Williams' England was a pastoral one. In 1969 (when Burroughs was living in London), Williams settled at Corn Close, an estate in the North Country of England. Williams was led there by the work and suggestion of Basil Bunting, particularly Bunting's poem *Briggflatts*, a poem that electrified many readers when it appeared out of the English North in 1966. If Burroughs' England is the South, Pop, surface, fast, glossy, schizophrenic, urban and international with an eye toward Paris/New York, Williams' England is Northern, earthy, gnarly, slightly daft, Anglo-Saxon, tweedy and rural. Corn Close was the aristocratic country manor gone backwoods. Williams' experimentalism comes not from the sophistication of the international avant-garde, but from the primitivism of folk art, the plain talk and homespun wisdom of the back roads. Williams resisted the urban. Williams stated "I have turned more and more away from the High Art of the city and settled for what I could unearth and respect in the tall grass." Burroughs found his inspiration in the exact place that Williams turned his back on and closed his ears to.

Late in their lives, Williams and Burroughs were the eccentric old men of American Letters, but they came by their eccentricity differently despite similar backgrounds. Both men were clearly at the forefront of the experimental art community of the post-WWII era. In a side note, this is the great triumph of Black Mountain College. Black Mountain incorporated both Williams and Burroughs into its creative vision. There was an international sophisticated experimentalism as well as a backwoods funkiness to the place that was unique in the twentieth century.

To return to that seemingly odd dinner in 1965, Williams writes that dinner ended with a Shaker lemon pie baked by Johnson. Williams remembers Burroughs muttering, "Hey, man, that is the craziest lemon pie. I mean groovy." As Johnson had baked two pies, Burroughs returned to his apartment with a small gift from Williams and Johnson. Now it does not get more classic, more simple, and more homespun than Shaker lemon pie. In fact, it is so old-school that you would be hard pressed to find a restaurant serving it nowadays. Williams specialized in such acts of archeology, both literary and culinary. It is funny how Williams portrays Burroughs as a stereotypical Hippie or Beatnik. Burroughs' talk is all hip clichés, "man," "craziest," and "groovy." Williams' critique of Burroughs and the Beats is subtle here. One reason Williams never published the Beats and Burroughs is because he felt they got distracted by hip fads. In Burroughs' case, this would be the Pop Art, rock music, underground newspapers, and

Scientology of Swinging London. I suspect that Williams would have admired *Naked Lunch*'s excavation of the lost era of 1910 small town Americana and arcane drug slang, but he would have disapproved of Burroughs' infatuation with the "groovy." Burroughs' *Naked Lunch* and other writings could use more Shaker lemon pie: the homespun, the retro, the old school. More small town Americana, less warmed over European experimentalism exemplified by The Composite City and Interzone. Williams feasted on just such literary comfort food and created works that stuck to the ribs and minds of generations of readers. So on that night in 1965, Williams fed Burroughs well and no doubt provided Burroughs with some much needed food for thought as well.

DAVID ANNWN

MUSTARD & EVENING PRIMROSE—
THE ASTRINGENT EXTRAVAGANCE OF JONATHAN WILLIAMS' METAFOURS

Jonathan Williams' magisterial *No-nonse-nse* (Mt. Horeb, WI, 1993) features the subtitle: *No-nonse-nse: Limericks (Invented in Ireland c. 1765), Meta-Fours (Invented During the Non-Summer of 1985 in Lower Stodgedale) and Clerihews (Invented in 1890 by Edmund Clerihew Bently [sic]) by a Perdurable "True Descendent of Aristophanes and Catullus" Jonathan Williams.*

Certainly, 1985 seems to be a pivotal moment in Williams' creation of this form. Two years previously, clerihews were JW's 'rage' as witness *Les No-Account Contes de Mont le Conte Par J. Clerihew Williams, Who Distills Them* (1983), *62 Climerikews to Amuse Mr Lear* (1983), and *The Fifty-Two Clerihews of Clara Hughes*, (1983). In *Blues & Roots/Roots & Bluets* (1985), featuring poetic crystallisations of conversation heard along the Appalachian Trail, hardly a single metafour appears.

Yet, actually, the metafour was no late or fugitive flash in this writer's poetic pan. As early as June 17th 1963, in *Lullabies Twisters Gibbers Drags*, this fierce satire surfaced:

WHITE ANGLO SAXON PROTESTANT INVOCATION; OR, DON'T LET A WET W.A.S.P. GET HIS SHIT HOT

from commies and sheenies
and bull-dickied darkies –

good Lord, deliver Us![1]

And, early on, there's something which drew the poet to the muscled musicality and stentorian vigour of subversive anti-mottos:

LAWLESS WALLACE ÜBER ALLES

How the ripple-effect of words, the trilling of consonants and drawn-out 'A's, kicks in there and the quartet of words fall with instinctive rightness previously, in:

La lune rode up,
    a white slice, right

and

GET HOT OR GET OUT

Yet it was clear that by 1987, the form was proving so seductive, it was becoming the focus of small books as in: *Two Meta-Fours*, Woodland Pattern Book Centre, Milwaukee. And a year later, it is dominating the collection: *Dementations on Shank's Mare, Being 'Meta-Fours in Plus-Fours' and a few 'Foundlings'* (1988). A year on, the hyphen is dropped in *Metafours for Mysophobes* (1989) and again in *QUANTULUMCUMQUE* (1991). The form persists through *No-nonse-nse*, 'Amuse-Gueules for Bemused Ghouls' in *Blackbird Dust* (2000), *Kinnikinnick Brand Kickapoo Joy Juice* (2004), 'Meta-Fours,' to the first section of *Jubilant Thicket* (2005), and the list is far from complete.

Yet what to make of this quadratic obsession? Pierre Joris senses that these quadriform inventions are crucial to Williams' achievement and that he is 'the meta-fours' switch hitter.[2] Jeffery Beam writes revealingly that: 'Using a new form, of his own devising, the "Metafour", Williams proves there is something new under the sun. And that the new is usually found in the glory of the remaindered old'.[3] And elsewhere, Jim Cory writes that metafours 'Typically … offered the poet's wry take on things banal'.[4] Michael Hrebeniak judged that Williams' '"Meta-Fours" are exemplary; energies emerge cleanly and conversationally, forging an entire world-vision by transforming nonsense into sense'.[5] It's worth dwelling a little on that transformation of 'nonsense into sense' since, in the prefatory note for *Dementations on Shank's Mare*, the metafourist himself wrote:

The poet's fascination with his dotty invention, the meta-four continues. Its only 'rule' is that each line have four words—all punctuation and capitals are eliminated except for possessive apostrophes. The result (when it works) turns sense into nonsense and gets the mind so off-stride that you don't know whether you're coming or going. And you don't distinguish 'prose' from 'poetry'.[6]

Hrebeniak laudably concentrates upon Williams' forays into the flux and, that which is commonly called, the detritus of ordinary to forge new lines. Yet, Williams stresses the de-stabilizing and apparently nonsensical nature of the finished articles, not their source.

In *Metafours for Mysophobes*, he extends his thoughts:

> After all these ruinous decades writing 'poems', I have had to invent a form that doesn't seem like poetry at all: the Metafour. It's crazy, it's nonsense, it's the anti-poem, it's the impure-poem, etc. But it strikes me that it can be read, dammit, because the line is strangely fresh. Count it out: four words in every line. You must be kidding? Say whut? Mr. Edward Kennedy 'Duke' Ellington told us: you got to say it without saying it. I think, actually, I understand that. This is all, at the moment, I can hope to bring to the flensed reader. It allows me to tell little stories; it allows me to move prestissimo from here to there; it affords a formal pleasure that is curiously hard to figure.[7]

By the time of *QUANTULUMCUMQUE*, (meaning 'the least that can be said'), Williams is foregrounding that 'least'-ness, (recalling Niedecker's *condensery*), and speed, the *prestissimo*:

> Today's huckster now has about 15 seconds in which to sell soap—30 seconds strain the attent of the mobocracy. The wastrel poet … may not have but 5 seconds. He therefore alerts his words: you guys better creep in, crap and creep out, like starting now: DO IT!

He will still be re-working and dovetailing these words re metafours fifteen years later. Compression, speed, seeing the new in the old, that repeated 'nonsense' (we must remember his dada tendencies), de-familiar-ization of the language, disorientation, (partly created by the dropping of most orthographical referents) and formal pleasure all stay at the front of his mind.

Around the time of *QUANTULUMCUMQUE*, he summed it up to me thus: 'Francis Bacon the painter said, "What I really want very, very much to do is the thing that Paul Valéry said, 'To give the sensation without the boredom of its conveyance'". And I think that's why the things I do are usually so abbreviated and quick'.[8]

Like Bacon then, he sought to short-circuit our appreciative processes. These poems, like Bacon's work as Louise Cohen has described it, 'arrive straight through the nervous system and hijack the soul'.[9]

In the wake of Joyce and Stein's achievements, American poetry during the 1940s and '50s abounded with experiments in unpunctuated verse and poetry, some of it in lowercase, some of it using four words to a line. We think of W.C. Williams, (JW's 'spiritual father'), Zukofsky, e. e. cummings:

> mr u will not be missed
> who as an anthologist …

and Don Marquis:

> i heard a spider
> and a fly arguing
> wait said the fly
> do not eat me …

All provide examples that might be said, at first glance at least, to resemble Williams' invention of the metafour.

Perhaps a closer exemplar might be glimpsed in James Laughlin's sig-nature typographic metric, an achievement Williams linked to the poetry of Catullus, Martial, Propertius and Ovid. Laughlin's formal experimenta-tion led to couplets measured by sight, in which the second line is no more than two typewriter spacings distinct from the line that precedes it. These free-flowing lines, mainly unpunctuated, often remind one of the 'back and forwards' flickering of meanings in metafours:

Some People Think

that poetry should be adorn-
ed or complicated I'm

not so sure I think I'll
take the simple statement

in plain speech compress-
ed to brevity I think that

will do all I want to do.

Yet each of these examples, are, in their own ways continents away
from Williams' mature work. Witness:

this revelation to be
stamped on a grapefruit
BE CONTENT WITH FORM

When I heard him read this poem from *Metafours for Mysophobes* at
the October Gallery, London, what struck me was the intense passion in
his voice, his fierce and tender emphasis, as, his open hand pushed down
miming the 'stamping', and he read the third line four times, each time
with a different set of stresses: first 'CONTENT' as that which is contained,
then as being fulfilled, sated, and so on. The varied reiteration was giving
an auditory equivalent what we couldn't see: the poem as verbal and graphic
object combined, a series of signs for our complex engagement, for our eyes
to flicker backwards and forwards over. It sent my mind back to his pub-
lishing of the first *Maximus* poems:

one loves only form
and form only comes
into existence when
the thing is born

It was a statement of 'revelation' and the poem is a wonderful 'at-one-ment', Williams' reiteration revealing each segment of inherent thought glittering. In his search through ordinary ideas and words he was always looking for 'fire-points, the garnet crystals'.[10]

There is no precise typology of metafour other than their four-ness and ebullience; by their very nature they are multivalent, roiling and hybrid lexical forms but one can remain attentive towards different tendencies and lights inside the crystal.

In *The Loco Logodaedalist in Situ*, the poet reminds us of his own and his then partner, Ron Johnson's, addiction, from at least 1963 onwards, to the kind of word games: anagrams, palindromes, acrostics, cut-ups, Tom Philips-like 'cut-aways' and concrete works of Ian Hamilton Finlay and Dom Pierre-Silvester Houédard. Some notable results of this immersion are Johnson's *Io and the Ox-Eye Daisy*, *Eyes and Objects* and *Radi Os*. In writing of Williams' *QUANTULUMCUMQUE*, Jeffery Beam called the work 'concrete poetry with the concrete elasticised'. Precisely. Such a poem is 'this revelation' ...[11]

To reprise: 'Edward Kennedy 'Duke' Ellington told us: *you got to say it without saying it*'.

up the flue up
the flue you're going
up the flue and
then you get judged
i really believe that

In this metafour from *QUATULUMCUMQUE*, the elliptical slide sets in with the run-on 'up/the' repetition. Reading backwards and forwards, trying to get a footing, we find no intro, no contextual clue to where or when or how, and no subject nor object other than 'you' and 'flue'. It reminds us of Williams' referencing of Judith Thurman's words: 'Start as near the end of a poem as you can'.[12]

To re-visit, '... *got to say it without saying it*': The poet's take on Ellington's words might strike one at first as an insouciant Scaly Mountain Zen koan, comparable with the jazz musician's inexpressible swing and *esprit* expressed only in the throes of music. In its original context, (*Music is my*

Mistress), the phrase has two different senses. William Morris Jr. thought Ellington's *Deep South Suite*, performed at Carnegie Hall in 1946, much too timid in its protest about the suffering of black communities. Morris made a plea for clarity on this score but Ellington thought it 'good theatre' and, in reply, made the statement about saying without saying.[13]

Of course, 'up the flue' says it all the more effectively for keeping its criticism subliminal. The speaker in the poem is confounded, is judged, by their own unselfconscious and simple-minded expression, the flatness and atonality of 'i really believe that' after the chimes of 'you' and 'flue'. There is, additionally, a very soft but insistent subliminal resonance: 'up', 'flue', 'you're', 'you', 'judged', like an 'invisible' image emerging from a Magic Eye 'deep vision' painting , and the shape that sound assumes finally is 'jew', especially taking the soft German 'j' as in *juden* into account, and the fate in 'flues' for millions. Think back on Williams' anger against the Anglo-Saxon prejudice against 'commies and sheenies'. The poem flares, saying it with sonic undertow rather than openly and all the more powerfully for that. Additionally, the holocaust is just where the speaker's outrageous, fairy-tale-telling doctrines have led in the past. Ellington writes of the story-telling impulse behind creating music and that 'the audience didn't know anything about it but the cats in the band did'.[14] And Williams again on the metafour: 'It allows me to tell little stories'.

The two flowers which give their titles to this study both answer to the rule of fours. When the seeds of the quadri-petalled and sepalled mus-tard flower are ground, they create an astringent; in food this provokes and excites the palate (like amuse-gueules, those bite-size hors d'œuvre selected by the chef). The petals are typically arranged either like the chi-asmus of 'X' or 'H'. Regarding the Evening primrose family (*Onagraceae*), too, most of its anatomy occurs in 'fours'—four petals, four sepals, etc. This is the family of the Sundrops and other yellow-flowered evening primroses.[15]

When a really hot mustard kicks in, you concentrate. After-effects are as important as first taste and burn. Which is the best? Gourmets differ: Maille Dijon; Gulden's Spicy Brown or Inglehoffer's Original Stoneground and, then again, others say the best and hottest is Russian. Williams, in his Old Testament prophet mode, never tired of telling us: *GET HOT OR GET OUT*. It seems an irony of the first magnitude that *No-nonse-nse* should have been produced in Mt. Horeb, WI, home of the Mustard Museum and the world's foremost collection of mustard memorabilia.

> The Museum also is home to hundreds of items of great mustard historical importance, including mustard pots and vintage mustard advertisements.[16]

Creation and reading in depth demands strenuous effort: the heat of effort and complete commitment in the words. We remember his chastisement of Richard Brautigan's poems:

> It's too thin. Off to a Vic Tanney gym, words! And a few months of Mr. Rexroth wouldn't hurt you either. Then, if you insist on coming on quite so simple, do it in a way that might interest people who have listened to the beautiful clarities of Scarlatti and Schubert ...[17]

He liked words to work for their keep. With the cutting of most punctuation, no clause remained 'subordinate' to other, no personal name privileged over the world of things: all parts of the poem are to strive equally for attention, flowing, flickering and rippling back and forth, and, with each flex and re-arrangement of syntactic structure, new discoveries.

The metafour was whelped out of travail and discontent with the prevailing literary cultures of the U.K. and U.S in the 1980s. 'Poetry,' Williams told us, 'seems to have got out of whack. I want poetry "that's got a whang in it."' 'Whang' as in:

1. A thong or whip of hide or leather.
2.
    a. A lashing blow, as of a whip.
    b. The sound of such a blow.
3. *Vulgar Slang.* The penis.

tr.v. , whanged, whang·ing, whangs.

1. To beat or whip with a thong.
2. To beat with a sharp blow or blows.

v. whanged, whang·ing, whangs.

v.tr. To strike so as to produce a loud, reverberant noise.

v.intr. & n. To produce a loud, reverberant noise.[18]

In looking for poetry with whang, Williams, like Pound, Olson, Robert Duncan, Dahlberg, and Guy Davenport, often re-visited the archaic: Martial's epigrams, Juvenal and Aristophanes' satiric jibes against his contemporaries—all these have whang. For Richard Owens, the metafours specifically cast our minds to the Classical satirists:

> Looking at only the range of his work as a poet, the achievement is broad in scope, the earlier work marked by a gravity informed by Olson, and the later work—especially the Meta-Fours—saturated with the scathing wit of a Juvenal or Martial.[19]

In Aristophanes' comedy, *The Acharnians,* when we first meet the hero, he has a bad case of the blues; his delights have diminished to four (τέτταρα), but his reasons for outrage are so multitudinous, they beggar description and so he creates a word to convey this (ψαμμακοσιογάργαρα), literally 'sandhundredheaps'.[20] Compound words used as a dramatic device often feature in the plays and Williams' use of portmanteau and compound words, (indebted also to Joyce and Rabelais), 'Climerikew', 'Logodaedalist' etc. is striking. Williams also loved exploring weighty German compounds such as 'Südstaatenschriftstellerin' in *A Subtle Mississippian Riposte.*[21] But it is chiefly in the mustard-hot invective and ironic anger that we hear Aristophanes:

glory be to god
for jesse helms jesse
hates fags jesse hates modern
art now that one
thinks about it jesse's
just like most people
in north Carolina and
everywhere else ...
The rage grows until:

> he has the law
> on his sidewinder snake
> in the grass that
> he is whether he
> will brake for us
> poets and artsnakes is
> another matter thank you
> jesus thanks a bunch

In the final eight lines, the reader is thrown and thrown by three ellipses, the first seemingly sliding sinuously, seamlessly, into sideways glossing on Helm's character but incorporated into the one curve of the poem, to that mock ambiguation of the Janus-faced 'thank you' and the stinging rebuttal of the Christian far right.

Above all, Williams finds whang in spades in Catullus' *Carmena*; one of the metafourist's favourites was LXXXV:

> *Odi et amo. quare id faciam, fortasse requiris?*
> *nescio, sed fieri sentio et excrucior.*

The Latin doesn't use end-rhymes. Its syntax is far more flexible than English. Catullus relied on techniques like hyperbaton, anaphora and chiasmus for structure. In the lines above, four verbs compete for position, vie for dominance in sound. 'Chiasmus' refers to the crossing-over effect that this causes.

In the special edition of *Metafours for Mysophobes*, there is a holographic metafour written inside the endpapers:

> if Michelangelo had used
> a roller he would
> have gotten the ceiling
> done quicker reckons kitaj

It is, naturally, an irreverent joke and provocation—a slap in the face—for all bourgeois art-lovers. In terms of an up-date of chiasmus, one need only note the 'Mi' of Michelangelo and the 'aj' in kitaj, the relation between 'if' and 'kitaj', the verbs 'used' and 'done', the slight off-chime between 'would' and 'done', 'roller' and 'quicker', the velars of 'got ...' and '... ing' and 'the positioning of the two artists' names. This is without mentioning the quick master's staccato of distinct 'o' sounds, stretching the resources of language: '... lo', 'roll ...', 'gott ...', 'done' and 'reckon', that almost demonic whiplash, that 'whang', in the tail of the poem with 'qu' 'ck' 'k'.

As Eric Mottram wrote:

> Williams concentrates in making music and speech rhythms work with visual coordinations and disjunctions. His urge, increasingly, is to condense to the satire of epigram (his longer poems are often branches of epigrams) ... brief acts of what Joyce termed the verbivocovisual on the word. His ear for people's speech—ours as well as theirs—enables him to record impulses to idiosyncrasy he finds around him into poems of discovery rather than acceptance.[22]

It's that poem-as-discovery as well the whiplash of scornful satire and an almost instinctive mastery of technical skills outside the Anglo-American orbis that I want to emphasize in my relation of the metafour to the archaic. Williams' metafours remind of Gustaf Sobin's words concerning an ancient Ionico-Massalian potter:

> ... the potter was giving free play not to his own whims or fancies but to the vibrationary flow of yet unregulated energies ... [his lines] rise, plummet, exult—convulsively ... like a freshly released creature. If anything, they seem alive. Here we're very close to a vision of existence that, after being rapidly suppressed, would have to wait two and a half millennia to see itself reasserted. ... We might be reminded, too, in the realm of modern aesthetics, of Klee's definition of art as Gestaltung: as form in the perpetual process, or act, of formation.

We remember Williams' words:

> *Charles Olson made a vigorous effort long ago to teach me ... poetry is a process,* not a memoir.[23]

Indeed, Sobin continues:

> Or Olson's interpretation of the poem as a 'high energy con-
> struct' ... These indeed are archaic canons ... Within that vision, the
> world ... erupts continuously out of an irrepressible point of origin.
> An iridescent chaos, as Cézanne once put it ...[24]

The metafour form is alive and unpredictable; it's supremely suited
for the kind of free-play, exultation, high energy process and flexible control
which such impulses bring into being.

It might be tempting to write that Williams brought the verve, play
and lubricity of popular forms like clerihews and limericks to the intense
formal acuity of Objectivism and Minimalism, as if he was a card-carrying
member of either movement. Certainly this poet mentioned the limerick
most often in relation to the metafour:

> The meta-four, like the limerick, is a form that seems to provoke
> a certain lubricity.[25]

Such postmodern usage of traditional forms reminds of John Ashbery's
homages to Edward Lear; it has also prompted some unwisely to christen
Williams' work as 'minor' or 'miniaturist', the which terms reveal a poverty
of critical attention. Even in using the limerick, a form seemingly shaped
by its metrical hook, this poet has always subtly broken metrical constraints.
Williams' impatience with the sense that English speech can be scanned in
regular iambics is revealed in his disagreement with John Wain in *The Loco
Logodaedalist*. If, as readers, we're into metrical scanning, rather than the
counting 'it out' that the poet advises, the metafour finds itself as seamlessly
at home with variable feet as with stentorian anapests and with simple
trochees as sprightly iambs. More, Williams, just as Zukofsky subverted the
norms of received prosody, uses the metafour to disrupt each of these meas-
ures and, hence, catches our reading minds off-stride. Consequently, just
like the 'young bugger from Dent', in reading the metafours, we often don't
know whether we're coming or going.

If I have dwelt too long upon the vituperative and strenuous aspects of metafours, their satirical mustard-hot bite, one shouldn't forget their humour and awe. Guy Davenport writes:

> Look hard at the satires in this volume: their pungency and sass are not irresponsible, nor their wit flippant.[26]

If there is enough serious humour and exertion in Williams' metafour for anyone's taste, there's also affection, melancholy and, occasionally, querulous peace after long struggle.

> was that a golden
> eagle on the power
> line checking the audubon
> almost had to be
> I've waited 60 years

There are the explosive quips, explosions, 'foundlings' and one-offs:

> home sweet sweaty home
> or:
> one move you're chutney

and, like the sudden rise of a grace-note that lingers on the ear, there are the serene 'why-try?' lines, the ease of givens, the precisely beautiful:

> bucket of blue smoke

At such times, Williams' words on remembering Basil Bunting are recalled:

> solid, common, *vulgar* words

> the ones you can touch
> the ones that yield

> and a respect for the music …

Meta—indicating change or alternation, transcending or going beyond, occurring or situated behind or drawing from that which follows. The directional ambiguity is arresting; that metafour's pun with 'metaphor', the sense that signified and signifier are calmly one, just as a green thought resides inside green shade, these should need no gloss.

> The evening primrose opes anew
> Its delicate blossoms to the dew;

Thus John Clare, *the* man of his generation to bring the poet's eye back to the soil and sedge, to notice the growing particularities. Williams knew about Clare's attention, his marking the nightly extravagance and delicacy of the flower opening, each of his syllables a bud.

Mustard and evening primrose; to bring their names together might seem an oxymoronic bibelot. Mustard provokes. Evening primrose, in its turn, soothes and placates mood and swelling. Yet both flower-words can be nouns and adjectives simultaneously. They can be shades, plants and colours at once. There's even a plant which combines them: Mustard evening primrose, (*Camissonia californica*).

Ubi sunt …? As his metafour spells it out:

> post modern gardening is
> me and the weeds!

Like the four-petalled *Camissonia*, a plant of opposites combined: No postmodern poet so polyphonous: so riddling and clear, so beautiful and savage, so uproarious and enigmatic, so tender and taunting all at once and all the more felt for that. His words were 'wielded like scalpels to rid minds of debris and dead wood'.[27] Master maker. Lord Electric-Eclectic. Colonel Mustard of the Yorkshire Dales—we can only approximate the truth.

As the man himself would have known, ('amen and then some'), the night between the 25th and 26th January is sacred to Saints Timothy and Titus, of St Amarinus, martyr, Apollo the hermit, and the wonderfully named Poppo of Stavelot, Prejectus, bishop of Clermont and Polycarp of Smyrna. (He loved the unwieldy, ridiculous and incense-encrusted names and once spent five minutes asking me about the Welsh saint, St Cybbi and repeating 'St Guppy' over and over to himself, laughing in disbelief.)

Over that 25th night of January in 2009, lost somewhere between the year of the Pig and Ox, my mind cast abroad in troubled sleep, I dreamt that someone had introduced a bunch of roving delinquents into our house and that they were running amok: breaking, shattering, smashing. Family and friends were blaming me for my anger at the havoc. Unaccountably, there for the first, perhaps only, time, I noticed, standing off to the side, the unmistakable, tall figure of Jonathan. He was busy signing the back of one of the shattered pictures, and adding for good measure a metafour which, I realised, no-one had seen and, unless I could get to it, no-one ever would, and which I was desperately trying to read and memorize as I woke.

[1] *Lullabies Twisters Gibbers Drags* (à la manière de *M. Louis Moreau Gottschalk, Late of the City of New Orleans*) [Presented by] the Macon County North Carolina Meshuga Sound Society, Jonathan Williams, musical director, Highlands, (NC): The Nantahala Foundation, 1963.

[2] pjoris.blogspot.com/2008/03/jonathan-williams-1929–2008, accessed 29.01.09.

[3] Rear flyleaf, *QUANTULUMCUMQUE*, French Broad Press, Asheville, N C, 1991.

[4] authortree.com/9781556592027 – 18k, accessed 29.01.09.

[5] www.guardian.co.uk/books/2008/jun/06/culture.obituaries, accessed 29.01.09.

[6] *Dementations on Shank's Mare*, Truck Press, New Haven, 1988, p. 1.

[7] *Metafours for Mysophobes*, North & South, Twickenham and Wakefield, 1989, p. 5.

[8] *Prospect into Breath*, North & South, Twickenham and Wakefield, 1991, p.55.

[9] Louise Cohen, *The Times*, September 9, 2008.

[10] *The Loco Logodaedalist in Situ*, Cape Goliard Press, London, 1971, p. 34.

[11] Rear flyleaf, *QUANTULUMCUMQUE*.

[12] *Jubilant Thicket*, Copper Canyon, Washington, 2005, p. 4.

[13] See Bret Hayes Edwards, 'The Literary Ellington', *Representation* 77, Winter, 2002.

[14] xiv jstor.org/sici?sici=0734-6018(200224)77%3C1%3ATLE%3E2.0.CO%3B2-X, accessed 29.01.09.

[15] archive.org/stream/wildflowerseasto00reedrich/wildflowerseasto00 reedrich, accessed 29.01.09.

[16] www.mustardweb.com, accessed, 29.01.09.

[17] *The Magpie's Bagpipe*, North Point Press, San Francisco, 1982, p. 78.

18 www.thefreedictionary.com/whang, accessed 29.01.09.

[19] damnthecaesars.blogspot.com/2008/03/jonathan-williams-1929–2008.html, accessed 29.01.09.

[20] en.wikipedia.org/wiki/*Aristophanes*, accessed 29.01.09.

[21] See *Louis Zukofsky, Or Whoever Someone Else Thought He Was*, North & South, Wakefield & London, 1988, p.37.

[22] Professor Eric Mottram in *Niches Inches*, Dentdale, 1981, p .3.

[23] *The Loco LogoDaedalist in Situ*, London, Cape Golliard, 1971, p. 32.

[24] Gustaf Sobin, *Luminous Debris: Reflecting on Vestige in Provence and Languedoc*, University of California, 1999, p. 141.

[25] *Jubilant Thicket: New and Selected Poems*, Copper Canyon, Washington, 2005, p. 4.

[26] Guy Davenport *Jonathan Williams, Poet*, The Asphodel Bookshop, 1969.

[27] *Lullabies Twisters Gibbers Drags* (Nantahala Foundation, Highlands, 1963 p. 1.

ERIC MOTTRAM

AN INTRODUCTION—"STAY IN AND USE BOTH HANDS"

Jonathan Williams is one of the finest American poets of this century. That should be enough to say but it is not. These days he finds it difficult to find a publisher for his books, other than himself: a sufficient comment on the state of publishing on both sides of the Atlantic. He has asked for an introduction from a constant reader who has been under his tutelage at least since purchasing *The Empire Finals at Verona* in 1963; when Williams actually performed the Stan Musial poem in that book, poetry began to be realized in a new way. In the Olson "Funerary Ode" he says that "the poem is no place for polite usage only," and not surprisingly March is his month: " ... engendering green in the groundwork we work / to prepare a Spring in ourselves; to air the sound / in ourselves." Probably rightly, he has given up preparing it anywhere else; he might modestly be surprised that he still prepares it in others. He names Olson Orpheus; in his Elgar poems Orpheus is Eros; but then that pairing that makes for a necessary home is to Williams also Orphic—an alternative to those isolations instanced as the voice of the bardic executed floating head:

> ... whose juices come
> from the hill
> and spill into me
> and make me a month's mouth—
> a goat-foot in new greenery
>
> I love you and would
> care for you—

Williams' technique, if anyone still does not know, is nonpareil. As *The Times* (London) reported him in 1970: "Poetry to me is a kind of field—a place in which things happen. Our dear old friend Freud said wit is the playground of the mind. I'm interested in poetry as a playground. I'm interested in walking across the page, making football moves across the field." The past poets are active in him: "Tradition is in us / like the sun / 'Sin is / separation.'"

Dionysos unnerves with destructive skills as well as through nature and erotics, the presence of body as an extension of mind, mind of body. But Williams is adept, in day to day conduct as well as in his poetry, at the camouflage of gentility for purposes of invasion. Decorum holds Eros in art and good manners. In each book there lies a recognition that in releasing Eros we may well sink beyond creative individuality into freakishness, madness, religious mania, nymphomania and artistic self-regard—let alone the crude political ego-mania of certain Southern senators. Williams knows, too, that the Stonewall Riots of 1969 in the United States were only a tactical victory, a cultural explosion rather than a cultural change—a phrase of his in a letter to *The Times* (New York) in 1968. But it is doubtful if he would use the word *culture* much nowadays, if at all—for the same reasons that he writes: "The words *male* and *female* must have been invented by the same crowd that talks about Truth and Beauty." If you believe in variety and range of pleasure to defeat abstraction and enslavement to current fashion, you have to reach deliberately the rich alienation from stupidity and impotence Williams' poetry articulates.

The present selection from work published between 1969 and 1981 is expressly for the British, who certainly need it. Our tribal nationalism despises his definition of erudition—a knowledgeable set of passions for skill and individuality, a range which for him is enlivened with Mahler and Midler (Bette), Samuel Palmer and Ronald Books Kitaj, Mervyn Peake and Theakston's 'Old Peculier' [sic], Ross Macdonald and *Franklinia alatamaha* (and Wm Bartram's drawing of it), Oldenburg and Ruggles. His language does not so much stabilize this exuberance as guarantee its selective joys in another kind of athletics. Appreciation without greed or imposition is as rare as love without the will to domination and submission, as he is well aware.

Williams is fond of being useful by prefacing his books, and lists of his books, with pronunciamentos from admired language masters in every field. Here is a short one culled from two interviews he gave with Tom Meyer in 1974 and 1975:

I am a poet and a man who lives by Catullus's little song, "Odi et Amo."

Sex is one form of heat, poetry another. Our encounters are never entered without openness ... Poetry is about paying close attention to the particulars and not going moralistic, diffuse, intellectual, remote. "Every man in his life makes many marriages," said Sherwood Anderson. Not with lovers only, but with beloved plants, hills, sacred places, animal spirits, rivers, etc....

Poetry is not under obligations to Sociology. As a matter of fact, I agree with one of Charles Olson's primary preachments: the poet's only obligation is to make fresh lines.

Play is far more, finally, instructive than Deep Talk ... Decorum is an operative word.

We choose to live on the margins of this society and have somehow managed to do so. "Living well is the best revenge," someone said.

Decorum in poetry is the good manners not to waste the reader's time, space and energy. Williams concentrates on making music and speech rhythms work with visual coordinations and disjunctions. His urge, increasingly, is to condense to the state of epigram (his longer poems are often branches of epigrams), clerihew, pun chains, palimpsests *in parvo*, brief acts of what Joyce termed verbivocovisual on the word. His ear for people's speech—ours as well as theirs—enables him to record impulses to idiosyncrasy he finds around him into poems of discovery rather than acceptance. This is part of his admiration for creative idiom that moves fearlessly into the eccentric contrary to the centricity of consumer-spectator society and its replacements of taste by fashion and money. His humanistic politics begins here, applying himself to the frontiers of what the bourgeois fears as 'bad taste,' or the freed body striving for survival against that sado-masochism which passes these days for the social. The poem of decorum is therefore exuberant and sophisticated, agile and jovial. But social criticism is everywhere, a proper intolerance which often takes the form of a geniality barely masking a loathing for hypocrisy, cruelty and ignorance: Pope's Dullness.

The poem that is also a product of walking, music of all kinds, and photography cannot afford to neglect good boots, good performance skills, and good lenses. A product, too, of various forays into the necromantic realms of restriction and abstraction. The trained man with a Rolleiflex and a Mamiyaflex organizes his eyes with fundamental technology against the unruly mass of men in noisy desperation. The decision as to how much subjects are posed is, naturally, the point at which the note to his *Portrait Photographs* begins a short discourse on selection and record. In his note for *Photographs by Raymond Moore*, Williams intimates a lifelong position— that the photographs are photographs, "images in service to Seeing. Not in service to Sociology, The Class System, And Excess of Rationality, Cosmic Adumbrations, Self-Expression, Masculinity, Document, etc., etc." He should know: he is a firstrate photographer (we can ignore the rude, footling review of *Portrait Photographs* in *The Listener* by a mainliner of British Cultural Control). Williams also says of Moore, he is "a man constantly informed by music"—and the poet, too, listens as much as he sees. As a performer of his own poetry, he transmits his masterly timing of the lens to a gifted speaker's timing of the voice. But it is also a comedian's gift for wit as a means to reveal, briefly and suddenly, both pretensions and the void under them. "Am I saying that art is one of the best ways to salvage one's days on this planet?" he writes, as a "North Carolinian/Cumbrian person"— "Blame it on my Welsh ancestors and let's go back to the images."

Williams accurately claims that he has "absolutely no known audience— except a very few friends who are not bored silly by this odd substance called Poetry." You notice the word *substance* and then you notice that the few include—on record—Buckminster Fuller, Guy Davenport, William Carlos Williams, Bunting, Robert Kelly, Robert Duncan, Gilbert Sorrentino, Hugh Kenner ... One reason we like him is that he plays on our storage systems and our memories of pleasure and abhorrence, without clamping us in a vise of dogma. His wit is a disclosure, a way to make us feel good by creative participation in an art. Nature is not witty; we can be; sight and speech combine in the Williams poem to make a phenomenology of perception as professional as it is honest. How many poets can make us laugh into a state of involuntary abandon, and then return to the causes? Sometimes he condenses perception into a means for a guffaw at a rather obvious recognition, but rarely, and it is usually at the expense of some literary or sexual pomposity.

He has received some good appreciations: the *Truck* issue for his 50th birthday, Ken Irby's article in *Parnassus*, the *VORT* issue he shared with Fielding Dawson. But the best introductions are his own selections of his work in books like *Elite/Elate Poems, Selected Poems 1971–75* (1979), an excellent system of entrances, settings, and poems, and let it be said immediately: few poets have that joy in their ability which destroys artistic egoism. Perhaps living double-housed in Highlands and Corn Close has given a necessity to know exactly where he is? The poems, re-read from their earliest appearances in the 1960s, have an urgency which moves—given the time we live in—the need both to appreciate and resist environments. He is fond of making lists of what he likes, or boxing up maxims, turning oracular statements like some breviary. But his prosody itself is a resistance to both the imitative laxities of 'open field' poetry and the dull bondage of Hardy, Thomas and Frost, or the Auden and Lowell ironies which dominate official British poetics. Williams could be a rejuvenatory resource. Concrete poetry, found poetry, treated texts, the clerihew, riffs, Sitwellian systems of rhyme, meticulous limericks—he is as professional an inventor as Picasso or Ives.

But this North Carolinian/Cumbrian person is also a valuable appreciator and interrogator of Britain. Davenport wrote in his introduction for *An Ear in Bartram's Tree* (1969):

> A pattern of artists emerges—Blake, Ives, Nielsen, Samuel Palmer, Bruckner—and (if we have our eyes open) a whole world. It is a world of English music, especially Edwardian Impressionists and their German cousins Bruckner and Mahler, of artists oriented toward Blake and his circle but going off by centrifugal flights into wildest orbits, men like Fuseli, Calvert, and Mad Martin. The poet's admiration for Edith Sitwell will have something to do with this exploration of English eccentricity, and the poet's Welsh temperament, and, most clearly, Blake himself. The artist is aware of a heritage not only because, like the rest of us, he recognizes it in his origins and values, but because he is consciously adding to it.

This is why Williams moves among us like an ideal anthropologist who does not disturb the natives at their rites, but with an amazed judiciousness even eats some of their food, and actively likes Balfour Gardiner and Arnold Bax. Everywhere he walks and drives he stalks the British object (Barbara Jones was an early London friend), ear and eye collecting with an explorer's delight and apprehension at being up the Amazon. Sex is everywhere—"I haven't seen the territory yet that can't be sexualized or examined for its poetic cuisine, or its birds, or for its dialects." He delights, too, in artists' burial places and in epitaphic epigrams for their demises—not to idly memorialize but to ensure that the elite do not depart without greeting and recognition, and to re-establish a certain hierarchy of value, clear, too, in his foreword to *Untinears & Antennae for Maurice Ravel*: "The function of poetry, according to Louis Zukofsky, is *to elate and record*. I have no argument and can offer no improvement. For me each poem is both elegy and celebration. A poem is a linguistic, phonetic, graphic object."

Williams is American in his inclination to de-centered openness to form and subject; British—may we say?—in his love of that which resists levelling: the note for *Adventures With a Twelve-Inch Pianist Beyond the Blue Horizon* (dedicated to Bette Midler) includes: "If male friendship is not a subject that interests you (in which case you are a super-cosmic titanism from a distant congeries of galaxies, like H.P. Lovecraft) … you should be listening to Pat Boone or Ike Turner or Oral Roberts." This poet is ready to be amazed, but he remains as alert on watch as a Mailer patrolman, ready to kill in the world of signs. Increasingly his poems curtail into their own worlds and then flash steady compressed signals—as if lengthy discourse merely spread towards some blurred vanishing point. The poems move toward something like photographs, in fact—silent images to be silently gazed at (the series of poemcards as objects, the Furnival series punning visually and verbally on Anton Bruckner, Gertrude Stein and others of the elite), as we gaze at the gazes of the artists in *Portrait Photographs*. The satirical gaze of Williams' poems frequently engages outlawed sexualities, and challenges the faked ignorance of the self-consciously respectable and uptight. But the sexual poems are also strategies for holding together the body's loves and sensuousness in language. Tenderness is not exposed to vulgar sentimentality but firmly embedded in the complexity of its origins. Where the pornographer fantastically isolates the body's needs from the practical and social, Williams respects the total perceptive scene: things as they are, with allegorical meaning resisted. In the *VORT* issue he speaks of "neighborliness to materials … communities … ecosystems."

JONATHAN WILLIAMS/JEFFERY BEAM

INTRODUCTIONS TO *QUANTULUMCUMQUE*

NOTA

Please, take into consideration the poem as

radiant gist
a laughter in the mind
wisp-of-the-will
silver snippet shard
light-motif
adumbration
deliquescence
nuance
kernel and cotyledon
still point/fire point
sound-bite
lapsed synapse
headline
footnote
tessera
ear wax/ear wane
nest
nooz plash
signpost
exhalation
whiff
charm
oddity singularity
epiphany verity

eternal silence at the heart of sound
swivet
trash masher–and-compacter
vivacious miasma
ordure from chaos
voozjha day
fignificant storm
simple mercy simple blessing

Today's huckster now has about 15 seconds in which to sell soap—30 seconds strain the attention of the mobocracy. The wastrel poet (this nogoodnik with nothing at all to sell to any Respectable American Maller) may not have but 5 seconds. He therefore alerts his words: you guys better creep in, crap, and creep out, like starting now: DO IT!

I assume the following literary persons have it right:

> There are always so many more interesting things to do than read poetry.
> —John Ashbery

> Start as near the end of a poem as you can.
> —Judith Thurman

The present is timeless. I have said it before. President Bonzo-Ronnie took time with him when he went off to swing in the banana trees of Bel-Air. One used to complain because nobody answered one's handwritten or personally typed letters. Now must people don't even answer messages on their answerphone. When they do, you know full well that these denizens of New York and Los Angeles have not the attention span to understand what you are saying to them. Better to talk to a rhododendron bush, then go soak one's head. Alors, the maker recommends slicing up bananas to consume with these humble wordflakes, thus insuring potassium for the brain to keep it functioning. Starting now!

JW
Highlands
New Year's 1990

Finally, last night I got to sit down with *QUANTULUMCUMQUE* ... or did it sit down with me? It is not language and poetry as we know it; yet it is not anti-poetry or gibberish. Certainly, it is more fun than a barrel of Jesses. To wax a bit academic let me quote the first lady of unpredictable thought, Elizabeth Sewell:

> This is what we [are] looking for just now, a kind of thinking with the body, freedom and mobility combined with the experience of some intuitive make-believe way of understanding things by dancing them. Like a game, and unlike art, its accent is on doing rather than making. It is not rational, yet it is not out of control ... If someone could remind us, however, it would tell us something of this other half of ourselves which nobody educates now, so that it grows up in wild ignorance or sinks into atrophy ... Irrationally perhaps, one feels that dancing would be a way there, if only one knew how.

Only Jonathan Williams could produce such a book as *QUANTULUM-CUMQUE*. Without him our sense of ourselves would be immeasurably boring. These poems are too much fun. Many will want to run and hide. Beware, no rock can save you. Others will bring out their not-so-dusty white robes and hoods and start prancing. Give up fools! The enemy is too strong!

QUANTULUMCUMQUE signals the end of Modernism, Post-Modernism, Objectivism, Minimalism, and all other ISMS. No wonder Communism is in a bad way. Spies must have warned of Williams' project-in-the-woods. These poems are Democracy in action.

Jonathan Williams, metathetic metaphrast, begins this volume with a plea asking the reader to consider the poem everything from "radiant gist" to "still point/fire point," from "whiff" to "oddity singularity," on to "simple mercy simple blessing." Can the average reader understand the inevitability of this work? Can I? Can you?

Using a new form, of his devising, the Meta-four, Williams proves there is always something new under the sun. And that the new is usually found in the glory of the remaindered old. Subtitled "Sub-Aesthetic Poems," *QUANTULUMCUMQUE* (meaning "the least that can be said") is Concrete Poetry with the concrete elasticized. An earlier self-criticism called it "A BREAJOR THAKEMROUGH."

It is truly impossible to take these poems out of the context of the page. Their juxtaposition is an emotional roller coaster. Call out the therapists! Exile the critics! The interplay, the intercourse, the inner course they take is what it is all about. Read them, sneeze on them, whatever you will. It's said that Rilke can change your life, but whether you knew a cantankerous, nangy poet of the Appalachians and the Dales could, is another thing coming.

Jeffery Beam
Golgonooza at Frog Level
Orange County, NC
November 1990

JIM CORY

WE WERE ALL BEAUTIFUL ONCE
(OR) NEVER BARE YOUR SOUL TO AN ASSHOLE

A late William Carlos Williams poem called "The Act" describes a backyard encounter between neighbors. A woman cutting roses is urged by the man who lives next door to spare them because "they are so beautiful."

Agh, we were all beautiful once, she said,
and cut them and gave them to me
in my hand.

The poem turns on what reads like (and presumably was) a direct quote, five words that summarize with bitter resignation life seen from the vantage of age. Dr. Williams, an intrepid reporter, never ceased recording and collecting overheard speech, portions of conversations, and stray sentences. Around these he built some of his best poems.

Jonathan Williams, a fan and friend of WCW and like WCW a believer in "the democratic idiom," built on Dr. Williams' innovations, moving the oft-neglected and sometimes scorned genre of the found poem in new directions. More than for any other poet in the post-modern schools descending from Pound and WCW, JW made the found poem central to his enterprise. A man of broad interests that were also often arcane, he used as his compass an intelligence hyper-alert to irony in all forms and as his shaping tool a wry and engaging wit. He believed discovery was at least half the process of creation. All the ways he invented to use found materials complemented his passion for assembling lists of quotes into books, his fascination with outsider artists and his lifelong interest in photography. His was the art of the unnoticed, the discarded. "I haven't seen territory yet that cannot be sexualized; or, examined for its poetic cuisine, or its birds, or for its dialects," he wrote, in the collection *Elite/Elate*.

That territory was essentially anyplace with which he was unfamiliar, and there anything seen, heard or overheard was fair game. Into his poems he worked graffiti ("Ass is Nice" reads a poem called "Lipstick Sign under the Concrete Bridge over Middle Creek"), epitaphs, road signs, headlines ("Nancy: Together We Can Lick Crack"), maps, intercepted postcards, answering machine messages and much more. The content of the local phone book became a list poem titled "Selected Listings from the Western Carolina Telephone Company's Directory," and includes individuals named O.U. Muse, Zero Webb, and Lily Quiet. An entire poem consists of nothing but the stranger names among Kentucky's towns. Examples: Hell for Certain, Disputanta, Bugtussle.

Like WCW, he found grace, wit and insight in what sophistication would not ordinarily deign to notice, let alone record. Ransacking the culturally invisible and intellectually obscure for rough diamonds, retrieving the inventions of the untutored, was to some extent what he was about. Consider, for instance, this message, resurrected from a tombstone in an English graveyard and titled "On the Stone of Aaron Isaacs, Easthampton":

An Israelite,

in whom
there was
no guile …

That eight word elegy is not only a model of economy but a banquet for thought on the subject of anti-Semitism and its discontents.

Of course the point was far more typically humorous than elegiac. Often JW charged quoted material with irony by composing a title two or three times longer than the actual found poem. For instance, "raised manholes / for next mile" is almost meaningless without its title: "ADUMBRATIONS OF MEPHITIC PHANTASMAGORIA PRODUCED BY A ROADSIGN IN MILD & SUNNY KIRKBY LONSDALE." Title and text combined gesture to the lasciviousness Freud noted was never far from human thought. The text of a poem titled "Piedmontese Easter Sunday Home Truth" offers this bit of folk wisdom, picked up somewhere:

never bare your soul
to an asshole

The rhyme, no doubt, appealed.

JW published many books, chapbooks and broadsides of his work in a long and varied writing life. Out of this corpus, *Blues & Roots/Rue & Bluets*—its title borrowed from Charles Mingus, its method from anthropology—offers perhaps the best overview of his approach. The book contains all manner of found poems, including road signs ("EAT/300 FEET," and "O'NAN'S AUTO SERVICE"), epitaphs ("LIVED ALONE / SUFFERED ALONE / DIED ALONE") and a phonetic approximation of the sounds a pileated woodpecker might make feasting on dogwood berries. But in a handful of the poems in *Blues & Roots* JW took the whole idea a step further. Rather than appropriating what was stumbled on and already notated in some form, or even what was accidentally overheard, he sought people out—namely fellow residents of the Southern Appalachians—interviewed them and pared their musings on life, love, and liquor into stripped down post-modern forms that owe as much to the authenticity of the speaking voice as they do to his skills in arranging what he heard into lines and stanzas:

took me a pecka real ripe tomaters up
into the Grassy Gap
one night

and two quarts of good stockade
and just laid there

So begins "Custodian of a Field of Whiskey Bushes By the Nolichucky River Speaks": In poems such as that or in "Old Man Sam Ward's History of the Gee-Haw Whimmy Diddle" or "The Hermit Cackleberry Brown, On Human Vanity": JW refashioned verse into a vehicle in which the unrecorded and unheard finally have their say. Where poetry is often seen as exalted speech delivered downward from on high, these poems are sourced from below. They are common—to invoke that ultimate pejorative of British English—and therein lies their authenticity, their eloquence and their power, which is similar to the power of documentary film or outsider art.

In the latter third of his writing life JW created a kind of poem called the meta-four, the only real rule of which is that each line contains four words. Into this almost always untitled form he poured all kinds of quoted and overheard language, to wit:

an edinburgh publican has
a sign over the
bar that says if
assholes could fly this
would be an airport

thereby offering further proof to the aesthetic argument that poems are everywhere around us, if only we open our eyes and ears.

Baffling how few followed JW down the road of found poetry, or, I should say, down any of the many trails he blazed for it. Maybe that'll change as fashionable obscurity collapses in on itself. Or did he do it so well, in so many ways, that to attempt to emulate his achievement could only result in something second tier?

Hard to say. He knew that, just as in everyday conversation, raising a laugh, or only just an eyebrow, was the surest way to arouse interest and hold the reader to the page. JW is one of the few poets whose work is genuinely funny, but the whole point, of course, is that poetry must never take itself too seriously. When it does, no one listens.

JONATHAN GREENE

JONATHAN WILLIAMS—TAKING DELIGHT IN TWO WORLDS

Thinking of Jonathan Williams, I remember reading an essay by Heinrich Zimmer in *The King and the Corpse* that set out to rescue the word "dilettante" from its unfortunate current day pejorative meaning and restore its original meaning of "taking delight." Jonathan knew how to take delight in the panoply of what interested him.

He lived in stark contrast to today's world with the weight put on a dry professionalism, being a "specialist" in one small territory, becoming an expert in the art of self-promotion. For poets, it seems that 99% become teachers as their vehicle of sustenance with the attendant creation of a small tribe of student groupies. Then outward to network with similar folks at meetings of the Association of Writers and Writing Programs. Jonathan "networked" before the word existed, but often across disciplines and in altruistic fashion. Who knows if Guy Davenport would have ever met the photographer Gene Meatyard without Jonathan telling them they lived in the same town and should look up one another. Hundreds of other examples of this generosity should be in the record.

In the past poets led different lives: one might marry money (Pound) or be a priest (Hopkins, R.S. Thomas) or doctor (Williams) or banker (Eliot) or work in insurance (Ives, Stevens). Or take the other route and honorably be a "Bohemian" and perhaps agree with Thoreau (via his reading of Indian philosophy) that living in semi-poverty was the proper lifestyle for concentration on the higher calling of Nature and Art.

The route for Jonathan: to take to heart the George Herbert saying that "living well is the best revenge"—and he lived well though often without the means that would make that an easy task. Often he was a mendicant for Art as publisher of his Jargon Society books and his begging bowl was out, scrounging the means to publish the next book. My wife, who for a time was Jargon's Treasurer, called those pleas for money "whine-o-grams."

He had no real feel for the preservation of money and as soon as some appeared, he knew beforehand how to spend it.

His wide-ranging passions and interests were omnivorous. Literature, photography, hiking, food & wine, folk art, music were just a few of his serious preoccupations. If we just wanted to zoom into music and his wide and eclectic taste, just look into what is filed under M: Mahler, Magnard, Martinů, Moeran, Mompou, Mingus, Monk. For starters. The last two paragraphs on the original LP of Mingus' *Ah Um* is a quote from Jonathan that ends, "Poetry and music are for those with straight connections between ears, eyes, head, heart and gut."

For many years Jonathan divided his time in these pursuits between Scaly Mountain, North Carolina, and Dentdale in the Yorkshire Dales of England. Who knew that both would be "found" and become trendy years after he was "in situ" in both places.

From both places he could venture forth on hikes—in the Smokies and the whole Appalachian Trail here, and throughout the Dales and other long walks in Albion. And more than once he took off to walk in Germany's Black Forest. In fact all that hiking punished his feet (he always seemed to be breaking in a pair of new hiking boots) and might have led to the painful peripheral neuropathy that he suffered from at the end of his life.

There are many ways Corn Close (the house in the Dales) and Sky-winding (the house in the Nantahalas) mirror similar worlds that would have the tropisms to feed Jonathan's interests. They both have good views and are happily away from the snobbism of the "centers" of civilization (big cities) he scorned. Both have a feeling of genuine warmth and good taste. At both places there would be bouts of drought and water troubles. Both have roads to houses that UPS trucks cannot manage with ease.

In England, JW would have the hiking guides by Alfred Wainwright (*Walks in the Howgill Fells* and others) and handy at Skywinding was the *Guide to the Appalachian Trail in the Great Smokies, the Nantahalas, and Georgia* by Lionel Edney, Rufus A. Morgan, and Henry B. Morris. In both places he would naturally *kvetch* about some of the locals, though he was quick to celebrate others as well. It was only natural Jonathan would buy and display facing outward on his living room mantelpiece the *Born to Kvetch* book by Michael Wex.

He had a keen ear for the dialect of both places and you can see the results in his poetry, especially in *Blues & Roots/Rue & Bluets: A Garland for the Southern Appalachians* and *Shakum Naggum* where he has some work in Cumbrian dialect. Both books are in part homages to the old-timers like Rufus Morgan who climbed Mount LeConte in the Smokies 173 times and Allen Beresford, "the remarkable Yorkshire hill farmer" who died the day after Jonathan photographed him "in Oughtershaw in Upper Wharfdale" and it is that photograph that graces the cover of *Shakum Naggum*.

His collecting of regional craft and folk art went on in both residences. In England he collected walking sticks and shepherd's crooks; in America pottery and traditional folk art. He was an early collector of "naive" artists of which Kentucky has its share.

In *Blues & Roots* I often liked the long title with the short poem—in many cases a "found" poem. If he had not had the ears to hear or eyes to see these, then for all of us they would have been "lost" poems. A prime example:

MRS. SADIE GRINDSTAFF, WEAVER & FACTOTUM,
    EXPLAINS
THE WORK-PRINCIPLE TO THE MODERN WORLD

I figured
anything anybody
could do a lot of I
could do a little
of

mebby

Ah, we all do what we can. Jonathan did way beyond most.

KENNETH IRBY

"america's largest openair museum"

We have here two of the latest and most striking evidences of Jonathan
Williams' diverse and remarkable accomplishments as poet and publisher,
photographer and prose stylist. Robert Kelly has called him the creator of
"america's largest openair museum"—and this means the exhibits, the guide,
the earphone commentaries, the buildings, the gardens, the grounds, every-
thing. No one does this better. Add that he truly does know *everyone*; and
keeps up with the latest in all the arts, sports, popular and arcane culture
and lore, and the grand gossip of both the United States and Great Britain
(at least); is the greatest enthusiast and promoter for the "really marvellous
'minor' or fifth-rate ignored writer" or painter or composer or whatever,
since Kenneth Rexroth; is the Compleat Traveller, and Chronicler of the
Compleat Traveller—and no one better to hike with; manages a correspon-
dence of upwards of 50 letters a week (there was once a plan to bring out a
selection of correspondence, one letter for each day of a certain year, but
the book has alas never appeared); is the living exemplar of Lucius Beebe's
often-reaffirmed article of belief: "I don't ask for much, only the best of
everything, and there's so little of that"; and for over 25 years has published,
and kept on publishing, some of the most notable writers and artists of our
time (while still remaining friends with most of them), producing a series
of books unmatched for elegance of design. Boris Pasternak used to insist
that life in order to be life continually has to exceed itself. It would seem
that we in Spectator America have come to expect, demand even, that a
poet in order to be a poet always has to do *something else*. But everything
that Williams has done, and always so well, we could otherwise expect hap-
pening in These States only "when the man in the moon / comes down in
a balloon," if then—to quote that other great North Carolina poet of the
complex actual, Charlie Poole. Now, all this has been said of Williams
before, and by people well worth paying attention to—but it always does

need to be repeated, and repeated again. Against the unending flood of information and the relentlessly shortening memory and attention span, our common lot, he has made an edge of wit and humor and intelligence and enjoyment, of exact collection and recollection, of what *tells*, offered in like share. For above all, he is a *poet*. Even, no, *mostly*, what he would probably never feel easy with, would always shy away from, Whitman's "folks expect of the poet … to indicate the path between reality and their souls." Just in that quickest catch *between*, maker in act, shared in the catch.

Elite/Elate Poems—in which title it may be remembered that elite also refers to a typewriter type, and derives from a Latin verb meaning to pick out, to choose, from an Indo-European root *leg-*, to collect, also with various derivatives meaning to speak, including dialect and Logos; and that elate, from the Latin to carry out, to lift up, has the root *tel-*, which also means to weigh, with derivatives referring to *measured* weight, thence to money and payment, so that we are also in the company of talent, and toleration, and extol—: "poems chosen and lifted up, neighbors and citizens," as Thomas Meyer says in his jacket note; poems picked and measured. This collection is made up of five sections, each a previously published book, totaling very close to the same number of poems as pages (taking *Zat's That Rollo!* as one poem, there are 220; and 224 pages, numbered or blank). In addition to Meyer's jacket note, there is an introduction by Guy Davenport; both are of considerable import. And there is a central portfolio of 12 photographs (made a baker's dozen by the cover take of Little Enis and Company) by Guy Mendes, providing completely independent but consistently apposite counterpoint images to the surrounding words. Following the mode of his two previous large collections—*An Ear in Bartram's Tree* and *The Loco Logodaedalist in Situ*—the author has given us "In Lieu of a Preface" another series of notable, rare, and select quotations from the most amazingly diverse sources.

Furthermore, each section is provided with prefacing and/or concluding commentaries and/or notes, making an immediately engaging and variously revealing tapestry of *setting*: place, circumstance, history, method, identification, theoretical rationale, companions of the spirit. It must be said that Williams' talents are displayed as amply in these settings, and in the titles of the poems, as in any other aspect of his art. In fact, he has an absolute, unexcelled *genius* for titles (which I, for one, envy unreservedly).

For the immensely complex, simultaneously multidimensional result (so admirably constructed that one is instantly drawn into it without any difficulty at all):—POEM (the central irreducible diamond-like artifact), plus TITLE (more often than not another poem in its own right; and of course the *real poem* is always the *unit* of the "title" and the "text"), plus SETTING, gathered then in a BOOK (more than almost any other poet that comes to mind, Williams writes to be read in a *book*), and that in turn gathered in a larger COLLECTION of several books (with its further accompanying remarks and embellishments by yet others)—for *all this,* even "america's largest openair museum" may not seem enough, like the fig leaf in the old joke, to cover what we have. Whatever and however, museum, encyclopedia, *Gesamtkunst,* three-ring circus and sideshow, or Mallarmean *Livre,* a tour of the premises is in order, section by section—bringing to bear consideration of his other work, as well.

The five sections of *Elite/Elate Poems: Pairidaeza, Imaginary Postcards, Adventures with A Twelve-Inch Pianist Beyond the Blue Horizon, a Celestial Centennial Reverie for Charles Edward Ives,* and *Untinears & Antennae for Maurice Ravel.* The first two are predominantly English in setting or source, the last three American. *Pairidaeza,* is subtitled *A Celebration for the Garden at Levens Hall, Westmorland,* the title itself being an Old Persian or Avestan word for enclosure, a circumvallation, the root of the English word paradise, which was first a garden (as John Evelyn—one of the inspirers of Levens— in his *Diary* for 11 Apr 1645: "The garden is rather a park or paradise, contriv'd and planted with walkes and shades"; and Milton in *Paradise Lost,* iv: "where delicious Paradsise, / Now nearer, Crowns with her enclosure green"). The poems are prefaced with a "Perambulation" (very carefully picking up again the root *per-* in pairidaeza/paradise), telling us, as Williams is always careful to do, about the poetic method used, and the authorities for its use, and the sources, and the history of the place honored (with a quick disquisition on the art of the topiary), and the nature of the author's involvement with it; as well as a tribute to the art, and the tradition of that art, of Ian Gardener, whose lithographs accompanied the text in its first publication. These are *found* poems (one of Williams' favorite quotations is from John Clare: "I found the poems in the fields and only wrote them down"), selected and arranged from seventeenth- and eighteenth-century accounts of the garden. A number are concrete or *visual* poems, set out in mimetic, metonymic patterns (of course the poems are all visual objects on the page, but the reference is to those whose special impact cannot be appreciated viva voce). The whole is meant as a tribute to the original gardener, as an artist (the first poem, for instance, entitled *An Orthographic Scattering of Bulbs of the Rare Narcissus, Topiarius Gallicus, In the Oak Avenue of "The Great Aire,"* is a display of M. Beaumont's name, in 19 different spellings and types, spread in careful broadcast down the page).

Many people have objected that poems in order to be *true* poems have to be "in one's own words" (*own* by intensity, presumably—one does wonder how any word can be actually *owned*). Williams, while certainly continuing to say things himself, affirms a tradition of finding one's voice "outside," in which the emphasis is on operations of precise attention, selection, and placement, rather than "inspiration" or vatic seizure. (Williams has often said that he makes poems *out* rather than *up*—thus providing a perfect replay to the question: "is that a real poem or did you make that up?") In his introduction to a sequence of poems selected from case histories in Havelock Ellis' *Studies in the Psychology of Sex* (Part II of *Loco Logodaedalist*), Williams discusses all this in some detail. Insisting that *"poetry is a process, not a memoir"* and that "'art' is in 'raising the common to grace,'" he cites with approval the Scots poet Thomas A. Clark on the way he had gone about working with Samuel Palmer texts. Clark's words are worth giving here:

> Years working in a short space via haiku, epigram, W.C. Williams, Creeley, Concrete, etc., the trouble was, how to distance it from one's own mind. The language became more and more self-referent and "obscure" in the worst sense. So I've been making poems using texts which were "outside my own head," and treating them in different ways: permutational, fragmentary, etc. ... I set about experiments like cutting columns in half, reading quickly across columns, or placing frames over pieces of prose. I think that knowing to look at all and knowing what to look for is rather a lot ...

In Barry Alpert's interview with Williams in *VORT* (#4, Fall, 1973), the following interchange took place:

BA: *Were the materials you found in Havelock Ellis via the rectangular cutout discovered more or less at random or did you find things you already had in your mind*

JW: *Well I think that's the only thing you do find; i.e., what's already there … I think it's very much like Thoreau says, he could spend the rest of his life concentrating on a square yard of Concord earth and there would be enough going on … There's enough in that to keep him going.*

Then, speaking specifically about *Pairidaeza* material, Williams goes on:

I used the "facts" and just recombined, took bits, you know, it's a kind of bouquet—bouquet garni … just an attempt to work with the whole metaphor of clippings, like clipped greens. I have a poem called "Clipped Greens" in which the typography is clipped in various ways. Just the word "clipped greens" has been clipped in different ways. It's a rather simpleminded but very delightful thing to do. Again, a naturalist's approach to things.

When one comes to look at the actual poems at hand in *Pairidaeza,"* apropos the "that's the only thing you do find; i.e., what's already there" above, one must remark on the convergence of the seventeenth-century English of the texts, especially the spelling, with the Appalachian materials in Williams' earlier *Blues & Roots/Rue & Bluets.* If we look at this from *Pairidaeza*:

The Storm Of Early October 1701

it is such a thing as hath not
bene in this Country in no
ag of man

thier is butt one ocke tree butt
it is a very good one
and al sheffeard too butt
it stod

bemun is very much disturbed about is trees
he wants stakes

hear will be aboundance
of fier wood

and then look at this from *Blues & Roots* (from the section "Common
Words in Uncommon Orders"):

From Uncle Jake's Carpenter's
Anthology of Death on Three-Mile Creek

Loney Ollis
age 84
dide jun 10 1871

grates dere honter
wreked bee trees for honey
cild ratell snak by 100
cild dere by thousen

I nod him well

we can see and hear (and feel in the case of the English piece that we are
about to enter one of M.R. James' stories) exactly what Guy Davenport was
talking about in his introduction to *An Ear in Bartram's Tree*:

What Jonathan Williams found in England, Wales and Scotland was
not a second heritage (as it might seem to a casual glance) but the heritage
in which he was raised from the beginning … as perhaps only a citizen of
Appalachia can know and in fact there is another poem in *Pairidaeza* that
exemplifies this continuum perfectly:

A Country Wordsman from the North Carolina Hills
Looks at Levens and Shapes the Language in His Own Way:

'ARY   TOE   PIE?

which carries this footnote:

> This little sonic metaphor does not seem far-fetched to me in the slightest. Any imagination capable of turning a bush into a corkscrew or a "Judge's Wig" or a rabbit is able to consider making a pie out of toes.

In all of which most *definitely* echoes the injunction in *The Nostrums of the Black Mountain Publican* in *Blues & Roots*:

DON'T EAT NO
HAIRPIE
ON FRIDAY!

And this but further underscores what even a casual browsing of *Pairidaeza* would make clear—that, as Williams says later in *Elite/Elate Poems*: "I haven't seen the territory yet that can't be sexualized" ("or," the rest of the sentence adds, "examined for its poetic cuisine, or its birds, or for its dialects").

The next section, "Imaginary Postcards," is made up of 40 "Clints Grikes Gripes Glints" celebrating the Yorkshire Dales, followed by a set of notes and an afterward, in which Williams tells us: "This combination of topography and typography is calculated to open a determinedly small world to mental travelling ... the landscape revealed is largely an interior one." Coleridge's dictum, "thought follows the line of the mountains," certainly might be an appropriate epigraph. But that this "small world" is also definitely material and tangible is stressed in the *VORT* interview: "They're essentially based on *things* that one sees or experiences or finds in living in the north of England. It's this kind of almost stupid wandering through a landscape and being amazed." (Stupid is *not* a word one would think of using in connection with Williams' work, whatever else one thought about it!) Here is an example of the terrain revealed:

A Regional Specialty is Suggested
By a Careless, Coprophilous Sign-Painted
On the A-650 North of Leeds:

MANURE
BROWN
EGGS

which receives this notation:

When recently observed, nettles were beginning to obscure the bottom
line. Seasonal variations in poetry have been too little considered.

These are, like so much of Williams' work, a traveller's poems (predominantly a *peripatetic* traveller's poems)—postcards that a Blakean mental traveller might send back. One may remark on a continuing fascination with postcards through all of Williams' books—those collected in *Lines About Hills Above Lakes*; the picture-postcard images reproduced in "The Plastic Hydrangea People Poems" in *Loco Logodaedalist*; the old messages presented as found poems on p. 134 and p. 198 of *Elite/Elate Poems*. There is even a tribute paid to this fascination, by Edwin Morgan, in his postcard contribution to the *Truck*/Gnomon 50th birthday volume for Williams (1979).

This is of course a part of Williams' much larger, on-going concern with the visual in poetry, and the interpretation of the visual and the aural—a concern that is perhaps even more insistent and variously evident in his attention to *signs* (again, a traveller's attention). More than half a dozen poems in *Elite/Elate Poems* are sign texts or make use of sign texts (on pp. 58, 64, 73, 111, 126, 187, and 210); a wall plaque is cited on p. 59; p. 62 presents an imagined sign; p. 69 (!) gives us an elaborate graffito/statistical chart; p. 76, a label. The earlier *Blues & Roots* is full of signs, one or two probably as well-known as any of Williams' poems; for example:

John Chapman Pulls Off the Highway
Towards Kentucky and Casts a Cold Eye
On the Most Astonishing Sign in Recent American Letters:

O'NAN'S
AUTO
SERVICE

It may be wondered whether this passion for noticing and transcribing odd signs, and as part of literature, is not a particularly *American* trait— Burma Shave verses flash by—or English *language*, at any rate? Graham Peck, the American artist, traveller, and writer (whose *Two Kinds of Time* remains perhaps the finest book written about World War II China), was first in China in the mid-1930s. His account of his experiences, *Through China's Wall*—a book well informed throughout with a most salutory sense of the absurd—records a number of truly remarkable English-language signs; e.g., this, from Chungking during the winter of 1936–37:

FALSE EYES AND DENTAL PLUMBING
INSERTED BY THE LATEST METHODISTS

and this, which would certainly be right up Williams' alley, from Changchung:

THE BLUE SKY AND ART STORE

(alas, it had been long closed, so its wares could not be sampled); and another, for a Japanese nightclub in Peking:

THE WHITE P
ALACE

which could be placed next to Williams' even more elaborate example of creative enjambment in *Blues & Roots*:

Paint Sign on a Rough Rock
Yonside of Boone Side of Shady Valley

    BEPREPA
    REDTO
    MEETGO
    D

Peck and Williams are both men of a developed artistic sensibility and sense of humor (New England on the one hand, Appalachian on the other, both honed internationally)—the kinds of attentions that pick and present the signs are not dissimilar. Reading *Through China's Wall* today one may very naturally take the quoted signs as poems, quite beyond their intended 1941 function as bits of socioeconomic color. But of course the major difference between the sign in Peck's book and in Williams' is that Williams *does* present it *as a poem.* For the existence and development of such an art as his, the creative role of the reader is crucial, something Williams' never stops saying:

For something as common and ordinary as

    EAT
    300 FEET

to suffer transmutation into something more than linguistic fool's gold requires a pact with an inspired reader.

But even more important is the creation of the context in which it is claimed: *this is a poem*—the surround that very exactly determines how the precise selection is to be viewed. What Stephen Scobie has said about Williams' colleague Ian Hamilton Finlay applies in every regard to Williams as well:

In many of Finlay's works, the poetic activity consists largely of establishing ... the "field" (sometimes literally) of "being a poem." Within this field, one concise image—often reduced to a single proper

name, number, or fact—can extend its significance in a witty and con-
trolled play among the levels evoked by the context. In such minimal
art, as the range of choice narrows (for both poet and reader), so the
quality of choice becomes more important, for it is only within the
most rigorous limits that the assertion of "being a poem" can be main-
tained and validated.

The most fascinating aspect of this in Williams' case may be his use
of *titles*. Certainly in "Imaginary Postcards" their operation is of considerable
complexity. In the first place, all the pieces are in one sense actually titles,
since they are inscriptions for postcard "pictures" we are asked thereby to
imagine. At the same time, in a strictly formal sense—as determined by the
location on the page and the use of italics throughout the rest of *Elite/Elate
Poems*—there are *no* titles at all, only numbers. Nonetheless, often there is
an operative title, set a noticeable distance above the text and serving to
introduce it—and often much longer and more elaborate, the "poem" func-
tioning rather as a punch-line (e.g., pp. 40, 57, 67). In some instances this
operative title is the setting for a text which is a quotation (p. 55); in others,
the solitary text itself is made up of both a setting/title and a quotation (pp.
54, 74). In some cases the title, or an additional title, is to be found in the
notes (pp. 47, 61, 64—the text of p. 47 consisting of the title and author
of an imaginary thriller); for p. 53, though there is no title, half the total
text—the answer to the question/riddle can only be found in the notes.
And later on in *Elite/Elate Poems* (p. 131), we find this poem:

(April 13)

Title

planh
on an
onan-
ist's
wrist

where the "real" poem is the one we are called on to imagine by the title
that *this* poem is (which we project as a title because it is so entitled!). This

persistent, total interpenetration of what is title, poem, text, context, note, commentary, actual, imaginary, etc., etc., throughout Williams' work is one of the most notable features of his art.

"Imaginary Postcards" is followed by a selection of photographs by Guy Mendes. Besides the enjoyment they afford us by their own elegant accomplishment, they also serve to shift the focus of the local back to the United States, while still suggesting the England we have just visited—as in the "Lexington 1974" depiction of two chairs (much less ornate but very similar to the pair of "Carved Walnut Chairs. English, early eighteenth century." in Plate 1, Fig. 6, of the *Furniture* article in the 11th edition of the *Britannica*). Though Mendes' images and Williams' poems function entirely on their own, in two cases they do share the same subject matter: "Campton, Ky. 1974" lets us see the sculptor, Edgar Tolson, who speaks in Williams' poem on p. 205; and the cover photograph gives us a view of Carlos Toadvine (and friends), the subject of "Who Is Little Enis?" (pp. 104–05).

While thus diverted by Mendes' picture, we might turn aside from our tour of *Elite/Elate Poems* to investigate the portrait gallery of Williams' museum, as represented by the book of photographs under review. This extraordinarily handsome volume of 2¼" x 2¼" tipped-in color prints of poets, painters, photographers, and composers, each with a facing note of identification and characterization, allows us to look at 30 "friends in the arts with faces too interesting to be missed even by a poet on the run," from William Carlos Williams to John Jacob Niles. Williams' photographs are an important part of his oeuvre. For years he toured the country in a VW bug, giving combination poetry readings, cross-culture group-gropes, and slide shows, bringing light and delight to the benighted. This reviewer first had any idea of what Louis Zukofsky looked like (at a time when that was a matter of some curiosity to him) from such an event in Berkeley in the mid-1960s; was first introduced to the wonders of Louis Sullivan's late-period, small-town Midwest banks; first had a glimpse of Walt Whitman's tomb—riches not forgotten. The present portrait selection, in addition to providing a great deal of pleasure just to wander about in it, is valuable to look at in connection with poetry. The photo of WCW in *Portrait Photographs*, for one instance, is the same that the "Elegy for a Photograph of

William Carlos Williams in Loco Logodaedalist" addresses. It does help to *see* the red dahlia the poem refers to, but nothing in the photograph alone could prepare us for the end of the poem:

> You taught us to
> scrape all the leaves off the Bottom of the Barrel,
> because the Leaves can equal
> the Sacred Red Anemones of Osiris
> falling in the Blue Waterfalls of
> Lebanon—
>
> and you knew it

One only hopes that eventually photographs from Williams' architecture and birth- and burial-place series will be published too, and as impressively as these portraits.

The 35 poems of "Adventures With a Twelve-Inch Pianist Beyond the Blue Horizon" were written in the Spring of 1973 while the author was visiting poet at a number of Winston-Salem colleges—one poem a day between Spring Equinox and Shakespeare's birthday, as example and impetus for his students. Dedicated to Bette Midler—on being told that her visitors were poets, she replied: "I hope you write hot ones. I like 'em hot."—they are not so simply just poems of the relentlessly sexual ("variously satiric and randy, about pederasty," as Guy Davenport says in his introduction) as, even more deeply, poems of longing and arousal, spring paeans, indeed. "It may be that the satiric spirit is always in defense of some deep and unquestioned love," concludes Davenport.

The range is from

The New Gripping Sleazo-Western at the J&J Newstand:

HARD ON
THE TRAIL
OF TAIL

to
Hornstein (1898–1973)
simply heeding
the Daimon's
bidding

something
whirring in the woods

and back again on the trail. Williams has argued (in the *VORT* interview) that sexual material in poetry "needs many techniques to keep it from being platitudinous, too easy, too indulgent." A deeper problem with "hardcorn-poneography," however, is: where is the *heart*? In his *Paris Review* interview Christopher Isherwood proposed: "We're not afraid of what's called pornography, but we are terribly afraid of what we call sentimentality—the rash, incautious expression of feeling." Some ten years back, in a review of *Bartram* (in *Caterpillar* #10), Robert Kelly asked if Williams were not afraid of his own tenderness ("& no business of mine to pry, since he would turn our eyes outward so well"); and Guy Davenport, introducing the same book, felt: "Pathos must appear in comic socks or not at all." Next to all this the following lines, the beginning of "Lexington Nocturne" in the present volume, should be considered:

don't you
don't you want to

a gentleman doesn't ask young men
questions like that;
he probably begins with reveries on the French word
tendresse
and how much better it is than our own

tendresse,
what you find in Adagio
of Rachmaninov's E minor Symphony
after the Largo, which was so

> rapacious
> and full of longing ...
> sacred *longing*:
> to be *long*, to *belong* to the company of those
> who trust the holiness of the heart's affections ...
>
> and to be long gone
> up the dirt road to Eros,
> as prone to the emotions as Sebastian,
> full of his arrows ...

Certainly, though the definition in these next lines may be questioned (though recognizing the *vir* in *virtue*):

> this is not just semen up your ass,
> this is class, is areté, this is how
> you learn to be a man

the restraint and exactitude of the whole account and the intensity of the actual *touch* in:

> thus I see you as your eyes open in the Lexington dawn
> and put my hand in your hair and
> let it hang
> just an instant
> there
> and let that be all
> for then

are undeniable. (The image of the hand in the hair appears very early on in Williams' poetry, in the elegy for Rainer Gerhardt, "He Was Alone When He Died," in *Loco Logodaedalist*, and reappears in the first March 4 section of the suite, "Strung Out with Elgar On a Hill," also in that book—this is a work remarkably similar to "Lexington Nocturne" in situation and expression of "feeling.")

Afraid of tenderness? no, though neither could one ever expect

Williams to be rash or incautious in expressing *any*thing. And comic socks? well, not *always*, though always *returned* to, persistently. It is rather *restraint* that is the keynote throughout: restraint, and courtesy, candor, precision, self-awareness, care and respect and equality of treatment for all of the complex actual—a gentleman's virtues, in short, entirely of a piece in the man and his work. Russell Banks, in the *Truck*/Gnomon birthday volume, has used the word *grace* to speak of Williams: "a kind of politeness toward the universe"; Robert Kelly, in the same collection, has called it *gentility*: "to respect, as the renaissance dukes were said to, the proportions and graces of the actual.… Gentility is kind, is behaving how it ought to." Williams himself, in his *VORT* interview, sums it up:

> I think that poetry is probably a branch of manners. Who would say that—would Confucius say that? I don't know who would say that, but one could almost … It's a kind of neighborliness that I like. Again, communities … ecosystems ….

And this is also a matter of *subject*, of subjects, of the immense *range* of material, information, people known, Williams deals with and keeps in measured motion, the greatness as *inclusion* of the work—as the *heart* of manners.

Both of the last sections of *Elite/Elate Poems* are dedicated to composers, honoring respectively the centenary birthday of Charles Ives and of Maurice Ravel, linked, other than by the affection of the poet for their music, only by Ives' denunciation of Ravel's work as being "of a kind / I cannot stand: / pleasing enough, / if you want to be / pleased." The selections of "A Celestial Centennial Reverie for Charles Edward Ives', (The Man Who Found Our Music in the Ground), "have been chosen from Ive's own writings and then "pushed around" by the poet. Part I, "Zat's That Rollo!," offers two pages of highlights from the memos on the *Concord Sonata*, without any basic alteration. Part 2, "Essays before a Sonata," presents 91 brief excerpts from the book of that title (on the same piano sonata), rearranged into concise, short-lined, Imagism/Objectivism-derived poems. Williams tells us in his introduction that his intention has been "to work motifs I find there into new forms … there may be something there he didn't quite realize he was aiming at. I'll make my own noises—with some of his words."

This is very much in the manner, or in the mood, at any rate, of Ives' continual quotation and remoulding of quotation from other music in his own compositions—with a great variety of tone, from homey musing to crusty invective to democratic affirmation to cosmic exaltation. The results are often things we might imagine Williams saying himself frequently enough, as: "always doin' something'— / doin' somethin'/ *within*"; but there are other pieces that Williams would clearly be far less likely to say "on his own":

> cherished thoughts, sacred communities
> now vanished,
>
> yet America is not too young
> to have its divinities
> beneath our Concord elms—
>
> of humblest clay,
> "instinct with celestial fire"

yet all are things that Williams obviously has *wanted* to say, a basic testament of belief in Ives' guise.

Maurice Ravel has been honored by Williams various times before (the 93rd birthday piece in the *Elgar* sequence, for one example); in the 40 poems of *Untinears & Antennae* he appears in person only once, imagined staring in amazement at his own excrement, but his presence has been felt by the poet throughout, "always demanding something more exalté." These *elegies and celebrations* (also the title of a Williams volume of 1962) are arranged as carefully to complement, reflect, and heighten one another, to face, to follow, and juxtapose by theme and tone-leading, as any book of poems of recent letters (as Edward Dorn's *Hands Up!*, say, or Gerrit Lansing's *The Heavenly Tree Grows Downward*, or Robert Grenier's *Oakland*). There are homages and dirges, acrostical portraits, signs, postcards, hales and farewells, "Vulgar, Trivial, and Exalted," dedicated to notables as diverse as Joseph Pujol, *Le Petomane*, and John Coltrane, James Broughton and Art Blakey. There is an elegy arranged, in the fashion of Ives sequence, from the mysterioso words of the photographer, Ralph Meatyard; there are two facing pairs of vales opening the suite, very quiet, very restrained, of that apparent simplicity which Jarry characterized as complexity refined, synthesized, drawn taut; and there are all the varieties of multiple-word-play highjinks we always expect from Williams, as the following, where the title serves as a sideshow barker's cry to rivet our attention just before the curtain is flung back to reveal the label on the invisible offering:

A Scientific Breakthrough!
Now, For the First Time:
An Instant Aphrodisiac and A Laxative,
Artfully Combined,
With the Senior Citizen in Mind
& Based on An Ancient Chinese Medical Formula
(for Paul Metcalf)

PRUNE TANG

But the crowning achievement, and one of the finest poems of Williams' entire career, is the last poem of the book, honoring the 300th anniversary of the building of the Quaker meeting-house, Briggflatts, drawn on the words of the poet, Basil Bunting (as a preface one might look at the five-years-earlier poem on Briggflatts in *Loco Logodaedalist*). It is a truly noble *ars poetics*, a fit response to the demand of Ravel's spirit for the Exalted:

whether it is a stone next to a stone
or a word next to a word,
it is the *glory*—
the simple craft of it

and money and sex aren't worth
bugger-all, not
bugger-all

solid, common, *vulgar* words

the ones you can touch

the ones that yield
and a respect for the music ...

what else can you tell 'em?

Williams has many times been praised as a *light* poet, that is, as a writer—indeed, perhaps our *greatest* writer—of *light verse*. Now, there is no doubt, at least not in my mind, that he is one of the funniest and wittiest writers alive. But any such qualification as "great poet of light verse," "great concrete poet," "Great Gay Southern Gentleman Poet," etc., etc., no matter what praise, inevitably means that the writer is to be taken as being something less than simply *a poet*, the real thing, true *makaris*. ("If you're capable of writing a quote funny unquote poem, it's somehow an implication that you can't write anything else.") And in this case, ignores the other areas of Williams' work than the quick, deft, satiric, humorous—the serious, the elegiac, the visionary strains present throughout the poetry, from the beginning. It is true that there are many kinds of poetry and areas of experience that Williams simply does not take on. He does not work in the longer forms, nor the epic nor mythopoeic modes. He is not concerned with the ideal or the abstract, the "big subjects." The poems are not written to fit into some "grand design" nor to prove some "higher truth." Very little in the way of politics and economics appears; no such causes are espoused. Except for "the Revolution of the Word," the poetry is not "At the Service of the Revolution" (in actual effect, however, it may be so). Nor is it poetry of total, overwhelming *seizure* (but certainly is "hot, celebratory, and juicy"); contrast Robert Duncan: "in a poem you don't get to drive the car." But reading through the entire body of Williams' work it simply will *not* do to characterize it as *light* in any sense of being frivolous or "merely entertaining" or lacking in intensity—though other senses definitely *do* apply: bright, quick on the feet, unencumbered. Or as Edward Dorn put it in the Preface to his *Hello, La Jolla*:

These dispatches should be
received in the spirit
of the Pony Express:
light and essential.

Though the critical use of these terms later in the book should also be noted:

Rauschenberg's Untitled (Early Egyptian Series)

Some viewers might imagine
art is worth its weight. A work
which depicts that expectation
but which is essentially light
is Brilliant and worthless.

Some people have concluded that there is a geographical difference in the essential weight of Williams' poetry. Robert Kelly, in his 50th birthday piece, has argued that, though Williams brings to bear "an identical enthusiasm and rapt eye, faithful vocabulary, brain full of scherzo" when he writes about England, nonetheless:

> the results are not at all like those dozens of quickstep books that have made his american reputation. We dont [sic] laugh in the same way, though the pretenses and inadvertencies detected are just as ridiculous as those of Possum Bottom, N.C. Instead we feel, or I feel, a closer trembling of the veil. It is a Masque of Yearning to rehearse the world, and fondle it part by part, in and out of humor.

The point is well taken, but at the same time it must be pointed out that this "closer trembling of the veil" and "Masque of Yearning," a verge of revelation in the attended physical world, is also very much present in Williams' American work, starting long before he ever went to England—as in *The Grounds*, from *The Empire Finals at Verona*:

Lusters, stir the row! Poe's
Valley-of-the-Many-Colored-Grass became
the Vale of Arnheim. Potomac's Valley shall become
a domain we create, inchoate
scene where snows wane
and bulbs burn under the winter ground.

At the margins of thought, on the margins of the river, the winter
surrenders to the hosts of Great Venus.

Or witness the coming of the rattlesnake god in *The Familiars*; or this,
in the heart of the Appalachians:

> I do not know the Ironweed's root,
> but I know it rules September
>
> and where the flowers tower
> in the wind there is a burr of
> sound—empyrean … the mind
> glows and the wind drifts …
>
> epiphanies pull up
> from roots—
>
> from "The Deracination in Blues & Roots"

Whether about England or the United States, Williams' non-satiric,
non-erotic poetry deals with some sense of "otherness" (of course this is true
of *all* the poetry, finally)—exaltation, awe, immense quietude, transfigura-
tion—before Nature. As the elegiac poems again and again find their exact
term of bidding farewell in a natural object, most often a plant, a growing
thing. Part of this is an intense poignancy felt in the face of the transitoriness
of all things (and so his deep share with Delius); part—but it is really all
the same—a kind of native Buddhist sense of Emptiness. For Williams, too,
"the idea of emptiness engenders compassion"; and

> a few utterly quiet scenes, things
> are very far away—*'form
> is emptiness'*
>
> comely, comely, love trembles
>
> and the sweet-shrub

which also *has part* in a visionary tradition of *seeing through* Nature, which would have been encountered in American Transcendentalism as well as in the English masters Blake and Palmer—the elder Henry James finding the Shekinah on the trolley car; or Ives of Thoreau, that "he knows now/ he must let Nature / flow through *him.*" So, definitely, other senses of *light* apply: angle or aspect of view; illumination; enlightenment; animation or liveliness of the eyes; the guiding spirit in each human being.

Williams' is a *contemplative* poetry, attentive upon the entire world before the clear senses, intention in abeyance except to be "scrupulous to the momentary actual," in Kelly's words; and of the exact sudden light flash of wit, image, word-play, revelation—not a meditative poetry, concerned with turning thoughts over and over. It is very much a poetry of what Ford Madox Ford called, in that neglected masterpiece, *England and the English* (1907), *assoupissement*, "a bathing in the visible world"—and of Ravel's *sites auriculaires*. In the preface to his most recent collection, *Glees ... Swarthy Monotonies ... Rince Cochon ... & Chozzerai for Simon* Williams tells us:

> From Corn Close I daily look out across the valley to a group of Scotch pines in a field of grass. The light in Dentdale is unusually dim and the pines are inconspicuous and unremarkable. But, let the late sun shine its rays up the dale and the trees become transfigured, with the forms of the foliage and the trunks of the elongated shadows endlessly fascinating to the eye. Everything is seen "in a new light."

For Williams' work, too, it is fit for us to use the title William Carlos Williams gave to a book of short stories, in the fullness of its intended meanings: *Make Light of It.*

Jonathan Williams is one of the most considerable poets of our time. His work may be returned to again and again, with ever renewing delight in the fineness of its workmanship. In conclusion, the following words of Virgil Thomson on Williams' revered master, Maurice Ravel (quoted in Hoover and Cage's 1969 study of Thomson), are humbly offered as also providing a characterization of Williams that does him no disservice—for he, too, is at once an intellectual by his tastes and an artisan by his training and his practice. He is not a bourgeois nor a white-collar proletarian nor a columnist nor a priest nor a publicized celebrity nor a jobholder nor a political propagandist—but simply and plainly, proudly and responsibly, a skilled workman.

CHARLEY SHIVELY

TOILING IN THE BULLPEN—THE BLUES OF COLONEL WILLIAMS

Jonathan Williams jumps avidly through the mind: I see him pictured in
Blue & Roots/Rue & Bluets: A Garland for the Appalachians: Pan rests (a pie
pan) pied, laying back-packed piper (or is it another?) his walking stick,
hooves (or shoes?) big feet, tweed hat hands. Day and night he dances those
Appalachian smoky Blue Ridge Mountains. The satyr plays flute; his glans
landscape flute.

I like the flavor, remember riding along the Blue Ridge Trail going
south after midnight through the mountains. Charles River was hanging
out—his whole torso out the car window. Thought for sure he'd fall.
Coming back alone he wrote a poem lying naked in water, rocks, getting
them off something brings it out there, something delivers, something not
shown in *Deliverance*. But found in Delius' music: Jonathan's "Reflections
from 'Appalachia'" captures the calm goat wildness: wilderness trail music
musing:

> Dawn songs in the dews of young orange trees;
> and ranging orisons; and wordless longings
>
> sung in tranquility's waters sliding in sun's
> light;
>
> and benisons sung in these trees ...
>
> (from *An Ear in Bartram's Tree*)

In case you think I kid about the goat business just follow Jonathan's
lines through a set of love songs written out of Aspen, Colorado: "a
goat-foot in the new greenery" and translated Mahler: "I do wander in the

mountains / and ease my heart in the highland" (in *The Loco-Logodaedalist in Situ*). He plays the same in a Greek Scene, along the Trojan coast, "The Honey Lamb":

Eagle-eyed, spies
swoops
swishes into town

ponders, whether tis nobler
to bullshit, brown
or go down
on
    that catamite cat, Kid Ganymedes,
                         mead-mover,
erstwhile eagle-scout
bedmate

        (Anthologized in *Angels of the Lyre*, edited by Winston Leyland)

Out, open and early, Jonathan Williams has made himself a lightning rod for the dirty and ugly of the straight world. He read with Tom Meyer in Boston's Charles Street Meetinghouse. Somehow out of the hills came a Jesus Freak (really cute kind) who interrupted the show. Tom was reading delicately, deliciously, sweetly. The khaki clad stud shouted from beneath the brass pipe organ bank: "Don't you see, what you do is sin the eye of God." I loved the view: just think of every blowjob, fuck or whatnot as done in that great cavity called "the eye of God." Instead of exploring the mucous optical sex scene, voices of reason drove the nut out. Jonathan, of course, had the last best words from his Mae West series: "If your cock's as big as your mouth, honey, / I'll see you after the show."[1]

Nothing like that every happened before (or since): Jonathan brought it with him. Likewise at the reception afterwards: the gays lavishly outnumbered the straights, and in an effort to dominate things the latter turned all conversation to baseball. (They ignored my request to hear only those sport stories detailing sexual irregularities.) In a beautiful demonstration of his technique, Jonathan drew them all out (the drinking helped). They became more and more grotesque as they replayed great ball plays from the past. Caseys at their bat, falling out one by one, they realized they were being taken. Finally only Bill Corbett (self-appointed Boston local literary heavy) remained in action: utterly mad in his virility, frantically gesticulating baseball plays in the faggot parlor. We gasped.

The straight men misunderstood Williams' baseball (as they do that of Jack Spicer). In their twelve-year old delirium, they miss the curve Jonathan throws, "Toiling in the Bullpen":

ball game's same as
sex is;

viz:
   who can untrack
           the frozen rope
                that falls inert
     in the rapturous pasture?

Those "six-time champions / of the Class-D / Crapioca / - Grapefruit League" unfortunately—or maybe fortunately—never catch on to camp plays.

One of the lessons of Charles Olson was to go out and be with the people and the landscape: himself in Gloucester, Ed Dorn in Santa Fe or Pocatello, Idaho, Jonathan Williams in Highlands, N.C., or John Wieners in the gay glitter ghetto. You have to throw yourself entirely into the space; snobbery and condescension (the previous material of American poetry) had to be forgotten absolutely. The projection of [open] field poetry includes the land as well as the line.

For a queen those hills can be hard and cruel. Once traveling all night through the mountains to visit a lover at Camp Gordon, Georgia (Jonathan has a postcard reprinted from the camp mess room), the hostile police stopped me; they figured I was an up-all-night drunk (everyone drank across the state line Horseshoe Valley). The valley and the hills mean meaness. Just last December I went from Atlanta where the gay bookstore rejected *Fag Rag* (because of Black faggots pictured there) on to Huntington, West Virginia & Ashland, Kentucky. All I could feel was snobbery hearing a queen talk about the installation of a new bishop and a wine-cheese party with Thunderbird and Velveeta. ("What," I said, "no saltines?") This is no easy track to run, field to hoe, form to find. As the photograph/sign says: "STOP, The Area Ahead Has the Worst Weather in America. Many Have Died There from Exposure. Even in the Summer. Turn Back *Now* If the Weather is Bad." Someone has used the sign for a practice target. (*Blues & Roots/Rue & Bluets*)

So, while I was out on the land, I went coon-hunting with my brother-in-law: dogs & studs chasing *furr* down the creeks and hollows of southern Ohio. He got over six hundred skins last year; and I didn't turn a single trick while I was home. He was showing me his fighting cocks, they kill each other. "It's cruel, maybe / but that's the way the world is," he said. Jonathan's poetry touches that cruelty and grotesquerie.

The politics of Appalachia and of faggotry are actually a lot alike. David Morris in a review of the regional literature finds two main tendencies: "one, to romanticize and two, to Gothicize." Jonathan veers at times towards the gothic in his perception—a Gothicism that would deny "the humanity of the people by portraying the daily life of the people as dark, distorted, sexually kinky, cruel, animal, brutal ... savages with mystical powers" (*Win*, 18 March 1976). The landscape is celebrated; the people appear as so much transitory scum. Which is all to say I can't go all the way with the politics of "The Plastic Hydrangea People Poems" in *The Loco-Logodaedalist in Situ*.

While making political demands of the poet, I might add a note about Narcissus. I just love him. After all, the great Marcuse instructed our generation to learn the lessons of Orpheus and Narcissus—a little bit of singing and a little bit of self-love. Jonathan does love to be mentioned, photographed, drawn—and even quartered I suspect. An immense attention to his self-images dangles over each book—he has collected over 70,000 replies to his letters—including the wonderful one of Lester Maddox on official Georgia Governor's Mansion stationary: "Same to You."

His concentration on image and self-image has marvelous results. The books from Jargon Press (Jonathan's as well as others) bear the unmistakable touch of a great designer bringing every facility to communicate the poem/message. The book like the poem can suddenly light up in neon, sing in dulcimer or symphony orchestra, fold up accordion-like or explode in a postcard from Dealey Plaza. Book, picture, sign, music, symbol, word, song, line, melody—they all shine with an unmistakable Jonathan Williams net.

Much more in the thing itself than anything else, Jonathan in love and hate, returns again to Catullus' *"odi et amo"*:

I detest and I lust

O Great Catullus
with you!

in the world
up to the hilt

(from *The Loco-Logodaedalist in Situ*)

---

[1] Editors' note: Compare Shively's original version of the story in his piece with John Mitzel's "Jonathan Williams: An Appreciation," earlier in this volume. Editor Jeffery Beam queried Tom as to the true story. His reply: "I was reading. Khaki was the heckler's attire. But he was at the back of the sanctuary, cute or not, can't attest. The crowd almost immediately hounded him out of the building, and the voice clearest among them was Bill Corbett's. Although the Mae West quote appears in both 'tellings,' it's nothing I remember and could well have been a remark Jonathan made later when he had the podium—or was it pulpit?" And a day later, this added: "What has come to mind (hesitate to say memory) about the Boston Legend was that the 'heckler' asked me if the love poem I'd just read was about another man. I said yes and then he made the remark about sin etc."

MICHAEL McFEE

"RECKLESS AND DOOMED"—JONATHAN WILLIAMS AND JARGON

Once, while spelunking through the dim stacks of a university library, I found myself facing a vein of poetry books—slim volumes, tightly stratified. I was surprised to discover, near the end of my survey, several early books by Jonathan Williams, which are usually highly prized collector's items locked away by jealous curators in rare-book rooms. I extracted one, opened to the title page, and found it inscribed in the author's flowing hand: "ODI ET AMO and that's all she wrote!"

"I hate and I love": for Jonathan Williams—once self-described as "poet, publisher, essayist, hiker, populist, elitist, and sorehead"—as for his epigrammatic source Catullus, that is indeed all she wrote. "He is," says Guy Davenport, "what used to be called an enthusiast, and his array of enthusiasm would take a committee of lesser souls to see." More than any genuine man of letters—a sparse class these days, among which Williams constitutes a uniquely vigorous genus—he has devoted himself to propagating these passions, "finding the writers and others worthy of our enthusiasm and husbandry," sustaining the scattered community of "homemade genius." Williams inherits the mantle of Parson Weems and John Chapman, Whitman and Pound, all broadcasters of radical seed: men of individual visions, peculiar and sublime. "We are talking about one-man bands," Williams once remarked, "not a whole cultural apparatus."

Perhaps the most public forum for Williams' affections is the Jargon Society, which he founded in 1951, deriving its name "from the Old French, jargon, defined by Olivier Messiaen, particularly, as 'a twittering of birds.'" Characterizations of this nonprofit, tax-exempt organization abound, most from the pugnacious pen of its founder, as in this "Statement of Purpose" (1960): "The purpose of a writers' press like Jargon is reckless and doomed. It is to make coherence in the avant-garde community—a community which is snide and sullen and generally deserving of the rock-bottom place it holds in America. Regardless of what they say ('they' being poeticules, criticasters, kitschdiggers, or justfolks) I believe the writing of poems to be more than a minor art and the only way to impress this upon a distraught American attention is by stating and restating the main traditions of the few poets who move us from generation to generation." With a typically forthright and double-edged pitch, Williams concludes: "There are always a hundred people to tell you what's wrong with what you're doing and why it shouldn't be done. There isn't that much time to argue. The accomplishment of the press, modest as it is, is the only answer to give. I am interested in acquiring patrons for specific projects. You name it, from the listing herein. To ask for sums less than $100 for sponsorship is hopeless. $100, or $1,000, is not very much money, assuming you believe the practice of poetry is more important than making pink plaster flamingos to cheer the birds up while they bathe and sing."

In the quarter-century since, Williams has continued to hate—"One has to put up with my Welsh evangelist's harangue, and that I preach and inveigh against the Laodiceans, the Crapioca Pudding Conspiracy, The Tenured Professors With Minds Like Tire Salesmen, etc., etc."—and to love, cultivating his Eden of writers, patrons, and books. The result is nearly 100 Jargon titles, including classics like *The Maximus Poems of Charles Olson*; in Gilbert Sorrentino's words, "A Jargon book is typically a perfect synthesis of writing, graphics, and design; it is a pleasure to hold and read." This is no modest accomplishment. How did Williams—in his early 20s—initiate such a distinguished series?

"Our first few books," he said in a recent conversation, "were made possible by a small legacy from the will of a friend in northeast Georgia— around $1,500. I had already done a few pamphlets at Black Mountain College"—four, in fact—"and with that money we were able to bring out Kenneth Patchen's *Fables & Other Little Tales*, Charles Olson's *The Maximus Poems/1–10*, Robert Creeley's *The Immoral Proposition*, and my *Four Stop-pages/A Configuration*." A total of 1,250 copies were produced while Williams was serving as a medic in Germany; today, according to J. M. Edelstein, Jargon bibliographer and Chief Librarian at the National Gallery of Art, some individual volumes are worth almost as much as the original legacy. "At that point," Williams continues, "I faced three options: to become a publisher, and develop Jargon; to buy a Porsche; or to buy a small

Max Beckmann painting in Stuttgart. I chose the Celtic path of misery and service to humanity, and I've been begging ever since."

Williams' "begging" is more an individual than an institutional matter: patronage is an honorable tradition at Jargon. "Foundations have an inherent distrust of us, and vice versa," he says, a polite echo of his passionate *Green Corn Thru a Cow; or, Where Were You When the Culture Explosion Hit the Fan?* (1965). This pamphlet displays Williams at his most vitriolic, denouncing foundations ("It is their business to find me and the others, not vice versa: to hell with them"), renouncing readings and other distractions, and demanding "support to get on with the job. There are some things that no one else in the country is so prepared to do, by training and by talent. *ipse dixit*." Fortunately, the rest was not silence, as Jargon's (and Williams' own) ample bibliography prove.

Such a rejection of conventional small-press life-support systems leaves only one route for the determined publisher: work, work, work. Constant individual effort; a steady investment in tire rubber and shoe leather, elbow and axle grease; a willingness to go solo and above all to go, make disciples, "preach the orphic gospel"—these are the givens. In his introduction to Williams' first selected poems, *An Ear in Bartram's Tree* (1969), Davenport speaks of the wide-flung "network" of American culture, concluding: "For a decade now Jonathan Williams has made it his business to go from point to point on this network: there has been nothing like it since the mediaeval scholars who for want of any other communication wandered from university to university. His long zigzag trips can easily be explained by noticing that he is a publisher of books unwelcome to commercial publishers (who are closer to the grocery business than to that founded by Gutenberg); by invitations from universities to read, show slides, lecture on book design, architecture, and poetry; and by the fact that to know artists and poets one has to go to Pocatello, Id., and Pippa Passes, Ky."

Williams once estimated that he traveled 40,000 miles a year during the 1950s, and even in the mid-1980s he and fellow Jargon editor Thomas Meyer keep moving. "We were on the road pretty constantly from late February to mid-May," Williams reported. "We hit every major city between Highlands and Boston by car, and then made a trip to the southern tip of Florida." Is the circulation worth it? "Sure. If you go out, give readings, and show books and travel a lot, you'll run into people who want your books.

Our demographic profile is very obscure, but our readers are probably like the people we publish: eccentric, isolated, and very passionate."

Highlands is the small western North Carolina town where the Jargon editorial trust resides during the cool months—a mountainous hour or more southwest of Williams' native Asheville, only a holler from Georgia and South Carolina. During the summer Jargon operations shift to Corn Close, Dentdale, Cumbria, England; and though the workload and especially the travel are lighter, "we still spend half our time on Jargon, and try to print one book a year when there—British writers."

Williams rarely generalizes about the logistics of producing Jargon's books, British or American, because in the words of the Society's executive director, Tom Patterson—"each book is its own special case. For example, with our recent book of John Menapace photographs, *Letter in a Klein Bottle*, only a very few presses in the country could handle the specifications for things like varnished prints. With some small presses, all their books look pretty much the same, in size and format. That's just one of the things that sets Jargon apart: each book is different, every work is an art object, and everything is a special case." Despite Jargon's widespread editorial base, and the fact that Patterson and its business office are in the Piedmont, North Carolina city of Winston–Salem several hours away, and the fact that its production center is usually in Charlotte, another hundred miles away, Williams has never thought of changing his system: "It's not very efficient, perhaps, but it gets done." He's particularly proud of his association with Heritage Printers in Charlotte and its president, William E. Loftin, "an honorable Presbyterian technocrat. I was almost their first customer back in the late Fifties, when we did Denise Levertov's *Overland to the Islands*. We've done about 30 titles since. Technically, in terms of production, we don't have to bow to anyone; in fact, everybody else uses Heritage now—Knopf, Book of the Month, you name it. Our new Niedecker book is as good as anything you'll see in the country."

That book is another of Williams' longtime pet projects, *From This Condensery: The Complete Writings of Lorine Niedecker*. Williams' promotional copy lifts the form to feisty heights: "Not only is Lorine Niedecker the best recent American female poet—she is one of the best poets period, living or dead, male or female. There are only 1,423 Americans who will listen to such talk, but, for them, we are delighted to be publishing this book of hers." *From This Condensery* also provides an instructive contrast with Jargon's origins. "It was easier in those days," Williams admits, "when I did everything. I could get 50 people to give $25 each and we could print a book—50 special editions, and 450 trade copies. The Niedecker will cost around $20,000 for 2,600 copies—which means we'll have to sell them for around $30." Early Jargon titles listed for a few dollars. "There's just no way around the price, and even so, it takes very long for a book to break even.

"But that's not really the issue. It sounds idealistic, but I'm not into profit or loss. The point is, to get these books published." As Williams has said elsewhere, "There are still a lot of people that seem to need attention . . . strays and mavericks, the generous, the non-adventitious; i.e., those afflicted with both vision and craft." His presentation and preservation of visionary work is at once shrewd and naive—though, in the words of William Harmon, one of Williams' few academic advocates, "The Lilies of the Field Know Which Side Their Bread Is Buttered On."

"What I've been trying to do," Williams says, "is to make adult versions of Oz and Tolkien and L. Frank Baum for my own shelves. I wanted books that would be as special as the sacred books of childhood, that would have the same allure and excitement."

Much of that excitement, for a Jargon book, is visual: The books are beautifully designed, often by Williams himself. The production is equally fine; as Williams said in his interview with William Corbett in 1976, "I have been loudly criticized for making the books precious objects. Some people say, well look, multilith is as good. Get it out for a dollar. Alas, I've never felt so abject.... My books have often cost as much as a bottle of whiskey. And I've always felt that once in a while you could forego the case of beer, or the bottle of Jack Daniels, and invest in Robert Duncan, or Ronald Johnson, or whomever it happened to be. A book may happen once every four or five years. I insist it has to do with desire. The desire that really excellent readers have, and the kind of enthusiasm and passion that reading can inspire. Our friend Pound says that the only reason he bothered was in order to enforce his desire. He was able to do a few things for a few people. Revive a few reputations. To insist that certain things be brought to people's attention. And this was all it amounted to. This was it. This is all one man can do."

No matter how busy Williams may be as modern-day Gutenberg, goliard, or scribe, kindling the fires of literary desire, his correspondence is faithful as the tides. He once guessed that he wrote 50 letters a week— "when I'm not in an automobile every day; the letters keep the network going"—and still maintains a comparable pace, with those who write back. "I spent $82 at the post office today," he commenced during our conversation, a fact for which the Highlands postmaster must bless his lucky meter. Williams' postage fuels terse, funny Jargon postcards; generous letters, on the Jargon stationery printed with its clouds of marginal witnesses; and, for the elect who help sustain the network, a handsome photocopied edition of his writing for the year. This private postal forum for his wit and affections is tended no less diligently than the Jargon Society: It is part of the same wide-ranging impulse "to keep the network going."

Williams once said, "Poetry is about all that is singular, eccentric, loving and hating." That certainly describes his own distinctive work, as writer of poems and essays and letters, as photographer, as epicure, as connoisseur of music and sports, as well-traveled apologist for "the gospel of beauty," and above all as publisher. However shin-splinting its climb has been, the Jargon Society has come to attract some well-deserved attention, winning a Carey–Thomas citation from *Publishers Weekly* in 1977 and such notices as this one in *The New York Times*: "Jargon has come to occupy a special place in our cultural life as patron of the American imagination. But however attractive the books are to look at, and they are justly collector's items, the chief pleasure they afford is the intellectual shock of recognizing an original voice ignored by sanctioned critical opinion." And the force behind Jargon's success has been, is, and ever shall be Colonel Jonathan Williams himself, whose tenacious support of individual visions has produced, in J. M. Edelstein's words, "not just beautiful books but a new literature." As a fellow Williams, Dr. William C. of New Jersey, wrote him nearly 30 years ago, "Dear Jonathan: Don't let the 'glum days' get you, I for one would feel lost without the genius of your publications. It's a strange thing about 'the new,' in which category I place what you do, at first it shocks, even repels, such a man as myself but in a few days, or a month or a year, we rush to it drooling at the mouth as if it were a fruit, an apple in winter."

RONALD JOHNSON

JONATHAN (CHAMBERLAIN) WILLIAMS

Jonathan Williams was born in Asheville, North Carolina, to Thomas Benjamin and Georgette Williams, a lively couple who soon moved the family to Washington, D.C. They were straight from the gracious strictures of Southern Semi-aristocracy (yet stubborn mountain folk to the bone). Williams' father was a multi-gifted self-made man, and his mother a talented decorator. In Washington, Williams attended that most British and Episcopalian of schools, St. Albans, attached to Washington Cathedral, and left with acute Anglophilia and a lifelong taste for cathedrals.

Consecutively, without taking a degree, he studied art history at Princeton, painting with Karl Knaths at the Phillips Memorial Gallery in Washington, etching and engraving with Stanley William Hayter at Atelier 17 in New York, and the whole range of arts at Chicago's Institute of Design. Then, in 1951, he returned to his native North Carolina mountains where the Bauhaus-influenced school, Black Mountain College, was in force with poet Charles Olson as rector. There, he distinguished himself on the softball team, hosted rambles through Southern drawing and dining rooms as well as drive-in cinemas, once dropped a pot of asphalt on a raw canvas from his room window, became friends with what were to become some of the best-known painters, poets, composers, and dancers of today, wrote his first signal poems, and began to produce a series of the finest examples of the bookmaker's art since William Morris.

To publish poetry alongside the work of contemporary painters, photographers, and typographers, he founded the Jargon Society in 1951, and he has remained its editor, publisher, and designer up to the present—with some ninety titles to his credit. He has taught at the Aspen Institute for Humanistic Studies, Maryland Institute College of Art, the University of Kansas, Wake Forest University, North Carolina School of the Arts, Salem College, Winston-Salem State University, and the University of Delaware.

He has held fellowships and grants from the Guggenheim Foundation (1957–1958), the Longview Foundation (1960), the National Endowment for the Arts (1968, 1969, 1970, 1973), and has received an honorary degree from Maryland Institute College of Art (1969).

One of the happiest legacies of Ezra Pound is the idea that any healthy society is in debt to its imaginative gadflies. Jonathan Williams is one of the wittiest and most daring. Precocious, with early influences ranging from Edith Sitwell, Kenneth Patchen, Robinson Jeffers, Kenneth Rexroth, and William Carlos Williams to Charles Olson, Robert Duncan, and Robert Creeley, Williams has created a distinctive line, sure of foot in a stream of syllables, clearly witty in the splash of its consonants—a line well informed by ear and eye, though innocent of metrics.

He has been deemed "democratic" by William Carlos Williams, "our best Greek poet" by Guy Davenport, "salty" by James Laughlin, "unequalled" by A. R. Ammons, "Indispensable!" by Buckminster Fuller, a "joyous laborer" by James Dickey. Robert Duncan calls him a "veritable male Marianne Moore"—and Thomas Lask says, "of all the Black Mountain poets (teachers and disciples alike), Jonathan Williams is the wittiest, the least constrained, the most joyous." And also a satirist.

The typical attender of Williams' heretofore unexpected undercurrents, founts, and sidelights of art would find all of the above to be true. The person behind all this hoopla is the crafter of an athletic style, each phrase to be read as if it were a basketball swishing through a net, each dribbled syllable contributing to a never-before-seen game of words. It is true that his more curious stretches of restless imagination may depend for their resultant point on humor dropped in the totally unsuspecting lap, but as poems they are always easy on the tongue and sharp as chitchat in a barber's shop. All get up and go, he sets us straighter. He has learned, the listener leans back to hear, from both socked fly balls and Charles Olson's "And the mind go forth to the end of the world." He knows that each one makes an arc.

Alert for eccentrics, roadside cafes with the accent over the *f*, stray-cat-scratched wisdoms of the urinal, foibles and follies, slips of the tongue, seers and doers, masters of schtick and spiel from sidewalk to bedroom and back, he seldom errs with eye or ear. This kind of Catullan spunk may be side by side with deep, moving, bucolic lyrics, one after another extolling the cow bells and cuckoos in Mahler, or Thoreau coming on a muskrat.

Here, puns are a kind of *gloire*; musics of the spheres may be traced through the relation of *o*'s and *a*'s both stressed and muted throughout what seems but brusque statement and rude sentiment.

Amongst this ruckus, Jonathan Williams' strength as a poet lies in a nearly tireless questioning of the extra-traditional lyric, in a time that believes with him that "form is only an extension of content" (Robert Creeley's words). If we take lyric in its first sense as song from a lyre, then we understand that in Williams' poetry, from the early book *Jammin' The Greek Scene* (only published in scraps and pieces), in which he turns up rather like Edith Sitwell playing Ovid on the saxophone in a New Orleans dive, to the masterly later poems written one each to movements of Mahler symphonies, his words present themselves, one after the other, as equivalents of notes of music plucked still ringing from the air. He stands as one always in dialogue with Orpheus himself.

In the splendid books clustered around *Jammin' The Greek Scene*, *Amen/Huzza/Selah* (1960), and *Elegies and Celebrations* (1962), the reader's ideas of music are stretched to include the lilts of energetic local speech, speech furthermore in terms vastly unconscious, yet honed to his most polished, terse wit. The intensity of psychic thrust in these poems is undiminished after two decades. "Enthusiast" and "The Distances to the Friend" (both elegies to older writer figures) are poems in which "song sweats through the pores" and the depths of one man swim before us "stifling all repulsion" "into the sounding keyboard."

Although published in 1959, his first widely remarked book, *The Empire Finals at Verona*, was written largely after the three books noted above. It includes the poems Williams wrote in correspondence with Louis Zukofsky at the time they both decided to translate Catullus—Williams in the argot of American jazz and Zukofsky after the sound of Latin. The volume also contains some of the best sports poems ever written, and surely some of his most democratic, witty, and lovely work:

> mute, flat on the planet,
> eyeing a jet-stream eight miles out,
> full of fall-out, waste and fragrance
> from Nevada

going out to seed the plankton,
sink atolls
and burst
            the livers of great whales.

This book contains three especially fine short lyrics: "Autopsy," "A Vul-
nerary," and "The Grounds." The first is Walt Whitman's autopsy report
and contemporary newspaper obituaries. The second is Williams at his most
sparely beautiful, in a poem dedicated to Robert Duncan; while the third,
under a feisty epigraph culled from an Edward Dahlberg letter, stakes itself
out squarely on the boundaries of Eden—a place he is to return to often in
later work.

With *In England's Green &* (1962), he continues to walk this new
imagined realm, propelled by Blake although arm in arm with Emerson
and Thoreau:

in the monocular sunlight
three miles wide
lid to lid.

Note also, in this book, the end lines of a Southern poem titled "Cob-
webbery," which is among the best of Williams' recreations of common talk:

Maw, rip them boards off
the side the house

and put the soup pot on

and plant us some petunias
in the carcass of the Chevrolet

and let's stay here
and rot in the fields

and sit still.

In that soup pot seems to stew the nurture of the whole blasted South, to Williams' mind, a pap of spiders. "Cobwebbery" indeed. The concluding poem of this volume is called "The Familiars," which relates a strange myth of a poet-planted "Rattlesnake Master" who takes "masses of rattlers large as washtubs" "into the crevice into / the central den." From this inner center, perhaps Jonathan Williams' Eden, words shed their skin to hear in a world where *paine* is become *paean*, and where common experience is scripture plain as birds singing in a tree. He finds a spot where each bud or bulb or den is literally a "crawl" of exits. It is a wonderful tale.

Since these books of the early 1960s, Jonathan Williams' productions have multiplied, sometimes to the point of ephemerality. Among this work, his *Mahler* (published first in 1967, then further expanded in 1969) stands paramount in its sustained maturity and lyric zest. These splendid poems were written both out of a long early listening to the music of Gustave Mahler during a time when Jean Sibelius was the darling of the concert hall, then a further compressed listening during the months of May and June of 1964 at his mountain home in Highlands, North Carolina. In a complex series of intro-, retro-, and circumspections, the images appear in interlacing circles like the first drops of rain on a reflecting pond, deceptive as to depth. Certain of these images appear to float through whole gilt clouds of unknowing that some black (or even ever bluer) empyrean might support. Witness from two movements of "Symphony 5":

II. *Stormily agitated*

to be a block of flowers
in a wood

to be mindlessly in flower
past understanding

to be shone on
endlessly

to be there, there
and blessed

III. *Scherzo*

one two three
one two three

little birds waltz to and fro
in the piano

at Maiernigg on the
Worthersee

and up the tree:
cacophony

one two three.

Every page bears the stamp of Williams' rangy intelligence, from local reference, to Eros Creatrix, and back to the heart. This collection has justly remained Williams' most popular book with critics, fellow poets, and readers alike. Yet one might equally praise *Blues & Roots/Rue & Bluets* (1971), which the author called a "Garland for the Appalachians" of "common words in uncommon orders—conversations quoted exactly but cast into line to reveal their native invention." Along the way there are also road signs, more snakes off the road, and a lot of whittling on porches. Take "The Hermit Cackleberry Brown, On Human Vanity":

caint call your name
but your face is easy

come sit

now some folks figure theyre
bettern
cowflop they
aint

not a bit

just good to hold the world together
like hooved up ground

thats what.

These poems should sit on our shelves alongside *Uncle Remus* (1880),
a book Jonathan Williams' father used to read to company. Alone, they
would make another poet's reputation.

No one should miss, either, "Excavations from the Case-Histories of
Havelock Ellis" (published in the 1972 selected poems *The Loco Logodaedal-
ist in Situ*). The title is unusually direct for Williams, and what he unearthed
in these texts is by and large his most direct work to date—if also his most
dark. Stark history after stark history is revealed, each in a kind of Piranesi
of closets. Their only kin are such as Henry James's "The Jolly Corner"
(1908), long snatches of Proust, and Poe at his best. One "History" reads
baldly: "it is a dark crimson / it affords me relief." It could be the burnt
scraps of Count Dracula's memoir. Another affords this little vision of hell:

the sight of the naked
    river,
        increased by
    a young Turk smoking
        below the waist.

We have no other poems as naked (and smoking) as these.

At the height of his career, what later explorations might we expect?
Not since James, certainly, has there been an artist so in touch with every-
one, so aware (a lesson he learned, as did Olson, from Edward Dahlberg)
that style could be built soundly. Grit and vision seem to sum up the career
of this strange man. His support of other artists is unparalleled in our time.
Because of this younger man, some now undenied elder masters have been
published again, among them, Kenneth Patchen, Louis Zukofsky, Basil
Bunting, Stevie Smith, Mina Loy, and Lorine Niedeker. He has also repub-
lished early editions of Olson, Creeley, Duncan, Levertov, and many others.

At his table one can meet anyone from Buckminster Fuller to William Burroughs, and often at the same time.

The fate of multitalented men, from Leonardo da Vinci to the composer Lord Berners who dyed tumbler pigeons shades of mauve, cerise, and chartreuse, all for delight of a guest, is often that their art is not comprehended by more direct minds. It may be, though, peeping through exactly these so often cranky, cross-grained, quirky minds, that one focuses best on a complex time. It is easy to imagine a future critic's zeroing in on Jonathan Williams as a window to what could comfortably be called a "period." Jonathan Williams is like Ezra Pound and Ruskin before him, that rare breed of proselytizing exemplar to whom each act of art constitutes an impetus for freedom.

THOMAS MEYER

JW GENT & EPICUREAN

The whole dream of democracy is to raise the proletarian to the level of stupidity attained by the bourgeois.
—Gustave Flaubert

America is a mistake, a big mistake!
—Sigmund Freud

We are the last first people.
—Charles Olson

Words. Words. Words.

Like his master before him, like Edward Dahlberg, Jonathan Williams is a delver of words. Some old, some new, and some blue. Salty, simple, elaborate.

What he looks for first in them is not the power to move, or to name, that comes later, rather he looks for the power to delight as they sound in the mouth, thrumming the lips, wiggling the tongue, and rattling the teeth.

Even the smallest glossary made from his personal lexicon provides us with a chrestomathy; a *chrestomathy*: a bit of useful knowledge about these phenomena called Jonathan Williams.

So I would like to mention some, as a way of beginning, just a few of *his* words from that category I'd call **Gob-Stoppers**, words guaranteed to "shut your cake-hole" as the Geordies of Newcastle, England say.

aposiopesis

A sudden burst of silence. Or "Shut my mouth wide open!"

Consider for a moment a man who titles a recent book of poems *Apo-siopesis*, and when that draws a blank, a man who, in explanation, provides you with an alternate pronunciation: *apo-si-oposis.*

That takes self-confidence in these matters so supreme that it borders upon insouciance. If not Zen.

enchiridion

"A handbook" meaning literally "in the hand": there is not a word, a phrase, an idea, a poem of Jonathan Williams' that he has not held in his hand, has not pressed with his thumb, spit upon and polished on his shirt-sleeve. Here is a man for whom the world cannot be the *world* until it is palpable, until it can be handled. Or is itself a "handle." And here we come to the spring and source of Jonathan Williams' Grand Paternity: William Carlos Williams, who told us, "a poem is a machine made out of words."

A Jonathan Williams poem usually fits in the palm of your hand and has very few moving parts.

They sometimes glow in the dark.

cathexis

Out of embarrassment when Freudian psychoanalytical theory was introduced to English; that is, when the works of Sigmund Freud were translated, it was decided to dress up his simple homespun German terms in Greek buttons and Latin bows to make them into a Jargon. So that the German *besitzung* became *cathexis*, when in fact it was almost, nearly, albeit false, a cognate of our English "beset," "being set in the middle of it all," being filled suddenly and passionately, filled to overflowing with the quality of a thing, to be overwhelmed. Besieged. To be possessed. For Jonathan Williams, the ultimate state of grace. To glow: "An apostle who does not glow, preaches heresy ..." The poet is quoting Arnold Schoenberg, in the *Rondo-Finale* of the "Symphony No 5, in C Sharp Minor" from *The Mahler Poems*:

Schoenberg: "I should
even have liked to observe
how Mahler
knotted his tie,

and should have found that
more interesting and instructive
than learning how
one of our musical bigwigs composes
on a quote sacred subject
unquote

... An apostle
who does not glow
preaches heresy."

kepology

That which is said, or spoken of, discussed, or "taught" in the garden, or the orchard. As opposed to the market place, or the center of the town, well away from the hustle and bustle. That which becomes discourse when we "loaf & invite the soul," to quote Jonathan Williams quoting Walt Whitman.

The word belongs to Epicurus, of whom the great Friederich Nietzsche said: "Never has the voluptuous been so modest." And with whom in mind he wrote:

Reason is crisp and businesslike—a flood
That gets us all too quickly where we want to be ...

To think about things in solitude makes sense;
To sing about things in solitude is very silly ...

And so I come in my meandering to the title I have given these remarks:

J. Williams, Gent. & Epicurean

Epicurus was a Greek philosopher who bought a house with a small adjoining orchard in Athens late in the fourth century BC. This became the headquarters of his operation. And there he taught and had his offices, as it were, rather than downtown, which was the usual location for all such businesses.

He allowed women to attend his seminars and conferences. This was considered unheard of at the time.

He once advised a young man, "Get into a boat and sail away, as far from culture as you can get."

He also said: "Yes, a man with sense will speak in public, but only when asked."

For 21 years I have been Jonathan Williams' compatriot, companion, and amanuensis; I was very pleased when I was asked to say something about him this evening.

Words. Words. Words.

This Johnny Appleseed, as Buckminster Fuller dubbed him, who delves for words in books, has also dug for words, for the poems themselves, under the cabbage leaves, among the dog roses, between the clumps of blue chicory along an interstate.

He is fond of quoting John Clare's remark:

"I found the poems in the fields and only wrote them down."

A man is most eloquent—Dante proclaimed in *La Vita Nuova*—who uses the speech of ordinary men. The secret, Dante knew and Jonathan Williams knows, of the vernacular, of the way we talk, is its openness, its alert sensual tones (its vowels actually). To raise the common to the estate of the uncommon by the grace of language is certainly one of Jonathan Williams' prime æsthetic passions.

There is a great and necessary honesty of heart required in all this.

I am reminded of the rumors spread abroad about Epicurus during his own lifetime: They said no man was kinder than he was ... but that he talked dirty.

The more obvious earthinesses aside, Jonathan Williams finds in the dirt of his scrutiny words like: *gee-haw whimmy-diddle, slop-jar, popskull* which are in their way as exotic as *logodaedelist, heuristic, hermeneutics*, given the lives that engage us day after day, shopping at K-Mart, watching *Entertainment Tonight*, eating a Big Mac.

But the true Epicurean—and not just the "party animal" so often and so mistakenly called Epicurean—embraces it *all* precisely because for him or her there is nothing else, absolutely, resolutely **nothing else**.

The true Epicurean takes the crap, the glitz, the Bud Lite along with the Gabriel Fauré, the woodland path, the mountain sunset, the eau de vie Framboise.

For Epicurus tells us:

> All thoughts have their origin in sensations and depend upon the coincidence of things, their likenesses, and their coming together or coming apart; and sometimes (he concedes), sometimes thoughts will have something to do with thinking.

Or as William Carlos Williams so tersely put it:

"No ideas but in things."

It is the life of **attention** which is life itself for the Epicurean, the panoply of detail and experience.

I remember a friend Jonathan Williams and I were visiting in Dorset saying: "What a splendid thing a day out with Jonathan is. Most people don't notice anything, but Jonathan notices everything!"

Or is it—as Oscar Wilde might observe—that what Jonathan Williams notices **becomes** everything. His attention when it focuses centers. There is no background, foreground, or middleground. There is only what is there—a kind of "in-your-face" phenomenology.

Pay attention. Close attention. Is his credo.

For attention is the highest form of delight.

Epicurus confesses:

I do not know how I would be able to decide what was worthwhile if I abandoned good food, making love, and stopped listening, shutting my eyes to everything.

Which brings to mind an observation made by Clement Freud, British journalist and politician, and the grandson of Sigmund Freud:

If you give up sex, and if you give up smoking, and drinking, and eating well, it's not that you live longer, it just seems longer.

These antiphonal comments on Epicurus are part of the Jonathan Williams canon. If ever there were a living breathing proof of hypertexuality, it is he.

The Compiler of Lists. The Chronicler of Day Books. The Maker of Itineraries.

To quote Jonathan Williams is to quote him quoting someone quoting someone else.

The world is a mare's nest of interlocking details, an endless network spread out like a patchwork quilt, so dense and so extensive that it is unlikely that any hierarchy, any ranking of things can finally survive the glorious welter of particularities.

Hence it is the function of attention to isolate for a moment the single, luminous detail. Hence the lists, the compendia, the dispatches which constitute Jonathan Williams' natural form, poetic and prosaic.

Such a total belief in things, in the delights of material reality, and the ceaseless reporting of this results in a pure Epicurean disposition.

Just as it results in a shunning of the eternal and all ultimate convictions.

Close and passionate scrutiny combined with an unflinching curiosity develops in a man or a woman a sensibility which will dig its claws into everything questionable about this life.

And he or she is eventually overwhelmed with an aversion to big moral words and sweeping gestures.

In a pinch, I am describing Jonathan Williams the gad-fly, the satirist, the exploder of balloons. While we are startled and amused by his observations and pot-shots, we seldom, in this day and age, in this culture, feel anything but the quick sting of their recognition.

And we miss an essential aspect of an intelligence like Jonathan Williams'.

A quality that Nietzsche describes as crucial to an Epicurean sensibility, but more often than not obscured by the action of that sensibility:

> Whenever I hear or read Epicurus I enjoy the happiness of antiquity. I see his eyes gaze upon a wide, white sea, across rocks at the shores that are bathed in sunlight, while large and small animals are playing in this light, as secure and calm as the light itself and his eyes. Such happiness could be invented only by a man whose eyes have seen the sea of life's details become calm, and now they can never weary of that surface and of the many colors of this tender, shuddering skin of the sea.

The same might also be said of Jonathan Williams, except that when we read or hear him, we enjoy the flickering, happy light of Jeffersonian democracy, not antiquity.

And we see his eyes gaze out, not upon the sea, but out upon:

> A vast expanse of green meadows and strawberry fields; a meandering river gliding through, saluting in its various turnings the swelling, green, turfy knolls, embellished with parterres of flowers and fruitful strawberry beds; flocks of turkeys strolling about them; herds of deer prancing in the mead or bounding over the hills …

That next passage describing what is today Franklin, NC comes from the great eighteenth-century botanist, William Bartram, one of Jonathan Williams' acknowledged mentors—of language and of character. A perfect *adagietto* upon which to end my remarks.

But I think the last words should be those of the gent and Epicurean himself.

This short passage follows almost directly upon the one from William Bartram, it appears in an essay called "A White Cloud in the Eye of a White Horse." And such juxtapositions are the stuff art is made from:

The town of Cherokee in the Qualla Indian Reservation is one of the outstanding abominations in the U.S.—a horrendous conglutination of bears in cages, junque shoppes, genuine Indians jogging about in pseudo-Navajo headdresses made in Hong Kong out of plastic; reptile gardens; and millions of decorticated modern American white folks (only) in duckbilled caps and air-conditioned automobiles looking (as far as the ends of their bony, blue noses) for the Lost America.

REVIEWING

JONATHAN WILLIAMS
IMAGE GALLERY: 24 PHOTOGRAPHS

Charles Oscar, Black Mountain College, 1951.

Cy Twombly, Black
Mountain College,
1951.

Joel Oppenheimer,
Studies Building
at Black Mountain
College, 1951.

Katherine Litz, Black Mountain College, 1951.

Lou Harrison, Black Mountain College, 1951.

Robert Creeley, Mallorca, 1953.

Stefan Wolpe, Black Mountain College, 1954.

Kenneth Rexroth, San Francisco, 1954.

Louis Zukofsky, Brooklyn Heights, 1955.

Paul Metcalf, Massachusetts, ca 1955.

Mina Loy, Aspen, Colorado, 1957.

Bob Brown, ca 1958.

Ian Hamilton Finlay, Little Sparta, ca 1966.

Lorine Niedecker, Milwaukee, Wisconsin, 1967.

Thomas Meyer, Penland, North Carolina, 1969.

Ralph Eugene Meatyard, Lexington, Kentucky 1969.

Paul Metcalf, Massachusetts, ca 1970.

From left to right: Basil Bunting, Russell Banks, Dan Gerber and Thomas Meyer, Northumberland, 1970.

Harry Callahan, Providence, Rhode Island 1971.

Basil Bunting, Northumberland, late 1970s.

M.C. Richards, Skywinding Farm, North Carolina, 1979.

Sandra Fisher, How Gill Fells, England, 1986.

Georgia Blizzard, Glade Spring, Virginia, 1988.

RICHARD DEMING

PORTRAYING THE CONTEMPORARY—
THE PHOTOGRAPHY OF JONATHAN WILLIAMS

While he will be remembered as a Black Mountain poet and the publisher of the Jargon Society, Jonathan Williams initially went to Black Mountain College, that kiln of avant-garde aesthetics, in 1951 to study photography with Aaron Siskind and Harry Callahan, artists whom Williams had first met earlier that same year in Chicago at the Institute of Design. Williams had already left Princeton at this point, convinced the school was too stultifying and conservative. Given the range of Williams' abilities and creative intellect—that he would find traditional university study too confining, too overdetermined and overdetermining—is not at all surprising. In the 1950s, Black Mountain College, which offered a central site of community for figures from Merce Cunningham to Buckminster Fuller to Stefan Wolpe, seemed to be the only place able to accommodate the explosion of possibilities for imagining artistic production that were forming at that moment for the broadening field of the American avant-garde. When Williams arrived, the poet Charles Olson was the school's chief administrator—as loose a role as can be imagined—and Olson made clear in all levels of pedagogy that the self was any artist's true instrument. "I take it wisdom, like style, is the man—that it is not extricable in any sort of statement of itself," writes Olson in *Against Wisdom as Such*. "But [truths] are," he insists, "in no wise, or at the gravest loss, verbally separated. They stay the man. As his skin is. As his life. And to be parted with only as that is" (68). For those of Black Mountain, the art in any and all forms was inseparable from the person and from one's way of being in the world.

Interestingly, but perhaps also frustratingly, certain of Williams' roles get more attention than others. Along with the school's other famous alumni, Jonathan Williams was one of the quintessential hyphenated cultural workers of the last fifty years. As the publisher of Jargon, Williams directly changed the face of post-War American poetry. Not only did he launch or sustain the careers of Russell Edson, Robert Creeley, Louis Zukofsky, and Mina Loy, but he logged thousands of hours and miles, distributing the work across the United States and Europe, placing books into people's hands. Measured against Williams' Herculean efforts, today's bloggers have it easy. As a poet himself, Williams was a bit of a coterie author, though never quite as neglected as he was made out to be, given the friends, fans, and well-wishers who would make pilgrimages to North Carolina to pay homage. Williams counted Hugh Kenner, Russell Banks, and David Hockney among his company of interlocutors and supporters. However, the role of Williams' that seems to get the least attention is his role as photographer. Williams' talent was for the portrait photograph, and he took hundreds of these over five decades, primarily of authors, artists, and musicians, who lived and worked outside of the mainstream—figures such as the poet Basil Bunting, the outsider artist Howard Finster, and the master of Southern Gothic photography Ralph Eugene Meatyard. Despite two published collections of portraits—*A Palpable Elysium* and *Portrait Photographs*—Williams' abilities as a photographer remain undervalued. Engaging Williams' photography reveals insights into his work as a whole as well as indicates the various ways that he participated in shaping the culture of the artistic avant-garde, particularly of the 1950s.

If Williams' identity as a man of arts and letters is hard to categorize, he was not alone at Black Mountain. In describing the project of the school, Mary Emma Harris writes in *The Arts at Black Mountain College*, "Throughout its history Black Mountain was concerned with the nature and meaning of form in art, in institutions, and in lives and with ways to keep those forms alive, vulnerable, and responsive" (244). During Williams' time at the school, John Cage and Robert Rauschenberg, among others, appeared at Black Mountain for summer visits. Rauschenberg, who had been a student at the college just a few years before, famously blurred together the possibilities of painting and sculpture in his combines, assailing any delineation of rigid categories. Cage transformed music, incorporating not only silence and dissonance, but also the material properties of instruments and recording procedures and chance operations into his compositions. For artists and writers connected to Black Mountain, distinctions of form, genre, and mode all offered boundaries that were meant to be transgressed or dismantled in order to free the imagination. Perhaps the epitome of this conflation of the arts was the now famous performance in the summer of 1952 of Cage's *Theater Piece No. 1*, an event that was the precursor to art "happenings" of the 1960s and '70s that included an improvisatory, spontaneous collusion of all the arts represented at Black Mountain—music, dance, painting, writing—that, orchestrated primarily by Cage, occurred. Harris has assembled a sketch of this indescribable theater piece:

> A general summary of recollections places Cage on a ladder reading either lines from Meister Eckhart, a lecture on Zen Buddhism, the *Bill of Rights*, or the *Declaration of Independence*; [M. C.] Richards and Olson reading at different times from another ladder; [Merce] Cunningham dancing in and around the chairs—he was joined in his dance by a dog, who as an interloper, created his own time brackets; Rauschenberg either standing before his paintings or playing scratchy records of Edith Piaf and others at double speed on an ancient windup phonograph with a horn loudspeaker; [David] Tudor playing a prepared piano and a small radio; and either Tim LaFarge or Nick Cernovich (possibly both) projecting movies and still pictures upside down on slanting surfaces at the end of the dining hall [where the event was staged]. (228)

If one tenet of Black Mountain held that an artist's obligation was to close the gap between art and life, then categories and distinctions between and among forms of artistic expression and production would be demarcations that needed to be dismantled. Since this ethos was the dominant condition of Williams' aesthetic education, the insufficient attention to Williams' photographs and his identity as a photographer means that there is a great deal more to discover in terms of thinking about Jonathan Williams and what his work signifies. Moreover, Williams has taken not only the most famous but the *definitive* portraits of Robert Creeley, Jack Spicer, and countless other writers and artists. The cultural and historical importance of these images means that Williams must be taken seriously as a photographer in that his work constructs the human face, and thus the mythology, of a radical strain of American avant-gardism.

It might be said that Williams himself contributed to the undervaluing of his talents or significance as an image-maker. For instance, in the introduction to *A Palpable Elysium*, a volume collecting many of his famous color photographs, he asks that the "professionals" regard him as "a literary gent who takes the odd tolerable picture" (9). We might not take such self-deprecation seriously, however, because this demurral was a recurring rhetorical maneuver of Williams'. This gesture would unfortunately shape how people encountered the photography, regardless of the strength and composition of the various images. Portraitists often struggle against the fact that their subjects can over-determine the reception of the image. In other words, viewers respond to the content, accepting it too often or too readily as simply being a representation of how things are—the content overwhelming the form. With Williams, this would mean that his photographs might be seen by some as simply (or merely) providing visual record of the artists and writers he supported, and the photographs are merely a means to that ends of promotion.

Williams did, however, see himself as a writer first and foremost. "What I am is a writer who has been very enthusiastic about photography ever since I studied (a smidgen) with Harry Callahan at Black Mountain College" (*A Palpable Elysium* 6). This enthusiasm is not to be underestimated, though: his impressive photography collection includes work ranging from Frederick Sommers to Ralph Eugene Meatyard to Gerard Malanga. Williams would also provide introductions and essays to published collections of work by many of these photographers. His personal collections of contemporary photographs (now housed primarily at the Beinecke Library of Yale University) and his essays, while representing his taste also illustrate that Williams remained a lifelong student of the art. As is true with many artists, the attention to the work of others bore fruit in Williams' own art.

From Callahan and from Siskind, Williams learned, as he has described it, the fundamentals of using the Rollei camera he owned, but he would become closer to Charles Olson and that poet's maximal enthusiasms for what language can accomplish. If in terms of skills, one cannot say Williams learned from his teachers more than the rudiments in terms of how to take a photograph, one can suggest that he learned about art itself and its possibilities as a way of life—a form of perceiving the world and participating directly in the shaping of that set of perceptions. Since the Black Mountain pedagogy emphasized experiential learning by doing, learning by discovering rather than through direct didacticism, Williams learned a form of attention that comes with a dedicated observance of details and particulars. Siskind especially helped Williams to think of the connection of particularities to one's inner life. In commentary accompanying his portrait of Siskind, whom Williams described as one of his last mentors, Williams writes, "Siskind and his abstract expressionist pals [...] were among the first to show us that our innermost feelings can be found in the commonplace debris of the world, that they can be limned on walls and in stones and bits of stonework" (*A Palpable Elysium* 94). The world seen this way becomes a legible text of the self in the process of experiencing the world and responding emotionally to its intrinsic forms. In this sense, enthusiasm as a measure of the promise of one's own imaginative investments was a lesson that Williams discovered at Black Mountain College and would continue to shape his artistic ideals for decades to come.

Williams had not chosen simply anyone to become his mentors: Callahan and Siskind, both already fairly well known in the art world by 1951, would become arguably the two most important photographers of the mid-century. Siskind in particular came to be seen as the artist who brought Abstract Expressionist aesthetics impulses and ideals into the realm of photography in his ability to create images of objects that would isolate formal qualities and abstract possibilities of concrete particulars. Coils of rope, the grain of unfinished wood, the loops of a snail's shell, all offered Siskind a way of considering abstract form as part of daily experience. In this way, Siskind's photography would endeavor to distill objects to some essential sense of their form as form itself.

The lesson that Williams derived from Siskind is that for a good photographer, the world reflects back the possibilities of the self. Considering a photograph of Siskind included in *A Palpable Elysium*, we can think about how this ideal manifests itself in Williams' thinking about portraits, as he tended to photograph people rather than objects. In Williams' portrait of his former teacher, Siskind's face is a quarter turned from the camera, his glance soft but direct in the way that suggests he is not looking at something specific (95). Clearly, Williams does not capture Siskind in the middle of some larger motion. In most of Williams' portraits, the figures have an almost palpable stillness. They are unhurried, indicating not only Williams' care as a photographer, but also something about what he was trying to express in his subjects. Moreover, the center of the image disappears almost completely into a shadow. Why is it that the center of the image in the portrait is so dark? The most clearly defined feature is Siskind's right eye, which is the furthest thing from the viewer. A photographer, it can be argued, captures one's own self in the act of seeing. Thus, attention as an end in and of itself—an attention to our various forms of engaged and engaging attention—was what Williams learned from Siskind and Callahan, as well as Olson. Siskind's interest was objects, but Williams finds similar possibilities of expression in living people. That is why Williams' portrait of Siskind is also, paradoxically, a representation of Williams' perception of his subject, which is why Williams' portraits convey a kind of intimacy: the subjects reveal him even as he reveals them to the viewer. To Williams' credit, the portraits are rarely so sentimental. Indeed, in the Siskind portrait the fact that the foreground is so dark suggests something about the fact that what is nearest to us is the most difficult to discern and that one sees always with one eye in the light and one in shadow.

Guy Davenport said of Williams and his photography, "The color slide, descendant of the magic lantern, is still the most charming disseminator of culture, and Jonathan Williams is its master. He is the iconographer of poets of our time, and of the places and graves of poets gone on to Elysium" (*An Ear in Bartram's Tree*). Davenport's claims about Williams' photography indicate how a viewer might perceive the work in cultural and historical terms. If the portraits are iconographic, they create an authority by which to disseminate the importance and values represented by those figures in the photographs, values that might otherwise go unrecognized. Indeed, Williams specifically photographed his peers and those writers and artists—including Mina Loy and William Carlos Williams—who provided the contemporary foundations for his specific aesthetic genealogy. The photographs create a value for these authors, and that value then legitimates these figures who are often outside mainstream marketplace or institutional interests. Williams conveys authority to his subjects by means of the photographs and this authority reinvests itself in his work.

For an image to create its own authority, it must insist on itself. In Williams' portraits, we see a recurring formality in the poses and situations, which might convey veneration and be why Davenport sees the images as iconographic. Rarely are the people in the photographs smiling or laughing or crying. While the images have a form of intimacy, we never see the people in an elaborated social context, interacting with others. Perhaps because the only relationship being expressed is between the subject and the photographer taking the picture, there is a tendency for the people in the photographs to be by themselves and to be either confronting the viewer or turned away from the gaze of the viewer. That is to say, the people in the photographs that Williams takes—from Robert Duncan to Denise Levertov—are rarely engaged in an activity other than establishing a relationship with the photographer. The formality, call it a form of distance, may be what is so decidedly masculine about Williams' photographs and is the means by which the images manifest their authority, through their seriousness and their emotional coolness.

"Cool" may not be the most precise word since it often implies some negatively marked withholding of emotions. I mean it in the way that Miles Davis played "cool jazz" in the 1950s. In Williams' foreword to the *Aperture Masters of Photography* volume that collects Callahan's most famous images, he remarks on the stillness of those photographs: "Harry's a quiet man; where do you find any noise in his photographs? A little surf is all I can locate" (12). Williams goes on to suggest that Callahan's photographs are best viewed while listening to *Musica Callada* by the Catalan composer Frederic Mompou. Mompou's work is impressionistic and built on careful, fragile melodies for solo piano and he has been described as a successor to Claude Debussy. One can take Williams to be suggesting that Mompou's quiet, contemplative work for solo piano creates sympathetic conditions for viewing Callahan's images in such a contemplative mood. However, while Williams' portraits may not be as seemingly contemplative as Callahan's photographic meditations on his wife Eleanor's nude figure, for instance, Williams' images do find ways of capturing a stillness that marks the people he photographs. One telling difference between Williams' portraits and Callahan's is that the latter consciously intends an artfulness that a viewer would immediately recognize. Williams, on the other hand, is much less evident in the artifice of his photographs. The subjects, though posed, are not elaborate tableaus. The people in his pictures are people first, subjects second. Yet, to miss the artfulness altogether is to not look at Williams' images carefully enough.

Important critics of photography such as Roland Barthes and John

Berger have argued that the force of these images comes from the act of choice that conveys significance to whatever is photographed. "In an initial period," writes Barthes in his seminal work, *Camera Lucida*, "Photography, in order to surprise, photographs the notable; but soon, by a familiar reversal, it decrees notable whatever it photographs" (34). The camera names its own authority, this way. One result of Williams' photographic authority was that he became perhaps the primary chronicler of Black Mountain in the 1950s, his images developing into the foremost representations of the writers connected to Black Mountain. His portraits of Olson and Creeley and Duncan have become the most famous taken of these authors and he would also go on to take the definitive photographs of Lorine Niedecker, Louis Zukofsky, and Jack Spicer. This interesting question is not that he took strong, recognizable photographs, but that Williams' camera served as a way of determining value for these writers. In many ways, the sheer formal seriousness of attention evinced by these photographs conveys some of that importance to those artists and authors being represented. That the figures are presented in powerful ways as serious subject, the viewer is persuaded to see the people that way as well. The power of photography in terms of its ability to persuade is generally true, but Williams clearly was aware of how to make use of a photograph's rhetoric to legitimate his avant-garde community.

In the Black Mountain images especially, which are some of the earliest examples of Williams' mature work, Williams' portraits represent not only a countercultural intensity, but a masculinist vision of the writers with whose company he kept. In Williams' most famous images this form of physical power is often literally foregrounded: Olson's massive form, shirtless, hunched over a writing table with a gourd at hand; Creeley as the dark-eyed, "Spanish assassin," or Creeley perched atop a broken toilet, the painter Dan Rice at his side, peeking out of a barrel; Joel Oppenheimer growling at the camera while Francine du Plessix stands with feet planted and arms defiantly akimbo. All of these images serve to represent a playful but fierce artistic temperament as the essential environment of Black Mountain College. At the same time, the emphasis on physicality, coupled with Williams' characteristic cool, make the image specifically masculine.

It would be worth considering in another context what the specific function of this masculinizing plays in Williams' production of photographic documents of Black Mountain that are utilized to introduce the personas of Black Mountain College into literary and artistic communities at large. This particularly gendered set of documents would indicate the influence of Olson even on Williams' photographic work. Although there were a number of gay or bisexual students at Black Mountain in the 1950s (including Williams, Michael Rumaker, John Wieners, and Franz Kline) the environment was overwhelmingly hyper-masculinist. As Michael Davidson shows at length in *Guys Like Us: Citing Masculinity in Cold War Poetics*, Olson's poetics and pedagogy were deeply masculinist and given his sway and influence during his tenure as the school's rector, it makes sense that this ideology would assert itself in others (36–40). In *Black Mountain: An Exploration in Community*, Martin Duberman cites his interview with Williams in which Williams says categorically, "It took me a long time to get out from under [Olson]" (384). Williams is speaking specifically about Olson's influence on his poetry, and yet for anyone connected to Black Mountain, art and life—aesthetics and worldviews—were continuous and interdependent. The patriarchal ethos would manifest themselves in the photographic representations of these authors in almost unavoidable ways.

Once outside of Olson's aura, Williams would take portraits that were not so strongly gendered as his Black Mountain pictures, but as I have indicated they do maintain a coolness and a reserve that are in traditional terms coded as masculine. Even the color values of Williams' images are muted or keyed low. If a photograph enacts the photographer's identity, becoming the screen by which to discover how he or she sees, then are we to see the images as being Williams' desired reality—that is, the photographs become allegories of his desire—or was this a reflection of Williams' own complex versions of how to be both masculine and gay? These questions are not easily resolved to be sure, and yet if Davenport is correct in his idea that Williams' photographs disseminate a form of culture, the questions of what and how the visual markers of identity are circulated become relevant in terms of the cultural work Williams' portraits—or any portraits for that matter—accomplish.

Although different arts, there are certain commonalities that poetry and photography share, according to Williams. He writes, "Poets and photographers do not necessarily believe in public audiences or constituencies. They believe in *persons*, with affection for what they see and hear. They believe in that despised, un-contemporary emotion: *tenderness*" (*Magpie's* 84). What if we were to take this idea of tenderness as a poetics of Williams' photographs? Immediately, there is a productive tension in that the images are not evidently tender. So, the question is, what is the idea of tenderness working in his photograph, and might it reveal an idea of attention as being both a tendency and a form of tenderness? Again, this complicates the photographer's relationship to the people he photographs and makes the masculine vision far more nuanced. Williams' assertion indicates the simultaneity of the public and the private and suggests that the images are private, intimate perceptions that are made public. In that sense, the images resist being made into generalizations—it is the photographer's relationship to that person being photographed that is of paramount importance. But in looking at Williams' portraits one engages not only what tenderness looks like, but how it *sees*. This is a communicable tenderness, something like a binding empathy that forms the possibilities of community. In looking at these portraits, one stands in Williams' place, becoming the proxy for the relationship established within the photograph without ever losing one's own sense of self.

There is a famous story about Picasso's portrait of Gertrude Stein and his response to someone who thought that Stein did not look like what Picasso had painted. "She will," he replied. What has always intrigued me about that exchange is whether Picasso meant that the portrait was ahead of Stein in the way that Stein believed the contemporary should be. Or did he mean that the image would become so famous that people would be unable to see Stein except through the lens of his painting? Artists, in a sense, create history before it happens. In numerous biographies, memoirs, and retrospectives of the avant-garde of the post-War period, Jonathan Williams' photographs serve as quintessential representations of the era as defined by the topography of artists' faces. His concept of the contemporary, also defined by what was outside established or institutional values, was made historical in part through the persuasive, inquisitive authority of his camera. Through his camera's lens, he helped disseminate new aesthetic possibilities by the camera's ability to establish value through its gaze. The images that he created with his camera helped fashion an avant-garde community as a collective of individuals—each a face that enabled the work to be seen as human, as seeking to create the world as both subjective and objective at the same time—local and private, public and shared.

WORKS CITED

Barthes, Roland. *Camera Lucida*. Trans. Richard Howard. New York: Hill and Wang, 1981.

Davenport, Guy. "Introduction." *An Ear In Bartram's Tree*. By Jonathan Williams. Chapel Hill: University of North Carolina Press, 1969. N. p.

Davidson, Michael. *Guys Like Us: Citing Masculinity in Cold War Poetics*. Chicago: University of Chicago Press, 2003.

Duberman, Martin. *Black Mountain: An Exploration in Community*. New York: Dutton, 1972.

Harris, Mary Emma. *The Arts at Black Mountain*. Cambridge, MA: MIT Press, 2002.

Olson, Charles. "Against Wisdom as Such." *Human Universe and Other Essays*. Ed. by Donald Allen. New York: Grove, 1967. 67–71.

Williams, Jonathan. "A Callahan Chrestomathy." *Harry Callahan*. Aperture Masters of Photography. Köln: Könemann, 1999.

———. "The Camera Non-Obscura." *The Magpie's Bagpipe*. San Francisco: North Point Press, 1982. 82–86.

———. *A Palpable Elysium*. Boston: Godine, 2002.

VIC BRAND

BURR, SALVAGE, YOKE

A starry vocabulary, adjectives and epithets, orbit around Jonathan Williams: with "toughness, affability, stamina, a sense of mission and a touch of madness", he is an "imaginative gadfly," "a one man band of exacerbated 'injuns'," and "the best comic poet writing in English":[1] He has made a great motion in the world, in his goings and comings, on foot and by car across America. He seems to have known—or tracked down—everyone, and they in turn have rendered the tribute of description, repaying his generosity of spirit with words of effusive praise. The rarity of Williams' trajectory through the culture seems to demand elaboration. If you haven't heard of him, it's not because he hasn't been trying to get the word out about Jargon Society. Buckminster Fuller called him "our Johnny Appleseed."[2]

Throughout the 1950s and '60s Williams toured the country—"to move among a dormant public to seek out the many thousands of alert readers whose tastes are not served,"[3] crisscrossing America in a series of old gas-guzzling family Pontiac station wagons crammed with books published by his Jargon Press as well as seven or eight other small presses. The press began in 1951, ahead of a boom in small presses that arrived in the 1960s. Jargon sought to promulgate American poetic voices that weren't otherwise heard.[4] Jargon, later incarnated and institutionalized as the Jargon Society, soon came to supply a tenuous and influential artistic diaspora with an outlet, as well as a thread of community. In the beginning Williams looked to James Laughlin's New Directions as a model, and at times the two presses shared authors like Kenneth Patchen and Robert Duncan. As Robert Dana noted in his study of small presses, "each press reflects ... the character of its founder, its presiding spirit." Williams' admiration for artists has been Jargon's only compass and agenda. Even the Society's own writers—sometimes those who appear in the same volume—will object to others who appear under the Jargon imprint ("I've discovered most of the people I publish despise each other."⁵) But Williams has persevered in publishing whomever he believes should be seen and heard.

Jargon's output has dropped off since the 1970s, when it was publishing four or five books a year. Williams himself notes that "a press does have a kind of shelf life.... I don't think you're right on top of things but maybe fifteen or twenty years, in terms of what other people are thinking."⁶ But Jargon continues to print, its most recent volume being Mark Steinmetz's *Tuscan Trees* (Jargon 104; 2001). Williams *is* Jargon, and its artistic direction mirrors his own vector through space. Today Jargon's reputation ranks with other venerable independent publishers, such as New Directions, City Lights, and Black Sparrow.

The Jargon Society advocates the American extraordinary: the unknown, the unique, the dedicated and obscure. Consider its contributors: Charles Olson, Paul Metcalf, Harry Callahan, Art Sinsabaugh, Ralph Eugene Meatyard, Guy Davenport, Louis Zukofsky, Raymond Moore, Clarence John Laughlin, Mina Loy, Buckminster Fuller, John Menapace, Robert Creeley, Doris Ulmann, Denise Levertov, and Guy Mendes. Williams' challenge was to find an audience for them. Wealthy benefactors, collectors, friends, and contributing artists bought a majority of Jargon's wares, as well as audiences at the hundreds of readings Williams performed around the country. And yet he admits that he "distrusts public attention and the city"⁷ —Williams the cantankerous apostle. He has often compared Jargon's audience to the Lamed-Vav Zaddikim "the thirty-six anonymous and mysterious pious men, to whose humility, just deeds, and virtues the world owes its continued existence."⁸

While struggling against inertia in the populace, he has also struggled as a publisher with the idiosyncrasies of his artists: they have been temperamental, overprotective, sensitive, skittish, or ornery. Art Sinsabaugh nearly backed out of a project because of differences of opinion over book design; Clarence John Laughlin refused to participate in an exhibition of Southern photographers curated by Williams. Since publishing with Jargon does not mean great fame or wealth (which have never been the point), the only thing at stake is the art itself. Ultimately, though, his artists and writers recognize Williams as a kindred spirit and come to trust him with their passion.

Although Jargon publishes to address the mainstream neglect of new and original poets, it exists primarily because Williams wants to make beautiful objects. From the beginning, Jargon has united word with image. Jargon 1 (1951) consisted of a poem by Williams accompanied by an engraving by David Ruff; Jargon 2 (1952), a poem by Joel Oppenheimer and a Robert Rauschenberg drawing. Williams has always aimed to create books that evoke the wonder that he felt as a child while reading the *Oz'* books, Kipling's *Just-so Stories*, *The Hobbit*, and *The Wind in the Willows*. He has cited "the book as a kind of childhood desire. ... I want them to be as entrancing as those. I don't think I'd bother if I didn't feel that way."[9] The work of William Blake and the graphic poems of e. e. cummings and Kenneth Patchen are Williams' more mature touchstones.

Following in the steps of these visual poets, Williams trained in part to be an artist. He quit Princeton in 1949 after three semesters and went to New York, where he spent the spring of 1950 studying at Surrealist print-maker Stanley William Hayter's *Atelier 17*. When Hayter closed the atelier to return to Paris, Williams moved on to the Chicago Institute of Design, where he studied typography. In July of 1951, Williams followed photographer Harry Callahan from Chicago to Black Mountain College. At the time, photography "just seemed like one of the things to know about ... the camera seemed a very plausible substitute for drawing, which I couldn't do very well."[10] At Black Mountain he befriended Callahan and Callahan's friend Aaron Siskind; but Williams was pulled irretrievably into the gravity of Charles Olson, poet and rector of the College: Williams traded camera for pen.[11]

Black Mountain College in North Carolina played host in its later history to a community of the artistic avant-garde, including poet Robert Creeley, choreographer Merce Cunningham, painter Robert Motherwell, composer John Cage, and visionary architect Buckminster Fuller. The College began in 1933 as a progressive educational institution that emphasized community, democracy, experience, and the arts. Under Olson's direction, until its closing in 1956, the name "Black Mountain" became synonymous with a poetic movement that rebelled against a growing formalism in American poetry. Robert Creeley, Denise Levertov, Ed Dorn, Paul Blackburn, and Robert Duncan—with William Carlos Williams as their elder statesman and Olson's essay "Projective Verse" as their manifesto—all worked under Black Mountain's influence. Olson declared to Williams: "The artist is his own instrument."[12] And with that challenge, Williams embraced a quintessentially American do-it-yourself aesthetic. With no one else willing to publish Olson and his circle, Williams willed into being the publishing venture known as Jargon, at first for the purpose of publishing Olson's *Maximus Poems*. (The idea for Jargon only predated Black Mountain by two weeks: Jargon 1 was a single printed sheet that Williams issued in San Francisco, with art by engraver and fellow Atelier 17 student David Ruff, who later did printing for City Lights' Pocket Poets series.)

Beginning in roughly 1958, Jargon began to attract work from well-established art-photographers.[13] California-based Wynn Bullock (whom Williams described as "a luminous man, with a windy, cloudy, lovely nature"[14]), Henry Holmes Smith of Indiana University, Frederick Sommer in Arizona, and Callahan all began contributing photographs to be used as frontispieces for books like Henry Miller's *The Red Notebook, The Maximus Poems,* and others (see bibliography). As word spread in the photography world, other artists began to seek out Williams to support Jargon's work. Jerry Uelsmann, '70's master of the composite image; one-time Light Gallery director Charles Traub; the godfather of photography curators, Beaumont Newhall; novelist/photographer Wright Morris; Ansel Adams and Carl van Vechten, all were enthusiastic fans (one of Adams' letters to Williams opens "Dear Genius …").

Jargon's first, thorough integration of text with image came with *On My Eyes* (Jargon 36; 1960). Eight of Callahan's abstract nature photographs—fallen leaves, spider-webs, reeds in water—were interleaved with poems by Larry Eigner, a Massachusetts poet of "sparse elegance."[15] Callahan taught and photographed in Chicago with Art Sinsabaugh, Art Siegel, and Aaron Siskind, then moved to the Rhode Island School of Design, where he became Chair of the Department of Photography. While in transition from Chicago to Rhode Island (with an extended stop-over in Europe), he sent his selection of photos to Williams for *On My Eyes*. Callahan claimed that the eight shots were "not a choice at all," being the only nature shots left in a "catch-all box" after he had packed up.[16] *On My Eyes* was a first for publisher and photographer both, being Callahan's first appearance in print.

Like Callahan's selection of prints, Jargon's pairing of artists was serendipitous and inevitable: "I wonder why I chose to put some of those people together," says Williams, "and then, I don't wonder."[17] A similar combination of text and photography was *Six Mid-American Chants* (Jargon 45; 1964). Williams was preparing to reprint a selection of prose-poems written in 1918 by Sherwood Anderson, author of *Winesburg, Ohio* (1919), who had died in 1941. During a visit to Chicago Williams saw Art Sinsabaugh's banquet-camera photography of Indiana landscapes, which convinced him that only an enormous 19 x 55 cm edition could put Anderson's lyrics in the proper context. Sinsabaugh and Williams rekindled their association, which would later result in an invitation to Sinsabaugh to photograph England's Yorkshire Dales, where Williams lived for parts of the year. *Chants* was one of only a few publications, other than exhibition catalogs, to feature Sinsabaugh's work in his life-time. Charles Olson's reaction to the gargantuan tome: "My God, it's like a train, like getting a train for Christmas, even including the tracks ..."[18]

Since the 1960s Williams had hoped to include artists' monographs among Jargon's publications, in the vein of *Aperture* magazine. But Jargon did not produce any completely photographic editions until *The Appalachian Photographs of Doris Ulmann* (Jargon 50) in 1971. The book began "a quiet revival"[19] of the Park Avenue socialite's pictorialist studies of the Southern rural poor. It impressed no less than Museum of Modern Art photography director John Szarkowski as "beautiful, moving, and true"[20] and the book was sold in the museum's shop. The *New York Times* noted that "the recovery of Doris Ulmann's portraiture is typical of Jargon's cultural husbandry."[21] Jargon is an ongoing salvage, like Williams' photographs of tombstones, a monument to memory. Neglected Modernist poets Louis Zukofsky and Mina Loy also have him to thank for preserving their work from mainstream amnesia.

Two Kentuckians, Ralph Eugene Meatyard and Guy Davenport, are among those whose reputations were established under Jargon's flag. On one of Williams' visits to Kentucky, he traveled with the photographer and the author to meet Thomas Merton, monk and poet,[22] after which Meatyard and Merton struck up an immediate friendship and collaboration that was eventually documented in the book *Father Louie: Photographs of Thomas Merton* (Timken Publishers, 1991). Davenport and Williams had long been friends, having met in the early 1960s at a reading Williams gave at Haverford College. Davenport floated the idea of publishing a book-length poem, and through a frequent correspondence (collected in *A Garden Carried in a Pocket* [Green Shade, 2004]) of stylistic one-upmanship Davenport became Williams' "principal colleague ... (h)e already knew more about my poetry than I ever did."[23] That long poem, *Flowers & Leaves* (Jargon 46; 1966), was Davenport's first original, non-scholarly work in print, and frequent contributions to Jargon's catalog followed, as well as introductions and prefaces to Williams' own works.

Davenport also wrote prefaces for Meatyard and co-curated a major retrospective of the photographer's work at the International Center of Photography (2005). An optician by day, Meatyard had studied with photography masters Van Deren Coke and Minor White; his work had been published in *Aperture* and *Art in America*, and shown in New York and at Tulane University. He had turned the front of his optometry store into a gallery where he held exhibitions of his and others' works. Williams liked Meatyard—"he was terribly normal ... he fascinated me because I knew so little about him"[24]—and he notes, "once in a while you want to print somebody you have doubts about or don't really understand ... I'm trusting my ears and my eyes."[25] A Meatyard photograph appears on the cover of *Flowers & Leaves*, and he is responsible for the author photo of Davenport;[26] additionally several of his pictures were considered but finally not used for the cover of Walter Lowenfels' *Some Deaths* (Jargon 32; 1964). But Meatyard's magnum opus, ten years in the planning, was interrupted by his death from cancer in 1972. Williams had been in correspondence with the photographer up until the time of his death and subsequently worked with Meatyard's widow to complete *The Family Album of Lucybelle Crater* (Jargon 76; 1974), the seminal work of an artist of "extraordinarily ambitious ideas."[27]

In the text of *Lucybelle Crater,* Williams cogitated: "You ask why it is so hard and perhaps so futile to write about photography, or to describe any medium in terms of another? Simply, that things are *obvious* or they aren't there at all".[28] In spite of the "futility" of the effort, Williams has written persistently on the subject of photography, yoking words to images: in his unused preface to Emmet Gowin's *Photographs* (1976); his essays on Callahan and the British photographer Raymond Moore;[29] and, since 1960, his commentaries and reviews in the photography magazine *Aperture*. His essay collections, *The Magpie's Bagpipe* (North Point, 1982) and *Blackbird Dust* (Turtle Point Press, 2000), are littered with observations on cameramen like Sinsabaugh and Louisiana symbolist Clarence John Laughlin.

When he speaks of photography, Williams is eloquent and enthusiastic. In 1961 Williams served as an *Aperture* guest editor, assembling a feature, "The Eye of Three Phantasts," that surveyed the work of Laughlin, Wynn Bullock, and Frederick Sommer. Upon its publication, editor Minor White wrote to Williams that "Henry Holmes Smith is enthusiastic about your article; says it is the best piece of writing on photogs that *Aperture* has ever printed. And I tend to agree ..."[30]

Of his own work, Williams has said, "Jargon is a small effort. Yet I think it stands for something. That's all that's important ..."[31] His are artists in the bud or in the dust, salvaged by a fellow outsider. He is an artist of the first order, all the more unique because his artistry lies in his ability to fashion a beautiful bibliographic object from the work of others. His tenacity in his mission is almost Greek in its tone: like Pheidippides, he has run innumerable miles to bring the city news of action on its borders; he persists like a Sophoclean hero, calling for the audience that his artists deserve, even while laboring under the knowledge that few will respond. Yet the risk has returned reward, and several major artists have him to thank for their first foothold in the culture: Olson, Callahan, Meatyard, Davenport, among others. While "The Mainstream" runs muddy and full of fish, Williams and Jargon have stood in the mountains, tapping the root of a clear spring. Without them, we would probably not die of thirst, but it would be hard to recognize the taste of fresh water.

JARGON PHOTOGRAPHIC BIBLIOGRAPHY

(Listed by Jargon series number; edition information where available)

13a. *Amen/Huzza/Selah*. Poems and photographs by Jonathan Williams. "A Preface?" by Louis Zukofsky. (1960; edition of 700; limited edition of 50 signed copies)

13b. *Elegies and Celebrations*. Poems by Jonathan Williams. Preface by Robert Duncan. Photographs by Aaron Siskind and Jonathan Williams. (1962; edition of 750)

17. *The Suicide Room*. Poems by Stuart Z. Perkoff. Drawing by Fielding Dawson. Photograph by Chester Kessler. (1956; edition of 200; 25 hardcover, signed & numbered)

22. *The Red Notebook*. Henry Miller (holograph manuscript with drawings). Photograph by Wynn Bullock. (1958; edition of 2,000)

24. *The Maximus Poems*. Charles Olson. Photograph by Frederick Sommer. (1960; edition of 2,000; limited edition of 101 bound copies, of which 75 copies are numbered, and 26 copies are lettered and signed.)

27. *Sonnet Variations*. Poems by Peyton Houston. Photograph by Henry Holmes Smith. (1962; edition of 1,000)

28. *A Laughter in the Mind*. Poems by Irving Layton. Photograph ("Frog & Flower") by Frederick Sommer. (1958)

29. *1450–1950*. Optical poems by Bob Brown. Photograph by Jonathan Williams. (c. 1959; In association with Corinth Books; a facsimile reproduction, first published by The Black Sun Press in 1929; edition of 2,0000

32. *Some Deaths*. Poems by Walter Lowenfels. Introduction by Jonathan Williams. Photographs by Robert Schiller. (1964; edition of 1,500)

33. *A Form of Women*. Poems by Robert Creeley. Photograph by Robert Schiller. (c. 1959; edition of 2,000; in association with Corinth Books)

35. *A Red Carpet for the Sun*. Poems by Irving Layton. Photograph by Harry Callahan. (1959; edition of 1,000)

36. *On My Eyes*. Poems by Larry Eigner. Introduction by Denise Levertov. Photographs by Harry Callahan. (1960; edition of 500)

45. *Six Mid-American Chants*. Poems by Sherwood Anderson. Eleven photographs by Art Sinsabaugh. Preface by Edward Dahlberg. Postface by Frederick Eckman. (1964; edition of 1,550)

46. *Flowers & Leaves*. A poem by Guy Davenport. Photograph by Ralph Eugene Meatyard. (1966)

49. *The Poems of Alfred Starr Hamilton*. Introduction by Geof Hewitt. Drawing by Philip Van Aver. Photograph by Simpson Kalisher. (1970)

50. *The Appalachian Photographs of Doris Ulmann*. Introduction by John Jacob Niles. Preface by Jonathan Williams. (1971)

55. *A Long Undressing: Collected Poems 1949–1969*. Poems by James Broughton. Photograph by Imogen Cunningham. (1971; also in limited edition of 100, signed)

57. *Just Friends/Friends & Lovers: Poems, 1959–1962*. Poems by Joel Oppenheimer. Photograph by Bob Adelman. (1980)

64. *St. EOM in the Land of Pasaquan*. "As told to and recorded by" Tom Patterson. Foreword by John Russell. Photographs by Roger Manley, Guy Mendes,

and Jonathan Williams. (c. 1987; edition of 4,000; also "patron's edition" of 100, leather bound, numbered, and signed by authors and photographers)

70. *Bad Land.* Poem by Richard Emil Braun. Photograph by Frederick Sommer. (1971)

73. *Spring of the Lamb.* A "wild Welsh tale" by Douglas Woolf. "Broken Field Runner: A Douglas Woolf Notebook" by Paul Metcalf. Two photographs (covers) by Ralph Eugene Meatyard. (1972)

75. *Some Particulars.* Poems by Thomas A. Clark. Photographs by Bart Parker. (1971)

76. *The Family Album of Lucybelle Crater.* Photographs by Ralph Eugene Meatyard. Texts by Jonathan Greene, Ronald Johnson, Ralph Eugene Meatyard, Guy Mendes, Thomas Meyer, and Jonathan Williams. (1974)

77. *The Sleep of Reason.* Mardi Gras photographs by Lyle Bongé. Texts by James Leo Herlihy and Jonathan Williams. (1974)

78. *The Middle Passage (A Triptych of Commodities).* Text by Paul Metcalf. Photographs by Guy Mendes. Designed by Jonathan Williams. (1976)

82. *Who is Little Enis?* Catullan ode by Jonathan Williams. Photograph by Guy Mendes. (1974; edition of 500 signed copies)

84. *Eyes and Objects (Catalogue for an Exhibition: 1970–1972).* Poems by Ronald Johnson. "A Gallery Goer's Foreword," by John Russell. Photograph by Ralph Eugene Meatyard. (1976; edition of 1,000)

89. *The Photographs of Lyle Bongé.* Introduction by A.D. Coleman. Afterword by Jonathan Williams. Writings by Lyle Bongé. (1982)

91. *Elite/Elate Poems.* Selected poems 1971–1975 by Jonathan Williams. Introduction by Guy Davenport. A portfolio of photographs by Guy Mendes. (1979; 1st edition of 150, signed by JW and specially bound, with original Mendes print, "Home, Cow and Country!" laid in; 2nd edition of 850, bound in paper)

95. *Heart's Gate (Letters between Marsden Hartley & Horace Traubel 1906-1915).* Edited and introduced by William Innes Homer. Photograph by Aaron Siskind. (1982)

97. *Letter in a Klein Bottle.* Photographs by John Menapace. Introduction by Donald B. Kuspit. Afterword by Jonathan Williams. (1984)

104. *Tuscan Trees.* Photographs by Mark Steinmetz. Text by Janet Lembke. (2001)

107. *Last Man In.* Poems by Richard Emil Braun. Cover photograph by Ron Nameth.

111. *The Neugents: Close to Home*. Photographs and text by David M. Spear. Afterword by Jonathan Williams. (1993)

112. *Blithe Air: Photographs from England, Wales, and Ireland*. Photographs by Elizabeth Matheson. Illuminations and pyrotechnic display by Jonathan Williams. (1995; edition of 1500, of which 50 in deluxe edition, signed and slip-cased, with original print laid in.)

[Special thanks to Michael Basinski, Steven Watson, Thomas Meyer, and especially Jonathan Williams.]

SOURCES

Bain, Robert and Joseph M. Flora, ed. *Contemporary Poets, Dramatists, Essayists, and Novelists of the South: a bio-bibliographical sourcebook*. Westport: Greenwood Press, 1994.

Contemporary Authors Online, Gale, 2006. Reproduced in *Biography Resource Center*. Farmington Hills, MI: Thomson Gale, 2006. *http://galenet.galegroup.com/servlet/BioRC*.

Dana, Robert. *Against the Grain: interviews with Maverick American Publishers*. Iowa City: U of Iowa P, 1986.

Davenport, Guy. *The Hunter Gracchus and other papers on literature and art*. Washington, D.C.: Counterpoint, 1996.

"David Ruff," *Wikipedia*. http://en.wikipedia.org/wiki/David_Ruff

Greene, Jonathan, ed. *A Fiftieth Birthday Celebration for Jonathan Williams*. *Truck* 21, Gnomon Press, 1979.

Harris, Mary Emma. *The Arts at Black Mountain College*. Cambridge: The MIT Press, 2002.

Henderson, Bill ed. *The Art of Literary Publishing: Editors on their Craft*. Yonkers, NY: Pushcart, c1980.

The Independent (UK), January 12, 2005.

The Jargon Society Archive, The Poetry Collection, University of Buffalo Library.

Johnson, Ronald. "Jonathan Williams." *Dictionary of Literary Biography*, vol. 5, edited by Donald J. Grenier. Gale: 1980.

The Library catalogs of Emory University and the University of Buffalo.

Meyer, Thomas, ed. *A Garden Carried In A Pocket: Guy Davenport [and]*

Jonathan Williams; Letters 1964 –1968. Haverford, PA: Green Shade [and] James S. Jaffe Rare Books, 2004.

New York Times, February 15, 1957; November 21, 1971; and January 12, 1975.

"Stanley William Hayter." *Contemporary Artists*, 5th ed. St. James Press, 2001. Reproduced in *Biography Resource Center*. Farmington Hills, Mich.: Thomson Gale, 2006. http://galenet.galegroup.com/servlet/BioRC.

Williams, Jonathan. *Blackbird Dust: essays, poems, and photography*. New York: Turtle Point Press, 2000.

————. *The Magpie's Bagpipe: selected essays of Jonathan Williams*. Edited by Thomas Meyer. San Francisco: North Point, 1982.

————. *Uncle Gus Flaubert Rates the Jargon Society in One Hundred Laconic Présalé Sage Sentences*. The Hanes Lecture. Chapel Hill: Hanes Foundation, Rare Book Collection/University Library, University of North Carolina at Chapel Hill, 1989.

NOTES

[1] Herbert Leibowitz in the *New York Times*; Ronald Johnson in *The Dictionary of Literary Biography*; Robert Creeley and Gilbert Sorrentino in Greene, respectively.

[2] Quoted in *Contemporary Authors*.

[3] *New York Times,* Feb. 17, 1957.

[4] "We publish the best we know to please ourselves and our friends, and to confound our enemies." *Blackbird Dust*, p. 118.

[5] Dana, p. 192.

[6] Dana, p. 221.

[7] *Uncle Gus Flaubert …*, p. 2.

[8] Ibid.

[9] Dana, p. 196.

[10] Dana, p. 202.

[11] Williams continued to make photographs, which appear alongside his poetry in *Amen/Huzzah/Selah* (Jargon 13a; 1960) and *Elegies and Celebrations* (Jargon 13b; 1962). Usually made with a Rolleiflex that he bought with Siskind's help, his photographs are portraits of friends or influences—their faces or their head-

stones—and include eccentric architecture. *Portrait Photographs* (Gnomon Press, 1979) and *A Palpable Elysium* (David R. Godine, 2002) collect and comment on a number of these.

[12] Dana, p. 204.

[13] Nearly all of these photographers had connections to the pioneer of photographic education, Laszlo Moholy-Nagy and Chicago, through either his New Bauhaus or the Institute of Design. Harry Callahan and Aaron Siskind would then have had close professional connections to all of them.

[14] *Magpie's Bagpipe*, p. 89.

[15] Mark Perlberg, quoted in *Contemporary Authors Online*.

[16] Letter, Harry Callahan to Jonathan Williams.

[17] Interview with the author.

[18] JW, "Homage to Art Sinsabaugh," *Aperture* 95. Reprinted in *Blackbird Dust*. Also good for a rowdier account of JW's relationship with the photographer.

[19] *New York Times*, January 12, 1975.

[20] Letter, John Szarkowski to JW.

[21] *New York Times*, November 21, 1971.

[22] Davenport recalls this meeting vividly in his book *The Hunter Gracchus* (Counterpoint, 1996).

[23] *The Independent* (UK), Jan. 12. 2005.

[24] Interview with the author.

[25] Dana, p. 220–221.

[26] A contribution of which Davenport was unaware until the book was in proofs, offering further evidence that Jargon's pairings were mysterious yet always somehow appropriate.

[27] *New York Times,* January 16, 1994.

[28] Draft of "Cogitations" from *The Family Album of Lucybelle Crater*.

[28] In *Harry Callahan* (Aperture, 1999) and Moore's *Murmurs at Every Turn* (1981).

[30] Letter, M. White to JW, November 28, 1961.

[31] Henderson, p. 126–127.

RECOLLECTING

JAMES JAFFE

JONATHAN WILLIAMS, JARGONAUT

Jonathan Williams died a week ago, on Sunday, March 16th, in Highlands, North Carolina, just past his 79th birthday. Three score years and nearly twenty would be a sufficient span for most lives, and beyond the expectations of most people, but hardly enough for a man of Jonathan's generous reach. As I've come to learn, however, the length of a life isn't apportioned according to our virtues, or our vices, our accomplishments, or whatever remains of our capacity to make and create; or even our capacity to enjoy ourselves. Life is arbitrary, and it will take you out no matter how much head or heart you have left. Jonathan had both, and, amazingly, a healthy liver, and the odds were still in his favor.

I met Jonathan in the early '80s, not long after I started collecting the publications of the Jargon Society, which he began back in 1951, during that legendary Summer Institute at Black Mountain College, where, at the recommendation of Harry Callahan, he had gone to study photography. It was at Black Mountain that he met Creeley, and Dawson, and Duncan, and Olson, and Oppenheimer, to mention only a few of the poets whose books he would soon publish. Jonathan eventually tired of talking about Black Mountain, but it's where he got his big push.

Jargon 1, Jonathan's *Garbage Litters the Iron Face of the Sun's Child* is dated June 25, 1951. Jargon 2, Joel Oppenheimer's *The Dancer*, with a drawing by Robert Rauschenberg, was printed for a dance recital by Katherine Litz at the YMHA in New York on December 23, 1951, but by December 17th, Jonathan was mailing a copy from Highlands to his best friend from St. Albans, Stanley Willis. *The Dancer* notes that "JARGON is Proteus: experiment, collaboration: any media, for use now." That was Jonathan, and Jonathan stuck to that creed his whole life, non-stop, until infirmity finally brought him down.

When Jonathan caught wind of my interest in him, he asked me to join the board of the Jargon Society, and before I knew what hit me I was driving down to Winston-Salem for the annual meeting. I don't know what Jonathan was thinking; no doubt that I had money, and that I could be of use. Perhaps he thought I would become a patron, a benefactor, another generous soul who would support him and his good works, who would help him make all the things he wanted to make, just the way he wanted to make them, so that the rest of the world—or as many of them as had the propensity to find them—could discover them, too. Or maybe he was just curious, and wanted to meet a new collector who had taken such a keen interest in him and the Jargon Society.

Katherine Litz
Joel L Oppenheimer
Bob Rauschenberg

j a r g o n   t w o

is for Katherine Litz, & on the occasion of her dance recital at the YMHA in New York, 12 23 51.   verse by Joel L Oppenheimer, drawing by Bob Rauschenberg; set & printed by The Sad Devil Press at Black Mountain College, N. C., in Bauer Bodoni types on a Bristol paper, in an edition of 150, designer & publisher of the Jargon series: Jonathan Williams. inquiries, etc. to him c-o Box 518, Highlands, N. C. JARGON is Proteus: experiment, collaboration: any media, for use now.

Jonathan Williams

At the time, I only knew Jonathan through his works, but to me, they were marvelous, every last one of them. I'd spread them out where you could see them, and they dazzled me. They were more varied than the publications of any other "private press," and although each one was different—unique and curious in its own way, never uniform—they were all unmistakably the work of this one extraordinary man; and all of them were as personal and personable as he turned out to be. I wanted to meet Jonathan as much as I wanted to own all of the books he'd written or published. And it was spring, and spring is the best time to be on the road heading south.

Jonathan wasn't a "fine printer," and the Jargon Society wasn't a fine press in the traditional sense. Jonathan wasn't derivative or devotional; he wasn't a disciple; and although a collector, he wasn't interested in books no one reads. He didn't aspire to be a craftsman; he didn't print the books himself, and he certainly had no desire to set lead type on a hand-press all day. There was nothing hermetic about Jonathan; however rusticated he may have appeared at times. He wanted to make things happen.

The Jargon Society was a reflection of its publisher, its publications the prismatic refractions of his interests and enthusiasms. And yet it wasn't all about Jonathan, the way so many private presses are all about their printers, whose publications are barely more than a pretext for yet another repetitive expression of their particular aesthetic. After all, Jonathan named it the Jargon "Society" not the Jargon "Press." It wasn't about putting his stamp, his signature, on everything. And as such the Jargon Society differed from other literary private presses in being radical and democratic, in giving each book its own identity, its own idiosyncratic form. Jonathan never sacrificed a book, or its author, to a single concept. He didn't identify himself or his books with a favorite format or formula. Jonathan's books don't all look alike anymore than the poets he published looked alike. For all their affinities, the books Jonathan published were allowed to be as individual and independent as he was himself.

Whether Jonathan found them, or they found Jonathan, one way or another, Jonathan knew more interesting people than anyone I ever met. Miraculously it seemed to me, he even knew "the deliciously named V. E. G. Ham," one of the most brilliant and entertaining undergraduates at Sewanee while I was there. It turned out that Gene (Van Eugene Gatewood Ham) was a cousin of the wife of a friend of Jonathan's in Kentucky. But it figured that Jonathan would have known Gene. Jonathan had a knack for knowing remarkable people. It seemed he could put his ear to the ground, or cock his head to the wind, or just open the morning's mail and something original would come to hand. Jonathan had a nose, a sharp eye, and he paid attention; he discerned and distinguished the ordinary from the extraordinary; and unselfishly, he spread the word.

Jonathan always had more ideas than he could realize, and he never seemed to run out. There were plenty of books that should have been done, but couldn't be done without big grants or generous contributions from friends, most of whom realized that their contributions were supporting him as well as underwriting the costs of the books. Some books were simply too expensive for him to produce himself—like the monograph on the photographs of Art Sinsabaugh that Jonathan had envisioned and hoped to publish nearly forty years ago, but that was finally published by someone else in 2004, and I suspect, not as well as Jonathan would have done it.

There are more than a few libraries around the country waiting for books that Jonathan announced a long time ago but was never able to publish, wonderful books that would have enriched our lives, if only Jonathan had been able to find the money. Books like *The Selected Poems of Bob Brown*, designated Jargon 34; or *The Selected Poems of Mason Jordan Mason* (Judson Crews), slated to be Jargon 54; or *Eyes in Leaves: A Tribute to Guy Davenport*, which was planned—in the '70s!—as Jargon 90. The problem was—the problem always is—that most people with money want to use their money to make more money; they don't want to make beautiful things that don't make money—like books. Jonathan took a loss on almost every book he published, but it didn't stop him.

Jonathan cared about making good books and making them right; and he didn't much care whether they sold or not. He didn't expect much from the public, and would have agreed with Oscar Wilde that "The public have an insatiable curiosity to know everything, except what is worth knowing." Jonathan had his own vision, his own tastes, and his own standards, and he lived by them. He would seldom compromise, even if it meant that a book he dearly hoped to make wouldn't be done, even when it was a book he himself had written, like his book on Southern outsider art—the book as he wanted it to be, not the book that was eventually published. When it came to books and life, Jonathan knew what he wanted to do, and how he wanted to do it. And he did it, obstinately, and beautifully, whenever possible.

Jonathan peddled his publications, too—in person—starting in the '50s after he returned from Germany where he had served as a conscientious objector. (On second thought, I have a black-letter poster for a reading he gave there, and I'd be willing to bet that he started selling books while he was in Germany.) Jonathan would drive his VW bug around the country, giving poetry readings and trying to sell those beautiful "classic" Jargon publications: Creeley's *The Immoral Proposition* (1953) and *All That Is Lovely In Men* (1955); Duncan's *Letters* (1954); Olson's *The Maximus Poems* (1953–1956); Levertov's *Overland to the Islands* (1958); McClure's *Passage* (1956); Oppenheimer's *The Dutiful Son* (1956); three books of Kenneth Patchen's: *Fables* (1953), *Hurrah for Anything* (1957) and *Poem-scapes* (1958); Zukofsky's *Some Time* (1956); and of course Mina Loy's *Lunar Baedeker and Time-Tables* (1958).

I have a photograph of Jonathan sitting in his VW bug in the mid-1960s, with a copy of Sherwood Anderson's *Six Mid-American Chants* (1964), illustrated with the panoramic mid-western photographs of Art Sinsabaugh on his lap. Jonathan was only 35 years old. Fifteen years later, a collection of photographs called *JW, on the Road Selling that Old Orphic Snake-Oil in the Jargon-sized Bottles, 1951–1978* (Visual Press, 1979) was published to commemorate Jonathan's 50th birthday. Jonathan was still at it, going strong, although by then he was driving a VW Rabbit Diesel.

The wonder is that Jonathan was able to accomplish so much as a publisher; the pity is that he wasn't given the means to do more. Jargon's publications are a perpetual testament to Jonathan's desire to make things of worth, and to introduce worthy poets and artists to the world. Many of them are breath-taking examples of what Jonathan was able to do with modest means, determination, and self-sacrifice. Over the years, more than a few beloved books and photographs were sold—at disadvantageous terms—in order to subsidize the next Jargon publication, to make the next project possible, or just to pay the household bills.

What Jonathan did with what he was given was prodigious, and I've been talking only about Jonathan the publisher. Jonathan's publications represented only a fraction of what he did and what he might have done had he been given the time and the money to realize his ideas. In addition to

JW on the Road in California, 1965. Photo by Brooke Elgie..

being a publisher, he was an endlessly inventive poet, a brilliant photographer, an early champion of some of the best modern photographers—Clarence John Laughlin, Aaron Siskind, Ralph Eugene Meatyard, and Frederick Sommer—not to immediately mention some of the other wonderful photographers he introduced me and many others to: Raymond Moore, Guy Mendes, John Menapace, Elizabeth Matheson, and David Spears. Jonathan was also one of the earliest, most prescient, and least exploitative exponents of Southern outsider art.

Jonathan also had a rich and full personal life—perhaps more than one when you consider that he lived half the year in Highlands, NC, and the other half in Cumbria, England. And it was a life that Jonathan shared, as he shared himself, his wit, his humor, his sense of friendship and conviviality. Looking at all the occasional postcards, letters, ephemeral publications, even solicitations for money for the Jargon society that Jonathan created in so many myriad forms for over forty years, I doubt that a day passed without Jonathan sending something to someone, something unique and irrepressibly enlivening. It was a wonderful life, carefully made more gracious and hospitable by the poet Thomas Meyer, Jonathan's wise and irreplaceable partner of forty years. It was as enviable a life as one could imagine, and almost unimaginable in today's cannibalistic world.

To put it plainly, Jonathan was the most civilized man I ever met, notwithstanding his distaste for Bach; and the times I spent in his company, at his family home in Highlands or the cottage at Corn Close, have been among the most memorable and nourishing experiences of my life. And when it was time to leave, Jonathan always gave you a push in the right direction. My son will remember our ploughman's lunch at the Shepherd's Inn in Melmerby long after I'm gone, and he'll always remember Jonathan, who told us to go and showed us the way.

We were fortunate to have Jonathan as our guide. We've all been fortunate to have Jonathan as our guide.

When I heard that Jonathan had died, I wrote to Peter Howard at Serendipity Books in Berkeley. I thought he would want to know. Peter's response was worthy of Peter, and worthy of Jonathan, whose obituaries for his own friends are the finest of their kind. I can't imagine a more fitting tribute: "I met him only once, on the hustle for money for a book, but I knew all along his publications were the most remarkable of any in the USA in his lifetime. Early for the writer, always beautiful. Who can always be first and always beautiful?"

As it turned out, during the nearly twenty-five years I've known Jonathan, I built my collection, I became Jonathan's bibliographer and published a checklist of his work; I published his correspondence with Guy Davenport; I was of some use. All in all, I managed to do less than I might have done, or than Jonathan might have expected of me. Like so many others who knew Jonathan, I got far more than I ever gave. And for that I will always be grateful.

Amen. Huzza. Selah.

KYLE SCHLESINGER

THE JARGON SOCIETY

The Jargon Society did not begin with Charles Olson's mighty *Maximus*, but with a much more modest idea. Before heading down to Black Mountain College from Chicago in the early fifties, Jargon's founder, Jonathan Williams, went to San Francisco where he met mentors Kenneth Patchen, Robert Duncan, Kenneth Rexroth, and Henry Miller for the first time. It was there that he also met his contemporary David Ruff, a painter from New York who ran The Print Workshop between 1950 and 1955. Ruff taught etching and engraving, published some poetry (mostly Patchen), and gained notoriety in the Beat scene for printing Lawrence Ferlinghetti's own *Pictures of a Gone World*, the first book in the infamous City Lights Pocket Poets series, in 1955. It was no marvel of printing (the poems weren't so hot either), but City Lights quickly became one of the most commercially successful literary publishers in San Francisco.

The lesser-known, although far more significant publication to emerge from The Print Workshop wasn't even a book, but a piece of ephemera produced on the fly. Ruff's 1951 collaboration with Williams, whose "Patchenesque" poem met Ruff's image on a small, single sheet of yellow paper, is perhaps best described as a handbill. Ruff carved his image into copper plates (the same form of relief etching that William Blake used to create his own illuminated poems more than a century earlier) and printed the text from handset Lydian type, a distinct calligraphic sans serif designed by Warren Chappell for American Type Founders in 1938. Its publication on June 25, 1951 in an edition of just fifty copies marks the beginning of one of the greatest of the great postwar American private presses.[1]

I bet more people will read this poem within a day of its online debut than the sum of readers who have seen the first edition (published nearly six decades ago):

GARBAGE LITTERS THE IRON FACE
OF THE SUN'S CHILD

blue water strokes red rock.

on this petrific core of Spring,
god massages gentle space
into a wondrous foliage of thickdark peace.

now! leaves and thens unfold,
in glorious gloryings
unseeable twilights, intangible Saviors
air drapes a silver in the trees.

the red rock smiles in the blue water.

one bubble lifts
and lays its message on gold fog:
windstruck,
above the sunsets of the Snake.

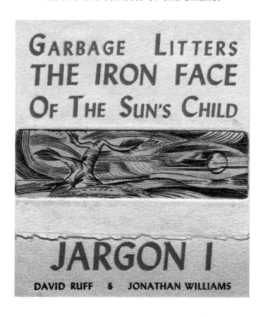

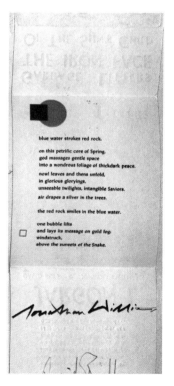

While the Jargon Society may forever be marked by Williams' stint as a student at BMC, what did not change (paraphrasing Olson) was the will to change. Faced with the constant financial pressures that so often come with private press ventures, one wonders why Williams (unlike Ferlinghetti) didn't pimp his past by publishing books that would cater to the interests of BMC enthusiasts? Or sell nostalgic kitsch to tourists in Asheville? Or peddle high-end works of art by BMC alumni in a New York City gallery? True to the ideals expressed by BMC's founder John Andrew Rice, who said that "... all college should be in tents—when they fold, they fold," Williams moved on, taking with him the ideas, rather than the commodities, the College had to offer. In fact, he was pretty much done publishing the Black Mountain poets (as such) by the mid-sixties when he was a young man still in his mid-thirties. Given the same opportunity in San Francisco, Ferlinghetti made City Lights Books a tourist destination, a spectacle amongst the sites and hype.

Williams stayed true to the integrity of private press culture (spawned by William Morris and his Kelmscott Press in the late 1800s) by making it his business to publish the poets he wanted to read in the form that he wanted to read them regardless of their commercial viability. While there were deluxe editions from time to time, these were the exception rather than the rule. It seems likely that these were primarily designed to be sold to special collection libraries and private collectors in order to raise money for the press's populist publications (not an uncommon practice). One of the characteristics most often admired in the Jargon Society is the unique design, uncompromising manufacturing standards, and use of high-quality (not extravagant) materials—not sumptuous, just well made. Williams claimed to have lost money on almost every book be published, and relied on the support of grants from individual benefactors and organizations to keep afloat. The range of poets and artists whose energy and ideas gained the support and admiration of Williams is staggering.

In stark contrast to Ferlinghetti's idea of branding his authors by shoveling content into templates devoid of personality, Williams wasn't interested in creating the illusion that he owned every book he published; in other words, the books themselves became active and unique contributors to the Society by the fact of their being in the world rather than byproducts of it. It's always struck me as ironic that the Beat values espoused in City

Lights books (freedom, self-expression, non-conformity, spontaneity, etc.) come in such boring packages. One of the most satisfying things about seeing a bunch of Jargon Society books together is the differences between them. No rules, no template, no formulas, no reruns; each book is built around its content.

Williams' friend, painter Paul Ellsworth is credited with suggesting "jargon" as the name for the private press. He defined "jargon" as his "… own speech. My language, as opposed to the tribe's language." *Jargonelle* is a spring pear indigenous to France, and the OED defines "jargon" as the "inarticulate utterance of birds, or a vocal sound resembling it; twittering, chattering" or "unintelligible or meaningless talk or writing; nonsense, gibberish. (Often a term of contempt for something the speaker does not understand.)" One of the principles Martin Duberman stressed in *Black Mountain: An Exploration in Community* is that in a community, one loses one's self while discovering what one means by 'self' in the company of others. It was also practical to be a 'society' or 'organization' in the sixties because it made it easier to obtain nonprofit status, become tax-exempt, and receive support from the National Endowment for the Arts and other sources of funding.

From the outset, Olson's aversion to Patchen and Dahlberg's projects suggests that if Jargon was a society it was not necessarily an idyllic one, nor did the society purport to advance a unified aesthetic or politic. In Williams' words, if there is any commonality between Jargon's authors, it is that they are "homemade," "nonacademic," "non-urban" writers working on their own terms.

James Jaffe put it nicely when he wrote, "The Jargon Society was a reflection of its publisher, its publications the prismatic refractions of his interests and enthusiasms. And yet it wasn't all about Jonathan, the way so many private presses are all about their printers, whose publications are barely more than a pretext for yet another repetitive expression of their particular aesthetic. After all, Jonathan named it the Jargon 'Society' not the Jargon 'Press.'" Quite unlike other publishers who chose to name their companies after themselves (David Godine; Alfred Knopf; Peter Blum, et al.), Williams' "society" modestly diffuses the spotlight, illuminating the network of writers, artists, and artisans involved in every book.

Williams' father, Ben, who had been the class poet at Hendersonville's

Fruitland Academy when he was boy, had a lifelong interest in the dialect and vernacular speech of the South. He read *Uncle Remus, Porgy*,[2] Roark Bradford's *Ol' Man Adam an' His Chillun* and *Ol' King David an' the Philistine Boys*, and John Charles McNeill's *Lyrics from Cottonland* to him as a child. Lore, dialect and folk culture, particularly that of rural North Carolina where Williams lived a good part of his adult life, are as much a part of Jargon's evolution as is the international avant-garde. Like Duncan, Williams cherished the books of his childhood. Critic Walter Benjamin claims that "… every passion borders on the chaotic," and cautions bibliophiles, whose passion "… borders on the chaos of memories." Williams' library was more than a reflection of his intellectual pursuits; it was a working map of personal history. As a boy growing up in the South, his affinity for writers like H. P. Lovecraft and August Derleth brought him to Ben Abramson's Argus Bookstore, where he stumbled upon James Laughlin's New Directions books. He henceforth read everything Laughlin was publishing. In 1947, he left his elite secondary school where he worked as the editor of the school newspaper and served as captain of the tennis team to attend Princeton University.

As a student in New Jersey, he read about Patchen's disability in Miller's pamphlet *Patchen, Man of Anger and Light* and decided to contact Laughlin about the ailing writer, then wrote directly to Patchen himself offering to work as a secretary for free. Much to their mutual benefit, Patchen accepted the offer, and Williams went to Old Lyme, Connecticut, to spend a month and a half with Kenneth and his wife Miriam. Williams would type for five or six hours a day what Patchen dictated from bed. That manuscript, *Fables and Other Little Tales* (1953), became the first substantial book published by the Jargon Society (aside from Williams' self-published titles).

Persuaded to some degree by Patchen's anarchist ideology, Williams tired of his Ivy League surroundings, dropped out during his sophomore year, and headed north to New York City's Greenwich Village to learn etching, engraving, and printmaking. With a background in painting, a passion for the literature published by New Directions, an ongoing interest in Blake, Edward Lear, Lewis Carroll, and Stéphane Mallarmé, it is easy to see how his interest in publishing really took off when he eventually arrived at the Illinois Institute of Technology[3] to study typography, etching, and photography. It was there that he befriended painter Paul Ellsworth, who became an early collaborator

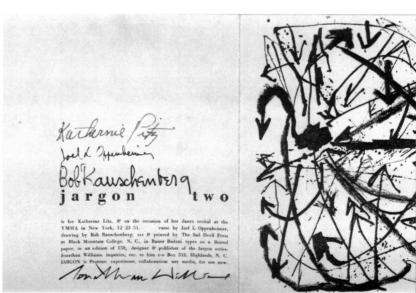

in the spring of 1951 when the two began exploring relationships between words and images. At the time, the Institute served as a haven for Jewish and other refugees from Europe, such as the great designer and photographer László Moholy-Nagy, a former instructor at the Bauhaus, and the Institute's current director. Williams studied typography under Lorna Zerner who had worked directly with the great typographer and book designer Jan Tschichold. He met potter and radical educator M.C. Richards, then serving as the head of the faculty at BMC, when she came to the institute to persuade students to enroll in a school known as a retreat for "free love, communism, and nigger-lovers." Signs began pointing back to the South.

Unsatisfied with student life in the windy city, Williams confided in his photography professor Harry Callahan, who put him in touch with his friend, Abstract Expressionist photographer Aaron Siskind, with whom he planned to co-facilitate a workshop at Black Mountain in the summer session of 1951 (Callahan later asked Siskind to join the faculty at the IIT, which he did, and went on to help establish one of the most innovative centers for the art of the book in America, Visual Studies Workshop in Rochester, New York). After his visit to San Francisco (discussed earlier), Williams enrolled in their summer course, the climate agreed with him, and he signed on for the autumn semester when he would begin studying under Olson.

Using the printing press on campus, Williams published the works of other students at the college, including Joel Oppenheimer and Robert Rauschenberg's collaborative broadside *The Dancer*, his collaboration with Ellsworth, and other student works by Dan Rice and Victor Kalos. Writers Fielding Dawson, Ed Dorn, John Wieners, and the illustrious Francine du Plessix Gray, were also his classmates.

Williams' quixotic days at BMC were cut short by the draft. After numerous attempts to gain conscientious objector status, he had to choose between up to five years behind bars for dodging the draft or the army. He chose the latter, and with the help of a sympathetic chaplain, Williams was transferred from his original post at a rifle company in Fort Knox, Kentucky to Stuttgart, Germany, where he worked at a hospital. Shortly after he arrived, he looked up the address of Dr. Walter Cantz, a printer in the city who had worked for Laughlin. Using a small inheritance left to him from a fellow soldier and friend named Charles Neal, he made a decision to take his vision of book publishing to the next level.

the maximus poems / 1-10

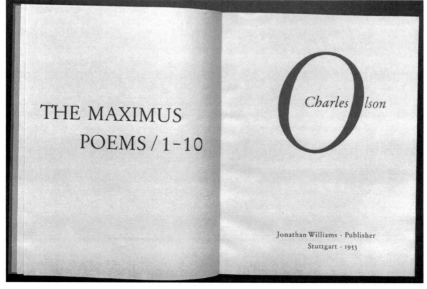

Dr. Cantz's workshop wasn't far from the hospital, and Williams' slight responsibilities afforded him adequate time to work with Cantz and Olson on the first edition of *The Maximus Poems I–X* (1953) as well as on Louis Zukofsky's *Some Time* (1954). Williams' first book of his own poems, *Four Stoppages/A Configuration* with graphics by Charles Oscar was printed in another shop across town, while Patchen's *Fables* (1953) and Creeley's early book, *The Immoral Proposition* (1953) illustrated by René Laubiès, were produced by a printer in nearby Karlsruhr. Without a doubt, these five books form the bedrock of what the Jargon Society was to become, and had Williams chosen never to publish another book, his accomplishments would be more than commendable. Of course, this was only the beginning.

Upon return to Black Mountain from Germany, he was delighted to be appointed the College's publisher, but BMC was bankrupt and about to close its doors forever after only twenty-four years of existence. The early books brought considerable attention to Williams and other emerging "outsider" artists of the era, setting a benchmark for the private press renaissance that began after WWII in America.

Other landmark books of the 1950s included Creeley's *All That Is Lovely In Men* (1955) and *The Whip* (1957); Duncan's *Letters* (perhaps my favorite book from Jargon, designed and printed by Claude Fredericks in 1954); Denise Levertov's *Overland to the Islands* (1958); Michael McClure's *Passage* (1956); Paul Metcalf's first book, *Will West* (1956); Oppenheimer's *The Dutiful Son* (1956); three books by Patchen: *Fables* (1953), *Hurrah for Anything* (1957) and *Poem-scapes* (1958); and of course Mina Loy's *Lunar Baedeker & Time-Tables* (1958).

Williams wasn't a printer, nor so far as I know, did he aspire to be one. This was one clear division between the Jargon Society and most private presses of the earlier half of the twentieth century. When he was starting out, there were artists' books, but no one would have called them that then. The Jargon Society didn't print or bind their books on the premises as did private presses of the past. Everything was outsourced.

Curiously enough, the design of the Jargon Society books does not reflect the direct influence of the Bauhaus, Swiss, or New Typography in any obvious way, nor do Williams' photographs resemble those of the Abstract Expressionists, nor do his mature poems appear to be derivative of Olson's or Creeley's. Despite his study with an all-star cast of European and American artists, Williams' aesthetic is singular.

Williams boldly calls the shots, and has produced over a hundred titles, including the first books by Lyle Bongé, Peyton Houston, Ronald Johnson, John Menapace, Thomas Meyer, Art Sinsabaugh, and Gilbert Sorrentino. He was also the first to publish the poetry of Guy Davenport and Buckminster Fuller, and responsible for the first American editions of Denise Levertov, Irving Layton, and Mina Loy. He brought British language artists Thomas A. Clark, Simon Cutts, and Ian Hamilton Finlay to a new audience. Their influence on Williams' imaginative bookmaking can be observed in *Fourteen Poets, One Artist* (poems by Paul Blackburn, Bob Brown, Edward Dahlberg, Max Feinstein, Allen Ginsberg, Paul Goodman, Denise Levertov, Walter Lowenfels, Edward Marshall, E. A. Navaretta, Joel Oppenheimer, Gilbert Sorrentino, Jonathan Williams, and Louis Zukofsky with drawings by Fielding Dawson). Because no two are alike, every book is, in its own way, a collaboration. The editors of Flood Editions have transcribed and published Duncan's correspondence with Fredericks when they released a trade edition of *Letters*. This captivating exchange demonstrates that book design, like writing itself, is an activity that requires a great deal of negotiation, revision, and correspondence.

Williams once commissioned Doyle Moore of the Finial Press to design and produce a concrete poem by the Scottish poet Edwin Morgan entitled the Siesta of a Hungarian Snake.

Since the book doesn't have any text, as such, I suspect that Morgan or Williams gave Moore a concept, rather than a manuscript, to interpret an edition with the assistance of his students in the Graphic Design Department at the University of Illinois at Champaign-Urbana. The Jargon Society Archive, housed in the Poetry Collection at the University at Buffalo contains five unaccredited mockups most likely produced by students. Communication Design Professor Tony Rozak, a former student of Moore's, told me that Williams often sent work to Moore, who would in turn bring projects to class. Rozak didn't remember Morgan's book in particular, but said that it was the kind of assignment that Moore often introduced to workshops.

The largest mockup is incorrectly titled THE SIESTA OF A SLEEP-ING HUNGARIAN SNAKE by "John" Morgan, "printed by Jonathan Williams, Highlands, North Carolina." Of course, the verb "printed" should be replaced with "published" because it was Moore and his students who did the actual printing. Part of the jargon that came out of the small press revolution of the sixties was the difference between being a publisher and an actual press operator (and it's not just an issue of semantics). For the first time, a publisher who had never seen or operated a printing press could say "I run a press" and be understood, but I digress ...

In this mockup, one sheet of transparent vellum lays over the poem, printed on smooth cream paper that is both folded and stapled into a black folder. The "poem" or "text" is an instable hodgepodge of S's and Z's that form the visual-acoustic shape of a snake's snoozing sound. The second largest mockup features a textured brown cover with a small serpentine spiral. A sheet of vellum covers the handsome title page and the red spiral reappears beside the gray title on deckled cream-colored stock sewn into the cover. Here, the poem is attributed to the correct author, and the colophon, "Printed as Jargon 1964, by Jonathan Williams ... " comes closer to an accurate description of the publisher's relationship to the printer, but doesn't quite do the trick. Inside the "sSZsZssZSZszS-ZszZSzsZSzszsz" recombination is printed on four layers of vellum that are pleasantly disfigured by the minutiae of misalignment between the leaves. The last page is printed in red on heavy cream-colored stock. The title page is grand but overwhelms the tiny text that begs for greater entropy. There is also a smaller version that is quite similar, with two exceptions: the text only appears on one page, and is purpose-

THE SIESTA OF A SLEEPING HUNGARIAN SNAKE   by JOHN MORGAN

printed as JARGON 1964 by Jonathan Williams, Highlands, North Carolina

lessly covered by a piece of vellum with a red printer's device. Like the first mockup, the S's and Z's are printed in a hodgepodge of fonts strung together by a thin purple line that curves through the slithering letters.

The most successful mockup is an accordion fold, but much longer than any of the others. Here the "ZSsz" combination begins in microscopic letters and as the pages unfold, the letters grow larger and larger until they slither (crop or drop) off the page, spiral, and dissolve at the tip of the tail. The title page is printed in blue and black sans serif allowing the tip of the poem to protrude ever so slightly below while the jacket combines an array of energetic wood type in beige with the title in blue running up the body of the "Z" that runs the length of the page.

Steve Clay's Granary Books of New York City and Simon Cutts and Erica Van Horn's Coracle of Ireland are two of the most inspiring small press operations active in the world today. Jargon's spirit has moved through dozens, perhaps hundreds of small presses, leaving a living legacy in its wake. In markedly different ways, Granary and Coracle's own histories blossom, while both pay homage to Williams' model. To varying degrees, all publishers are cultural sculptors, stone soup alchemists with a taste for the bizarre. The inherent flurry of correspondence between artists, writers, artisans, distributors, critics, readers, and fellow travelers puts the publisher at the center of an ever-widening network of relationships, or as Clay put it in his introduction to *When Will the Book be Done?* (2001): "The first item that I identify as a Granary Books publication was actually published by Origin Books in 1986—*Wee Lorine Niedecker* by Jonathan Williams. It embodies several elements that remain important to me now, some fifteen years later, among which is an acute awareness of the 'book' as a physical object. I write this in quotes because the work in question is not a book *per se* but presents a short poem by Mr. Williams, printed on a small piece of card stock contained within a printed envelope which is enclosed within yet another printed envelope. As such, its references include Williams' own Jargon Society ('the custodian of snowflakes'), a press which made ample use of a diverse array of publishing formats including folding cards, broadsides, postcards, pamphlets and books. The Jargon Society was one of two or three publishers which loomed behind the emerald curtain at the fore edge of my imagination as possible exemplars for an entity which had not yet been conceived."

The publisher is responsible for much of the mingling and coordination between parties whose relationships have an unfathomable effect on one another in the present and the course of the future of the arts and culture at large. When I sent Jonathan Williams some of the first books I published at Cuneiform Press nearly ten years ago, he responded with great enthusiasm and praise: *it's always interesting to see what happens when a young publisher gets the bug ... there's no telling how everything turns out.*

[1] According to Susan Finnel Ruff, David Ruff met Jonathan Williams when David was working with Stanley William Hayter at Atelier 17 in the Village in the late forties. Probably 1948 or 1949. The same sources also describe Williams meeting Patchen and his wife Miriam in New York and visiting when they were staying in Old Lyme, Connecticut. David and Holly left NY for San Francisco at the end of September, 1950. The Patchens followed and lived with David and Holly until they found a place they could rent. Sometime after that Jonathan also moved west.

[2] Williams' father was a friend of DuBose Heyward who used to summer in Hendersonville and was the author of the novel *Porgy*. Heyward's wife adapted the novel into a play which inspired Gerswhin's 1935 opera, *Porgy and Bess*, later adapted into the 1939 movie.

[3] Williams, and thus his biographers, always stated that Williams attended the Chicago Institute of Design. László Moholy-Nagy opened a design school the New Bauhaus in 1937. Due to financial problems the school briefly closed in 1938 and reopened in 1939 as the Chicago School of Design. In 1944, this became the Institute of Design. The Institute of Design became a part of Illinois Institute of Technology in 1949, becoming the first institution in the United States to offer a PhD in design.

THORNS CRAVEN

THE *WHITE TRASH COOKING* STORY

I graduated from Washington & Lee University in 1962. The 50th reunion of my class was held in the spring of 2012. W&L reunions are probably like most, but my fiftieth presented a particularly enjoyable opportunity for me. W&L has an organization, Friends of the Library, which holds its annual meeting during the reunion weekend. The Friends invite a member of the 50th reunion class to speak to that meeting about their library, and when I got the notice of that invitation and a solicitation to nominate a classmate my wife encouraged me to raise my hand.

I wrote to the chairman of the Friends and told him that if no better candidate emerged I was available and willing to speak to the annual meeting about "Poetry, Photography & White Trash Cooking: My Life as Treasurer of the Jargon Society." I got the assignment.

I treasure that call to review my years of service and servitude as Treasurer of the Jargon Society, the great gift of friendship that Jonathan Williams bestowed on my wife Perry and me, and to have control of the podium to tell the story of the first and last commercially successful venture of Jargon, Ernie Meckler's wonderful cookbook, *White Trash Cooking*.

The following is the portion of my speech to the Friends of the Library of Washington & Lee University devoted to the adventures related to the publication and sale of *White Trash Cooking*.

The early '80s were enormously successful for Jargon's publications. Many books, many get-togethers, many bills. From the beginning there were no employees of Jargon, but in 1984, Jonathan hired Tom Patterson to be the executive director. Tom is a writer/art critic/curator and has paid particular attention to "outsider art." Jonathan was essentially bringing in a deputy charged with supplementing his own activities in traveling, finding, recording, and preserving the work of individuals who either shunned or ignored attention.

One of Tom's assignments was to assemble and mount an exhibition of Outsider Art and that was accomplished in Winston-Salem in 1985. As was our custom, the Jargon Board of Directors scheduled its annual meeting during the time of this exhibition. Board meetings were generally more social events than business ones, but Jonathan generally reported on projects planned and underway and during this period we were always recruiting new board members and friends who might make significant financial contributions to support the publications and exhibitions. At this meeting, however, we were running out of steam, and I recall that Whitney Jones and I were worn out with the hand-to-mouth existence that we had been leading for the past few years, and we wanted to direct the conversation to the reality of our circumstances.

Our board meetings were directed by Whitney. Our financial patrons were never shy about expressing their preferences, and as the meetings went on, Jonathan usually swiveled in his chair until his back was turned on the rest of the board and his gaze was fixed on the ceiling. As we talked about winding up a long and glorious run, it seemed like the life of the Jargon Society as it existed then was coming to a close. Our principal backers said they had put in about all the money they wanted to spend and that if we couldn't find other supporters, we should shut down. Jonathan tolerated this conversation as long as he could, and then, ignoring what had been said, put a small cardboard box on the table and said he would like to show us something. Inside the box was the raw manuscript of *White Trash Cooking*, the recipes and photographs of Ernest Matthew Mickler.

Ernie fit the mold of almost everyone who had been found and preserved by Jonathan and Jargon. He was from northern Florida, and despite his MFA from Mills he spent his life as an itinerant caterer. He was collecting recipes and taking pictures as he went, and at every dinner he served he would ask hosts and guests if they knew anyone in publishing who would be interested in his book. Once they heard the title they generally changed the subject. And Ernie had gotten the same response from the major cook book publishing houses—change the title and we might be interested, but there is no way we would publish a book called *White Trash Cooking*.

That changed at a dinner party in Key West where a guest who was involved in publishing medical text books heard Ernie's pitch and told him that the book might be just the thing to interest his friend Jonathan Williams. That started the box on its journey to our board meeting.

Jonathan said he understood that Jargon fundraising was exhausted. His first thought was to try to solicit investors in the project, but realized this was inconsistent with our non-profit status. So he turned to the idea of borrowing the necessary funds from friends of Jargon, 10 at $2,000 each was his first pitch. His enthusiasm was sufficient to bring us back from the edge of dissolution and inspire two board members to write checks sufficient to cover the expense of an initial run of 5,000 copies.

One of the lenders, Phil Hanes, asked that he be provided with as many as 300 copies as soon as they were printed. Phil had an enormous Christmas list and he wanted to send copies to all his friends. We managed to satisfy his request and copies went all over the country as Phil's Christmas greeting to his friends. Those friends included Harper Lee, William Fulbright, Helen Hayes, North Carolina's Governor Jim Hunt and Senator Jesse Helms. Lots of influential people were looking at the recipe for "Big Reba's Rainbow Icebox Cake" that year, and they were sending Phil thank you notes and telling their friends.

Shamelessly using those notes as blurbs, review copies went out around the country. I think *Vogue* might have been the first magazine to give a little notice to *White Trash Cooking,* but it was soon followed by *USA Today, People,* and all the places you would like to be mentioned. Before long, Ernie was cooking chicken feet on the David Letterman show and we had two more runs of 10,000 copies each. And now we were starting to get calls and letters from the publishers who had said "no way" to Ernie a short time previously.

Dealing with good fortune was such a novel experience for Whitney and me that for a while we enjoyed it. Having money come pouring in and being able to pay our bills on time and in full was exciting. But we knew we were on a wave and we had no idea of when it might break. For the long term, we wanted to get the books into the hands of an organization that had the means, ability and interest to keep it in print and on shelves in bookstores.

As we fielded inquiries from Random House, Bantam, Workman, and many other specialty publishers, we decided to go to New York. We made appointments with four or five publishers over a two day period and presented ourselves to hear their pitch.

My most vivid memory is of sitting in a cramped office at Random House, Whitney and I along with four or five editors and editorial assistants, listening to them talk about how much they loved the book, about how much they wanted to buy the rights to print it from us, and how they wouldn't change that much—maybe tweak the title a little and take out the pictures, but "really, not that much." While we were talking a handsome man in a beautiful suit stopped and hovered in the doorway. The office fell completely silent and everyone gave devoted attention to this guy. He said, "I love your book," and then moved on down the hall. The cast in our room vibrated with excitement and told us that was a very good sign. "What would we expect for the rights? You're not going to make this an auction, are you?"

We took our leave and had a coffee downstairs before moving on to our next appointment. Whitney asked me if I knew who the guy in the suit was. "No idea." "Well, he is the hottest guy in publishing today. He doesn't read books, but he can feel them. Apparently he has felt *White Trash Cooking* and it feels good."

Then Whitney went on to give me this insight: "We've got them right where we want them. They have never met and dealt with anyone like us." "What do you mean?" "Well, you and I aren't going to get a dime out of this deal. And they have never met anyone who wasn't getting something." This analysis put us into a very good mood, and we went on to three or four meetings that were much like the first, absent the hovering man in a suit. We never met another one of those. We also never got a publishers lunch at the Four Seasons or drinks at the Algonquin. But when we got home we started getting letters offering $50,000, then $60,000 and going up. All of the offers made clear that the buyer retained the right to make changes in the content of the book.

As we were pondering all of this, wondering what to do, we were hearing on the one side from Jonathan that we could never agree to any changes, and on another side from Ernie who was getting 50% of the net on our sales and who had never had access to that much money in his life, do whatever you need to do to keep this stream flowing.

A wonderful thing happened. We got in the mail a 12–15 page proposal, bound in a dime store clear binder, from Phil Wood and Ten Speed Press. The proposal was cast to show why the only publisher worthy of taking on our book was Ten Speed. This was done mostly with photographs. There were pictures of the principals involved, most prominently the founder and publisher of Ten Speed, Phil Wood, a man whose wardrobe consisted of at least a hundred Hawaiian shirts, with matching ties for business occasions. There was a picture of the Ten Speed kitchen featuring their open refrigerator packed to bursting with all of the ingredients in the *White Trash* recipes. For me the coup-de-grace was the picture of their mail room which featured two waste cans. One was labeled "Trash" and the other was labeled "White Trash."

Ten Speed also offered substantially more money than anyone else, a higher royalty than anyone else, and proposed only one change in the book as we had produced it: the title page which identified the publisher as "The Jargon Society" would be altered to show that it was also published by Ten Speed Press.

That was all we needed. Let's make a deal. Unfortunately, Jonathan thought at this point we needed the services of a literary agent and he brought such a creature into our negotiations. I felt at the time like the captain of the QE II. We had gotten this ship into the harbor, up the river, and next to the pier, and now there was someone who was standing on the bridge saying "put that rope on that post over there," and "now give me 10% of everything you get out of this for the rest of your life." But it didn't seem to bother Phil Wood and Ten Speed, so we ended up signing a contract and looking forward to sales far beyond our 25,000. I think the total, 25 years later, is around 700,000!

It was not all beer and skittles along this road. But we were having fun and a steady flow of actual income made lots of things possible within Jargon that had never happened before. Jonathan and Tom were actually paid a small stipend for the work they performed. Printers of other books were paid in full. The Board of Directors held its next meeting in Berkeley, hosted by Ten Speed Press, and had a celebration featuring Ernie's cooking. Ernie wrote a sequel, designed with help from Jonathan and Tom and earned enough money that he bought a house.

Sometime during this sunny period, the occasional cloud appeared. As I understand it, the lady on the cover of *White Trash Cooking* was autographing copies of the book in a drugstore in her Alabama home town and somehow a lawyer got into the line. Before he was finished with his conversation with her, she had become, in the words of the letter he sent to Ernie, to the Jargon Society, and to our distributor, the Inland Book Company, "Your flagrant violation of this person's dignity and privacy has caused her severe mental trauma and chronic anxiety." We were directed to stop publication and distribution and to inform the lawyer within five days of what we were going to do to compensate his client for her damages.

Phil Wood and I talked about this development on the phone. He pointed out that the contract between Jargon and Ten Speed called for indemnification should Ten Speed be held liable for any action arising from publication of *White Trash Cooking.* I took a quick look at our contract with Ernie, the only contract with an author which Jargon had ever reduced to writing. It contained a clause in which Ernie agreed to indemnify Jargon. Phil told me that he and his lawyer had handled matters like this in the past and asked if we would let them handle this one. An easy "yes."

Ernie recalled that he had gotten permission to take the picture of our lady on the cover as she sold watermelons from the back of her pickup, and he knew that he had gotten that permission in writing but for the life of him he couldn't find it.

The first offer to go from California to Alabama was to pay our cover lady $1,000 and give her an all-expense paid weekend in Memphis. Rejected, and the attorney countered with a demand of $3.2 million. When we discussed this development, Phil Wood asked me where I thought the $3.2 figure came from. "Well, Phil. I see the lawyer at his desk. He's drinking a beer and he turns the bottle around in his hand. He looks at the label. '3.2, that sounds about right.'"

The case was dismissed with the payment of $50,000. The only consolation I could offer Ernie, who had this amount deducted from his future royalties, was that for the first time in his life he could afford it.

I can't recall how long it was before the next letter from a lawyer arrived. This one came from counsel to the Junior League of Charleston. Their claim was that recipes which had appeared in their famous cookbook, *Charleston Receipts,* appeared verbatim in *White Trash Cooking.* Phil called to tell me this and to give me the page numbers for the recipes. I looked them up and compared them to the Junior League book. The first thing I noticed was that they were similar, but it did seem that our book had margarine where theirs had butter. And the second thing was that they were mostly recipes for squirrel and possum.

Phil assured me that his lawyer did advise that recipes are subject to copyright. He reminded me to remind Ernie about indemnification, and he asked for suggestions about what to do next. I thought this situation provided us with a very good opportunity.

"Phil, I think you should get Ernie and go to New York or wherever you think would be a good place to be interviewed and hold a press conference. You can announce that the Junior League of Charleston is petitioning the US District Court in South Carolina to declare that they are the original white trash. You can add that you plan to invite all the members of the Junior League of Charleston to a cooking contest, our recipes for squirrels and possums against theirs."

Phil called me back to say that his lawyer wouldn't let him do that, and eventually $50,000 was offered and accepted and that lawsuit was dismissed.

Phil Wood died last year. A great man with a wonderful spirit. Just look at the list of books he published and you will conclude that. We had a long conversation on the phone several months before he died. During that chat I asked him if he had any regrets. "Only one. That we didn't go to New York and have that press conference."

Me. I've got no regrets.

TOM PATTERSON

IF YOU CAN KILL A SNAKE WITH IT, IT *AIN'T ART*— THE ART HISTORY OF A MAVERICK POET-PUBLISHER

Eddie Owens Martin (aka St. EOM): Five Pasaquoyan Masks, early 1980s, painted concrete, James Harold Jennings Amazon, late 1980s, painted wood.

[The following essay was originally written as a contextual backdrop for the exhibition *If You Can Kill a Snake with It, It Ain't Art: Selected Works from the Collection of Jonathan Williams* which I curated during what turned out to be the last year of Williams' life. The premiere venue was Appalachian State University's Turchin Center for Visual Arts, in Boone, North Carolina, where the exhibition opened on March 7, 2008, the day before Williams' seventy-ninth birthday. As it turned out, sadly, the occasion found him in deteriorating health and close to his home in a hospital where he remained for nine more days until his death on the night of March 16. The exhibition remained at the Turchin Center until early June and, at this writing, is on view at the Green Hill Center for North Carolina Art in Greensboro, North Carolina (January 23–March 22, 2009). This essay is envisioned as the central text for a color-illustrated catalog of the exhibition projected for eventual publication by the Jargon Society. Williams remained very much alive at the time of the essay's completion, and the concluding paragraphs provide a snapshot of his final months among us mortals. Accordingly, I've chosen to retain the original present tense, referencing Williams throughout as a still-living presence, as in many ways he will remain for those of us fortunate enough to have known him.

—Tom Patterson, January 2009]

To worship beauty for its own sake is narrow and one surely cannot derive from it that aesthetic pleasure which comes from finding beauty in the commonest of things.

—Imogen Cunningham, as quoted in
the introduction to Williams' *Blues
& Roots/Rue & Bluets: A Garland for
the Appalachians*

If you can kill a snake with it, it ain't art.
—Lyle Bongé

Lyle Bongé's bodacious zinger of an esthetic credo is one of the more memorable lines in Jonathan Williams' collection of favorite quotations, a bit of inspired nonsense reflecting a strain of southern-fried dada humor that Williams and Bongé both appreciate. Since it plays on the perennial issue of how art is defined, it seems a pretty good fit for an exercise that's all about Williams' eye and what attracts it.

Williams' literary and publishing endeavors have been fairly well documented and celebrated in print and in several exhibitions.[1] Less widely recognized and appreciated to date is the extent of his engagement with visual art, and the fact that he has been involved with art and artists for at least as long as he's been writing poetry. An examination of his career's visual dimension reveals important connections between his art pursuits and his more widely known efforts and enthusiasms. Something of the range of his visual sensibilities is reflected in the invariably handsome, always distinctive designs of the Jargon books he has published over the years.[2]

He has also maintained an active career as a photographer since the early 1950s, specializing in informal portraits of artists and writers and views of artists' graves and visionary-art environments.[3] Over the last sixty-some years he has been steadily collecting objects that have caught his sharp eye or been given to him by the many artists he has known during that extended interval. His collection is born of friendship as much as esthetic affinity, and the scale of its holdings is consistent with domestic space, always conducive to close viewing.

I've had the pleasure of getting to know this collection over more than thirty years of friendship and professional association with Williams and his companion, fellow poet Thomas Meyer. I've visited their mountainside home in Macon County, North Carolina, on a few dozen occasions, including five or six visits over the last year, specifically for the purpose of taking a more systematic look at what's usually displayed on the walls, shelves, floors and tabletops. I've inventoried more than three hundred pieces in the house and a smaller nearby cottage on the property, and from that number I selected about two hundred outstanding ones for the traveling exhibition *If You Can Kill a Snake With It, It Ain't Art*. In this essay I hope to sketch out something of the personal history behind this remarkably wide-ranging collection and comment on how it has evolved.

Williams' literary and visual interests have been intertwined from the beginning. The first artworks he found appealing were illustrations in his favorite children's books—L. Frank Baum's Oz series, Rudyard Kipling's *Just So Stories*, and Beatrix Potter's self-illustrated tales. Growing up an only child in Washington, D.C., he attended St. Alban's School, the prestigious private academy where senior contemporaries among the student body included Gore Vidal. Williams' memories of his six years at St. Alban's include classes in which art teacher Dean Stambaugh instructed ten or fifteen students in still-life and *plein-air* landscape painting and led them on field trips to the Phillips Collection. As an adolescent, before he began to cultivate literary ambitions, Williams aspired to be a painter.

In the early 1940s his parents bought a forty-acre farm in the Southern Appalachians where they built the house he still lives in, about ten miles outside the resort town of Highlands. His father, a North Carolina native and professional filing-system designer, gave the property the poetic name Skywinding Farm, and it initially served as the family's second home.

Skywinding Farm Gate, *late 1990s, Mark Steinmetz.*

Williams took advantage of their summers there by working directly from nature, sketching waterfalls and other features of the local landscape. Back at St. Albans in the fall, he made oil paintings based on these sketches. Surviving works from his teens also include drawings of scenes from Disney's *Fantasia* and a creepy surrealist landscape painting inspired by H. P. Lovecraft, a favorite writer in those years.

After graduating from St. Albans, Williams entered Princeton University. He recalls the year and a half he spent there as a fallow period for his painting but acknowledges having absorbed useful insights into Byzantine, classical Chinese, and Italian Renaissance art in the art-history classes. It was also at Princeton that he made his first forays into art collecting. He bought an affordable Henri Matisse lithograph of a woman's face from a traveling print dealer who regularly visited the Ivy League schools. And— as a "bribe" to keep him at his studies, according to Williams—his father bankrolled his purchase of Georges Rouault's aquatint etching *The Yellow Clown* from a New York gallery.

Williams used the Rouault etching as an excuse to meet a writer and artist whose work he had recently discovered, namely Kenneth Patchen. Having read of Patchen's interest in French Modernism, Williams wrote to him at his home in Old Lyme, Connecticut, and offered to lend him his fresh art acquisition. Patchen wrote back to accept the offer, and Williams hand-delivered the Rouault print to him. (Williams isn't sure when he finally got it back but thinks it was probably in the late 1950s.) Around the time of their initial meeting, Williams bought the first of several limited-edition Patchen books he has owned, each incorporating Patchen's hand-painted images.

Williams didn't like Princeton, and he dropped out in 1949, but he persevered with his art studies. Returning to D.C. for a few months, he briefly studied painting with Carl Knaths at the Phillips Collection. He spent most of 1950 in New York, living in the West Village and studying graphic art with Stanley William Hayter at Hayter's Atelier 17. Early in 1951 Williams left New York for Chicago, where he enrolled for one semester at the Institute of Design. It was there he produced his final statement as a painter—an untitled abstract-expressionist exercise he made by dropping a bucket of tar out a second-story window onto a sheet of white cardboard. He's still fond enough of it that it hangs in his home alongside some of his favorite contemporary folk-art pieces. Also during his semester in the Windy City, at the site of a Louis Sullivan building undergoing demolition, Williams found a fragment of Sullivan-designed terra cotta ornamentation, a segment of stylized vines in relief, which he subsequently framed and still prominently displays in his home.

During his brief stint at the Institute of Design, Williams made connections with several individuals who would influence his future creative trajectory. One was M. C. Richards, a writer who would later become a potter, and from whom Williams would collect a few distinctive vessels. Williams met Richards when she paid a visit to the institute on behalf of Black Mountain College, where she was then teaching.[4] She was a charismatic figure, and her presentation about the school left a strong impression on Williams. The other two key influences on his path to Black Mountain were photographers Art Sinsabaugh and Harry Callahan, who taught advanced photography courses at the institute. It was their work—Callahan's in particular—that prompted Williams to take an active interest in

Eleanor, Chicago, *Harry Callahan, 1953.*

photography. As a beginner at the medium, he was ineligible for enrollment in their Chicago classes, but Callahan and fellow lensman Aaron Siskind had been hired to teach under less restrictive circumstances that summer at Black Mountain. Williams followed Callahan's suggestion that he sign up to study with them there. Over the next few years Williams would buy the first of a number of prints he owns by these photographers.

Late in the spring of 1951, before settling in at Black Mountain, Williams traveled to the West Coast. During a visit to Big Sur he spent a few hours with Henry Miller, who gave him a small blue jewel of a watercolor. In San Francisco Williams collaborated with printmaker David Ruff, whom he knew from Hayter's New York atelier, to produce fifty copies of a broadsheet in which a copper-plate engraving by Ruff accompanied Williams' poem *Garbage Litters the Iron Face of the Sun's Child*. Williams doesn't think much of the poem, in retrospect, but the broadsheet became the first publication of the Jargon Press, an operation which from the start paired contemporary visual art and writing. Williams brought copies of Jargon #1 with him to Black Mountain, where he quickly began learning what he could about photography from Callahan and Siskind. A secondhand Rolleiflex that Siskind located for Williams became his primary art-making instrument, replaced in subsequent years by other similar cameras and eventually augmented by various Polaroid models.

More influential than any visual artist on the creative transformation Williams underwent at Black Mountain was poet Charles Olson, who taught writing and related courses at the college and had recently been installed as its rector. In interviews Williams has acknowledged the powerful impression Olson's poetry, dynamic personality, and teaching made on him as a young man still in search of his métier. Stimulated in part by Olson's classes, Williams began to devote increasing attention to his own poetic efforts and to his fledgling press, an enterprise that Olson encouraged. In Olson's classes Williams met fellow student Joel Oppenheimer, who had learned to operate Black Mountain's in-house letterpress. The two combined forces to produce 150 copies of the second Jargon broadsheet, in which Oppenheimer's poem *The Dancer* is augmented with a drawing by Robert Rauschenberg, then an art student at the college. The notebook-size, abstract drawing consists mainly of freehanded arrows pointing in myriad directions. Like many other works reproduced in subsequent

Jargon publications, it entered Williams' collection, although he sold it a few years ago.

Williams retained his student status at Black Mountain beyond the summer session and into the following academic year. In 1952 he and Oppenheimer collaborated to produce the third and fourth Jargon imprints—*The Double-Backed Beast* (text by Victor Kalos and drawings by Dan Rice, both Black Mountain students) and *Red/Gray* (poems by Williams and a drawing by Paul Elsworth, formerly a fellow student at the Institute of Design). Later that year, though, Williams' activities at Black Mountain were interrupted by the draft. Having been classified a conscientious objector; he was assigned to non-combatant work for the U.S. Army Medical Corps in Stuttgart, Germany, for a term ending in 1953. During that interval, he used an inheritance of $1,500 from a recently deceased family friend to finance small-edition Jargon books by Creeley, Olson, Patchen, and himself. Accompanying the text for Creeley's book, *The Immoral Proposition*, were drawings by René Laubies, a French artist whom Creeley knew and Williams met while in Europe. (Williams still owns a Laubies painting from the same period). Williams rendered the calligraphy for Olson's *The Maximus Poems/1–10*, and Patchen created unique paintings for each of fifty copies making up the special edition of his *Fables & Other Little Tales*. Drawings for Williams' book, *Four Stoppages/A Configuration*, were made by Charles Oscar, an artist he had met at Black Mountain.

Williams made one art purchase while in Germany, albeit at no significant expense. At a Stuttgart gallery he paid twenty-five dollars for a photograph by László Moholy-Nagy, which he sold about forty years later for a substantial profit.

After returning to the United States in 1954, Williams made Skywinding Farm his home base but over the next couple of years traveled often to Black Mountain, about 100 miles to the east. At the time the college was on its last legs, its population reduced to a bare-bones faculty and a handful of students. He made a number of photographs at the school in those years, and his Jargon Press published new books by Creeley (*All that is Lovely in Men*, 1955) and Olson (*The Maximus Poems/11–22*, 1956), both still teaching there. Black Mountain's final year, 1956, also witnessed Jargon's publication of four more books, including *Will West*, the first novel by Paul Metcalf, then living near the college. The other three were by poets who lived far from North Carolina and had no connection with Black Mountain—Louis Zukofsky, Irving Layton, and Michael McClure, for whose first book, *Passage*, Williams created special calligraphy.

Visual artists among Black Mountain's last holdouts included Joseph Fiore and Dan Rice, both nominally teachers at that time, as well as painting student Jorge Fick. A couple of Rice's works on paper from that period remain in Williams' collection, as do two small, later paintings by Fick. Rice provided drawings for Creeley's second Jargon book, and more than a decade later made drawings that Williams reproduced on the cover of Ross Feld's Jargon-published *Plum Poems* (1972). Rice's work bore the boldly gestural stamp of New York School Abstract Expressionism, two of whose leading exponents—Willem de Kooning and Franz Kline—had taught at Black Mountain in the years before Williams arrived there. Abstract Expressionism's leading critical advocate Clement Greenberg had also taught briefly at Black Mountain prior to Williams' arrival and Williams remembers reading Greenberg when the school was in its final months of operation.

After Black Mountain closed, Williams started to establish the pattern of geographically wide-ranging activity he would follow for the next forty years. Crisscrossing the country in a Volkswagen[5] loaded with Jargon publications, he offered them for sale at bookstores and universities where he arranged to give readings. Staying with friends and literary or art-world connections along the way, he subsidized his publishing efforts and his travels by collecting fees for his readings, soliciting paid subscriptions for forthcoming books, and occasionally selling photographs or other works from his growing art collection.

Photography began to occupy more of Williams' attention in the late 1950s, thanks in part to connections he made on another trip to the West Coast. He stopped on the way and met Frederick Sommer, then living in Flagstaff, Arizona; and shortly thereafter met Sommer's fellow photographers Ansel Adams, Wynn Bullock, Brett Weston, and Edward Weston, all living in or near Big Sur at the time. Williams acquired photographs by all of them, and he made his own photographs of them, as well as informal portrait shots of other writers and artists he saw during that trip. He revisited Henry Miller at Big Sur, and Kenneth Patchen, then living in Palo Alto, and acquired several Patchen watercolors of fanciful beings. Within the next

Mount Williamson from Manzanar, Sierra Nevada California, *1944, Ansel Adams.*

year he published Miller's *The Red Notebook* (1958), with drawings by Miller and an informal portrait photo of the author by Bullock; and Patchen's self-illustrated second and third Jargon books—*Hurrah for Anything* (1957) and *Poem-Scapes* (1958).

Williams also visited Los Angeles during that West Coast trip, motivated in part by a desire to see and photograph Simon Rodia's domestic yard environment known as the Watts Towers—Gaudiesque spires encrusted with broken crockery and rising above the city's Watts neighborhood. An Italian immigrant and self-taught architect, Rodia had several years earlier abandoned the site. Williams' visit to Rodia's Towers marked the beginning of an ongoing interest in vernacular art environments.

In keeping with his other activities of the early post-Black Mountain years, Williams published several books that reflected his growing interest in photography. Reproduced in the eleven other books published under his Jargon imprint from the late 1950s through the mid-'60s were images by

Bill Traylor: Untitled (terrapin), *1940s, ink, watercolor, and pencil on cardboard.*

his former teachers Callahan and Siskind, as well as photographs by Robert Schiller, Sinsabaugh, Henry Holmes Smith, Sommer, and Williams himself.

The latter part of 1957 and the beginning of 1958 found Williams back in D.C. and frequenting the Library of Congress in order to research the Etowah Indian Mounds, the 1,000-year-old remains of an important American Indian city and ceremonial complex on the Etowah River in northwest Georgia. It was a site that held special personal meaning for him due to its location on land that in modern times had been owned by his maternal grandmother Georgia Tumblin, until its acquisition by the Georgia Historical Commission and designation as a state historic site in 1953. In his youth, several years before he began collecting modern and contemporary art, Williams had collected carved stone tools and other artifacts he found on his grandparents' farm—objects that remain in his possession.

During the interval in Washington, Williams met Ronald Johnson, an aspiring poet studying literature at George Washington University. Their common interests and mutual attraction soon developed into a relationship as domestic and traveling companions that lasted for ten years, during which Williams' Jargon Press would publish Johnson's first book. From the late 1950s into the early 1960s they lived for periods of a few years or several months at a time in New York, North Carolina, and England. One of their early joint ventures, in 1961, was an ambitiously conceived hiking trip along 1,400 miles of the Appalachian Trail, from Georgia to New York State. The first of many extended walks Williams would take, it significantly influenced his view of the world and had a big impact on his work, yielding what he has referred to as his peripatetic poetic method: "always on the go, always on the look-out."[6] He took the same approach to collecting art— ears and eyes open, picking up what caught his attention and captured his fancy. The sources and subjects in his writings run the gamut from high culture to vernacular culture—"refinement" to "vulgarity"—a range also reflected in his visual esthetic, as evidenced by the art he lives with.

Late in 1961 Williams and Johnson made their first trip to England, which they liked well enough to continue living in London throughout 1962. Among the new friends and acquaintances they made there was American expatriate artist R. B. Kitaj, with whom Williams soon collaborated on a couple of publications: Kitaj created the wrap-around cover collage for Williams' book *Lullabies Twisters Gibbers Drags* (1963), and a series of sixteen silk-screens to accompany Williams' poetic sequence inspired by the music of Gustav Mahler. The latter collaboration, *Mahler Becomes Beisbol*, was issued in 1965 by London's Marlborough Gallery as a limited-edition folio. More than ten years later Williams' reproduced Kitaj's pastel portrait of British poet Basil Bunting as the cover of the Jargon festschrift *Madeira and Toasts for Basil Bunting's 75th Birthday* (1977).

Williams would return to England often over the next forty years, eventually establishing a regular summer residence in the Pennine Dales of Cumbria. His headquarters there since the late 1960s has been a farmhouse whose purchase and restoration he oversaw for its American owner Donald B. Anderson, an oil-company executive and arts patron from New Mexico.

In England Williams was also introduced to native British artists in whose work he took a strong interest, including writer and artist Mervyn

Peake as well as visual artists John Furnival, Glen Baxter, and David Hockney, all now represented in Williams' collection. In the 1970s Furnival made drawings for Thomas Meyer's *The Bang Book* and *Staves Calends Legends*, both published by Jargon, as well as three of the Jargon postcards Williams began publishing after 1975. Much later, in 1983, Baxter would provide the cover drawing and frontispiece for Williams' *The Fifty-two Clerihews of Clara Hughes*, which I published in Atlanta under the Pynyon Press imprint. And Hockney sketched an informal portrait of a mustachioed Williams smoking a cigar and looking intense—a drawing he gave to Williams.

The 1960s and '70s also brought Williams important new contacts among artists and literati back in the United States, including several he met during residencies at the Aspen Institute in Colorado and North Carolina's Penland School of Crafts. Three key figures whose paths he first crossed during those years—writer Guy Davenport (also an adept draftsman) and photographers Ralph Eugene Meatyard and Guy Mendes—all happened to live in Lexington, Kentucky. Williams took an interest in Meatyard's photographs after a mutual friend introduced the two men while Williams was visiting Lexington in 1960 or '61.

Davenport's mail order for a Jargon book in 1963 prompted Williams to strike up what became a long-running correspondence with him, and the two met in person for the first time in 1965.[7] In the following year Williams published Davenport's book *Flowers and Leaves*, which featured two of Meatyard's photographs including an author's portrait. In 1969 Williams reprinted Davenport's essay "Do You Have a Poem Book on E.E. Cummings?"—originally published in the *National Review*—as a sixteen-page chapbook illustrated with one of Davenport's drawings. That same year, Davenport's portrait drawings of Ferdinand Cheval and Raymond Isidore—the creators of visionary yard environments that Williams and Ronald Johnson had visited in France—appeared in Johnson's Jargon-published booklet *The Spirit Walks, The Rocks Will Talk*. One of Meatyard's photographs was reproduced on the cover of writer Douglas Woolf's *Spring of the Lamb*, a Jargon book from 1972. And in 1974 Williams published Meatyard's *The Family Album of Lucybelle Crater*, a book of deadpan portraits of the photographer's friends and fellow Lexingtonians (including Williams, Davenport, and Meatyard's wife) all wearing grotesque rubber Halloween masks.

Carl McKenzie: Devil Family with Serpent, *early 1980s, metal wire carved and painted wood.*

It was also in 1974 that Williams published his first collaboration with Mendes, a photographer, writer and—at that time—relatively recent graduate of the University of Kentucky. In the fold-out poster publication, *Who Is Little Enis?*, Williams' uproariously bawdy poem in homage to Carlos Toadvine, aka "Little Enis"—an overweight, alcoholic rhythm'n'blues singer who performed at strip clubs and honky-tonks in and around Lexington— is imprinted on a blue-hued, stylized phallus under Mendes' photo-portrait of Enis posed in front of his Cadillac. A few years later, in 1979, several of Mendes' photographs would be featured in Williams' Jargon-published collection *Elite/Elate Poems (1971–1975)*. Making another appearance in Mendes' cover photo, Little Enis poses with his guitar and a group of strippers in front of a Lexington strip-club marquee.

In 1965, during a visit to Kentucky's Berea College, Williams first saw the late Doris Ulmann's Depression-era photographic portraits of rural mountain people. Ulmann's assistant during her arduous travels in the Southern Appalachians had been John Jacob Niles, the American ballad singer and folk-music scholar. A visit with Niles in 1967 at his home in Lexington convinced Williams that the photos needed to be widely seen, leading to Jargon's publication of *The Appalachian Photographs of Doris Ulmann* (1971). Williams owns a print of one of the photographs, a portrait of "Aunt" Lou Kitchen at her spinning wheel, made after Ulmann's death, from one of her glass negatives archived at Berea.

Another region-centric photography book that Williams published in the early 1970s is *The Sleep of Reason* (1974), devoted to Lyle Bongé's darkly outrageous images of Mardi Gras in New Orleans. Like Williams, Bongé is a native southerner—in his case from Biloxi, Mississippi—who attended Black Mountain College. In 1964 he and Williams drove across North Carolina with the aim of collaborating on a book inspired by their travels. The project was eventually shelved, but Williams still has a couple of the photographs Bongé made during their travels, including one that eventually made its way into the Jargon-published collection *The Photographs of Lyle Bongé* (1982).

While continuing to pursue his photographic interests, including his own camera work, Williams began to pay increasingly close attention to contemporary variations on folk or vernacular art. As early as 1960 or 1961, not long after he first saw Simon Rodia's Watts Towers in Los Angeles, Williams visited folk potter Lanier Meaders at his shop in Cleveland, Georgia, about fifty-five miles from Williams' home in North Carolina. Making his wares with clay dug from a local river bank, Meaders carried on a tradition begun by his grandfather. Williams bought one of the comically grotesque face jugs for which the potter later became widely known. As evidence of Williams' sustained attention to such art forms, more than thirty years later he bought two more elaborate figural pots by Lanier's nephew Clete Meaders.

In 1969 Williams visited self-taught artist Clarence Schmidt's ridgetop environment in New York's Catskill Mountains. By that time Schmidt's slapdash seven-story house had been destroyed in a fire, but Williams recalls finding the artist at work coating the trees in his "Silver Forest" with aluminum paint, and he documented the visit in photographs.[8]

In Wolfe County, Kentucky, in the early 1970s, Williams met self-taught wood sculptor Edgar Tolson. A lapsed preacher who had fathered twenty-two children and served a year in prison, Tolson began making stylized figural carvings in the late 1950s while recovering from a stroke. In the ensuing years his work was discovered by art professors at the University of Kentucky and began to gain a national following. The tableau that Williams bought from Tolson, depicting Adam's and Eve's expulsion from the Garden of Eden remains one of the best and most important contemporary folk-art pieces in his collection.

Three untitled pieces by Ralph Griffin, ca 1990, painted wood.

William Anthony isn't a self-taught artist like Tolson or a number of others whose work Williams started collecting in the 1970s and 1980s, but Anthony's signature style plays on the figure-drawing mistakes most commonly made by people with neither artistic training nor talent. Williams' friend and fellow writer Gilbert Sorrentino introduced him to Anthony's work around the mid-1970s. Shortly thereafter Williams published Anthony's first book *Bible Stories* (1978), a satirical version of the Old Testament distilled into fewer than thirty pages of hilariously bad drawings and brief texts, with an introduction by Sorrentino. Williams would eventually acquire nearly a dozen of Anthony's drawings and paintings, and in 1988 he published the retrospective collection *Bill Anthony's Greatest Hits: Drawings 1963–1987,* with an introduction by art historian and critic Robert Rosenblum. Among its diverse offerings, the latter volume features Anthony's skewed renditions of famous artworks by Delacroix, Matisse, Munch, Picasso, Bacon, and other Modernist masters.

Without narrowing the range of his visual interests, Williams immersed himself in contemporary Southern folk art through the last quarter of the 20th century. During those years he added to his collection works by some three dozen self-taught artists from his native region, namely Leroy Almon, Z. B. Armstrong, Eddie Arning, Minnie Black, Georgia Blizzard, Vernon Burwell, Raymond Coins, Ronald Cooper, Granny Donaldson, Sam Doyle, Howard Finster, Harold Garrison, Russell Gillespie, Denzil Goodpaster, Ralph Griffin, Dilmus Hall, James Harold Jennings, Clyde Jones, Jacob Kass, O.W. "Pappy" Kitchens, Eddie Owens Martin (aka St. EOM), Carl McKenzie, Clete Meaders, Ruben A. Miller, "Sister" Gertrude Morgan, J.B. Murray, Leroy Person, W.C. Rice, Juanita Rogers, Nellie Mae Rowe, Mary T. Smith, William Cook Stanton (aka "Brother Rat"), Jimmy Lee Sudduth, Mose Tolliver, Bill Traylor, Fred Webster, and a few others.

Williams sought out most of these artists where they lived, not only so he could buy art from them, but also to get to know them with the aim of eventually writing about them and their work. A number of the essays, poems, and photographs that emerged from these encounters are collected in *Walks to the Paradise Garden,* an illustrated manuscript that unfortunately remains unpublished. Williams envisions his own core contributions augmented with additional photographs that Guy Mendes and Roger Manley made of some of the artists and their work, often while traveling with

Duck Woman of Orphiss: *Harold Finster, ca 1984, enamel on plywood cutout.*

Williams. Williams has declared the book too expensive an undertaking for the Jargon Society and none of the other publishers who has seen it has been willing to take it on, despite the widespread popular interest in folk and "outsider" art in the years since he became a pioneering enthusiast and champion of such work.[9]

Williams did much of his field work for *Walks to the Paradise Garden* between 1984 and 1987, as part of a larger, Jargon-sponsored endeavor called the Southern Visionary Folk Art Project, of which I was director for its three-year duration. In addition to researching and documenting the art of self-taught artists in the region, Williams and I also pursued his idea of establishing a museum devoted to such work, a notion that proved to be overly ambitious and was finally abandoned. Much of my own effort under the project's auspices centered on two artists from Georgia, Eddie Owens Martin and Howard Finster. As we wrapped up work on the project, Jargon published my book on Martin (*St. EOM in the Land of Pasaquan*, 1987), profusely illustrated with photographs by Williams, Manley, and Mendes. The similarly well-illustrated, as-told-to autobiography I co-wrote with Finster was eventually published by Abbeville Press (*Howard Finster, Stranger from Another World*, 1989). Williams' deep interest in this variously named, non-academic art is reflected in only one other Jargon publication, Paul Metcalf's *Araminta and the Coyotes* (1991), whose cover image reproduces a Mary T. Smith painting.[10]

Vernon Burwell: Black and white cat, *ca 1984, painted concrete.*

The zeal with which Williams pursued his interest in folk art didn't overwhelm his other visual-art interests. The early 1980s also saw the Jargon Society publish a couple of photography books (*The Photographs of Lyle Bongé*, 1982; and John Menapace's *Letter in a Klein Bottle*, 1984). Williams arranged for the posthumous reproduction of several late Philip Guston drawings as "illustrations" for Jargon's 1988 publication of Joel Oppenheimer's *Names & Local Habitations (Selected Earlier Poems, 1951–1972)*. More recently Jargon published two books of landscape photography— Elizabeth Matheson's *Blithe Air: Photographs from England, Wales, and Ireland* (1995) and a book devoted to Mark Steinmetz's photographs of *Tuscan Trees*. The latter volume appeared in 2001, the fiftieth-anniversary year of Williams' first Jargon publication.

With his birthday on March 8, 2008— one day after this exhibition opens at its premiere venue—Williams will mark the beginning of his eightieth year. As befits his advancing age, he has gradually slowed the pace of his activities, including his publishing endeavors. He still has a few other writers' manuscripts he would like to publish under the Jargon imprint, should funds become available, but his energy for pursuing financial support isn't what it used to be, and his ability to do so has been curtailed by health problems.

His most persistently troubling ailment is chronic numbness and pain in his feet, a condition medically diagnosed as neuropathy, which has limited his mobility since 1999 and put an end to the peripatetic travels that formerly drove his efforts. Nowadays he's a virtual hill hermit, rarely leaving his house. But Skywinding Farm makes for a comfortable and esthetically satisfying hermitage, furnished with the antiques his parents collected and otherwise largely decorated with his own art collection. If you get tired of looking at the art, you can always gaze out the big west-facing windows at the spectacular, sweeping view of northeast Georgia and the Nantahala Mountains. For company and all manner of invaluable assistance (not least of all culinary), Tom Meyer, Williams' poet partner of nearly forty years remains in residence, evidently in first-rate health and top literary form at a very young-looking sixty-one. Additional company includes H. B. (Hale-Bopp) Kitty, fabulous orange-tabby feline-in-residence, and frequent visitors, mostly longtime friends and cultural associates.[11]

Williams has accumulated plenty of laurels to rest on, and he certainly deserves a respite. Indeed, the Loco Locodaedalist appears to be reliably in situ at Skywinding until further notice.[12] His life has settled into a fairly steady daily routine that involves waking up around 9 a.m. and spending most of every day in a comfortable chair in the cathedral-ceilinged living room with a good view from one of those west-facing windows. Thus installed, he reads newspapers (*The New York Times* and *USA Today*), mystery novels, biographies, and some of his mail; sometimes takes phone calls; writes notes and maybe the occasional poem on a yellow legal pad; and watches daily news reports and selected sports events on the nearby TV. He augments the healthy daily diet that Tom Meyer provides with a mid-day vodka martini, a glass of single-malt Scotch whiskey before dinner and usually another one afterward, along with a cigar enjoyed while listening to recorded music— invariably classical or jazz—until going to bed around 10 p.m.

Living well—said to be the best revenge—has for Williams always entailed living with art. And what says more about a man than the art he lives with?

(BTW: Williams knows its bad luck to kill a snake. Especially with art, subject to damage and to be handled with care.)

—*Winston-Salem, December 2007;*
revisited January 2009

NOTES

[1] Some of the more informative and insightful writings on Williams' writing and publishing career include Joel Oppenheimer, "On Poetic Injustice," *Village Voice*, April 9, 1979, p. 8; Kenneth Irby," America's Largest Open-Air Museum," *Parnassus*, 1980; John Russell, "Jonathan Williams," *New York Times Book Review*, Feb. 13, 1983; Jim Marks, "A Jargon of Their Own Making: Williams and Meyer Have a Way with Words," *The Advocate*, Nov. 24, 1987; Susan Tamulevich, "Black Mountain Bard," July 1990, pp. 36–39; Jim Cory, "High Art & Low Life: an interview with Jonathan Williams," *James White Review*, Fall 1993, pp. 1–4; Tom Patterson, "O For a Muse of Fire: Jonathan Williams and the Iconoclasm of the Jargon Society, *afterimage*, March–April 1996, pp. 8–12; Jeffery Beam, "A Snowflake Orchard and What I Found There: an Informal History of the Jargon Society," *North Carolina*

Literary Review, vol. 6, 1997, pp. 16–27; Jeffery Beam, "Tales of a Jargonaut: an interview with Jonathan Williams," *Rain Taxi* online edition, Spring 2003, http://www.raintaxi.com/tales-of-a-jargonaut-an-interview-with-jonathan-williams/. [Also see the Jargon web site at http://jargonbooks.com/ for an unabridged version.] The most recent exhibition centering on the Jargon Society's publications (and including a limited selection of related art from his collection) was "Jonathan Williams and Friends," at the Asheville Art Museum, Asheville, N.C., Sept. 3, 2004–Jan. 9, 2005, which was accompanied by an illustrated, six-panel brochure including essays by Williams and the museum's executive director Pamela L. Myers.

[2] Jargon-published artworks by Ruff, Rice, Elsworth, Laubies, and Oscar, as well as a number of other artists' images reproduced in later Jargon publications, have either been sold by Williams or are included in the Jargon Archive, housed in the Poetry/Rare Books Collection at the State University of New York at Buffalo. See the collection's catalog *Jargon at Forty, 1951–1991*.

[3] Selected photographs by Williams have been collected in two volumes, *Portrait Photographs* (Gnomon Press, 1979) and *A Palpable Elysium: Portraits of Genius and Solitude* (David R. Godine, 2002).

[4] Black Mountain College was a small, progressive, arts-centered institution that existed near Black Mountain, North Carolina, for twenty-five years beginning in 1932. See Martin Duberman, *Black Mountain: An Exploration in Community* (New York: W.W. Norton, 1972, 1993); Mary Emma Harris, *The Arts at Black Mountain College* (Cambridge: The MIT Press, 1987); Vincent Katz, ed., *Black Mountain College: Experiment in Art* (Cambridge: MIT Press, 2002); and Michael Rumaker, *Black Mountain Days* (Asheville: Black Mountain Press, 2003).

[5] Editor Jeffery Beam notes: "Jonathan's crossings of the continent with books in his trunk are legendary now—sometimes described as being in a Volkswagen, sometimes in a station wagon. I queried Thomas Meyer as to the facts." His email reply on February 7, 2009: "Jonathan traversed this holy continent on several occasions. Coast to coast eight times? Twenty? Can't remember how many, the number is mentioned by him somewhere. The first forays (readings/preachings/sellings) were made in a Studebaker station wagon handed down to him by T. Ben [Jonathan's father, ed.]. Vague sense that there could've been more than one of these cast off family vehicles—always Skywinding station wagons. Then there came the VW sedan, gray and dubbed The Shadow, if memory serves. Early '60s. Succeeded by various VWs. The last full driven circuit (Skywinding to LA/SF/Seattle and back via NM/TX et cetera) off the top of my head was December to January 1978–1979.

By 1980 it was airplanes some or all of the various ways. You know, Jonathan had never flown, and was afraid to, until 1971. The virgin flight was in Don Anderson's personal Lear Jet. Nice introduction to sky ways." However, a new feature added to this volume, transcripts of interviews with North Carolina filmmaker Neal Hutcheson for the *Talking about Writing* video series, includes this quote from Williams: "In the '50s I'd inherit cars that my father had worn out, they used as much oil as gas. Mostly Pontiac station wagons. That was in the '50s. I think in the '60s was the first time I had my own car. It was a Volkswagen Beetle. By 1980, I had gone through about six … I think I must have crossed the US something like 43 times by car."

[6] *Blues & Roots/Rue & Bluets: A Garland for the Appalachians*, Grossman, 1971.

[7] Much of Williams' correspondence with Davenport was published in *A Garden Carried in a Pocket: Guy Davenport/Jonathan Williams, Correspondence 1964–1968*, Thomas Meyer, ed., Haverford: Green Shade, 2004.

[8] In *A Palpable Elysium: Portraits of Genius and Solitude*, pp. 44–45, Williams writes of his visit with Schmidt alongside a reproduction of one of his photographs, showing a detail from the Silver Forest.

[9] For detailed information on many of the self-taught artists whose works Williams has collected, see Jane Livingston and John Beardsley, *Black Folk Art in America, 1930–1980*, Corcoran Gallery of Art/University of Mississippi Press, 1982; Roger Manley, *Signs and Wonders: Outsider Art Inside North Carolina*, North Carolina Museum of Art, 1989; Alice Rae Yelen, *Passionate Visions of the American South: Self-Taught Artists from 1940 to the Present*, New Orleans Museum of Art, 1993; Paul Arnett and William Arnett, eds., *Souls Grown Deep: African American Vernacular Art in the South*, Vol. I & II, Tinwood Books, 2000, 2001; and Gerard C. Wertkin, ed., *The Encyclopedia of American Folk Art*, Routledge, 2004.

[10] For more information on the Jargon Society's Southern Visionary Folk Art Project see Tom Patterson and Roger Manley, *Southern Visionary Folk Artists*, a twelve-panel foldout brochure published by the Jargon Society, 1985; see also *Let It Shine: Self-Taught Art from the Marshall T. Hahn Collection*, High Museum of Art, 2001, pp. 54–55.

[11] About six months after Williams' death, H.B. Kitty went missing, never to return. Several domesticated cats in and around Scaly Mountain were killed by coyotes around that time, and H.B. is likely to have been among the victims.

[12] The reference is to Williams' book *The Loco Logodaedalist in Situ* (Cape Golliard/Grossman, 1971).

MICHAEL BASINSKI

SOME FACTS AND SOME MEMORIES—
THE JARGON SOCIETY ARCHIVE AT THE POETRY COLLECTION
STATE UNIVERSITY OF NEW YORK AT BUFFALO

The Poetry Collection is more than seventy years old. Our collecting policy of harvesting as much published poetry without bias from all corners of the English speaking world has resulted in an unmatched first edition and little magazine collection with more than 140 thousand titles. The Poetry Collection is twentieth century poetry's library of record. However, the Collection is much more than books and magazines. It boasts more than 150 manuscript collections. The collecting of manuscripts began in the late 1930s when Charles Abbott asked poets for donations of their work sheets, which were at that time simply food for the furnace. Because of Abbott's ability to see the future of scholarship, the Poetry Collection acquired the manuscripts of William Carlos Williams, Wyndham Lewis, and James Joyce and the Collection holds more than 400 Ezra Pound letters and, for example, Wallace Stevens' manuscript of *The Man and the Blue Guitar*. Obviously, the Collection's collecting line began with the Modernists. With this established tradition, manuscript collecting extended to the New American Poetry and a remarkable facet of that poetry were the poets associated with Black Mountain College. Central to the Black Mountain constellation of poets was Jonathan Williams and his Jargon Society, an independent publishing venture that made the names of Charles Olson, Robert Creeley, Joel Oppenheimer, Denise Levertov, and Robert Duncan, among others, common names in the halls and homes of the poem. The Jargon Society Collection and the manuscripts of Jonathan Williams reside in The Poetry Collection.

The Jargon Society Collection is the largest single manuscript Collection held in the Poetry Collection. As such, it is composed of more than 750 archival (clam-shell) boxes and more than fifty storage boxes of partially sorted archival material, which translates into more than 300 plus linear feet of manuscript material. Purchased in 1991, the Jargon collection is arranged in seven series: Series I. Manuscripts—Jonathan Williams (22 boxes alphabetized); Series II. Manuscripts—other (59 boxes alphabetized); Series III. Business records (17 boxes); Series IV. Letters to Jonathan Williams (487 boxes alphabetized); Series V. Letters from Jonathan Williams (13 boxes alphabetized); Series VI. Art and photographs (51 boxes); Series VII. Peripherals (64 boxes). The peripheral material includes posters, invitations to art openings and musical performances, random notes, random mailings, and all variety and sorts of miscellaneous material that offers context to the other specific archival material. Projects are currently underway to bring all of this material into full view. Do not hesitate to contact the Poetry Collection with your interests.

A quick review of Jargon authors teases the scholarly imagination. The archive includes research material relative to the study of: Charles Olson, Robert Duncan, Irving Layton, Kenneth Patchen, Ian Hamilton Finlay, Robert Creeley, Denise Levertov, Lorine Niedecker, Louis Zukofsky, Ronald Johnson, William Carlos Williams, Joel Oppenheimer, Basil Bunting, Tom Meyer, and then there are the Jargon visual artists, e.g., R. B. Kitaj and then there are the Jargon photographers, e.g., Eugene Meatyard, and etc., etc. The Collection is a treasure of research projects awaiting the twenty-first century scholar.

The Jargon Society would not exist at all were it not for Jonathan Williams. Born in Asheville, North Carolina, in 1929, Jonathan Williams was a poet, photographer, essayist and publisher. His highly regarded and eclectic Jargon Society started in 1951, the same year Williams became a student at Black Mountain College, and he, via the Jargon Society, remained actively engaged in the publication of books for over fifty years, which is to say the entire span of Jonathan Williams' adult artistic life. This monument should not overshadow Jonathan Williams the poet.

Williams was a poet who explored form and tone and temperament and all of form's potential, to which he brought his wealth of tone and personal temperament. Perhaps more than other poets from the Black Mountain tradition, Williams remained open to a poem that could contain the multitudes and the entire range of human experience. His artistic life was a collage and so was his poetry. It is, therefore, easy to define Jonathan

Williams as a poet. But to say what type of poet demands a neologism for a concrete, sound, field, Black Mountain, collage, humorous, Gay, Southern, progressive, Appalachian, and experimental poet and perhaps a few other isms and this and that and bricka brack to top off the JW poetic stew. A full, focused and scrutinizing study of the poetry of Jonathan Williams from his *Mahler* to his use of the aphorism and beyond is much desired and needed and would open an understanding of the complexity of the Jargon Society as an extension of Jonathan's poetry.

I had occasion to meet Jonathan Williams several times at the Poetry Collection. One might say, easily, that these were business meetings and, therefore, tense and anxious because they revolved around that decidedly unpoetic substance labeled money. Nevertheless, money and its softer terminology: funding and/or financial support was a necessity for Jonathan who worked with poetry outside of the academy. Somehow I found myself as a liaison between the University and the realm of poetry as manifested through JW. Over the years there were many phone calls. Jonathan's home needed a new roof or he needed photocopies of his Bunting letters or an installment check went astray. In fact, there was another Jonathan Williams who, at least once, received a check meant for our JW. We talked about the weather and he was always interested in our snow storms and we talked about sports. He knew all about the Buffalo Bills. He faithfully watched the Atlanta Braves on TV. He kept track of the Tour de France. I learned about drought and frost and ice storms in North Carolina.

I do remember his first walking into the Poetry Collection. It was history that moved into the room. He was not as tall as Charles Olson but taller than most people and imposing and commanding and with a deep aged and refined voice. Tom Meyer was his companion. The more I remember the more links appear in mind, like Wendy Kramer's project linking Jonathan's approach to poetry with that of Gertrude Stein's and when we were all sorting Jonathan's manuscripts, there was a poem with lines about a pan cake and Pan's cock.

I have decided that my foremost JW memory would involve Jonathan at a certain cocktail party. It was the celebration of the fortieth anniversary of the Jargon society, I think. The Jargon Board of Directors was in Buffalo at the Poetry Collection as were the Directors of the University of Buffalo Foundation. I recall Jonathan Williams, always the connoisseur, talking with Alice Wardynski. The conversation was about kielbasa (Polish sausage for you outsiders). Alice Wardynski's father began a flourishing Buffalo business making sausages and cold-cuts (*Don't give me that Baloney! I want Wardynski's!* was their jingle), and Alice Wardynski was much involved in the family business. Jonathan quizzed her about the perfect preparation of both smoked and fresh Polish sausage, about the exact time sausage should boil, about the exact amount of salt one might pinch into the water.

DALE SMITH

DEVOTION TO "THE STRANGE" –
JONATHAN WILLIAMS AND THE SMALL PRESS

For more than fifty years Jonathan Williams published from his home in North Carolina an extraordinary number of poets and writers, many claiming diverse affiliations to the poetic tribes that compose the heart of the New America poetry. The Jargon Society, a now-legendary small publisher, proved what single-mindedness and determination could accomplish in the world of American letters. Williams' exceptional legacy as publisher, provocateur, poet, essayist, and photographer maps out numerous possibilities available to other artists intent on keeping alive the various folkways and urbane intelligences that commingle in the local attention of the artist. In many ways he established a model for how to build a community of writers from the ground up. With James Laughlin, Lawrence Ferlinghetti, Amiri Baraka, Diane di Prima, and many others, Williams contributed to the fertile and energetic continuation of North American literature in a period of increasing cultural consolidation by the New York publishing industry. As a model of what a publisher can be, Williams certainly ranks among our greatest.

Through his work with the Jargon Society, Williams introduced many authors to print, including James Broughton, Basil Bunting, Robert Creeley, Robert Duncan, Denise Levertov, Paul Metcalf, Lorine Niedecker, Charles Olson, and Louis Zukofsky. His appetite for little known writers and photographers revealed him to be a man driven by a curiosity to possess perspectives formed in hidden details, exotic oddities, and introspective visions. His search for the hidden and over-looked spread from his publishing life into other orders of attention as well. Such a need to apprehend phenomenal details and to make them available to others should be instructive to any DIY publisher today. Instead of looking for strategically fashionable exemplars of the arts, Williams expressed preference for the unknown or forgotten. Not only did he publish the likes of Wisconsin poet Lorine Niedecker, practically unknown in the 1960s when Williams encountered her work, and Alfred Starr Hamilton, a New Jersey poet who lived much of his life in a Montclair boarding house, he looked at the world with a similar appetite for the disclosure of unknown things. In "The Poetry of Work," he writes:

> On a Pennsylvania dresser in my workroom in Highlands, North Carolina, I have six pots and vases: a Ch'ien Lung mirror-black; a tall Ming celadon; an alchemical form by M. C. Richards; a small, spotted Bernard Leach celadon; a plump, white piece by Toshiko Takaezu; and a polished black piece from the Santa Clara pueblo with eagle-feather design by Camillo Tafoya; on a wall behind them is a portrait of Charles Edward Ives, by W. Eugene Smith. A small quotation from the Shakers is pinned next to it: "No vice is with us the less ridiculous for being in fashion."

Discussing the publication of a book of graveyard photos by Lucinda Bunnen and Ginny Smith, Williams recalls:

> When I first looked through several thousand slides and several hundred prints spread over the refectory table here at Skywinding Farm, I asked: "Lucinda and Ginny, don't you think *Scoring in Heaven* is too strange even to be a Jargon Society book?" They thought that was the nicest question anyone had ever asked them. I was, of course, just kidding. I love to visit the Strange like some people love to visit the Country, as I say over and over again. The Jargon Society has, after all, been the publisher of Ernie Mickler's glorious amalgam of pig-grease and sass, *White Trash Cooking*. And of Tom Patterson's monument to the late, bodacious Eddie Owens Martin of Buena Vista, Georgia, *St. EOM in the Land of Pasaquan*. And we have espoused artists and poets as curious, visionary, "ugly," and far-off-the interstates as Bill Anthony, Glen Baxter, Ralph Eugene Meatyard, Lyle Bongé, Doris Ulmann, Alfred Starr Hamilton, Mason Jordan Mason, and Richard Emil Braun. Stephen King says somewhere: "I guess when you turn off the main road, you have to be prepared to see some funny houses."

Such devotion to "the Strange" gave Williams an impressive ability to punctuate art with intrusions of the unexpected. By listening to what was most delightful, he was compelled to present a complex body of work that gave insight to the American experience in all its wildness of form and attitude. Along with some of the most valuable poetry of the 20th century, Williams published Ernest Mickler's *White Trash Cooking*, which became Jargon's only commercial success. While today some small publishers carefully prepare catalogues as if they were constipated with a grand sense of their contribution to the world of literature, Williams provided a model of fertile introspection, showing us how to proceed according to the interests and desires of the publisher. Creative motive, for Williams, rested within individual perspectives and capacities for delight, not in some sense of social importance, publishing what others require.

In a letter to the editor of *The New York Times Book Review*, Williams once claimed that poetry readers could be counted "somewhere between the number of Ivory-billed Woodpeckers (several sighted in Cuba recently) and the number of California Condors." He observed too that "[t]he only poetry readers I have unearthed lately lived near Pippa Passes, Dwarf, and Monkey's Eyebrow in Kentucky; at Odd, West Virginia; and at Loafers Glory and Erect, North Carolina."

More recently Williams' poetry met a larger audience when Copper Canyon published his selected poems, *Jubilant Thicket*. In it we witness the hilarious and insatiable mind Williams possessed. With the ear of Basil Bunting, a regionalist attention to "the Strange," and an obvious commitment to poetic lore, Williams crossed the hayseed with the aesthete to retrieve such remarkable moments as this one:

Uncle Tot Harper
could talk
the tits
off a hog

farmed sheep
fifty years
under Crook
under Winder

and's done
nowt since
but natter

get
the good man
a gob-stopper
for Christmas

reminds me
Miss Stein said Mr. Pound
was a village explainer

ok if you're a village;
if not, not

In another selection of his work from 1972 called *The Loco Logodaedalist in Situ*, a sequence called "History" stands out for its wit and pliability. The "history" in question is Williams' adolescence, through which he delivers insights ranging from the profound to the naughty on lines that seem almost to float off the page:

History VI:

about 16 lying on the grass in the sunshine

one   his hand
                        with all his might

        opened,   exposed   manipulated
                                    the other's

            to this day
        a telescope

excites me

They

grew up normal men.

And also:

History XXI:

the organs of generation
imagine
the caprice of male captors,

urine

over my body,
limbs

in my face!

"The face he presented to the world was of an irascible crank, a loose cannon, a gadfly," said Williams' life-partner, Thomas Meyer, in a conversation with the *New York Times* after Williams passed in March 2008. "But as a publisher he was extraordinarily generous, always looking for the overlooked." Likewise, in his poetry, the overlooked occupied his attention. The masturbatory fantasies of youth emerged, giving wonder and joy with sympathetic laughter to experiences that often remain hidden in the backward abysm of memory.

As a young publisher and writer, Williams' example helped me better understand how to locate attention in many facets of life. The local competed with broader national scenes to help me become aware of the kind of poet I wanted to be—and the kind of publisher I hoped to become. I had to learn how to trust my own prejudices, too, and follow instincts and preferences that may not necessarily agree with the tastes of others. Williams' examples in his own writing and in the books he published helped guide my work. His sense of printed words on the page, too, led me to see book-making as an art that makes poetry present to readers according to the printed environments that support it. At the heart of American poetry for decades, Williams' legacy will be felt for many more to come.

WORKS CITED

Hevesi, Dennis. "Jonathan Williams, Publisher, Dies at 79." *New York Times*. March 30, 2008. Available http://www.nytimes.com/2008/03/30/books/30 williams.html?ref=todayspaper

Williams, Jonathan. *Blackbird Dust: Essays, Poems, and Photographs*. New York: Turtle Point Press, 2000.

Williams, Jonathan. *Jubilant Thicket: New and Selected Poems*. Port Townsend: Copper Canyon Press, 2004.

Williams, Jonathan. *The Loco Logodaedalist in Situ: Selected Poems 1968–70*. London: Cape Goliard, 1972.

RICHARD OWENS

IN CONVERSATION WITH JONATHAN WILLIAMS, 1 JUNE 2007

For nearly two years beginning in early 2006 I had the rare privilege of working with the Jonathan Williams/Jargon Society archive in the Poetry and Rare Books Collection at the University at Buffalo. Throughout this period I spent any number of hours in the calm of the closed stacks sorting through dozens of previously unopened boxes, tasked with the responsibility of separating the choice from the chaff—print proofs, manuscript drafts of poems or literary correspondence from telephone bills, cigar wrappers, supermarket circulars and such. The experience was a humbling one that underscored for me the extent to which Williams was indeed a living library. Later, when word circulated in March 2008 that he was finally gone, it was thus consoling to see CA Conrad appropriately acknowledge this: "It's like a library burned itself to the ground while we were sleeping."

Any archive is necessarily incomplete and the library that contains it even more so. Rather than calling our attention to what is present the materials within an archive generate distance, becoming increasingly unfamiliar. Further, in Williams' case—with his literary archive housed at the University at Buffalo; his photography archive at the Beinecke; and his correspondence to dozens of poets, artists and photographers scattered across a comparable number of libraries—Williams himself was the living institution through which one might approach these incomplete and spatially dispersed materials. And so it was the incomplete character of the archive and the scattered state of his papers that persuaded me to arrange the following interview and address questions the archive raised but refused to answer. More casual than formal or rigorous, the following conversation is transcribed from a phone interview with Jonathan Williams conducted Friday afternoon, June 1, 2007.

—Richard Owens

RO: You did a lot of hiking. I know you covered 1500 miles of the Appalachian Trail and you've done a lot of hiking in the north of England …

JW: Yeah, and all over France. Not all over, but I mean quite a lot in France. A certain amount in Spain. A certain amount in Italy. And a lot in the Black Forest. As they say, I used to get around.

RO: Mike Basinski mentioned that you were going to devote some time to the Tour de France.

JW: Oh, I love to watch that. That mainly occupies my daytimes during the month of July. Comes just after Wimbledon. Well I always have been kind of a sports nut, so I'm glad to be able to see these things.

RO: I think that's interesting. George Bowering was just in town and he delivered a reading last night. I think he's drawing perhaps off Jack Spice —but he's wildly interested in sports. And you're a poet that also holds sports central. They often seem to enter into your work. So maybe you can say something about the role of baseball in some of the work you've done. I think it was yesterday I was looking through *Long Taters* and the Yogi Berra quotes that pop up every once in a while …

JW: Yeah, well it's a game that makes very good sense and I've always been interested in it. I guess I went to my first major league game when I was quite young. It was the late '30s and I was … well, let's see. Not Babe Ruth. He either retired or wasn't playing anymore. Lou Gehrig was playing that day. So it was a pretty long time ago. And Spicer is fanatical about baseball. I guess I share some of that.

RO: You were among the first to actually champion Spicer and see him as an important figure long before he was given much attention. You were supportive all along and there's of course that gorgeous photograph of Spicer that you took. He's standing, I believe, on timber …

JW: Yes, large timber. Up in the redwood country. I've got other good pictures of Jack. I've got probably about five or six quite good Polaroids. As I may have said at some point earlier, Yale has acquired all of my photographic archive. They've acquired the transparencies, Polaroids, etc, etc. So we're in the process of getting that into their hands at the moment. It'll be at the library there. What is it called?

RO: The Beinecke?

JW: Beinecke. Can't even spell it probably.

RO: You know, I have this impulse to try and discuss everything and you've had a hand in everything ... I've been reading through a lot of the interviews you've done over the years and they all seem to focus on Jargon and I wanted to kind of try and move away from that and explore different areas ... It seems to me that central figures for you in your poetry have been Mahler, Bruckner, and then Charles Ives and a couple of other folks.

JW: Yeah. Yeah. That's true. I've been listening to a lot of late Romantic work lately. But then I never like to forget the jazz that I was brought up listening to. I went to New Orleans a number of times to catch up on that scene. And I spent a lot of time in the '40s and '50s in New York listening to jazz. So I kind of got around in those days, as they say. You know, I love jazz almost as much as anything else. But I never got very interested in pop music, I must confess. I haven't really listened to anything much after those kind of mild days of people like the Beatles and Simon and Garfunkel. That's about the last pop music I listened to. I just don't know what's going on with all this stuff that they play these days. Don't like it.

RO: Do you continue to collect?

JW: To some extent. Again, not like I did. Well, I've got a big collection. I won't run out of things to listen to for a long time. I just reencountered, for instance, a composer I've been ignoring for about twenty years. Isaac Albeniz. He doesn't seem to get much attention anymore, except for his one big glorious piece called *Iberia* which started out in life as twelve piano pieces and then he had them orchestrated. It's a stunning work. Since I'm not living in a city with any decent record stores, I don't know. I think there used to be one in either Durham or Chapel Hill. I think that was about the only one in North Carolina that you would bother with. There's nothing much available. And I guess there are even less stores now than there used to be. Places like Atlanta! Another reason not to go to Atlanta. There are probably no decent record stores at all anymore. That's a miserable place these days, I think. It's all I can do to watch the Braves play baseball. They're doing a little better than they might this year.

RO: How did you get drawn into the Army? It seems through interviews and other mention of it you were drawn into the Army by means of conscription.

JW: Yeah, I was drafted.

RO: During the Korean conflict?

JW: Yeah, I was at Black Mountain. It must have been about 1952 or something like that. I took a conscientious objector stance and got nowhere with that because it wasn't supported by the quote *peace* church. I went to an Episcopal school and was brought up that way. But I got no support from that church and I should have known better than to try the Roman Catholics. They were of no use. Finally, the only person who gave me any support when I was actually in the medical corps was a man with a wonderful name: Chaplin Kaplan. He was great. I don't know where it was, which Army base, but anyway they were going to probably stick me in jail if I wasn't careful and he said, well don't be ridiculous. Leave this man alone and transfer him to … Oh, when I was going to be transferred to the medics he was very instrumental in helping there. So, you know, I had a very successful military time. That was mostly in Germany. I was assigned to Stuttgart which was a wonderful place to be. That's when I published some of the first Jargon books.

RO: How were you able to do that? Did you locate a letterpress printer? It's really astonishing that you bring out the first Jargon books in Stuttgart.

JW: Well, it was, again, a bit of luck. I had any number of New Directions books. And just by looking at random here and there I discovered that one of the printers he was using was located in a suburb of Stuttgart. They were doing really excellent printing in those days. Laughlin, I guess, got tired of spending a lot of money. Back in the '40s and '50s he had some beautiful editions. Some of the best came from a firm called Doctor Kantz and the hospital I worked in was less than a ten minute walk from his plant. So I made myself known and told him that I had a book or two that I'd be interested in trying to publish. So that was a lucky thing that happened there. Who could have counted on that? And then I found two or three other printers, one more in Stuttgart and one in the village of Karlsruhe and I did a Patchen book out there with them that turned out pretty well. Well, like Olson's *Maximus Poems* I suppose is the best thing we did in Germany. Maybe the best of all is a book of Louis Zukofsky's called *Some Time*. I can't do any better than that. So anyway, being a corpsman in a locked psychiatric ward one of the things I did to stay awake at night was read proofs and read scripts and it was helpful. Didn't want to fall asleep necessarily. Some of those guys were *mean*. They were very—oh, what's the word they use—*antisocial* is the word I believe they use. But I was delighted to have all that stuff. I had a lot of spare time. I guess they gave us more time off than most people because we were under a certain amount of threat of being, you know, knocked in the head. So then I was able to go from Stuttgart down to places like Zurich where there were some interesting artists and interesting printers.

RO: Were you able to—well, I was wondering about this before. For as much as you love Mahler were you able to see any of the great conductors perform Mahler in Germany at that time? Klemperer or Horenstein or that sort of thing?

JW: Yeah, I saw Klemperer I think in London. Horenstein I think is a terrific conductor but I never saw him live. One or two of his Mahler performances I think are not to be equaled. The Third, the Mahler Third, is terrific. Oh, I've heard—let me see. There were one or two others at that time. Not sure I'm remembering very well today. But Stuttgart was very good for music. A lot of concerts. A lot of free stuff. A lot of very good church concerts that you could go to for nothing. There was the chamber orchestra, the Stuttgart chamber orchestra, which was one of the best in its day. There were one or two very good Bruckner conductors in those days. Let's see. Who would that be? He did a ycle, one of the earlier cycles.

RO: Furtwängler?

JW: No. It's later than that. But I mean he recorded everything. All of the symphonies. He was very good, this man.

RO: You seem to have had your finger on the pulse of not only music but art and you weren't in your thirties, you were in your mid-twenties and you knew precisely what was happening and you had a sense of what was important and what was not. Again, just looking through your papers and the various gallery exhibits you attended in the '50s in New York and reading the correspondence to and from you really underscores the fact that you knew what was going on.

JW: Well, I was lucky enough to be … I guess growing up in Washington, D.C., was a very good thing. I went to a lot of music there. And then when I got out of school, out of St. Albans school, you know when I went to Princeton there were other opportunities. Then, of course, I was in New York, oh, three or four years and that didn't hurt. Well I've always, like they say, been interested in things. I'm glad I didn't start out life in Atlanta. My grandparents had been in Atlanta. Happily my mother married and moved to Washington. A great place. Think of the number of museums available. Again, lots of them for free. And the Freer. Wonderful Chinese/Japanese collections. One of the best in the world. I used to go to the Freer quite a lot. I don't know. There was no excuse to be all that ignorant if you just kind of paid a little attention.

RO: Your father's collection of Chinese vases—Ming and T'ang dynasty—is that …

JW: It's within sight as I talk to you in a corner of the living room here. It's quite a beautiful collection. It was, I guess, put together in the middle of the 1940s. And that's when he did most of his collecting. Again, living in Washington, there were very good auction houses there and lots of collectors were in the diplomatic service of one country or another and, you know, they got stationed somewhere else and sometimes they got rid of their holdings. So had access to some very good things. And the friendship of some of the curators at the Smithsonian and the Freer Gallery. They would help him and educate him. Lots to know. But yeah, it's a lovely collection. I'm going to hang onto that one. It goes very well with the house. The house is like so much else. It's kind of a hodge-podge, but a good kind of hodge-podge. So you get that Chinese material. We have a lot of very good French furniture, English furniture, American furniture, Chinese furniture. So all of that is here. I hope in a way that this house can be maintained in some respect, you know. Hence the library is pretty much here. And a big collection downstairs of Outsider art and there's various other modern art. It would be nice to have that kept intact. Tom Meyer will, of course, attempt to see that this happens. So I hope that comes to pass. But the house itself is fairly remote. It has the views that haven't been intruded on really. You can see almost nothing but mountains—and in three directions.

RO: Sounds gorgeous.

JW: Well, it's not bad, as they say. Today I'm looking out the window hoping to see some rain coming. We haven't had rain for about a month.

RO: You mentioned Thomas. I'm curious. I think there's something interesting happening between your own poetic practice and Thomas' practice as a poet and I wonder if you can talk about how you first encountered one another.

JW: Well, let's see if I can get that clearly in mind. I think it was … I don't know. I was talking to a poet named Gerrit Lansing. We were talking, just talking the usual stuff. I said to him at one point, God, I said, I get really tired of these third-rate straight poets. That's about all you see. Aren't there any good gay poets? And I said, you know, I said I want to publish some. And Gerrit happened to have met Tom when he was up at Bard College and suggested that I write to him. So I did. I wrote to him and exchanged a couple of letters. And I told him of my desire to publish some gay writers and he said, well I have a manuscript that I can show you. And that was a book called *The Bang Book*. Have you seen that?

RO: Absolutely. Yep.

JW: Well, that was the first project and I thought that one came out very well. Had nice drawings by my English artist friend John Furnival. So that's kind of how it started. Like that. Write somebody a letter. And he was, well, tremendously bright for one thing. He comes from around the northwest. His parents and siblings grew up in Seattle. So he'd never really been to the east until he went to Bard. So that's how it all started, as they say.

RO: So when he went to Bard wasn't Robert Kelly teaching at that time?

JW: Yes. He had been for just not very many years at that point. Must be there forty-five years by now, or close to it. We went up to a celebration of his fortieth anniversary. That was maybe 2001 or 2002. Yeah. Robert is a wonder to behold. There's not as much of him as there used to be back in those days. And he's a tremendously bright guy. He always humbles me. You know a little. I know a little. But it seems like Kelly has read just about everything. I forget who it was that said he was under the impression that he was the last Englishman who had read everything of any interest. I think it's Thomas Carlyle that claims that and it may have been true. But anyway he [Thomas Meyer] was a student of Robert's and that was a very good thing for him.

RO: So where did you first meet? Was it up at Bard?

JW: Actually, I was teaching a couple of semesters at something called the Maryland Institute College of Art in Baltimore. So I was there. And I heard or read that there was going to be a concert of music by Carl Ruggles.

RO: And he's a figure that's important to you. Ruggles.

JW: Yeah. He associated of course with Ives. Anyway, I think it might have been his ninetieth birthday. I believe I'm right on that. It could've been maybe a little bit less than that. Let's say it was his ninetieth birthday and there was going to be this concert at Bennington. A couple of concerts, on a Friday night and a Saturday night or something like that. And I thought to myself, gosh, it's not all that far to get from Baltimore to Bennington. So I just mentioned that to Tom Meyer and he said, I'd like to go to that, too. So I went slightly out of my way and picked him up at Bard and off we went to Bennington and to those concerts. So that was the occasion. That could be the date. So that was the occasion. Later that year, let me see. We got interested in the idea of living together and we went down to Penland School that winter, in North Carolina, that craft school and spent a couple months there. Anyway, that's kind of where it all started.

RO: I'm also curious about your poetic practice and the way in which that intersects perhaps with Tom's practice.

JW: Well, we've always kind of written separately in a way, you know. And we don't discuss too much of what's going on in either's work. We obviously pay attention. And Kelly certainly thinks he's the best that he knows in that generation. He's always said that. Continues to. And Jargon's done some good editions of Tom's. But he's a much more learned kind of poet than I am. I know a lot of stuff, but … I'm very badly read. Somebody asked me the other day, what do you think of Jane Austen. I said, I don't know. So, I'm like that about a lot of people.

RO: But you know Ian Hamilton Finlay and his boy Alec Finlay and you've really promoted Simon Cutts and other folks.

JW: Well, I have an eye for that or ear for that and it seems I can be more useful doing that than hundreds of people with degrees in Virginia Woolf and whoever else. Let them go. Let them have it. Anyway, I don't know whether there's always people as invisible as Simon Cutts in England.

RO: And also Basil Bunting. There's a very peculiar connection between you and Basil Bunting. You somehow connected with what he was doing and really supported it, promoted it.

JW: Well, we had the good luck to be able to see him quite a lot over a period of about fifteen years. The cottage in England is only about three miles from the Quaker meeting house that he wrote a lot about. Briggflatts. He would go to Quaker meetings there whenever he could get down from the Tyne valley where he was brought up and to the Dales. And once we got established down there he would come and stay with us and a lot of times he would come on a Saturday in time to go to Sunday meeting and then stay the weekend and take advantage of being there and not leave until Sunday afternoon. So anyway, we were able to see a lot of Basil and he was a delight to have as a visitor. He knew a lot about whiskey and one can learn different things from different people. And I loved drinking with him. He's a great person to drink with. And the fact that he had known Pound as well as he had and any number of other people made him fascinating. So yeah, we miss him. It's hard to imagine that he died in 1985. Well, he was eighty-five years old that year but that's beginning to get to be a few years ago. Don't know what you do with time. I guess you put up with it.

RO: But your relationship to Bunting and other Brits. You really do your best to jump the pond and bridge the gap.

JW: Wasn't all that far to get to. Like they say, there's a lot out there. There's a lot of things to do if you're lucky enough to have very good health and things of that sort. There it is. That's one of Basil's favorite expressions. There it is.

RO: You also published the American poet Alfred Starr Hamilton's poems which I think is interesting. It was what, Geoff Hewitt that brought you to it, but you saw in Alfred Starr Hamilton something which was sort of important.

JW: Yeah, I was quite taken. He was like discovering some bizarre French poet of the nineteenth century, you know. As I say, I thought there was something quite marvelous about Alfred Starr Hamilton. Even if it comes from New Jersey. I don't know that part of the world very well at all. But I used to visit over at Dr. Williams' house. That was the only intimate experience I've had in that part of the country.

RO: Again, just looking at your early years at St. Albans, you were connected to poetry in a sort of meaningful way at a very early age. You started reading Patchen at St. Albans. You first encounter poetry yourself at St. Albans ...

JW: Well, I don't think I really did. There was no course. I didn't take any course. I got onto, as I may have said at an earlier time, I got onto Patchen through a bookstore in New York City. The Argus bookshop run by a man named ... let's see if we get his name ... well, the great bookseller of the '30s and '40s. First thing I found out, and this is so strange, I found out that this bookshop, the Argus bookshop, was a great place to find the work of H.P. Lovecraft, who I got onto before I got onto Kenneth Patchen. Then I went to the shop and I met the bookman and I said, people tell me that you have some more recent things of some of the writers of poetry and so on. He said, I'm very fond of Kenneth Patchen, of Kenneth Rexroth, Henry Miller, etc., etc. And I said, well, when I get finished with this Lovecraft I'll come back and get something from you. I was about thirteen or fourteen I guess when that happened. But there was no interest in poetry per se at St. Albans. But I thought I was pretty well educated there. Very, very conservative by nature. And that's okay. It doesn't seem like much of an achievement to me, reading *The Little Minister*. Do you know who wrote that? Sir James Barry. I think he wrote that child's book. What did James Barry write? *Peter Pan*. He wrote *Peter Pan*. So that's another interesting area. Ben Ingramson was this man's name, the bookseller. Those were the days when there were some really interesting bookshops around New York. And he was in the Village, in the West Village. He just had great stuff and his prices were very modest. And he had all kinds of contact with those people. He knew Henry Miller quite well. So that was great. It's not easy to find people like that anymore. I know very few booksellers. I know three or four that I like very much. But having said that I'm not in touch with a lot of them.

RO: You had a strong relationship with Ted Wilentz. And of course there's the Jargon/Corinth connection. But even before that weren't you wrapping books and kind of working at the Eighth Street bookshop.

JW: That's right. Yeah, I did that. Ted was a really fine person. I liked him a lot and enjoyed working for him. Yeah, I worked in the shop I guess about a year. It must have been the '50s.

RO: And you appear in *The Beat Scene* anthology edited by Elias Wilentz. And the Wilentz family at large is just a really interesting sort of thing. I found recently sketches of Basil Bunting by a "J" Wilentz and I'm not entirely sure if they're by Joan or by John.

JW: I don't know. Joan does quite a lot of drawing. It's probably her. I just received one on a postcard within the last week. I guess it was through Ted but—oh, what's the word—well she owns some of the rights to the Olson poems that the University of California has published. And every once in a while somebody will buy Olson and I'll get a check for twenty-four dollars and three cents.

RO: Now I'm thinking now about *Jammin' The Greek Scene*, the prefatory note that Charles Olson provides for that. I think it's such a wonderful note. He says a couple of things which in their own sort of way forecast the future on some level regarding your own poetic practice.

JW: Olson is extremely sharp about some things. He has a lot of wonderful remarks. Home truths which I love. The one that I keep coming back to, somebody said, Mr. Olson, you said one time that you make twenty-six dollars a year from poetry. He said, I meant to say in a *very* good year. Twenty-six dollars from poetry. And I believe him. One time I received a royalty statement from New Directions. Fifteen cents. I framed it. Have it in my library. J. Laughlin was famous for being a little close with his money but that beats anything that I know of. How much did it cost to cut the check? But the point is well taken. Twenty-six dollars from poetry. Olson, as I say, I really enjoyed his presence. We didn't do as much as we might have. He was rather demanding. And I didn't have the money. He was asking a little more of me than I could give him.

RO: In what way? As a publisher or as a poet?

JW: As a publisher. We did the *Maximus Poems* as well as we could possibly have done them. But, you know, not many of them sold.

RO: I'm kind of wondering now about the relationship between music and your own poetic practice. I mentioned this earlier, but Mahler and Ives are central figures to what you do and I'm particularly interested in Charles Ives and his role in your own poetic production.

JW: I guess it's really based on listening to the music. I had certainly done that a lot. It kind of rubs off, as they say. Now that cloud is going away a little bit now…. It would be interesting to know why certain composers or certain pieces are as influential on oneself as they are but I guess from the time I first heard Charles Ives I was really interested and there wasn't much of it to be heard in those days. Just enough, I guess. Things like the *Concord Sonata*. That was there. Then the symphonies slowly materialized. The quartets. The songs, which I think are often terrific.

RO: You have the "Celestial Centennial Reverie for Charles Edward Ives" and it seems his work on some level determines the way that poem appears …

JW: Well, there's lots of composers I like to do that with. I've thought about trying to do, instead of a Mahler book, a Bruckner book. Maybe I will, if possible. I'm sitting here looking at the sky and finishing off my favorite drink of the season, which is a dirty martini. You put the vermouth in the glass and then you put some ice in. Not that much. And then two big green Spanish olives. You put those in. And then you trail some of the juice, the olive juice, in the glass and that's that. It's very very tart and sour unlike a regular martini. But I really like them. I usually have one at this time of the day. Don't think you'd want to drink two or three. It's pretty strong. But that's what I do for alcohol during the day. Very tasty.

RO: If you don't mind, I wonder if you can talk about Ronald Johnson. I'm thinking about your connection to England and Johnson's first book, *Book of the Green Man*. That's a work which seems to me partially informed by your own poetry. His interest in Samuel Palmer and that sort of thing.

JW: Well, that's correct. We did a lot of walking that particular year together and we were going to see Palmer things. So it's not surprising he's talking about what he's talking about because I was doing it too.

RO: And prior.

JW: Yeah, I was just old enough. Not much older. But I think he turned into quite a good writer. I liked his work at the beginning and I liked it at the end. But this would not be the case with Tom Meyer. You wouldn't find him following my lead.

RO: How did you first meet Ronald Johnson? What were the circumstances around your first encounter with him?

JW: He was living near DuPont Circle in Washington, D. C., northwest there along Connecticut Avenue and I can't spell it out precisely I'm afraid, but he had an apartment and I knew somebody who was looking for an apartment. We knocked on his door and asked him if he could help us, if he knew of anything or anybody. So that was kind of a very casual sort of meeting. And that was in Washington, D. C. I was living there for about six months so we got to know each other, Ronald and I. Then he came down to North Carolina and spent some time down here and we got along quite well.

RO: So his first jaunt through northern England is with you.

JW: Yeah. That was a good walk.

RO: And of course there's the other Johnson—Ray Johnson. Recently

I was looking through Ray Johnson's correspondence. We don't have your side of it, but we have his letters to you at the collection and there are some very dear letters and you were connected to him for quite a long time.

JW: I suppose, but not very closely. I met him as he was passing in and out of Black Mountain, but he wasn't a student actually when I was there. He was a visitor. He had been a student. He was a likeable man. Ray Johnson himself was—what's a good word for Ray? Squirrelly, I suppose. He was really very eccentric. I mean, he wanted to make something out of nothing at any given moment which I sort of enjoyed. There was something French about him. Alfred Starr Hamilton. He struck me as curiously surreal and so did Ray Johnson. But I didn't know him very well personally. We had a couple of projects. We did two books together and I think he did drawings for a book of fables by Russell Edson. But he's got some terrific stuff. But he didn't get any attention, that's for sure.

RO: I wonder if we can talk about your connection to Lorine Niedecker. There are your photographs of Niedecker. I'm certainly interested in the photographs of Bunting and Briggflatts, but those photographs of Niedecker required you to travel out to Fort Atkinson to spend time with Niedecker. You're one of the few to have done that while she was alive. What was it like visiting her?

JW: Hard to say. Very quote *normal* unquote, you know. She liked to talk about rebuilding her little cottage and things of that sort. She wasn't terribly interested in talking about poetry and thinking back to the days with Louis Zukofsky and all that. She was very much a woman of her time and place out there in the Wisconsin countryside. It's hard to imagine people not being interested in her but most people do manage not to be interested and it continues on. Anyway, she was lucky to have Basil Bunting's attention like she did. And Louis Zukofsky's. People like Corman and so on.

RO: With Basil Bunting, with Simon Cutts and other folks like that—Ian Hamilton Finlay—you were also concerned with bringing British poetry to the US. I wonder if this is simply because you were in the north of England …

JW: It must have had something to do with being in the north. Most of those writers were there. Thomas A. Clark was somebody I quite liked for a while and still do. Do you know his work? Now there's some rain out there. That's what we need. What can poetry do to bring itself up to the needs of the weather? I can hear it out there. It's coming down. That's great. Even if it doesn't rain but five minutes, it's going to be something. But as I say, I like Tom Clark. He came out of a very basic kind of life. Not too far from Glasgow. Just down the river there. And I don't think Tom's family, any of them, were ever interested in anything like—quote—writing or poetry. He had to make all that stuff for himself and he did a good job of it. A very good job I think. And his ideas of what a book looks like, the size of a book and all that stuff, he's good at that. I've only seen him once in the last few years, but he's … He lived in England quite a few years, and said he couldn't take it any longer. He went back to Scotland. Not where he came from but on the east coast. I'd love to see him again. His wife is very nice too. She's an artist. Draws very well. Laurie Clark. She's done drawings for quite a few of his little books. If you see drawings it's usually Laurie. She's very good I believe. Very skillful.

RO: From your early twenties forward you've identified a number of interesting artists. And now I'm wondering about your relationship with, say, Guy Davenport. He's such a wonderful artist and scholar.

JW: I think I'm almost proudest of having dealt with John Furnival. English artist. I think he's a really wonderful draftsmen. I'm really pleased when we can do another book. He's wandered off. He gave up on living in England. He couldn't stand the Brits any longer. He's moved to the south of France, where he lives like a peasant. A very simple life. It's not an art colony or anything like that. His wife is a very skilled artist too. She does wonderful knitting and hence I have a great piece of hers that's a portrait of Samuel Palmer at the age of twenty she did. Her image is great. So I'd love to see her again. Maybe if we can kick my feet into submission.

RO: There that wonderful caricature of you batting that Furnival did for David Wilk's *Truck* magazine. The JW festschrift issue.

JW: O yeah. That's cricket. I love baseball, but Furnival is more interested in cricket.

RO: There's also a photograph of you at a football match and you're watching, I believe, Leeds play another team. Is that something you did regularly in England, attend soccer matches?

JW: Yeah. Back in the seventies we tended to go to football. Then it got quite rough in England for a while. There was a lot of fighting. It was rather violent and so people stopped going. Anyway, I've gone to quite a lot of cricket as well. It's a wonderful game. Much more complicated than baseball. I'm not sure ultimately it's a better game but it's very very complicated and not many people know what to look for.

RO: Which sport do you find yourself most connected to?

JW: Well I know most about baseball, which I've been looking at for quite a while now. I have some reservations about cricket, but baseball, I've been looking at that long enough to have a pretty clear sense of what it's about.

RO: The other day I was reading through *Long Taters*, your book of quotes. You're quoting, of course, Flaubert and Bunting, Clement Greenberg, and a number of others. But every once in a while these Yogi Berra quotes creep up. The quotes are priceless.

JW: Yeah. If Heraclitus had said such things.

RO: I'm also endlessly curious about your relationship with Mina Loy. Certainly the 1958 publication of *Lunar Baedeker & Time-Tables*. She phoned into the book launch. You held a book launch in New York. I think Duchamp attended that and others. She doesn't attend that. She's in Colorado. So I'm wondering how you first encounter Mina Loy.

JW: O dear. I think James Laughlin told me to my surprise—this is back in the fifties when Mina Loy was alive and living in Aspen, Colorado, with her daughter. Well, there were two daughters but she was living mostly with one of them. So somebody told me, well you can't ignore Mina Loy, can you? And I said, probably not. What do I do next? I drove to Aspen and arranged with her daughter to have lunch with them and so took it from there. We asked if we could do the book and they had a book they wanted doing. So that was that. Then came the second book, which had so many errors we finally got rather embarrassed over the fact that we published it at all.

RO: Thank god we have it. That's the only book that includes *Anglo-Mongrels* in its entirety. But that book launch. I read Mina Loy was upset—well, I guess she phoned into the book launch in New York and was upset with you for not hanging her constructions.

JW: I can't really remember what that had been about. I had nothing to do with making the exhibition. That was made by somebody at the bookshop on Madison Avenue. Books &c. You remember that one? Anyway, the manager or the owner or somebody more or less got out some bookcases and put books in there and that was that. I didn't have anything to do with ordering the show.

RO: Now I'm thinking about your own poetic practice and whether or not you've continued to produce work over the past ten years, say from 2000 forward.

JW: Yeah, I would say so. I don't find it's very different. I do what I always do. Sit down and put words on pages and scratch around a little. As I say, there's no agenda. I never have any agenda. That allows me space to do this and do that and not do *this*. I'm not very inclined to worry very much about theory and all that. But something goes on in some sense.

RO: Did Olson have you reading theory, historiography when you were at Black Mountain?

JW: No, no. He never did that. He may have for some people, but not for me ... I found him extremely agreeable ... But there's a slightly more interesting word than agreeable. But we got on well. Francine Du Plessix and myself were the only students of his that had any kind of university training, Ivy League or not. So that kind of set us apart from the others. But, as I say, I liked his attitude and the things he said. I think Francine got very cross with him. I suppose women, there were only a few. And he was very forthright. He was half Swedish and half Irish. As a result he talked a lot and he talked a lot of the blarney, as they say. But I didn't have a problem and I really miss having him around. He doesn't go away. He stays with you. I guess it's been, gosh. 1970. That's quite a while ago now. He was about sixty. He and Kenneth Patchen were done at about the same time at about the same age.

RO: You mention Du Plessix. She was among the early group that you befriended—along with Joel Oppenheimer and Fielding Dawson—and who you remained connected to for quite a long time.

JW: Francine, of course, she was in that class, summer of 1951, with me and, I think, Joel must've been there. Things were really poor. No money or food or anything.

RO: So when you started bringing out the first Jargon publications, you were setting these publications by hand. What's your relationship to the letterpress? Once you hit North Carolina, the Highlands, you let the Heritage Press do the work, but with the early publications you had your hand in the mix, maybe even setting some of the work?

JW: Well, not I, personally. We would pick somebody to do the setting. Some of those were extremely well done. Heritage Press was great, but it was rather predictable and we had to push them a little bit. They were not used to printing books of this sort and so we had to do a little pushing here and there. But they were wonderful to work with. I really liked those people. They did a lot of our books. Gosh, probably twenty-five or thirty. They did a lot. And they did them well. But we used to have to light the fires a bit every once and a while. They were a little bit predictable.

RO: What do you mean precisely by "light the fires"?

JW: Kick it around, as they say.

ROBERT J. BERTHOLF

THE JARGON SOCIETY AND CONTEMPORARY LITERARY HISTORY

Jim Lowell of the Asphodel Book Shop in Cleveland sold and distributed the early publications of the Jargon Society. He was an ardent reader of William Carlos Williams, had visited Charles Olson in Gloucester, gave D. A. Levy a safe place in Cleveland, and corresponded with writers in England and America. He knew Jonathan Williams and was an enthusiastic supporter of Jargon publications.

When I arrived at his shop in the fall of 1968, he became an immediate source for the publications and most of all news, especially impeccable literary gossip about the society and its writers. Conversations with him soon became documents of essential literary history because so little had been written about the writers whose books and pamphlets were so familiar to the store. He did not hesitate to say read this book, and this one, and please follow this magazine and that one also. In fact, the more I read and talked the more he was willing to talk, so visits to Cleveland and later to Burton, OH, were educational, directive and life changing.

He sold me a copy of Duncan's *A Book of Resemblances*, which I thought the most beautiful book I had ever seen, the two early installments of Olson's *The Maximus Poems*, Paul Metcalf's *Genoa*, Lorine Niedecker's *Tenderness & Gristle*, Joel Oppenheimer's *The Dutiful Son*, Louis Zukofsky's *A Test of Poetry* (he refused to sell me limited editions of Zukofsky's poems until I had read the *Paris Review* editions of *A*), Creeley's *The Immoral Proposition* and *All That Is Lovely in Men*, and, of course, Jonathan Williams' own books, including *Elegies and Celebrations*.

Many people have written about Jonathan Williams' curmudgeonly habits, his eccentric but informed ways of seeing and thinking, his natural habit of finding poems on billboards and menus, and, of course, his dedicated and persistent drive to support his view of the world in Jargon's publications. Being around him was also fun: the food, wine and conversation were always terrific. From the start, however, my main interest in Williams and the Jargon Society grew from my awareness that his publications constituted part of the literary history of American writing after 1945.

Williams left the Chicago Art Institute for Black Mountain College to study photography with Harry Callahan and Aaron Siskind, and ran directly into the powerful authority of Charles Olson, poet, and poetic thinker. Ten years before Donald Allen edited and published *The New American Poetry* (1960), Olson wrote and published his essay "Projective Verse" (1950). It took a few years for the implications of the essay to penetrate the writing of the new generation of writers, but when it did literary history suffered—or enjoyed, depending on personal views—a drastic break.

Olson's training reached back into the poetics of nineteenth century American writing and literary thinking, nurtured by F. O. Matthiessen, Frederick Merk and other professors in the new American Civilization program at Harvard. Though he disavowed the Romantic Imagination, even denying the writing of Emerson and Thoreau, he was baptized in the novels of Herman Melville, as well as familiar with the pragmatic thinking of Charles S. Peirce and John Dewey. His essay countered the literary traditions coming from T. S. Eliot—in fact most of the European Modernist assertion—that was in 1950 finding a new credibility in the New Criticism, with the poetry and essays of John Crowe Ransom, Cleanth Brooks, Robert Penn Warren, and others. He aligned himself with the poetic thinking of Ezra Pound—though there was a serious break with Pound over political issues—and the new writing of William Carlos Williams.

Olson, with Robert Creeley's support, argued for a poetry containing information, for a poetry which achieved its form as an extension of its content, for a poetry, then, which rejected predetermined structures. He also argued to expunge the egotistical "I" which he called "lyrical interference" as the centering, authoritative voice of the poem. Instead he thought the poet was an object like other objects in the field of action/information in which the poem took place, and was a participant in the resulting poem as a projection of that field of action. This position was radically against the position of the growing number of poets teaching and writing inside the protection and affirmation of academic institutions.

William Carlos Williams, who was closer to Wallace Stevens' concepts of the imagination than he admitted, thought so well of Olson's account that he quoted a long passage in his *Autobiography.* The Jargon Society published books for nine years amplifying Olson's concepts of achieved form and the Jargon idea of fine books and in these ways generated and cultivated the writing and thinking that Donald Allen named "Black Mountain Poetry" in his anthology *The New American Poetry* (1960).

From 1951 to 1960 the Jargon Society published books by central poets of the new American poetry, including Charles Olson, Robert Duncan, Robert Creeley, Paul Metcalf, Joel Oppenheimer, Michael McClure, and Jonathan Williams. The record is impressive and needs to be set out in more detail, though a full bibliographic record will wait for another publication. The two volumes of Olson's *The Maximus Poems* (1953) and (1956) set a standard for book design and printing that would be one of the signatures of Jargon publication. But the volumes also lead forward to joint publication with Corinth Books of New York of *The Maximus Poems* (1960), the volume which spread Olson's achievements to a wider audience and helped to define an era of American poetry.

Robert Creeley's Jargon publications followed a similar course from *The Immoral Proposition* (1953), *All That Is Lovely in Men* (1955), and *A Form of Women* (1958) to *For Love* (1962) by Charles Scribner's Sons, that began the transforming of Creeley from an interesting writer to a major poet.

In like fashion Robert Duncan's Jargon book *Letters: Poems 1953–1956* lead on to his trade publication with Grove Press, *The Opening of the Field* (1960) and fixed him as a rising poet in the San Francisco Renaissance of poetry but also a part of the group called by Donald Allen "The Black Mountain Poets," centered in Jargon's publications, Robert Creeley's editing of *The Black Mountain Review* and Cid Corman's editing of *Origin.* One small press and two journals made up the energy of the shift in direction of American poetry.

Jargon also published Michael McClure's first book *Passages* before he emerged as a main writer of the "Beat Generation," and Denise Levertov's first Jargon book *Overland to the Islands* (1958) initiated a series of trade book publications in the 1960s that made her a major literary figure. By 1958 she was in correspondence with Robert Duncan through the Jargon Society's ambience, and that correspondence lead to the decisively crucial discussion of the relations and interrelations of poetry, politics, and the Vietnam War. Joel Oppenheimer's early Jargon book *The Dutiful Son* (1957) developed into another later one *Names & Local Habitations (Selected Earlier Poems 1951–1972)* (1988), his column in *The Village Voice* and a distinguished career as a poet who used only lower case letters. Louis Zukofsky's first Jargon book, *Some Time* (1956), and then later *A Test of Poetry* (1964) brought the "Objectivist" movement of American poetry of the 1930s, where William Carlos Williams and Wallace Stevens were also active players, into the Jargon ambience before Zukofsky jumped ahead with the publication of his long poem *A* as a major poet, and who with George Oppen and Lorine Niedecker, beginning with her Jargon book, *Tenderness & Gristle: The Collected Poems (1936–1966)* (1968), brought a new discipline to the views of the objective status of the poetic line and the poem itself. Jonathan Williams' interest in and care for the British poet Basil Bunting was so admirable and actual that Bunting could not have written his late, grand poem *Briggflatts* (1966) without them and the attention of Tom Pickard.

Examples proliferate and though this essay cannot be definitive, some additional examples help clarify the lines of growth: Mina Loy's Jargon book, *The Last Lunar Baedeker* (1982), filled up a gap left in the older Modernist movement; James Broughton's *A Long Undressing: Collected Poems 1949–1969* (1971) brought a poet from the original, indigenous San Francisco poets into the Jargon world where Larry Eigner, with his *On My Eyes* (1960), and Canadian poet Irving Layton with his *The Improved Binoculars* (1956), and Kenneth Patchen's *Fables & Other Little Tales* (1953) were already settled residents.

Ian Hamilton Finlay's *The Blue and the Brown Poems* (1968) and Thomas A. Clark's *Some Particulars* (1971) focused Jargon's attention to the lineup of British concrete poetry. Paul Metcalf's *Will West* (1956) followed by *Genoa* (1965) brought the great-grandson of Herman Melville into the mix that Olson's studies in the American West had created. Ronald Johnson's *A Line of Poetry, A Row of Trees* (1964), Guy Davenport, *Flowers and Leaves* (1966), and Tom Meyer, *The Bang Book: Poem* (1971) and *At Dusk Iridescent: A Gathering of Poems 1972–1997* (1999) all exemplified the clarity and intelligence of the new in poetry; Tom Meyer also introduced a different discipline of seeing and writing initiated by Robert Kelly at Bard College.

Then there are the books of Jonathan Williams to fill up the record. The two early books *Amen/Huzza/Selah* (1960) and *Elegies and Celebrations* (1962), both Jargon books, are classic examples of Williams' electric style of picking up found lines and rearranging them in a poem. His sense of form inside the poem is as specific in two books published outside Jargon, *Mahler* (1969)—which might be Williams' most accomplished poetry—and *An Ear In Bartram's Tree: Selected Poems* 1957–1967 (1969)—matched by two Jargon books *Get Hot or Get Out: A Selection of Poems, 1957–1981* (1982), *Elite/Elate Poems: Selected Poems, 1971–75* (1979). He cultivated the views of an outsider, at times outraged, but also perceptive in his poems as well as in his support of folk art.

Literary history does not take place alone. Before he started publishing books, Jonathan Williams knew that poetry was integrally related to photography, painting, drawing, and music. Williams' first publication, *Garbage Litters the Iron Face of the Sun's Child,* contained an engraving by David Ruff, and Joel Oppenheimer's *The Dancer* contained a drawing by Robert Rauschenberg. Williams himself contributed the calligraphy for Olson's *The Maximus Poems 1–10,* while René Laubiès made the drawings for Creeley's *The Immoral Proposition,* Al Kresch the drawings for Levertov's *Overland to the Islands,* and R. B. Kitaj provided the cover for Williams' *Lullabies Twisters Gibbers Drags.*

Williams went to Black Mountain College to study photography so it is natural enough that photographs appear in Jargon's publications, Williams' own in Creeley's *All that Is Lovely in Men,* or Aaron Siskind's in Williams' volume *Elegies and Celebrations,* and Harry Callahan's in Larry Eigner's *On My Eyes.* Ralph Eugene Meatyard was a favorite of Williams, so his works appears in several books including Douglas Woolf's *Spring of the Lamb.* Jargon published Meatyard, *The Family Album of Lucybelle Carter* as well as Lyle Bongé, *The Sleep of Reason,* and *The Photographs of Lyle Bongé.* Including works of art was inside Jargon's commitment to publish beautiful, well designed books, finely printed. Late in his career Williams published a collection of his photographs with a commentary *A Palpable Elysium: Portraits of Genius and Solitude.* His portrait of Kenneth Rexroth could be Williams' signature photograph.

At the same time, Williams was equally enthusiastic about the music of Gustav Mahler, Anton Bruckner, Edward Elgar and at times Pierre Boulez—these and other musicians show up in his poetry, essays and correspondence.

The Jargon Society under Williams' direction developed its own ambience, and writers and artists communicated with one another mostly by letter. Olson's *Maximus Poems* were after all "Letters." Before and after "Projective Verse," Olson and Creeley corresponded often several times a day. Duncan and Olson provoked one another in their letters and Duncan and Levertov in their letters produced a massive commentary on poetics and the poets' response to the Vietnam War. Levertov corresponded with William Carlos Williams, Creeley with Levertov, and so on.

The letter was the medium of communication, and Jonathan Williams was tireless in keeping up the flow of the mail and when he had a chance to travel he expanded the ambience of the Society wider and wider. As a result, the Jargon writers left a massive record of their thinking, interconnections, their passions, personal and professional—in fact a rich deposit of the very best literary gossip and a huge assemblage of historical information.

A final note: When I went to Buffalo as Curator of the Poetry Collection in August 1978, the Jargon Society Archive had been appraised and was for sale in the manuscripts market. The Poetry Collection's focus on the poetry of William Carlos Williams and avant-garde writing of the Pound/Williams line created a necessity to bring the Jargon Archive to Buffalo.

There will be another time and place to tell the long story of the negotiations, compromises, even disputes, that made the purchase possible. Now I am more interested in saying that the papers are a huge reservoir of research materials to study how a small press managed its literary life, how one group of smart, articulate poets managed through their interconnections and their publications to define a kind of contemporary literary history. Smaller manuscript purchases followed and each gradually found relationships with the Jargon papers. Then the manuscripts of Robert Kelly arrived as a complement of the Jargon manuscripts for each had an ambience of publication and letters that went together, provided pieces of information that made the literary history possible.

With each smaller acquisition the larger collection "cured," and when the Duncan materials and his library arrived the archive revealed its greater depth and spread of the interrelations. The poets whose papers were in the library gave poetry readings, lectures, and came to talk about this and that. It was and is an active, living perhaps, archive day by day achieving its own history.

NEAL HUTCHESON

"INCLEMENTED THAT WAY"—JONATHAN WILLIAMS—
FINAL SCRIPT—TALK ABOUT WRITING:
PORTRAITS OF NORTH CAROLINA WRITERS

[The Neal Hutcheson Collection: Number: 05074-z at the Louis Round Wilson Special Collections Library at the University of North Carolina at Chapel Hill includes videotapes and other materials from Hutcheson's *Talk about Writing: Jonathan Williams* and *Jonathan Williams Selected Readings* (production completed, June 2001), funded by Jim Clark and the North Carolina State University Humanities Extension/Publications Program. The recordings feature Williams reading his poems; discussing writing, poetry, Jargon, and his life; and curiosities such as an appearance by H. B. Kitty—the Jargon Society mascot—and Williams showing off his thyrsus carved by Skip Taylor. The collection includes footage and the preliminary and final scripts from the NCSU Humanities Extension/Publications Program series, *Talk about Writing: Portraits of North Carolina Writers* and another Hutcheson film entitled *Mountain Talk*. What follows are transcriptions of Williams' comments during the sessions (transcribed and lightly edited by Jeffery Beam), the script of the final video, and the contents for the *Selected Readings*. The recordings and filmings took place in 1999 and 2000 at Skywinding Farm in Scaly Mountain.]

I was born the year of the Great Depression. My father came from Hendersonville, North Carolina … was running a stationery shop in Hendersonville. That failed, so … he got a job in Washington, D.C., must have been about 1932 … So I grew up in Washington … I had heard a little [of the way people talk around here] … I visited over in Henderson County as a child and then he bought this property when I was eleven, in 1941, and built this house and it was first occupied in 1942. We would come down here during the war years from Washington, D.C., where … my mother and I and usually an aunt or her mother would spend the summers down here and my father would come occasionally when he had a couple of weeks. He'd probably come twice. He'd drive down from Washington or take the train to Asheville, which was still running in those days. It was a very nice trip. You can read all about it in Thomas Wolfe's *Of Time and the River*. I think about the first hundred and twenty-five pages is the trip from Biltmore to wherever it is ... Washington or New York. It's quite good.

We built a kind of farmhouse, which is down the hill. Not the one that's immediately below us, which is kind of the guest house. We had a man who lived on [the property] everybody called "Tut." His name was Coolidge Burnette and he was the son of the man my father bought the land from. The Burnettes were a prominent family down here. My father wanted to put in apple trees and have an orchard, so Tut was in charge of that. So I got to hear him talk all the time—and his wife—so that's probably where it started. And he had kids, and his relatives around. It was a very distinctive way of talking, I'd never really heard that much of it. There were many more native people on the farms around here ... I guess the cost of everything up here has just run them off. Run them toward Franklin or run them down into Georgia, where things are much cheaper.

But by the time I was getting out of school, which would be 1947, I was pretty well-versed in it, I mean, I understood it pretty well ... Well, I remember in one of my books I credit Tut Burnette with something he said. How does it go, now? I was talking to him and said something he thought was very funny and he said ... They had this wonderful expression, "They Lord," which I guess is kind of like "thou," but, "They Lord, Jonathan. I'm just about tickled to death." And you remember things that are said that well. So I've got that in *Blues & Roots* at the beginning. That was 1944 if I got the date right.

But you'd hear wonderful expressions. There was a great talker across the road. His name was Ivan Owens. He was over there I guess, in the '50s. He was one of the best there was. He moved down into Georgia [to get] better medical care or something ... moving down into Georgia was going to be an advantage to him when he got older. I've got "Uncle Iv," as we called him, in three or four poems.

And there was a man over in what's now called "Sky Valley," in those days it was known as "Mud Creek." Sky Valley is a club. It's got the golf course, it's got the ski lift, it's got the tennis courts, it's got the restaurant and all that, and about five or six hundred houses over there, about a mile from here. Happily, it's on the other side of the mountain so we don't see much of it. But there was in those days one farmhouse over there and a big field of cabbage and on one of the slopes leading up to Rabun Bald which you see from Mud Creek, the second highest mountain in Georgia and a lot of trails up it ... There was a little cabin and there was a man in there who was known as, let me get it right, now ... Well, he was a hermit. And everybody called him "Cackleberry Brown." Have you ever heard that expression? Well, again, I thought, "Cackleberry? What's that?" And somebody said, "Well, some folks call him 'Hen Fruit.' 'Hen's fruit,' and it just sort of means 'egg.'" Cackleberry ... hen fruit ... egg. I thought, well, "That's pretty interesting," all this kind of, elaboration on simple words.

I wasn't exposed to very many people except the Baptist tribe on my father's side and also on my mother's side. She came from Atlanta, Georgia. They were very sort of middle class people at best, and talked very, very normally. I think people like that are sort of conservative by nature and the idea of colorful language doesn't occur to them. It kind of points at you if you use that kind of talk. But the mountain people just relished it. And, as I say, if I wanted to go to the waterfall and read a book, I'd pass by Uncle Iv's place and stop to talk ... Just, just to get it in my ears. He could talk about the weather for an hour. It was wonderful.

I miss it, because that's one of the things I liked best about the area, the dialect. I believe it's because there wasn't much learning, or book learning going on, people couldn't read and write, it throws you back on yourself. And talk is what developed, an ability, it's really wonderful ...

I didn't start trying to write it until I, I guess, basically ... a little bit in the '50s but those were the days when I was at Black Mountain and that kind of thing wouldn't have been very much on the stove. Charles Olson was cooking, frying other kinds of fish, you know. Very elaborate and intellectual things, and historical things. I don't think he had much interest in what the folks around were saying. But by that time I did have an interest, so maybe in the late '50s ... I guess the pivotal moment was taking the walk on the Appalachian Trail in 1961. It just seemed to be something to do. ... I did that for about four months, one of the nicest things about that was that we would encounter people all along the way ...

... I've always had books and always enjoyed them. In a sense I think something like the Jargon Society, the books I publish, I want to have the same kind of feel or passion about them as the childhood books ... if it's not exciting like that, or you don't feel good about it, you know, don't do it. I read so many books as a child. I guess that's where the interest in words really begin. I have to thank my parents for early exposure to reading ...

My father used to read me the first things I heard and they were in black dialect, he was very good at it ... a very skilled reader of dialect, particularly black dialect. I don't know why he was because Hendersonville never had very many black people—His mother ran a boarding house ... I can remember her, she was a wonderful ... she was good. She talked beautifully. So he would've been exposed to a few people like that. He would read Joel Chandler Harris—*Uncle Remus* of course. And I remember he read Kipling's *Just So Stories* very well.

Then he had a couple of favorites of his own—they were written by a man who is not very well known at the moment—he was a newspaperman from New Orleans and his name was Roark Bradford. He had two books telling Bible stories in back dialect. He was white, but he was a master of this form. He was just as good as Joel Chandler Harris and *Uncle Remus*, it's that kind of approach. I don't know how people feel about them now. I've read a couple of them to artist friends who are black and they thought they were funny and enjoyed them. It's like, can you use dialect of any kind without offending somebody—I suppose not. As I always say, offense is there, is provided, for those who will take same. You have to write what you write. It wasn't poking fun; just delighting in what was being said. One was called, *Ol' Man Adam an' His Chillun'*, which was later turned into a rather famous play and movie called *Green Pastures*, and the other one was called *Ol' King David an' the Philistine Boys*.

And I'd get those ... My father used to read those, they were party pieces. If there were people visiting, you'd eventually—if everybody'd had a few drinks—you'd get out those books and read a story. So that's one of the things I remember first is those two books—his books and Joel Chandler Harris', who was from Atlanta, a newspaperman, again. And whose house was maybe about four or five blocks from where my grandparents lived. He had a beautiful carpenter Gothic gingerbread house over on Gordon Street called "The Wren's Nest."

And there was a famous North Carolina dialect poet called John

Charles MacNeill. He came from somewhere down near Laurinburg. And he wrote in the black dialect. *Lyrics from Cotton Land* was one. It used to be the most popular book of poems that the University of North Carolina had ever published. I think it went through many many many editions. But it's pretty lightweight compared to these other people.

Obviously Roark Bradford had turned it into literature, as had Joel Chandler Harris, but as I say it took me a while to realize that I could do that too. I wasn't going to do it in the black dialect because I didn't have as good an ear for it as I had for the Appalachian dialect. Most of my experience with black people in the South was going to New Orleans and places like that, listening to musicians, local musicians play. So I had a little feeling for it. But I didn't have as good an ear for that as I had for Appalachian mountain country people.

After that it was the Oz books, which are full of strange names and places. I remember in 1939, I was ten years old, and I was in Woodward and Lothrop's department store in Washington. Naturally, like all good things it was on a remainder table in a department store. I still have the original copy with the price on it. And I bought a copy of the first edition of Tolkien's *The Hobbit* for 49 cents which I still have. So Tolkien was a big influence. I had that running around in my head. And Oz, I had all the Oz books, all forty or whatever. That's what my allowance went for, for two or three years …

Another thing that has become very important to me is found material—things that are outside of myself. A lot of that comes from walking. And I started walking, I thought, "Gee, there's the Appalachian Trail," you know. "Why not do that?" So like some crazy person I got started on the Appalachian Trail with Ronald Johnson, a poet friend. I didn't prepare for it … we walked close to 1500 miles. I just suddenly decided that was something to do. Started in May down near Dahlonega, Georgia. The southern terminus of the trail is Springer Mountain. And you go up Amicalola Falls, I believe it's called. You kind of take the trail up the side of the falls and get to Springer Mountain and then that's where the trail starts. So I did that for about, nearly four months, got about as far as the Hudson River, ran out of time, I couldn't afford any more time … one of the nicest things about that was the fact that we would encounter people all along the way.

The trail is not all that remote. In many places, it goes through farm country and you'd encounter people. Sometimes you had to go to a general store on one side of the ridge, maybe in Tennessee, or, you know, they'd have in your guidebooks, you can get food at six miles down on the Tennessee side. If you want such-and-such, you've got to go on North Carolina side, eleven miles. So you'd have to hitchhike down. And if it's a country store, there's always people in there talking. Sometimes you'd just get into conversation or sometimes you wouldn't, but I'd certainly register what was being said. If you look at the poems, particularly *Blues & Roots*, it's full of received conversation that I've done nothing except frame by the form of the lines. It's all out of somebody else's mouth, so to speak. I've tried not to intrude or make changes. I've pared it down a little bit.

I don't make much distinction. I like to find things, and then I like to make things. I don't particularly like to make up things, I just like to make things and they're usually things that I've found—either signs or conversation or words out of some stranger's mouth, which struck me as terrific.

The Appalachian Trail was where I got most of the material for *Blues & Roots*. Every day, I'd run into a few people. Someone working a field ... if we were walking in range, he'd want us to stop and talk. But that's the nature of mountain people, if you're doing something like hiking, they feel well-disposed ... except the guy who wanted to shoot us because we were near his still. But the other farmers would welcome a little break from what they were doing and a little news of the outside world. A lot of these people were living pretty far back in the bushes. I think that's something that people are always curious to know this and that. There's always a farmer who'll say, "Well, how many snakes have you seen today?" And I said, "Well, actually, I think I saw a black snake." He said, "We got more snakes than any other place I've ever been." You know, and they'd brag on how many snakes ... how dangerous they were. I mean, this is common practice. We heard that kind of talk quite often. So people are kind of proud and afraid at the same time. Brag on their snakes.

I keep coming back to the images of arrowheads, crystals, and bird song. It's just natural. Well, not entirely natural. You've got to work on an arrowhead. You've got to work to form it ... the wonderful sort of simplicity of it, and the crystal, again. Nature doing that work ... Jonathan Swift said there's not too much to poetry or prose; you just have to get the right words in the proper places. That could be said of baseball, you know. If you can't throw from shortstop to first, you better do something else. And if you can't get your words more or less quote right unquote, maybe you'd be better off making money. You know, doing something useful like working for an investment firm. Basil Bunting always said the interesting thing about poetry is that it has absolutely no value ... except in the way that a glass of water is valuable. It's free but it's very important when you want one, when you need one. And the same thing is more or less true of poetry. It's not going to make you any money, but it can maybe help you pass the time, which we all need on occasion, whether it's certain kinds of music or conversation or whatever ... There's so much silence involved with poetry. The silences are sometimes the most interesting parts of it. The way the thing is being put together. And the pauses. It's very interesting, as I say ... what we're just simply trying to do is make a kind of picture of the mind's music on paper.

I did a lot of it that summer, because I had time. There's always about an hour before dark if you're on a long hike when you've eaten your evening meal and there's some light and you either read or ... I got out my notebook and just started playing around and seeing what I could do with this stuff and I discovered that it wasn't too hard. But it took a lot of listening and you have to listen very, very ... So, I've gotten very, very good, I would say, at listening, and, as I say, I'm quite happy to more or less stay out of it.

This is nothing that poets haven't been doing for a long time. The nature and visionary poet John Clare, the Englishman, he said that he "found the poems in the fields and only wrote them down," which is a great way of looking at it.[1] Blake said he had received his poems and took no credit.

You never know when you hitchhike what's going to transpire. I used to do a lot trying to get to New Orleans to listen to music. It seemed relatively safe ... I did get into a strange situation in LaGrange, Georgia ... about one or two in the morning and I was standing in a town square. And this car came roaring, you know, into town. And I didn't know whether to put out my arm or not, but I decided I would. The car wasn't too bad but the guy was strange. I looked in the back and there were all kinds of knives and cleavers. And I said, "What's all that equipment back there?" He says, "I'm a butcher ... I'm taking all my tools and gear down to be cleaned up and I have a little place down here in the country." I asked him what his name was. He said his name was Jenneth Watson. I said,"Jenneth? Not Kenneth?" He said, "That's a family name." So, I've never forgotten Jenneth

Watson. And I was kind of glad to get out of his car. The more I talked to him, the less frightening he became. I mean, that does make you think, as I say, to have all that stuff back there. But I went on down to Nawlins.

Something that has always been is an interest in music, a serious interest. I know much more about the history of music than about the history of literature. This is not just European Western music, it's also American music, jazz. I used to go down to New Orleans in the late '40s and I heard some of those great players.

I don't know how much culture's left. Most of the people, you know, the native population that once was here are hardly here at all now. There are a few shopkeepers who have been in the same family for two or three generations, but I don't know where they've gone. I'm sure there's some, but I only know one or two people around Highlands who, are kind of authentic and speak as their grandparents [did].

And later I had the same experience in settling into the Yorkshire Dales and being exposed to the broad Yorkshire, as they call it, "Yorkshire Tyke," T-Y-K-E … a word that I've never quite understood what it means. It is kind of the patois. It's broader than anything that we have around here. It's much easier in England, somehow, I don't know why … England's a small place. You'd think with the television everywhere that the dialects would've gone, but they haven't. Even the kids … grade school, they talk as broad as their grandfather would … They know the difference. They can talk like television. But when they're in the family talking [among] themselves, they still are so thick that you really have trouble, even after being there for years.

Each Dale in the Yorkshire Dales has a slightly different accent. People who live two Dales away from each other sometimes have a little trouble understanding each other. The one that we are in is called Dent—Dentdale—which was occupied by the Vikings and the Norse for a long time. So there are lots of words that you learn. I mean, it's so different. They don't call hills "hills," they call them "fells," which is a Norse word. Clearing is a "thwaite." A cliff is a "scar." Everything is different. And it's wonderful … it's great! I've always loved to hear a new word or find a new word, and understand what it means … [yet] these people are not all that different. The people occupying Yorkshire are either Anglo-Saxons, like most of the people around here, or Celts—that's the Irish-Scottish strain … So the stock of the people is very similar and if you live there long enough you realize

... you begin to sense even more similarities. There's a kind of a dark Presbyterian sort of feeling about the Yorkshire people. They expect something terrible to happen. You can be walking down the road and see a farmer's wife that you've spoken to and say, "Lovely morning, madam." And she'll say, "Aye, we'll pay for it." She's thinking about December the nineteenth. Freezing conditions, and having to bring the sheep in. But this was nice, July. And I've heard mountain people greet each other around Highlands. "How're you, how're you today, Ed?" And he'll say, "Well, I'm no worse." There's this kind of fatalism that country people have. But it took me a while to feel like I was doing the Northern English accent. I can't speak it very well but I can certainly understand it and I know what the words [mean] ... most of them. But, as I say, it's very different to our ears.

A farmer was visiting a friend of ours up the Dale. He stopped and came in for a minute with a child, a young child, [age] one or two, who was yowling and carrying on. And he said, "Well, Mike, he, he's right nangy this evening." And I said, "He's what? Nangy?" I'd never heard that. It's sort of obvious, when you think about the sound of it ... the baby was very unhappy—unsettled. So "nangy" is a word that I've liked ... I've even called myself sometimes "The Lord Gnang." Put a G in front of it, like, G-N-A-N-G. Gnang! [Heard it] up in a little village above us called Gawthrop, which meant "home of the cuckoo" back in Medieval times.[2]

The place names in England are absolutely fascinating. You look at the map ... I think I'd rather read a map than most novels. Because there's more going on. I have a little fragment which I call a poem but others might think it's a little too brief and not enough going on, but ... It's just four words. "Hag worm haw moss." *Hag worm haw moss.* It does enough for me, I mean, the "hag," the A changes to "haw." Three letters. "Hag worm haw moss." And what that means is ... It's the marshy place on the side of the hill where the adders live. I mean, to translate it, you'd have to just about use that many words. But a "hag worm" is an adder. And a "haw" is the hill, and the moss is the marshy place.

But, you know, this is theoretically the English language. [Bad English?] Well, [no], just because it's not used in the sort of common, ordinary way ... As I say, most people have almost no conversation in them anymore, I don't know what's the matter. They're not used to talking to each other much anymore. It's quite startling how if you go to the restaurants in Highlands and listen to people … In the summer, there's a nice little French cafe run by *actual living* French people from the Southwest of France and it's very nice. They go back to Florida in the winter, unfortunately. But if you listen to conversations in there it's just staggering … Well, the poverty of the language.

A lot of Americans—I don't know—they just don't know how to talk. They have these strangulated voices, and in the South, a lot of them are too loud. You can hear halfway across the restaurant what somebody's talking about—which is not pleasant. But if it's older people, they're talking about their grandchildren, they're talking about the next cruise, and then they're talking about money. That's about all. You never hear any conversation about what people are reading or music or … the arts are just out of it. I guess people talk about movies sometimes. That's about it. And you can have that same experience all summer … Certainly, ideas are never discussed; and very seldom, politics. I guess those are things you don't talk about in America. Religion, politics, sex … at the table, anyway. But it's an impoverished situation and I don't care whether it's educated or uneducated, if somebody's got something to say that interests me, who cares, you know. *Who cares.*

[Uncle Iv] talked about the weather a lot. One time, he was taking a cow to pasture. He just stopped and we talked and talked about the crops and milk and all that sort of thing, and he said, after about an hour, he said, "Well, Mister Williams, I reckon … I can tell that I'm a-hesitatin' you. So I'll be seeing you later." So he wandered off. But "a-hesitatin'" is a wonderful expression. One time I took Stefan Wolpe, the composer who was at Black Mountain at the time to see the waterfall. European … born in Berlin … lived in Israel; then when he came to the United States taught in Philadelphia, taught in New York, and then was down at Black Mountain College when I was there in the '50s. Stefan had a fairly broad German-American accent. We stopped and I introduced him and [Uncle Iv] said, "Where are you from, Mister?" And Wolpe said, "I'm from Berlin, Germany. Do you know where that is?" And he said, "Well, no, I ain't ever heerd of it so I reckon it must be somewhere yon side of Asheville." Iv was a man who went on a cabbage truck one time to Atlanta and he got down there and didn't like all the people and said he'd never go to a city again. But his idea of where you went was to Franklin because he had some kin down there and he could stay the night. It's about, well, if you went across country … it would be about fifteen miles, so he would go and then the next day he'd come back. But he didn't like to go any further really than he could go and come and get back by dark. So that limited him to Scaly Mountain and Dillard, down the mountain. That's a steep walk. That's a very, very old-fashioned way of sensing where you are in the world. That's kind of the same way that the Greeks went about it … the idea of a *polis*, you know. You went out from the center to the edge and then you came back and it was very measured by one's physical capacity to get out … to be on the edge and get back. That's what city-states were about. Those are the only two kinds of dialect that I've ever really pursued.

Well, I don't know whether we raised that point in an earlier talk, but I've sort of figured out, I think, to my satisfaction that the reason [the native mountain folk] were so good was because book-learning and all those kind of things were hardly available and they had to work for daddy and no school after maybe the age of fifteen. So they didn't have what you'd call really much skill trying to read or trying to write, so, that throws you back on yourself … And so, talk is what they developed to a high degree of ability, I mean, it's really wonderful. But I haven't met a good talker in Macon County for years, really … Well, as I say, everything was much more individualistic in those days and people were more individualistic and conversation was more interesting because they had very little … They weren't reading books and they didn't know how to write very well. I still know people that are in that situation in the county, but I just think there were more … A lot of those people had a bit more personality and they weren't … sitting hour after hour looking at television and being exposed to all the stuff outside. Maybe that's not always a good thing. In England, it seems as though people have these things now, they've got all their media stuff. But they're much more rooted, it seems to me, in England than we are and it's much more homely and the people … take care of each other. It's much slower and it's not always about being entertained … I just can't stand it … I pick up *The New York Times* Sunday looking for the culture news and ninety percent of it's some blessed movie that I don't really want to see. I haven't seen a good movie in about fifteen years; I just have given up on it. I just can't … Who has the time? … There're enough distractions as it is. To get anything done I just have to live in the woods, I can't imagine any other way to get anything done. It's not easy even, having all the time we have available here.

We try not to go to Highlands more than twice a week just to get provisions and go to the bookstore and there's one place that's nice for lunch so we try to maybe do that once a week. Otherwise, I have no business in Highlands—it's three hundred shops selling stuff that nobody needs or people who live here need. So it's geared to a tourist invasion. I was reading *The New York Times* recently that Carmel, California, which is a place I visited in, well, almost fifty years ago, and was quite charmed by, as were a lot of people in the arts. Robinson Jeffers, the poet, lived there. The photographers Edward Weston and his son and Neal and ... Well, one, I'm forgetting, I don't know why, he's very good ... Brett. Brett Weston. Ansel Adams. Wynn Bullock ... I knew a couple of science fiction writers who lived out in Carmel Valley. I don't think they'd probably live there anymore because this report said Carmel now has a hundred and eleven art galleries. This is a town of about two to three thousand people. And the parenthesis was that each one is worse than the one before. And the daily influx of tourists is twenty-five thousand, every day, twenty-five thousand people coming into this town.

Well, I'm told that on a hot, July weekend, not necessarily the Fourth of July, there'll be five to ten thousand people in Highlands, and I think I believe it because ... it's almost impossible to walk down the street. And I don't know what those shops have in them, but I don't think there's anything much that I need ... the most honest shop has closed because the lady who ran it for about fifty years finally just got too old to keep doing it. That was a shop called "The Condiment Shop." Elizabeth Edwards ran it since about 1950 to now, but she's about ninety years old. It's hard work making jams and jellies and conserves and pickles ... I think it's hard to find people to help her. So that's gone ... after all, those were things growing in the mountains picked by local people and preserved and they were very good. She was wonderful ... those things were very, very good and people knew about them all over the country. But, as I say, that's about quote "the most authentic" quote unquote shop that Highlands had.

[Pumpkin butter?] I'm not sure that I have [tasted it]. Have you tried it? It's odd. The English really dislike pumpkins, and pumpkin pie, of course, well, they don't have. They don't have Thanksgiving, do they? But they are always making remarks about the Americans because of these terrible pies that they eat.

There's a woman named Ruby Vinson who's an old-time person and she's probably eighty but she's still cooking. She makes pastries and desserts for a restaurant up in Highlands. And she makes the best buttermilk pie that I know. And we had a Jargon Society meeting and I insisted that everybody try this pie, and one of the people said, [after] I said, "How you like it?" "Is this as good as it gets?" So we had one complaint, at least. But there's another pie that's called chess pie which is kind of like it. I couldn't tell you the difference, but it's rather similar.

We had delicious pumpkin pie from this little catering restaurant up in town called "Wild Thyme." Delicious. But guess who's in the kitchen doing most of the work? The owners are doing some of it and they're both highly trained out of the Ithaca's Culinary Institute [of New York]. So they have a lot of training. But their staff, the guys that are actually doing most of the cooking are three guys from Kathmandu in Nepal. So, as a result, you get all sorts of amazing soups—Thai this and that. [A] hot and sour soup that can be very good, and in their case, it is. And all kinds of preparations that are somewhat Asian, somewhat Italian, and French, a bit. So it's extraordinary, I mean, that Macon County all of a sudden has people like this, you know, operating, so, that's a good sign. It's a very good sign.

[I first came back here] about 1970, I guess we've been putting in a lot of time since. The big changes didn't come until in the '80s and then as of '90—the last ten years have been a lot of change. Well, it wasn't about half the size that it is now. All these little strip malls weren't here. And, as I say, I don't know what these shops have in them, but, it doesn't look ... as though there's much for me. It's either junk or it's very, very up-market stuff. Because there's two kind of people ... wandering the streets, mostly people up from, well, places like maybe Gainesville, Georgia ... certainly they're coming from places like Spartanburg and Greenville, South Carolina. Maybe they even come from Asheville. Just come for the day and wander about and they don't spend all that much money but, then, of course the [new] people who live here are, tend to be, very wealthy and it's a different breed. You don't see them much out in the daytime. But they shop, and there's some clothing stores up there that are like things you'd find in Atlanta or New York. There is a nice little bookstore which is run by somebody who knows what he's doing and his two assistants are … very well-read. They know what they've got, and they can order through Ingrams. If you want a book you can get it probably within three days. I don't know why this business about getting stuff overnight or two days from now is important. So, you want a book—you don't have to read it this week. It's another notion, you know. It's a way to spend money. FedEx—I'm perfectly happy with book rate which takes me back when I first started Jargon back in the '50s. Book rate was eight cents for the first pound and maybe twelve cents for every additional pound … most books would get out of here for eight and twelve, which is, what, twenty? Twenty cents. Now, it's, what? Maybe, three dollars, three-fifty? Four-twenty.

[The people in Highlands] were people like grocers. There've been two generations of Brysons doing that. A lot of people, local people were into real estate, even then. Trying to sell land. As I say, it's gotten absolutely wild. I think land around Highlands costs about what it might in a place like East Hampton out on Long Island. And there again, I hear people in East Hampton and South Hampton who're, who don't want to put up with the crowds, that come here all the time. So they're moving to places like Maine and northern New Hampshire and that's pretty drastic. Not only is it, you know, a terrible winter, but there's really almost nothing going up there. To go from that kind of society into the woods'll be hard for people.

But, as I say, there were real estate people, there were the usual things that a small town would need. A good hardware store. There were beauty parlors—a few. There were I guess two markets. The Potts family was very prominent. I think the permanent population in those days, about 1970, would have been about five or six hundred. And about probably half of those would have been people who came here and built second homes or summer houses and then liked it and decided to winterize them, and so the quote "native population" has never been all that much up on the plateau here. Most of the people in the county are down around Franklin which is a really sort of workaday place. If you need to get some tires, you go to Franklin. If you need to see an anesthesiologist, you go to Franklin. Lowe's is down in Franklin. Wal-Mart, Kmart, they're all down there.

The poetry didn't really start until I went to Black Mountain College. And before that I had gone to Princeton for a year and a half and I dropped out of Princeton because I just couldn't stand the people.

I did very well in prep school, I mean I participated fully—I was captain of the tennis team, I was captain of the soccer team, the newspaper, Prefect, you know, so I really enjoyed it. But, seeing all these upper middle-class establishment kids all thrown together into a place like Princeton was too much for me I felt very alien somehow all of sudden. Everybody there was like George Bush or James Baker—James Baker was a year younger than I—but those were the kind of people who were there and they were all going to go into daddy's law firm or The Bank. And it was going to be a life of country clubs and all that, and I just didn't want to spend the rest of my life doing that. All of a sudden I realized, this is not what I'm going to do and I dropped out of that and I'm very glad I did.

At Princeton, I was not very enamored of the place, but I got my work done there and I certainly hardly strained myself at all and I would end up with A's or B's. But, you'd see your lecturer once a week for an hour … so I didn't like the kind of distance I felt from people at Princeton … but I had heard about a college in North Carolina called Black Mountain so I signed up for that and went to the summer session in 1951. Actually Harry Callahan was teaching photography at the Institute[3] and he suggested I go to Black Mountain because he was going to be there that summer. He said he "also had a friend from New York who's going to come down and his name is Siskind and I think you'll like him, he's great." I did very much like him.

Well, the opposite was true at Black Mountain. I mean Olson would have classes after dinner which would start maybe at 8 o'clock. They would go until maybe the local tavern was about to shut down. People would rush to the local tavern, pick up beer, bring it back to the college, the class would continue, sometimes it would go through the next day … you could hardly fail to find out some things that were important to you from people of the caliber that we're talking about.

So, that's kind of how that all happened. So when I got to Black Mountain, ostensibly to study photography, I was introduced to this enormous man, Charles Olson. He was about the biggest man you've ever seen. He was bigger than Jesse the Body Ventura. He was about 6'9" … with more energy than a roomful of people. So, he kind of started me writing. He was excellent in the sense that he didn't insist that all of his students write his kind of poetry. He tried to bring them out of themselves. He was a good person to work with and he would give you tremendous numbers of books to read. It was very exciting. A very great man. That's hard, particularly because I studied with someone as massive and strong-willed as Charles Olson. It's not that he insisted you write like he, but his style was so overpowering—I had to get most of that out of there because I have a very different nature than Charles. You ran a risk being a student of his of being kind of smothered. You know, huge guy, and, as I say, he just was about the most energetic person that you'd ever encounter. I mean, he's just sparking all the time, stuff was happening all the time. He was here, he was there, he was in, he was out. I haven't met but one or two people in life who are like that. So that was very exciting to be with him.

I started writing the poetry ... in the summer of '51, with Olson ... I started having small books come out about 1958, '57 ... In my case I think it took about ten years to establish what you might call my own voice ... Putting together this selected poems of mine, I'm not taking very much out of the 1950s ... that's the first ten years that I wrote.

I had a lot of very good mentors. [Robert Creeley] ... came to Black Mountain as someone to teach and I was still in the position of being a student. But my contemporaries there, the one that I was closest to was Joel Oppenheimer. There was Fielding Dawson who's always been a friend ... I published a couple of little things of his at first but I haven't really followed his career. He's mostly a story and fiction writer and also, at one time, a very talented person with ink and a pen ... and collage, and so on. I did a book with him about 1960. *Empire Finals at Verona.* Very good images. It's got that great picture of Stan Musial and his famous crouch waiting for a pitch. That's a terrific drawing. Dawson came from a suburb of St. Louis called Kirkwood. I got to read that poem on television in St. Louis and Musial rang up the station and said, "Bring him over for lunch." He was in the restaurant business after he retired. So I got a free lunch out of Stan, which was great. One of the occasional uses of poetry. Let's see, who else ... Ed Dorn was somebody I never really knew very well. He was there. I was quite friendly with Michael Rumaker who turned into, again, a fiction and short story writer. He was in Olson's class. Later on there were a couple of people when I wasn't there much; John Wieners was a student. That's just about all, I guess. The summer of '51, Francine du Plessix Gray was in the class and I've kept up with her pretty closely. She was down here recently for that Black Mountain College symposium in

Asheville … was very good, I thought, on the night. So Joel Oppenheimer has died and Ed Dorn has died and Wieners has had a lot of psychological problems. His career has not been entirely happy.

Creeley is still very active. He'll be, I guess, seventy-four this year. But he's still full tilt. Full tilt. He was brought [to Black Mountain] by Olson to instruct and was there for about, I don't know, maybe two spring times.

I'd guess it was '54 and '55. And then he left. Went out west and got married for the second time to a woman in New Mexico and he lived out there for a quite a while. North of Albuquerque. Placitas. But I was particularly fortunate in some of the writers that I knew and from about the age of well, less than twenty … I went to see Kenneth Patchen who was very important to me. Went to see Kenneth Rexroth in San Francisco, a bit later than that. Went to see Henry Miller. Knew Paul Goodman. Knew Louis Zukofsky. So that's a pretty formidable bunch. And plenty of others, too. I had quite a lot of exposure to all of those guys. [They] could tell you where you were at and what you might try to get to. One of the most important things, I think, is knowing, so to speak, what to read and … reading the right poets. Someone like Zukofsky or Rexroth was tremendously read. Rexroth was an autodidact. I don't think he went to school. He was taught at home by Socialist intellectual parents in some place in Indiana where he grew up. Elkhart, Indiana. Like Edward Dahlberg, who was also an autodidact … tremendously, richly read … It's important that you know people like that. You can do a lot of it on your own but I'm still finding out books that I should have read fifty years ago. You know, why didn't I read that book, you know? Stupid. Somehow I didn't, so …

When I was at Black Mountain I got the call that I was going to be drafted. I had to fight that battle for about a year. Rather than go to jail in the state of Virginia I decided to accept the advice of some my mentors … they all said go into the medical corps, it'll be less damaging to yourself. And I think they were right.

You could go before a federal hearing officer and they had one at the post office building in Asheville. That's the county seat of Buncombe County. [He] had a marvelous name: Kingsland van Winkle. As in, Rip. And so I had this conversation and said that I was going to pursue a conscientious objector's position and so I did. So I was in Alexandria, VA—it must have been in 1952, because this thing was like January '52. Someone said "Well, this judge up here usually gives maximum sentence and you would probably go to jail for five years and you'd get some time off for good behavior." So I talked to several people. I talked to Patchen and Rexroth, who were both pacifists. Paul Goodman, who was a pacifist. Olson, who kind of leaned that way. And we talked to the War Resisters League which was an organization that was devoted to helping COs. They said if you can get into the medics, go for that. That's two years and you might find yourself doing something of use and [it] also might be interesting, depending on where they send you. They said of course, you might get sent to Korea, but maybe you wouldn't. So we decided we would approach the army authorities and my father got a lawyer and they said, sure, sure, he can go in the medics. Of course, when I was inducted, the first thing to happen was they sent me to Fort Knox, Kentucky, which was a rifleman's training place, so I had a little bit more fun. I refused to accept the weapon after a week or two. Then there was talk of court marshal and I went to several chaplains there. I went to the Episcopal chaplain; I had been brought up in an Episcopal school. He wouldn't support the position. Catholic chaplain wouldn't support the position. So I went to see the Jewish chaplain whose name was Chaplain Caplan which means chaplain, I think. And Chaplain Caplan was sort of a poetry nut, it turned out. He knew a lot about poetry. I gave him something I published and he said I'll get on the phone and get you sent to where they train the medics at Camp Pickett, Virginia. So, finally, I got into the medics. After training at Camp Pickett they sent us down to Fort Sam Houston [in] San Antonio, Texas. I had about three months studying. My category was neuropsychiatric technician so I trained to be an orderly on a psychiatric ward ... And then there was a short bit of training at Walter Reed hospital in Washington. From there, we were sent by ship from New Jersey to Hamburg. I went down to Stuttgart to what they called the Fifth General Hospital. I was working as a Neuropsychiatric Technician. That just meant I was working in the locked ward with some of the more violent and unpleasant patients. And that was all right.

It was interesting. It wasn't really dangerous, but, you always had the possibility that some psychopath would jump you if you didn't watch out very carefully.[4] And there were people who were very aggressive and hostile and deranged. A lot of people weren't, they were either in depression or some of them were malingering, as they called it ... trying to get out of the

Army by acting crazy. There were some of those always. There were people who were being restrained and put on electroshock therapy which wasn't very pleasant. I had to grab somebody by the left leg and be part of a team to drag him in there and get his head zapped. I don't know, I think they stopped that procedure, but at the time it was en vogue. It would certainly take the meanness out of somebody; there would be no more aggression for a while. But I think frankly it was often done on racial lines. You know, some big black dude with a bad mouth would find himself on that table quicker than somebody else. I'm sure that [was] part of it. There was an interesting psychiatrist who had been drafted. He was from New York, had a New York practice. He was gay, this black guy. So I saw quite a lot of him. Harold Trigg, I think his name was. I saw that he died. In the *New York Times* there was an obit maybe ten years ago. But he was a very charming, civilized guy. He hated all those career psychiatrists who had been trained down at Texas. He just didn't want anything to do with them. So there were odd moments like that. There were some great lesbian nurses. Really tough ones who were very nice [that] I liked. They seemed to gravitate to that particular ward for some reason. Well, they were pretty sturdy girls and we got along very well with them.

I had enough free time while I was in Stuttgart to publish Olson's first volume of *The Maximus Poems*, Robert Creeley's *The Immoral Proposition*, Kenneth Patchen's *Fables and Other Little Tales*. And a kind of big standing broadside folded sheet thing of mine, some poems with some drawings by a man named Charles Oscar who was married to the dancer Katherine Litz. So, I was fortunate. Instead of going to Korea like most of the medics I ended up in Stuttgart which happened to be the center of German printing … ten minutes down from the hospital where I was stationed … and got to go to marvelous places. Zurich and Munich and Paris. Majorca to see the Creeleys … so I have no reason to complain about my time in the Army.

Stuttgart was an extremely interesting place. Musically, it was one of the most interesting places in Germany. They had the famous chamber orchestra and they had the South Radio Symphony Orchestra. They had an opera, which wasn't bad. And lots of recitals. I heard really great people—Alfred Cortot, Clara Haskil—really wonderful pianists. I think I did about as well that I possibly could have done. I just got very lucky.

The only thing I knew was that New Directions had printed a couple

of books [with Dr. Walter Cantz'] print works in the same town as the hos-
pital, which was across the River Neckar from Stuttgart. Ten minutes away
from the railroad station downtown. So I immediately found out where the
place was and went down the hill and met those people and they told me,
you know, about all the terrific printers there were in Stuttgart, they'd
mostly come from places like Dresden and Leipzig. Those had been centers
of printing. But those towns were heavily bombed so a lot of people [had
come] to Stuttgart. It was bombed too, but not like those places. By the
time I got there in '52 they were still in the midst of rebuilding the down-
town. Typically, they had bombed the opera house, the art museum. They
seemed to have missed the railroad station but somebody said that's because
they wanted to keep the lines going, you know. So they left the enormous,
great … central station. But most of the cultural parts of town had to be
rebuilt. But it was a great time to be there. It was a very nice town. One of
the nicest cities I think I know …

Well, it's a tiny bit like Asheville in that it's got hills all around it and
in the case of Stuttgart, they're mostly vineyards. And they come right on
into the town … the country's very close at hand, you know. There's some
very nice architecture and people were quite friendly. We had to wear uni-
forms but that didn't seem to bother them too much.

Hamburg's up in the northwestern part … they've got a harbor. It's a
big port. That's the way we sailed from America and then back to I guess
the same place, I forget … New Jersey, somewhere. You'd go down to a
place like Frankfurt and then keep on going south and you'd get to maybe
like Heidelberg and then a little bit to the southeast would be Stuttgart.
And then if you kept on going to eastern Germany you'd hit places like
Augsburg, Wurzburg, Ulm. And then Munich. Then you'd be down in
Bavaria. If you went south of Stuttgart you'd end up sort of on the Swiss
border in the Bodensee. Lake Lucerne, is that what they also call that? I
think so. And then to the west of Stuttgart was Karlsruhe and then south
of that is like Baden Baden and Freiburg. And then you're at Basel. So you're
not too far from Switzerland there.

Well, Jargon really got its start. We had done a couple of broadsides
at Black Mountain but these were books so that's where it really happened.
And again the luck of being in a place where the printers knew so much,
they could teach me how to really do good books. I didn't have to work

with somebody who prints the newspaper in Asheville, who knew nothing. These were extremely skilled artisans. The books we did there look as good as anything we've done since. A couple of them are really my favorites; Olson's *Maximus Poems* … Zukofsky's *Some Time*. I don't see how we could have done it any better …

If Black Mountain had any money and had continued I would have done a number of publications for the college, been publisher to the college. It closed in '56, so then I was kind of on my own.

Jargon Society is a writer's press, a small press, started by me at Black Mountain College in July 1951 with the first publication being a, just a little folded sheet with a drawing by Robert Rauschenberg on the cover, a poem by Joel Oppenheimer dedicated to the dancer Katherine Litz. It was given to everybody at the college and Rauschenberg was given a supply, I was given a supply, Joel was given a supply. I think we sold about twenty-five which didn't pay for it … gave all the rest away. It's a very desirable item at the moment. For one thing, it was the first time that Rauschenberg had ever done an illustration for any publication. We didn't know that at the time but that's the first time he'd ever done that … I think it was in that Whitney Museum exhibition that he had a couple of years ago and it's worth big dough, you know. I've got one in our archive at the University of Buffalo … I don't have one here. I hardly have any of the early Jargon books, they're all up at Buffalo … they're so rare. Yeah, that thing's worth God knows. It's the first Jargon and it's the first Rauschenberg, you see, so it's a very desirable item. I think we did a hundred and fifty. Joel printed most of it. Joel Oppenheimer knew how to use a press and we did it up in this little shop that was at the college. Bought the paper from a paper company in Asheville and printed up some envelopes. It was a nice little item. It was well done. Two colors. Katherine Litz was a wonderful dancer and very active that summer. There was a production of, I think it was called *The Glyph*, a text by Charles Olson. Ben Shahn did the set, Katie Litz danced, music was by Lou Harrison. So that was a great occasion, I remember that. Lou Harrison's still active at eighty-two, eighty-three years old. One of the best American composers, so he's still on the job. Rauschenberg's still very active, I think … and Merce Cunningham is still active. So, track record's pretty good for a lot of these guys. They've lasted very well.

[The Jargon Society] is doing okay. Tom Meyer's *At Dusk Iridescent,* which is a gathering of his poems over a twenty-five-year period, came out this year and had a lot of attention, a very good reaction from a lot of people and a certain number of good reviews. So we're happy to get that out. But it's slowed down because, well, there again, I've slowed down some ... When Jargon was more active, that meant that I had to spend most of my time fundraising, and, you know, going places and having dinner parties and talking to people and trying to raise money. Well, after a while you just get beyond that. You don't want to do that anymore. So I haven't ... And then you have to send out newsletters all the time. Not just once a year but about three or four times a year to get people's attention, to get them remember what it's all about. And I've been sort of holding back on that front but I think in January we will get out a fiftieth anniversary newsletter and wave the begging bowl at them again, you know. And if they produce ... everybody's said to have a lot of money these days, so, I'd like to see a little of it, but it certainly hadn't come, well, it's not come if we haven't asked. The checks are not in the mail. We've got about four or five books we want to do and we have always been in that position. But all these things cost so much money ... any time you're putting out any kind of book ... probably a thousand copies is going to cost you ten thousand dollars, at least, just to produce ... this *Tuscan Trees*, the next book by Mark Steinmetz, his photographs. Janet Lemke text. It's going to be a charming book, but, like I say, it's at least in that figure, ten thousand at least. And that's a little hard to get your hands on. I've always liked the idea of the National Patron level which is a thousand dollars ... if people would give a thousand dollars a year. If fifty people would do that we would have no problems whatsoever, but I've never been able to get that figure up over maybe fifteen or twenty. And then there are people who are willing to give us a hundred bucks or occasionally five hundred but there're not that many of them. It's a constant search, and, I've just sort of tired of the search. But we'll keep doing what we can as we can.

There are no particular plans [for the fiftieth anniversary at the moment], but there had been talk of an exhibition at the Berg Collection in New York's Public Library. Oh, well, I first talked to the curator there back in 1996 and he was talking about the date of '98. Well, here we are in 2000 and there's still nothing concrete on the desk or on the table. So I've decided, if he wants to do it he has to get in touch with various booksellers and librarians and let them do it. I just don't want to … I can't involve myself with that much … what shall we call it? I mean, it's all just kind of like ephemeral and you know, nothing solid. There's nothing tangible in the offer. There's no dates, there's nothing clear. And after a while, I've just decided to back off from it. I'm sure there'll be something somewhere, we'll organize. That'll be fifty years after July of 1951. So … isn't that right? Yeah. Yeah, that's fifty years. It seems longer. About a hundred and twenty [books], something like that. Yeah, two or three a year. It adds up eventually. As I say, appetite changes.

I came back to North Carolina in January of 1954, and I started spending sometime here and sometime at the college. Jargon was just kind of getting started. Olson's book was available I think in '54. So we were trying to sell that. And also the *Black Mountain Review* was being published … we were trying to get it scattered around and sold, distributed. We worked on things like that and I was in Black Mountain quite a lot that summer.

But, with me it seemed the best thing to do was get these books out to the attention of people, so I got the idea that I would get in the car and take them all around the country, offer to give readings … and that worked, I did that for maybe the next eight or ten years, crisscrossing the country …

In the '50s I'd inherit cars that my father had worn out, they used as much oil as gas. Mostly Pontiac station wagons. That was in the '50s. I think in the '60s was the first time I had my own car. It was a Volkswagen Beetle. By 1980, I had gone through about six…. And I'd, you know, drive them all about a hundred and fifty thousand miles.

I think I must have crossed the US something like 43 times by car. I sort of hate to think about that, but it was nice at the time … The first time [the Asian flu] came through … was 1968 and I was in Aspen at the Institute, and I went sailing off to do a poetry circuit tour around the West. I got into Moab, Utah and I was so sick, I couldn't drive the car anymore. Just, I mean, it hit that fast. And it was called … the Asian Flu. That's the first time I think they'd ever used that term. When I recovered enough to get out of Moab, I had to stay in bed … I was staying in a motel and the woman who was running the motel was very helpful, she said, "If I were you, I'd go over to liquor store and get some bourbon or scotch and put it in some hot water and drink a couple of 'em and go to bed." So that's what I did, and I didn't feel too bad the next day. It seemed like the fever wasn't as bad. So I drove on to see friends in let's see, Prescott. Prescott, Arizona. The photographer Frederick Sommer and his wife. And I stayed there a couple of days and felt a little bit better, then drove to L.A., gave a poetry reading. Had to go back to bed. Went to Carmel, had the same experience. Went to San Francisco, got sick again. Went to Portland, Oregon, got sick again. Went to Seattle … The trip was about a month, the way it turned out … I figured it was going to be about half that time. But every time I'd get myself organized enough to give a poetry reading and talk to people I'd have a relapse … It was a strong, you know, I wasn't all that old. Forty, forty-one, something like that.

I still like VWs … this Jetta is a very good little car. They've got something I think, called a Passat that's bigger … But the new Jetta, I saw one in Highlands the other day. It's bigger than this one, somehow. It looks quite solid. It's as much car as I really want, and you get a little despairing when you see all this junk that people are driving, these personal tanks. They say they're safer. Well, they're not safer for people with automobiles … Well, I know there's a lot of them who don't seem to drive them very well … not used to that size vehicle and I mean, they have trouble making a turn … they're all over the road. You have to be careful up here because it's a two-lane road, the Highlands road, and plenty of places where you can get knocked off … down the mountainside. Plus, all the eighteen-wheelers, which service all these shops they now have in Highlands. There didn't used to be trucks like that out on these roads. And there's probably ten times the traffic that there used to be … It looks like the only thing that's going to stop over-building and too much growth is when they start running out of water in Highlands, which is not too far off, at this point. Because the population has doubled in ten years. The population's now two thousand, used to be 850 to one thousand for years … as long as people from Atlanta have the kind of money they have, they just keep coming and they're willing to pay a hundred and fifty thousand, two hundred thousand dollars, for lot with a bit of a view and then put up their two-and-a-quarter million-dollar house. And live just like they live in Buckhead … tear out the natural planting and spend fifty thousand dollars having landscape architects come in and put in stuff that's not even indigenous, in most cases, stuff that belongs in Florida. But there's no understanding these things.

I decided to use the station wagon my father offered me—the old

Pontiac—and try to go to San Francisco and place some books, try to sell some books, try to place some books and maybe live there for a little while. So I did that.

I wrote to some other small press publishers that I knew—City Lights, for instance, out in San Francisco … There weren't all that many Jargon books at that point, maybe ten. But that was the point, to sell these books … Must have been about September, October … drove across country, stopped here and there to meet people—in Taos, for one place. There was a writer there that Creeley knew—a kind of a strange, interesting writer named Judson Crews—who had all kinds of aliases and he wrote better usually under the aliases than his own name. No one knew why but one of his aliases was Mason Jordan Mason, supposed to be a somewhat sort of crazed black poet who maybe had disappeared into Namibia and was working for the Revolutionary Forces, you know, and there were many myths about Mason Jordan Mason. You knew that something was slightly dubious when he was theoretically translated into Germany by someone called Heinz Johannes Heinz. Mason Jordan Mason, I mean, it all sounded a little bit pat. I never met Mason but I did meet Judson Crews. I've always wanted to publish some of these Mason poems, I've got them in a drawer in there. For one reason or another, we just never did. I mean, they're pretty good. Rexroth of course always despised the Southern aristocratic poets. He says, "I don't know how good they are but they're a hell of a lot better than John Crowe Ransom and Allen Tate." And they are some pretty good poems in there … Maybe one of these days I'll sit down and look at it one more time. I've got some drawings that somebody made, so we got that far. There're only about a hundred poems, so it's just a question of whether you want to do twenty-five or fifty. I think that's probably all you want to do. They're good, there's no question about it. So that's a project that's been on the shelf for all these years. Might just try to dust it off and do it …

So I went on out to San Francisco and got a job wrapping—mostly '78s—at a rhythm and blues distributor, and that was fun cause I got to meet all the black disc jockeys in the Bay Area. You had Jumping George, Rockin' Deacon, and then somebody else. And they'd come in and get their review copies and talk to the owners. So I've always enjoyed wrapping records and wrapping books. I used to be quite good at it. (I worked in the wrapping department when I worked for the 8th Street Book Shop a little bit later when I was in New York in '58. I liked it better than just selling on the floor, somehow. I'd have to go to the post office, you know, push a cart down 6th Avenue or to the post office and do that stuff.)

I had enough money to live. In San Francisco there were a lot of blocks where you have kind of a passageway between two houses and inside the block there are a couple of little studios or structures. This was down on the Marina near the intersection of Fillmore and Filbert ... kind of down near the water. I paid all of twenty-eight dollars a month for this sort of railroad flat ... it went up some stairs and there was a kind of open balcony and three rooms. Twenty-eight bucks a month. Unbelievable. This was as late as 1954. Sounds more like 1934. Piece of luck.

There I spent time with Kenneth Rexroth whom I'd met before. Robert Duncan. Spent a lot of time with Duncan and the painter Jess and friends of theirs. Mostly, Duncan had a big circle of friends ... Robin Blaser ... What's her name, the photographer? She was a friend of James Broughton ... Imogen Cunningham. An older member of that group.

Michael McClure—we published his first book I think maybe a year later. I spent a lot of time with [Rexroth] and his wife. So there was a very active scene and there were a couple of very nice meeting places in North Beach, namely a bar that was called "The Place" which was run by two guys who had been at Black Mountain College earlier. One is a painter named Knutz Stiles who lives in Arizona now, and the other guy, at the moment I can't remember. I knew him but not very well. It was a very nice kind of Bohemian bar where you'd meet just any sort of person. Well ... Ginsberg was in there a lot that year. That's where I first met him, I suppose. Ferlinghetti was opening his bookshop, it was there. They were [exciting times]. Yeah. I met Jack Spicer and used to go to baseball games together. He was very sardonic, sometimes very amusing, sometimes terribly drunk person. But I liked him and we got on very well. I think he was a handful for a lot of people but I never had much trouble with him. So that was a very good year. Went downstate a month or so in Carmel Highlands. Had a friend who, again, had a cabin that could be rented for a little money ... by Point Lobos and met some very nice people. Wynn Bullock, the photographer ...

I believe I had two hundred copies of Ginsberg's first book, *Howl*. It was a dollar, but that didn't seem to provoke sales. I think it was too much for people at the time. I read it to some art students at the University of

Alabama and one young man got up and threw up over the balcony. I told that to Ginsberg and he was quite amused. We have a genteel tradition down here I suppose, at least that's the legend. My favorite poem about the south is a couplet by a terrible, terrible poet … He was called the "Bard of the Congaree" …

I sold a few copies of those [*Howl*]. I wish I had kept those. Course, I sent them back eventually to Ferlinghetti in San Francisco. The book in 1958—it cost a dollar. It's now selling in rare book catalogues for about 2500 dollars a copy. If I had 100 copies out in the shed I'd be in pretty good shape.

There can be some extremely unpleasant people writing poetry, we know that. I've known a certain number. Robert Duncan once said you have to believe in the muse and its power to channel through some really despicable people. He named a couple of names, I don't think I need to name them … I think we all know a couple like that, that you can't believe someone so awful could write a decent poem, but it happens all the time. I don't think there's ever very many good poets at any time. There must be about four or five thousand people who call themselves poets and you can get the list of their addresses out of the Poets and Writers Directory. Kenneth Rexroth once said that ninety percent of the worst people he knew were poets, and that poets these days were so square that they had to walk around the block to turn over in bed.

Now I'm reading Emerson and Thoreau, much more carefully than ever before. And I'm really impressed by Emerson—more so than Thoreau at the moment. Something about Thoreau's nature is slightly off-putting, I think. Apparently there were people in Concord, Mass. that'd see him coming down the street, they'd run and hide. He was a rather blunt, forthright guy, and it wasn't entirely a pleasant experience to talk to Mr. Henry David Thoreau … It's hard to find a sentence in Emerson that you don't want to quote. It's just extraordinary … there are people like Oscar Wilde who are certainly in the same class, but what you mostly remember that [Wilde] wrote were witticisms and epigrams. Emerson's range was much greater. He's almost the first American that can write with that much skill. Before that, we had guys who told stories like Fenimore Cooper. But you look at Emerson's reading … incredible. He read in German [and] I think maybe French. He read books … People just don't read books like that anymore—the history of Hittite religion and just on and on and on. I don't know how he had time to do anything. And he lectured all the time. He gave a public lecture about once a week. Incredible man. I've been reading a biography by Robert Richardson who has been at Wesleyan University but I think has retired. He's married currently to Annie Dillard and I believe they live in Hillsborough [North Carolina] now. It's called *Emerson: The Mind on Fire*. It's really a very good intellectual history of the man worth everybody's attention. I think it's a really important book and I've been learning a lot from it. So, of course, once you get past Emerson, there's other people that you've got to deal with. There's Margaret Fuller that nobody knows quite enough about. There's Bronson Alcott. That was a very interesting time up there.

Most of what I've been reading in the Emerson book has to do with some of his interests in people like Emanuel Swedenborg who's somebody that William Blake was interested in. A Swedish philosopher, but ... religious. Religious. He founded a sort of religion in the same way as the Quakers and the Shakers. But I don't know much about him.

Intellectual history is not anything that I've ever been all that interested in. But I suddenly define myself at this point in the game much more so. One's tastes in everything are constantly changing. There's a lot of music that until the advent of the CD ... half the repertoire that we have available now just didn't exist ten or fifteen years ago. There are composers that were absolutely unknown who were of major importance and now you can listen to them. So that's great. So that's why I don't go to the movies, I suppose, and run around town. Between CDs and reading a bunch of books and trying to write a few things, I'm more than occupied. It's nice to be busy.

But obviously I'm not as quick. It's one thing you find out with age that you just don't get things done as fast ... some of this is maybe like baseball, you can't throw heat anymore. It takes longer to do things ... Well, I suppose it has to do with all the electronics, is partially the problem. Every morning Tom comes upstairs and hands me a bunch of email, which I'm not particularly anxious to see because I had other plans for the morning, and then you ... suddenly this stuff intrudes on you. What you had planned to do at the desk is put off. Somebody yelling for this and that and the other and they want it now. Telephones I don't mind because if you live out in the hills it's nice to talk to people. I don't know about email, I mean, it's got its uses but it's also intrusive ... I don't know, it's kind of like post cards. But there again ... I don't know why everything has to be instantaneous.

What I do takes a long time to do and sometimes I get it done and I get it right but it's not like there's deadlines all the time. I think for commerce email must be very good. I'm not so sure how it fits in to the life of artists. I mean, you get them from people that you don't know who the hell they are and they want to know this and they want to know that.

We occasionally have had interns and sometimes it works and sometimes it doesn't. If you find one, send him up, you know. But the most able was a Chinese-American graduate student from Berkeley who was tremendously educated. He could do just about anything on a computer and didn't mind answering boring letters and rejecting manuscripts and he was great. He was [an] eighteen-wheeler running down the road. He stayed for about three months a couple of years ago and was a very delightful guy and we even imported his Japanese girlfriend from California for a couple of weeks so she got a little vacation. But, as I say, one or two have not worked out too well. But you never know till you try. But it's a good thing. We try to advertise occasionally for if anybody wants to live in the country and be exposed to a lot of music and books and conversation … and Tom knows a lot about cooking if anybody's interested in learning a little bit about that. There are a lot of things to be learned here. They have their own quarters and we feed them. But they've got to know about computers and probably have to know how to drive and stuff like that. Because you can't walk. If you want to get off the mountain you've got to, you know, be able to drive, at least.

Well, I suppose there must be some examples of [being a good writer without being an avid reader], but I'd be hard-pressed to tell you who they are. Of course, back in the days of the Romans, there wasn't much of a tradition for them to worry about. Catullus, I don't know how much he read. Most of those Roman writers that were interesting were of his generation or close to it. You know, Marshall and Horace and, well, let's see, who am I missing? Anyway, I suppose in the big scheme of things, there would only be people like Homer, and what's his name? Well, Herodotus. Hesiod … *The Works and Days.* I think it's very important.

You're vocabulary is not going to improve by conversation with most people these days. Most people have a vocabulary of about fourteen words with "like" struck between each one. Not a very interesting vocabulary …

Some people you read because their syntax is so good. Somebody like Jonathan Swift. I think Edward Lear is one of the most delightful people to read. [Not just] the nonsense … but his letters. He's got two volumes of letters that I ran into in England published early in the century. Absolutely stunning. They're just so charming. He's one of my favorite writers and one can learn a lot from Lear.

[Advice to a young writer …] Get a job. (pause) Well, read as much as you can and write as much as you can. If you do these things and you have a certain amount of skill and talent you're going to get better. Whether it gets you somewhere is another matter. I think I was better known in the '50s than now, because I simply insist on not living in big cities and being interested in marginal things. But, I don't think you do it for a big audience, or at least it never occurred to me to have a big audience for that reason. But I have plenty of friends and there's enough people out there who have some interest in what I do that I keep doing it. I don't think it takes all that many. If you're comfortable with what you're doing and want to do it, that's the good part. If you don't want to do it there's any number of other things to do in this society. We know that. But, it's a great way not to make money. It's one of the best.

An awful lot of people don't read as much as they used to or they don't read the older writers. That makes a difference. So, as I say, if you haven't read Emily Dickinson or Whitman or, let's add Mr. Emerson and Mr. Thoreau and bring it on down through Pound and Olson and people like that. Wallace Stevens and all that. On and on and on. I mean, there must be a hundred American writers that deserve to be read with some care by almost anybody. If people don't do that, they have trouble attaching themselves … it's a way to get into what's contemporary. It doesn't start, you know, like eight years ago when you bought your last automobile, I mean, there's stuff behind that, that's important to know about. And, well, again, there's so much else that people spend their time doing now. But, I don't know. Every time I read reviews in magazines and occasionally go to good bookstores there's a hell of a lot being published that's really very interesting, no matter what kind of writing you're talking about. I can't even keep up with mystery stories, which I like a lot. I'm constantly encountering really good mystery writers I've never read before. I must have found about five this year and I'm just astonished that I didn't know who the hell they were. That kind of reading is probably not going to help your vocabulary but some of them write extremely good English. A lot of them are British, but not all. No, I love that kind of reading. I think you should read everything. Serious things and totally frivolous things and cookbooks and record reviews and everything. Novels. I don't read much history, I don't read much about sciences. I probably read three or four books a week and that's about all I can handle. I like to wake up and read for about two hours in the morning … wake up about six o'clock and read till eight. Maybe read a half an hour at night and you can get through books pretty fast if you do that. But I would hate not to be reading all the time … I keep a quote book, as you probably know, and every time I see something that I think needs to be saved or preserved, isolated, I whisk into the computer and edit in. It's getting to be a big book.

There's going to be a book that's about three times the size of [*Quote, UnQuote*]. That only covers about, let's see … that goes up to about '91. So this will be a much bigger book, and then from '91 to now is yet another book. So these will be books of about two hundred fifty, three hundred pages each. All that's coming out of reading. No, I love to do that. Again, it's this business of finding things. I'm just obsessed with finding things all the time and of pointing them out, you know. Well, it's that formal thing, Olson says, "One loves only form" and somehow his eyes trained to kind of respond to those forms better than mine or whatever. No, it's great to find a word that's interesting or a sentence that's interesting. And so many people can do it, which is great.

[The future of literature in the United States?] Somebody just wrote a book about the collapse of American culture. It must be very popular because I read a review in *The New York Times*, tried to get the book and they'd run out of their first edition and were reprinting. So I think there must be a few people who are concerned about the culture as we know it. I don't know, like I said earlier one of the interesting things is that so many good books continue to be published whether anybody's reading them. Like I showed you the Coffee House Press three volume collected Paul Metcalf which sank without trace. We thought, finally, Jargon published six of his books and there are other people who published probably another six and we thought after about forty-five years maybe in that format we could sort of see them all, that finally people would begin to take him seriously. Except for his friends. Didn't happen. Didn't happen. So, a disaster. So, I don't know. I wouldn't speculate too broadly. I think that for the kind of work that I do and that interests me, we have an audience of maybe five to ten thousand people and that may be optimistic. I know there are people in New York who claim there are only five thousand serious readers of novels in the United States and that that's what they count on. They can just about break even if they can sell five thousand copies of somebody's first novel.

I used to know Wright Morris who's a distinguished person and wrote a lot of … took very good photographs. Wrote a lot of very good books about Nebraska. Mencken, I think, says, "How can you write a good book about Nebraska, you know? Who wants to go there?" There's a lot of that kind of talk. Wright Morris said he'd never sold five thousand copies of a book, and I mean, he was at it for, God knows, forty or fifty years. Won a lot of prizes. I don't know whether counting heads is good or not. It might be better just to go from one thing to the next and see what happens …

I don't know what's going to happen to this new book of essays but North Point Press published my last book of essays back about 1983 and they printed five thousand which might have been optimistic. They only sold about two thousand and … remaindered it. Which is really a good thing, in a way, for me, but not good for the publisher, because a lot of students and people without a lot of money pick those up off the remainder table for a couple of bucks. So they all got bought but the publisher got it in the neck and eventually failed as a press. I think Guy Davenport said it very well, "North Point Press died of excellence." True, probably.

So, as I say, I don't know how much appetite … how broad such a thing is anymore. But I don't think that much matters. It's great to be a publisher because you can exercise your will. You can do what you want to, and I think there's a lot to be said for that.

So I guess I'm not very interested in the money side of it. I get the printer paid and then we see what happens … we publish a book as excellent as Elizabeth Matheson's book of photographs that we did about five years ago [*Blithe Air*] and places like the *New York Times* will not even consider them, that means that we're restricted, essentially to people in North Carolina who have seen some of her work in art museums like Raleigh, Durham, Chapel Hill. So I think we sold maybe five, six hundred. That's ridiculous. I mean, we had fifteen hundred. And I thought, I don't think it's going to be hard to sell fifteen hundred copies of something as good as this. It's a wonderful book. But it's always been difficult to sell things in the United

States because it's such a big country and nobody's ever been able to solve the distribution thing, I don't know whether Amazon.com is going to solve it or Barnes and Noble. I'm old-fashioned enough to want to go to a bookstore and see the books, handle the books … like if I want to buy some jazz CDs, I want to look at them first, you know, and read the back. I want to handle the things. I don't care whether they come in fifteen minutes by Federal Express, I'd still want to do it the old way. I think there'll always be some people that want to do that. We'll just have to see. I don't think one should be put into the position of being depressed about things like this. There's no point. You either want to do it and do them, or, as I say, there're plenty of safe things to do. Really I've been doing this and losing money for fifty years and I'm still eating regular, as they say down South. It will always put a little wine on the table and pay for the oil bill. It's no way to make money but on the other hand it's a very nice way to live. The view's pretty good today in Western North Carolina, so it's not a bad place to live. And Jesse Helms is never invited here. With any luck, he won't knock on the door.

[Favorite epithets for myself?] Well, the Lord Gnang, I mentioned earlier that when I get in my curmudgeonly state, that seems very appropriate. Because the English language is so stodgy, I always call myself Lord Stodge, when I'm living there and am petulant. Lord Crudvigil of Dentdale is one I'm rather fond of. Always being vigilant against crud—it's always around us and endangering us. J. Jeeter Swampwater is a sort of Southern one that I like. J. Jeeter. Big Enis, in honor of Little Enis, the great left-hand, upside-down guitar picker of Lexington, Kentucky who always said he was a hundred and eighty pounds of dynamite with a nine-inch fuse. So those are a few but … oh, there's many others … I just love, I just like playing around with stuff like that. I've got names for most everybody else, too. No one escapes unscathed.

The point about walking is you start and you don't know exactly where you're going, or quite how you're going to get there, which is something that's also true in a poem. It's kind of like a stream of water that's finding its way down the hillside. That's one aspect of the form of the poem that interests me—how do you move from the beginning to the end, it's not always the same at all. So closed forms don't interest me very much except for silly ones like clerihews and limericks and such things, but those are just—I think they're great fun and I like them—but the thought of me being able to write a sonnet or a series of quatrains is very unlikely, I haven't got that kind of intelligence.

What's poetry about? Poetry's about, I think craft is perfected attention, and really it's paying attention that's the most interesting thing about it, and paying attention not just to the meaning of a word, but the look of that word, the color of that word, the weight of that word, there's multiple kinds of associations and qualities that each word has, that's what interests me.

Poets are people who listen to everything very carefully. And I certainly listened to the language of some of these mountain people as I walked up the Appalachian Trail. That experience taught me to listen to talk as they say, because my poetry has gotten more and more based on demotic speech based on, from everywhere. That's what I like about American language, it's from everywhere ... I'm liable to have any kind of language in a poem, whether it's Jesse Helms or it's Uncle Iv Owens who used to live across the road and spoke so beautifully. When people speak so well it behooves you to listen. It doesn't happen as much now of course.

In the late '50s, there was beginning to be an interest in Concrete Poetry, in which, these were poems which didn't necessarily have any sound. They were epiphanies, if you wish, or instances of a visual order which were so compelling at best that you regarded them like ... I suddenly realized that's another way of doing things ...

After a point you just keep on keeping on, you just do it the best you can ... My work has changed lately, my early work by my current standards is very prolix, is very expansive. Brevity is perhaps what I do best—I like to condense as much as possible, leave out as many words as possible, just really pare it down ...

[I] am more interested in not always sitting at the desk but going out and looking at things, that's where I find a lot of things, not by sitting at the desk or reading books.

When I read, I read very carefully and I try to ferret out things that other people will be interested in so I keep long quotation books. I really love the commonplace books and quote books ... They don't all come from scholarly or very serious sources. I'm always catching somebody saying something, you know, during a baseball game on television or something. Language is all around. One of the most important things is knowing what to read.

The rational mind hasn't got a lot to do with what I do. It's all about imagination, it's all about, as I say, music. Poetry is a kind of mind's music … If you want to be an intellectual and think, you know, don't read poetry. Read the phone book.

No matter what happens poetry is going to occur, sort of like dandruff, it just happens. There's always something. If there's not anything for a couple days I'll just read and look for things to put in the quote book … It's almost a sort of monastic existence. I like to stay home, I like to do these things …

I'm certainly looking for the sound. Again I'm quoting my mentors all the time because some of them got it exactly right. Zukofsky said first of all he was interested in the noise, the sound of the thing. So you've got to try to figure out what kind of noise the poet intended. And that can be hard, unless you've heard the poet himself, or [you've] got an extremely good reader, it's not as simple as you might expect … Charles Olson is somebody who comes much clearer when you read him correctly. He's a bit daunting otherwise because the poetry is so big, the lines are so long. There's so many pages. Same thing's true of someone like Robert Duncan. Music is maybe the first thing I'm interested in. Second, the classical reasons for writing poetry as Ezra Pound defined it, is to move, to teach, and to delight. So when you think about the poetry that you read and appreciate most, some of it doesn't teach you much, but to delight is probably the first, and to be moved is quite wonderful …

But, I think delight, probably, in my case is the first. And to be moved is also something quite wonderful. But those are classical reasons. And if one wanted to be sort of smart-ass about it, you'd just sort of say, "Well, I can't do anything better than this. I can't do anything else as well as this, so I'm going to do it." So I think that's you know, you're kind of stuck with it after a while.

Well, as I say, it's usually going to come because I think the sounds are organized so well. You have to read a lot of it, seems to me. It's like anything else you do well … If you read in public sometimes it takes you a long time to be able to do that. That's not as simple as it might seem. And you have to measure … Well, it's like baseball. If you didn't know anything about Ty Cobb or Babe Ruth or Lou Gehrig or DiMaggio or Feller … we can name twenty-five or thirty more. If you didn't know those people and what they'd accomplished and how they played it would be very difficult for you to know what's good and what isn't. Most baseball players are kind of average but if you're interested in something like baseball, you make it your business to know who the good guys were, or the great guys. Poetry, of course, you've got to go all way back into the Romans and the Greeks and the Egyptians … and the Persians. Not to mention the Chinese and the Japanese and all of these cultures. It takes a long time before you start to develop just a working knowledge …

J. Gordan Coogler, now it comes back to me, the name of the worst poet whose probably ever lived—J. Gordan Coogler, the "Bard of the Congaree." And he wrote one absolutely fantastic couplet: "Alas the South, her books have grown fewer / She was never much given to literature." It's hard to say 'ture' and get it into two syllables … this he said a hundred years ago and H. L. Mencken thought it was about the best thing he'd ever heard about the South, he despised the South … I don't think we are very literary people. Like the English. The English are practically tone-deaf, they don't have much ear for music but they have had a fantastic literary history. Most Southern writers are storytellers … and there are certainly some very good ones … Lee Smith is wonderful, her mountain dialect is the best I've ever run into.[5] She's really really good …

I'm interested in marginal people, ignored writers. I like to ferret out people like that, and I don't care where they come from …

I do not write, so to speak, a very public poem. There are not going to be that many readers who are going to take the trouble to find out what's going on in there.

I like the individuality of this work—the fact that it's not academic, that it's not overly schooled, and that people do this because … as a specialist in the marginal I think I need to keep my eyes and ears open in that direction. The center takes care of itself … that's all you have to say.

The mainstream doesn't interest me much. I like things on the edges that people don't pay too much attention to. I'm always happy enough to do that. And I'm still doing that. As Uncle Iv used to say, "I'm inclemented that way."

I think that for the kind of work that I do and interests me—we have an audience of maybe five to ten thousand people—that may be optimistic …

At the moment, we're putting together a new and selected poems which includes some of the dialect work and it's called *Jubilant Thicket*.

It's going to have a Harry Callahan photograph on the cover. I asked a poet from Philadelphia named Jim Cory to help me make the selection, which he did, and he made the groupings. He also has written a series of notes [for an] Introduction. And there's one section I like where he talks about these sort of found voice poems. "At other times, these spoken-word poems record adages, anecdotes, sagacious tidbits as: 'You live until you die if the limb don't fall.' In them, we encounter the paradox of ineloquence, which is verbal, and utterly non-literary. Williams gives us voices, visceral and transparent. If what they say seems somehow to speak to a whole culture and its traditions, its values, its ways, that's because he succeeds in drawing a character out of words. The auto mechanics summation regarding the problems of the engine entrusted to his care makes contemporary poetry appear sclerotic. He says, 'Your points is blue and your timing's a week off.' Perhaps, because he recognizes a pigeonhole when he sees one, Williams rejects the definition of himself as a quote 'Southern' unquote writer. He's no more a regional writer than a gay poet, or a (strictly speaking) folklorist, or a Black Mountaineer. Yet, the flora and landscapes of the South, its people, and their ways, remain a central concern and literary source. The fact that the various pockets of Eden he surveys and maps out are surrounded by backwardness and superstition by an ever-present subtext of race-hate makes them more valuable in his eyes and ours. Williams' South, his cornbread, sour mash, and outsider art, white and Afro-American." Yeah, that's pretty good. Well, let me read you just four or five out of *Blues & Roots* that we've been talking about.

I'm going to read some poems out of *Blues & Roots/Rue & Bluets*:

Essentially this book comes out of a long walk I took on the Appalachian Trail … and what I think I principally learned was the value of listening to what country people were saying and turning it into poems … Again, these are found things. All I had to do was write them down …

[Regarding *Blues &Roots*] [It was received] pretty well. It was published in New York with photographs. Have you seen that first edition of it? All I can say is, Duke University, the editor there was very interested in doing a new edition with a lot of extra material, so that was in the eighties. I think it came out about '70, '71, something like that, originally. I don't know, we didn't use the photographs because the man who took them, Nick Dean, really had sort of got out of photography, in a way, and he wasn't traveling down here, you know, to take pictures anymore. And so, I thought, well, let's just add some poems. And well, I don't know, obviously, some people like it. But I tend to write for enthusiasts and readers and there's not a lot in those poems that any academic could find anything to talk about. I mean, it's so ... I try to make it so clear that there's no question. And that's not ... They're not things to study, they're things to, basically, to enjoy. So the academics properly leave them alone.

Guy Davenport gave a, taught a class at the University of Kentucky about maybe fifteen, twenty years ago, and the only two poets under consideration were e. e. cummings and myself. And he said, "The students find your work much more obscure than they do e. e. cummings'," and I said, "This is impossible!" So, I said, "You've got to get me a time when I can come and read the poems to these kids," and having heard them, the mysteries kind of disappeared, you know, mostly. But they're obviously ... Most of them, except for the ones that are derived from signs, which don't have any music in them, they're all conceived musically, and once you ... It's very difficult with some poets, I recognize that. I mean, cummings is very difficult sometimes, but if you have heard him do it, it makes it a lot easier. heard him read a couple of times. He takes away a lot of the quote "difficulties." But I've always thought my work was not obscure, was not intellectually very trying. It comes out of a very sort of basic, democratic kind of situation. There are not a lot of ideas floating around in them, there's no philosophical tone. I'd like them to be of the same order as if you were interested in Indians and you go through the woods, you might find arrowheads. Somebody else interested in minerals, you might suddenly see mica and then maybe a bit of amethyst in connection with it. Things like that, where suddenly, little formed objects, you know. Or, on the other hand, if you're interested in birds, suddenly, you hear a wood thrush. Or the cardinal. Or the pileated woodpecker. I mean, you want to be able to know what that is, you know. That's a nice moment.

Taoism has a notion of dumbness in it, there's that aspect of it that I like. They're always talking about "pumpkinheads" and "gourds." So maybe at times you want to come on as dumb as a pumpkinhead. There's that aspect of it that I like. Simplicity is not easy, to pare it down as much as I do. Again, some people may think it's so pared down there's not enough there. I forget who said it but I always thought it was amusing, but someone said, "Always start as near the end of a poem as you can."[6] I think that's a good thing to think about. I've been in touch with poets who really preach the gospel of taking it down. Basil Bunting was great at it. he'd say of those seven lines I see about twelve words that really need to be there. And he'd show you how to get rid of the rest. If nothing else you haven't spent hours and hours and hours trying to read these things. They have to produce pretty quick. Just like the bird sings, about that same length.

I'm going to take them places probably that they haven't been before. Not necessarily just the Appalachian Trail but what interests me are people and … Well, a lot of the poetry of the last ten or fifteen years has been involved with what they call these days, I guess, "outsider art" or "self-taught art" or "naive art" or … Again, it's essentially people who live in the country who make things. Make odd things in the front yard or make odd things in the back yard for any number of reasons. I did this book with Roger Manley and another photographer named Guy Mendes who lives over in Kentucky.[7] And we spent about seven years, on and off, putting this book together and we interviewed about eighty-three individuals. Traveled from Virginia to Louisiana. Tennessee and Kentucky. And that book has got a lot of personal language in it. Some black, white, both. A lot of signs. Again, it's findings. So, I'm interested in finding people and places and … They tend to be off the beaten track or out of the mainstream. I mean, the mainstream doesn't interest me. It just doesn't. I like things on the edges that nobody pays too much attention to. I'm always happy enough to do that. And I'm still doing that, so, I'm, as Uncle Iv used to say, I'm "inclemented that way." That's a great word. I'm "inclemented that way."

[On "Bea Hensley Hammers an Iron Chinquapin Leaf on His Anvil near Spruce Pine, North Carolina, and He Cogitates on the Nature of Two Beauty Spots"]: I was living at Penland School, at the time. I was writing a big, long essay about crafts and the Southern mountains for *Craft Horizons* magazine. So I spent maybe a week at Penland … Well, this [book] was published in '69. I guess it had to be '67, '68. And I heard about Bea Hensley who was famous as a blacksmith. He could hammer … He had a way of playing tunes on the anvil, so, he was in great demand, you know. County fairs and he'd go around and play on this anvil. He made nice work. So I just went over there one morning to meet him and as he would say, he was "*bad to talk.*" So I'm bad to listen. (It's kind of the way that they say these days, "you so bad" ... It's that kind of jazz or hip-hop or whatever. But that use of the negative to make your point. Well, around here, they'll say, "So-and-so is bad to drink." You know. It means that they drink a lot.) I don't know whether you can compare [this kind of talk with "proper English," because this is an uncharted realm ... that kind of invective ... that's Elizabethan.

[On "Daddy Bostain, the Moses of the Wing Community Moonshiners, Laments from His Deathbed the Spiritual Estate of One of His Soul-Saving Neighbors"]: I heard this anecdote from somebody who had been there at the time and I think told it pretty carefully. Because the language is so exact and perfect. Anyway, this old man was a moonshiner and he lived very close to Penland.

[On: "Three Sayings from Highlands, North Carolina"]: Again, these were from life. All I had to do was write it down. Butler Jenkins was a caretaker I used to know. And Sam Cresswell, my auto mechanic ... I really don't know how you can say more with less words. Mountain people are either bad to talk or sometimes they're also so laconic that they hardly say anything, so, it just kind of depends on the mood.

[On: "Uncle Iv Surveys His Domain from His Rocker of a Sunday"]: Now, here we have our great man, Uncle Iv Owens. Get those feminists in here!

[On: "A Ride in a Blue Chevy from Alum Cave Trail to Newfound Gap"]: I like this poem because it puts several cultures in the same poem and we get a representative of a culture that doesn't have much to do with the Appalachians and how you confront it. In fact, I want to try to illustrate [it] somehow. Ideally, I would just get someone to drive me in an old car and film from the backseat. But I don't know how I'm going to do that. That's when you come down off of Mount Le Conte. That's a wonderful trail, the Alum Cave Trail. It brings you out back on four forty-one and then you've got to hitchhike. Well, I was hitchhiking, and he stopped. You never quite know if you hitchhike, what's going to transpire. I used to do it a lot when I was going to Princeton or trying to get to New Orleans to listen to music. I mean, it seemed relatively safe in 1950. But you sure don't see anybody hitchhiking around here, even local people that you can kind of recognize ... Because there's no public transportation, so you'd think there'd be more of it, but I don't think I've seen anybody hitchhiking in years … But, I hitchhiked from out here, at the entrance, all the way to New Orleans. It only took me overnight … Took about six or seven [rides]. But my luck was good, I mean, I just wasn't having to wait very long.

[Neal: Let me ask you about some words …]

A "dope" is a Coca-Cola. You used to be able to go into a soda fountain back in the, let's see … I certainly remember doing it in the '40s and '50s. You'd say to the girl behind the counter, "Honey, get me a dope." And out it would come, you know, it was the kind that you put together with the syrup and carbonated water. I haven't seen one of those machines in a long time. I guess they're almost extinct. Occasionally there'll still be a soda fountain, but they were great. Drug stores had them and would serve sandwiches and various kinds of concoctions.

Heard it in Georgia first, I think. Of course, that's a big Coca-Cola area. A lot of people … friends of my mother's, they would drink six Coca-Colas a day, it's kind of like the English with their tea.

"Sigogglin." Well, I don't know it but it sounds like you'd knock somebody "skygogglin." What was their definition?

[Neal: Well, this I got near outside Waynesville, and they said that means 'it's crooked'. It's "sigogglin." And they also gave me "slahntsways." For slanted. "Slahntsways." "Blackguard"?]

Well, nothing to do with the normal meaning of … How do we pronounce it in this country? So-and-so is a "blaggard." Like "blackguard" … it's sort of a villain. A villainous person's a … pronounced I think in England, maybe "blaggard." But it's "blackguard"? That's how you spell it?

[Neal: They say that when you're sort of disrespecting or abusing somebody.]

I don't think it's used much in this county. But they're using it. I don't think I've ever heard it. What county is that over there? Haywood … .Well, everybody, as I say, everybody's got some pet words.

[Neal: "Piccolo"? … A jukebox.]

A jukebox … Well, it just depends on the individual … a lot of people make their own words that nobody else knows about. Ernie Mickler, who wrote *White Trash Cooking*, had all kinds of wild words. There was one about his mother's cooking. Iv … Well, that business about Berlin was very good. "Yon way" meaning the far side of … Some people say "yan" around here instead of "yon." "Yan way." But you don't hear that much anymore.

There was a family of Vinsons lived in Scaly back in those days—I think there were twelve brothers and sisters who lived within a mile of here. And I think there's only one left. She's the lady who makes the pie. All of them have moved out or died and a lot of the … younger generation goes off to a place like Franklin, maybe becomes a barber … .where there's more steady work.

In the older days, Highlands was a resort … It started about Memorial Day and it finished Labor Day, so really it was only basically three months. You couldn't depend on the summer people, as they were called, to provide you with any income except for those three months, so that ran a lot of people off the mountain. Everything pretty well closed down—the market would stay open and the hardware store would stay open. Country club would close by middle of September. Now, of course, there's so much going on in Highlands that a lot of places will stay open through Christmas and they'll close … [Highlands] opens up again for Valentine's—it's a big weekend event—and then it's relatively quiet until first of April. But it's now basically a ten-month situation.

[1] Williams was very fond of this quote from John Clare.

[2] In the transcript Williams states that Gawthrop means "home of the crow" but in actuality it means "home of the cuckoo."

[3] Chicago Institute of Art.

[4] Apparently here Williams gives a description of duties, electroshocking people, etc., … which was not included in the texts the editor was given to transcribe.

[5] Lee Smith, the renowned North Carolina novelist.

[6] Judith Thurman.

[7] *Walks to the Paradise Garden* remains unpublished.

FINAL SCRIPT:
JONATHAN WILLIAMS—TALK ABOUT WRITING:
PORTRAITS OF NORTH CAROLINA WRITERS

[Reads poem: *Gary Carden Reports from the Coffeehouse in Sylva*]

It's like that great remark by Barnett Newman, the painter. He said, aesthetics is for the artists like ornithology is for the birds. Says a lot. I don't think about it too much. The rational mind hasn't got a lot to do with what I do. It's not that it's stupid or gibberish. It's all about imagination. It's all about, as I say, music. Poetry is a kind of mind's music.

Basil Bunting says there is absolutely no excuse for literary criticism. I can see why one would say that. If you want to be an intellectual and think, you know, don't read poetry. Read the phone book.

[Reads excerpt from the introduction to *Excavations from the Case Histories of Havelock Ellis* and poem "Dangerous Calamus Emotions"]

What's poetry about? Poetry's about—really it's paying attention that's the most interesting thing about it, and paying attention not just to the meaning of a word, but the look of that word, the color of that word, the weight of that word, there's multiple kinds of associations and qualities that each word has, that's what interests me.

It's not that you're a recording device plain and simple. Some poets feel that they are simply vessels through which things are being transmitted. Not always, because I am more interested in not always sitting at the desk but going out and looking at things, that's where I find a lot of things

Language is all around. If I hear it being used in a wonderful way I try to write it down quick, you know, to keep it.

No matter what happens, poetry is going to occur, sort of like dandruff, it just happens.

There's always something.

[Reads the third section from *In the Piedmont*: "Red Pig Barbecue #2, Concord]

Essentially this book [*Blues & Roots/Rue & Bluets*] came out of a long walk I took on the Appalachian Trail in the summer of 1961. Ronald Johnson the poet and I started at Springer Mountain, Georgia, and we walked to the Hudson River. It was about three and a half months.

The point about walking is you start and you don't know exactly where you're going, or quite how you're going to get there, which is something that's also true in a poem.

Poets are people who listen to everything very carefully. And I certainly listened to the language of some of these mountain people as I walked up the Appalachian Trail. It taught me, that experience taught me to listen.

[Reads poem: "Aunt Creasy, on Work"]

This is nothing poets haven't been doing for a long time. The nature poet John Clare, said, "I found the poems in the fields and only wrote them down."

Again, these are from life. All I had to do was write them down.

[Reads poem: "Three Sayings from Highlands, NC"]

I really don't know how you could say more with less words.

[Reads poem: "Sam Palmer's Watercolor Notations for the Sketch 'A Lane at Thanet'"]

Brevity is perhaps what I do best—I like to condense as much as possible, leave out as many words as possible, just really pare it down.

[Reads poems: "In Buncombe County, Thoughts in the Fields at Auvers, Sunt Lachrimae Rerum"]

What we're simply trying to do is make a picture of the mind's music, on paper.

I tend to write for enthusiasts and readers and there's not a lot in those poems that academics could find anything to talk about … They're not things to study, they're things to enjoy.

[Reads poems: "Always the Deathless Music; Three Choirs Festival, Gloucester Cathedral"]

They can be some extremely unpleasant people writing poetry, we know that. I've known a certain number. Robert Duncan once said you have to believe in the muse and its power to channel through some really despicable people … I think we all know a couple like that, that you can't believe someone so awful could write a decent poem, but it happens all the time.

[Reads poem: "August 22nd at Briggsflatt Burial Ground"]

Kenneth Rexroth once said that ninety percent of the worst people he knew were poets, and that poets these days were so square that they had to walk around the block to turn over in bed.

[Reads poem: "Orange County Blues"]

J. Gordan Coogler, now it comes back to me, the name of the worst poet whose probably ever lived—J. Gordan Coogler, the "Bard of the Congaree." And he wrote one absolutely fantastic couplet: "Alas the South, her books have grown fewer / She was never much given to literature." It's hard to say "ture" and get it into two syllables.

Well, things aren't as bad as they were a hundred years ago, but I don't find too many people interested in literature in a place like Highlands, NC, or anywhere else. I don't think we are a very literary people. Like the English. The English are. The English are practically tone-deaf, they don't have much ear for music but they have had a fantastic literary history.

Something Basil Bunting said is, the interesting thing about poetry is it has absolutely no value. He says except in the way that a glass of water is valuable. It's free but it's very important when you want one, when you need one. And the same thing is more or less true of poetry, it's not going to make you any money, but it can maybe help you pass the time.

I've been doing this and losing money for fifty years and I'm still eating regular as the say down south. I can always put a little wine on the table and pay for the oil bill. It's no way to make money but on the other hand it's a very nice way to live. The view's pretty good today in western NC, so it's not a bad place to live. And Jesse Helms is never invited. With any luck he won't knock on the door.

Reads poem: from *Imaginary Postcards: No. 14* "Three Miles of Glishy Slutch …"[1]

---

[1] Always introduced as his "Homage to Basil Bunting."

ADDITIONAL READINGS IN *TALK ABOUT WRITING*

"Dear Elvis"—excerpt from *Big Erma*
Reflections from Appalachia
The Lord, Working in Mysterious Ways ...
Dingle
Miss Lucy Morgan Shows Me a Photograph
Enthusiast
"Jesse Helms's high school principal was ..."
*Two Pastorals for Samuel Palmer, at Shoreham, in Kent: If the Night Could
    Get Up and Walk; One Must Try Behind the Hills*
A Ride in a Blue Chevy
Blues for Lonnie Johnson
Full Frontal Card of Mister E.M. Forster
Cobwebbery
To Carve in Wild Cherry, for John Jacob Niles
Kerry
An Aubade from Verlaine's Day
Dealer's Choice and the Dealer Shuffles
The Flower Hunter in the Fields
"So I asked Joe Tartt if he enjoyed the winter Olympics ..."
The Custodian of a Field of Whiskey Bushes
The Terrible Knitters of Dent

JW READINGS IN THE NEAL HUTCHESON COLLECTION

VOLUME ONE   **49 minutes**

Selected readings from *An Ear in Bartram's Tree*, part 1
        Section titles:

> *The Empire Finals at Verona*
> *Amen, Huzzah, Selah*
> *Elegies & Celebrations*

VOLUME TWO   **49 minutes**

Selected readings from *An Ear In Bartram's Tree*, part 2
        Section titles:

> *Lullabies, Twisters, Gibbers, Drags*
> (Miscellaneous poems)
> *Jammin' The Greek Scene*
> (Conversation about H.B. Kitty, the Jargon Society mascot)
> *Fifty Epiphytes, Epitaphs, Epitomes, Epigrams, Epithets-Fifty!*
> *The Lucidities*

VOLUME THREE   **56 minutes**

Selected readings from *Blues & Roots/Rue & Bluets*

VOLUME FOUR   **45 minutes**

Selected readings from *Elite/Elate Poems*
        Section titles:

> *Imaginary Postcards*
> *Adventures with a Twelve-Inch Pianist Beyond The Blue Horizon*
> *A Celestial Centennial Reverie for Charles Edward Ives*
> *Untinears & Antennae for Maurice Ravel*

VOLUME FIVE   50 minutes

The Loco Logodaedalist In Situ
Mahler
Get Hot or Get Out!

VOLUME SIX   58 minutes

Gless ... Swarthy Monotonies ... Rince Cochon ... & Chozzerai for
   Simon
Supa Dupa Inglaise Poems
The Fifty-Two Clerihews of Clara Hughes
Aposiopeses

VOLUME SEVEN   54 minutes

Dementations on Shank's Mare
Delian Seasons
No-No Nonsense
Quantulumcumque
Anathema Maranatha!

VOLUME EIGHT   32 minutes

Horny & Ornery
Kinnikinnick Brand Kickapoo Joy-Juice
Scumbags from Parnassus
Amuse-Gueules for Bemused Ghouls

Plus
Talk about Writing, Portraits of North Carolina Writers:
   Jonathan Williams   **26**
minutes
(including *Selected Readings*)   **18 minutes**

RICHARD OWENS AND JEFFERY BEAM

JARGON SOCIETY—A CHECKLIST OF JARGON SOCIETY

Aside from minor revisions and the inclusion of texts brought out by the Jargon Society since 1991, the list below is built on two publications: J. M. Edelstein's *A Jargon Society Checklist* (Books & Company 1979) and Michael Basinski's additions to Edelstein's list in *Jargon at Forty: 1951–1991* (The Poetry/Rare Books Collection, SUNY at Buffalo 1991). Unlike Edelstein's checklist and Basinski's additions, the list here contains only those titles appearing in the sequence beginning with Jonathan Williams' *Garbage Litters the Iron Face of the Sun's Child* (Jargon 1). Given space constraints, Jargon Society postcards, broadsides, billboards and other ephemeral items are not included here. These can be investigated further at the Poetry/Rare Books Collection, SUNY at Buffalo.

    1. Jonathan Williams. *Garbage Litters the Iron Face of the Sun's Child*. Engraving by David Ruff. San Francisco, 1951.

    2. Joel Oppenheimer. *The Dancer*. Drawing by Robert Rauschenberg. Black Mountain, 1951.

    3. Jonathan Williams. *Red/Gray*. Drawings by Paul Ellsworth. Black Mountain, 1952.

    4. Victor Kalos. *The Double-Backed Beast*. Drawings by Dan Rice. Black Mountain, 1952.

    5. Jonathan Williams. *Four Stoppage /A Configuration*. Drawings by Charles Oscar. Stuttgart, 1953.

    6. Kenneth Patchen. *Fables & Other Little Tales*. Karlsruhe, 1953.

    7. Charles Olson. *The Maximus Poems/1–10*. Calligraphy by Jonathan Williams. Suttgart, 1953.

    8. Robert Creeley. *The Immoral Proposition*. Drawings by René Laubiès. Karlsruhe, 1953.

    9. Charles Olson. *The Maximus Poems/11–22*. Calligraphy by Jonathan Williams. Suttgart, 1956.

10. Robert Creeley. *All That Is Lovely In Men*. Drawings by Dan Rice. Photograph by Jonathan Williams. Asheville, 1953.

11. Kenneth Patchen. *Poem-Scapes*. Highlands, 1958.

12. Louis Zukofsky. *A Test of Poetry*. New York, 1964.

13. Jonathan Williams. *Poems, 1953–1955*. Three volumes.

13a. *Amen/Huzza/Selah*. "A Preface?" by Louis Zukofsky. Photographs by Jonathan Williams. Black Mountain, 1960.

13b. *Elegies and Celebrations*. Preface by Robert Duncan. Photographs by Aaron Siskind and Jonathan Williams. Highlands, 1962.

13c. *Jammin' the Greek Scene*. Nota by Charles Olson. Drawings by Fielding Dawson. James Jaffe notes, "Approximately 4 proof copies were produced for a projected edition of 300 copies, but the book, with a cover designed by Fielding Dawson, was never published." Karlsruhe, 1959.

14. Robert Duncan. *Letters: Poems 1953–1956*. Drawings by Robert Duncan. Highlands, 1958.

15. Louis Zukofsky. *Some Time*. A song setting on the cover by Celia Zukofsky. Sutgart, 1956.

16. Joel Oppenheimer. *The Dutiful Son*. Frontispiece by Joseph Fiore. Highlands, 1957.

17. Stuart Z. Perkoff. *The Suicide Room*. Drawing by Fielding Dawson. Photograph by Charles Kessler. Karlsruhe, 1956.

18. Irving Layton. *The Improved Binoculars*. Introduction by William Carlos Williams. Highlands, 1956. Second edition includes thirty additional poems.

19. Denise Levertov. *Overland to the Islands*. Drawings by Al Kresch. Calligraphy by Jonathan Williams. Highlands, 1958.

20. Michael McClure. *Passage*. Calligraphy by Jonathan Williams. Big Sur, 1956.

21. Kenneth Patchen. *Hurrah for Anything*. Drawings by Kenneth Patchen. Highlands, 1957.

22. Henry Miller. *The Red Notebook*. Drawings by Henry Miller. Photograph by Wynn Bullock. Highlands, 1958.

23. Mina Loy. *Lunar Baedeker and Time-Tables*. Introductions by William Carlos Williams, Kenneth Rexroth and Denise Levertov. Drawings by Emerson Woelffer. Highlands, 1958.

24. Charles Olson. *The Maximus Poems*. Photograph by Frederick Sommer. Published in association with Corinth Books. New York, 1960.

25. Paul C. Metcalf. *Will West*. Asheville, 1956.

26. Robert Creeley. *The Whip*. Cover design by René Laubiès. Drawings by

Kirsten Hoeck. Highlands, 1957.

27. Peyton Houston. *Sonnet Variations*. Photograph by Henry Holmes Smith. Highlands, 1962.

28. Irving Layton. *A Laughter in the Mind*. Photograph by Frederick Sommer. Highlands, 1958.

29. Bob Brown. *1450–1950*. Photograph by Jonathan Williams. New York, 1959.

30. Jonathan Williams. *The Empire Finals at Verona*. Drawings and collage by Fielding Dawson. Highlands, 1959.

31. *14 Poets, 1 Artist*. Poems by Paul Blackburn, Bob Brown, Edward Dahlberg, Max Finstein, Allen Ginsberg, Paul Goodman, Denise Levertov, Walter Lowenfels, Edward Marshall, E. A. Navaretta, Joel Oppenheimer, Gilbert Sorrentino, Jonathan Williams and Louis Zukofsky. Drawings by Fielding Dawson. New York, 1958.

32. Walter Lowenfels. *Some Deaths*. Introduction by Jonathan Williams. Photographs by Robert Schiller. Highlands, 1964.

33. Robert Creeley. *A Form of Women*. Photograph by Robert Schiller. Published in association with Corinth Books. New York, 1959.

34. Bob Brown. *The Selected Poems*. Introduction by Kay Boyle. Drawing by Reuben Nakian. Jargon 34 was projected but never published.

35. Irving Layton. *A Red Carpet for the Sun*. Photograph by Harry Callahan. Highlands, 1959.

36. Larry Eigner. *On My Eyes*. Introduction by Denise Levertov. Photographs by Harry Callahan. Highlands, 1960.

37. Russell Edson. *What a Man Can See*. Drawings by Ray Johnson. Highlands, 1969.

38. Giuseppe Gioachino Belli. *The Roman Sonnets*. Translated by Harold Norse. Preface by William Carlos Williams. Introduction by Alberto Moravia. Cover by Ray Johnson. Collage by Jean-Jacques Lebel. Highlands, 1960.

39. Jonathan Williams. *Lord! Lord! Lord!: Traditional Funeral Music*. Handset and printed "for the friends of the Jargon Press" by Igal Roodenko. Highlands, 1959.

40. Gilbert Sorrentino. *The Darkness Surrounds Us*. Introduction by Joel Oppenheimer. Collage and drawings by Fielding Dawson. Highlands, 1960.

41. Lou Harrison. *Three Choruses from Opera Libretti: Jargon's Christmas in 1960*. Highlands, 1960.

42. Ronald Johnson. *A Line of Poetry, A Row of Trees*. Drawings by Thomas George. Printed by the Auerhahn Press, San Francisco. Highlands, 1964.

43. Paul C. Metcalf. *Genoa: A Telling of Wonders*. Iconography by Jonathan Williams. Highlands, 1965.

44. Buckminster Fuller. *Untitled Epic Poem on the History of Industrialization.* Introduction by Russell Davenport. Highlands, 1962.

45. Sherwood Anderson. *Six Mid-American Chants.* Photographs by Art Sinsabaugh. Preface by Edward Dahlberg. Postface by Frederick Eckman. Highlands, 1964.

46. Guy Davenport. *Flowers and Leaves.* Photograph by Ralph Eugene Meatyard. Highlands, 1966.

47. Merle Hoyleman. *Letters to Christopher.* Introduction by George Marion O'Donnell. Jargon 47 was projected but never published.

48. Lorine Niedecker. *Tenderness & Gristle: The Collected Poems (1936–1966).* Plant prints by A. Doyle Moore. Penland, 1968.

49. Alfred Hamilton Starr. *Poems.* Introduction by Geof Hewitt. Drawings by Philip Van Aver. Photograph by Simpson Kalisher. Penland, 1970.

50. Doris Ulmann. *The Appalachian Photographs of Doris Ulmann.* Introduction by John Jacob Nies. Preface by Jonathan Williams. Penland, 1971.

51. Thomas Meyer. *A Valentine for L. Z.* Highlands, 1979.

52. Peyton Houston. *Occasions in a World.* Drawings by Bob Nash. Penland, 1969.

53. Mina Loy. *The Last Lunar Baedeker.* Edited and introduced by Roger Conover. Designed by Herbert Bayer. Highlands, 1982.

54. Mason Jordan Mason. *The Selected Poems.* Introduction by Judson Crews. Photographs by Ron Nameth. Jargon 54 was projected but never published.

55. James Broughton. *A Long Undressing: Collected Poems, 1949–1969.* Photograph by Imogen Cunningham. New York, 1971.

56. James Broughton. *High Kukus.* Preface by Alan Watts. Drawings by Hak Vogrin. New York, 1968.

57. Joel Oppenheimer. *Just Friends/Friends and Lovers (Poems 1959–1962).* Photograph by Bob Adelman. Highlands, 1980.

58. Paul C. Metcalf. *Patagoni.* Iconography by Jonathan Williams. Penland, 1971.

59. Joel Oppenheimer. *Names & Local Habitations (Selected Earlier Poems, 1951–1972).* Accolade by Hayden Carruth. Introduction by William Corbett. Illustrated by Philip Guston. Winston-Salem, 1988.

60. James Broughton. *75 Life Lines.* Designed and produced at the Arion Press, San Francisco. Winston-Salem, 1988.

61. Jonathan Williams. *Lullabies Twisters Gibbers Drags.* Cover by R. B. Kitaj. Highlands, 1963.

62. Jonathan Williams. *Emblems for the Little Dells, and Nooks and Corners of Paradise.* Highlands, 1962.

63. Simon Cutts. *Seepages (Poems 1981–1987).* Winston-Salem, 1988.

64. Tom Patterson. *St. EOM in the Land of Pasaquan (The Life and Times of Eddie Owens Martin)*. Photography by Jonathan Williams, Roger Manley and Guy Mendes. Foreword by John Russell. Highlands, 1987.

65. Edwin Morgan. *The Siesta of the Hungarian Snake*. Several formats designed and printed by students of A. Doyle Moore in 1971 but never officially published.

66. Jonathan Williams, editor. *Madeira & Toasts for Basil Bunting's 75th Birthday*. Designed by A. Doyle Moore. Cover portrait by R. B. Kitaj. Highlands, 1977.

67. Guy Davenport. *Do You Have a Poem Book on E.E. Cummings?* Drawings by Guy Davenport. Penland, 1969.

68. Ian Hamilton Finlay. *The Blue and the Brown Poems*. Prefaces by Michael Weaver and Jonathan Williams. Notes by Stephen Bann. Calendar design by Herbert M. Rosenthal. Aspen, 1968.

69. Thomas Meyer. *The Bang Book*. Drawings by John Furnival. Highlands, 1971.

70. Richard Emil Braun. *Bad Land*. Photograph by Fredrick Sommer. Penland, 1971.

71. Ross Feld. *Plum Poems*. Drawings by Dan Rice. Accolade by Gilbert Sorrentino. New York, 1972.

72. Ronald Johnson. *The Spirit Walks, The Rocks Will Talk*. Drawings by Guy Davenport. Penland, 1969.

73. Douglas Woolf. *Spring of the Lamb*. "Broken Field Runner: A Douglas Woolf Notebook" by Paul Metcalf appended at back. Photographs by Ralph Eugene Meatyard. Highlands, 1972.

74. Jonathan Williams, editor. *Epitaphs for Lorine*. Frontispiece by A. Doyle Moore. Back cover by Ian Hamilton Finlay. Photograph by Diane Tammes. Penland, 1973.

75. Thomas A. Clark. *Some Particulars*. Photograph by Bart Parker. Highlands, 1971.

76. Ralph Eugene Meatyard. *The Family Album of Lucybelle Crater*. Texts by Jonathan Greene, Ronald Johnson, Ralph Eugene Meatyard, Guy Mendes, Thomas Meyer and Jonathan Williams. Highlands, 1974.

77. Lyle Bongé. *The Sleep of Reason*. Texts by James Leo Herlihy and Jonathan Williams. Highlands, 1974.

78. Paul C. Metcalf. *The Middle Passage (A Triptych of Commodities)*. Highlands, 1976.

79. Jonathan Williams and Thomas Meyer. *EPitaph*. Corn Close, 1972.

80. Jonathan Williams. *Pairidaeza*. Lithographs by Ian Gardner. Dentdale, 1975.

81. Simon Cutts. *Quelques Pianos*. Accolade by Ian Gardner. Highlands, 1976.

82. Jonathan Williams. *Who Is Little Enis?* Photograph by Guy Mendes. Corn Close, 1974.

83. Thomas Meyer. *The Umbrella of Aesculapius*. Introduction by Robert Kelly. Drawings by Paul Sinodhinos. Highlands, 1975.

84. Ronald Johnson. *Eyes & Objects (Catalogue for an Exhibition: 1970–1972*. Foreword by John Russell. Highlands, 1976.

85. William Anthony. *Bible Stories*. Drawings and texts by William Anthony. Introduction by Gilbert Sorrentino. Highlands, 1976.

86. Thomas A. Clark. *A Still Life*. With six variations on a Chrysanthemum of William Morris by Ian Gardner. Dentdale, 1977.

87. Peter Yates. *The Garden Prospect: Selected Poems*. Introduction by Peyton Houston. Illustrations by Susan Moore. Highlands, 1980.

88. Thomas Meyer. *Staves Calends Legends*. Emblem by John Furnival. Highlands, 1979.

89. Lyle Bongé. *The Photographs of Lyle Bongé*. Introduction by A. D. Coleman. Afterword by Jonathan Williams. Text by Lyle Bongé. Highlands, 1982.

90. William Anthony. *Bill Anthony's Greatest Hits*. Foreword by Robert Rosenblum. Flapdoodle by Jonathan Williams. Highlands, 1988.

91. Jonathan Williams. *Elite/Elate Poems (1971–1975)*. Photographs by Guy Mendes. Highlands, 1979.

92. Paul C. Metcalf. *BOTH*. Highlands, 1982.

93. Thomas A. Clark. *Ways Through Bracken*. Kendal, Cumbria, 1980.

94. Simon Cutts. *Pianostool Footnotes*. Kendal, Cumbria, 1982.

95. William Innes Homer, editor. *Heart's Gate (Letters Between Marsden Hartley and Horace Traubel 1906–1915)*. Introduced by William Innes Homer. Highlands, 1982.

96. Peyton Houston. *Arguments of Idea*. Highlands, 1980.

97. John Menapace. *Letter in a Klein Bottle: Photographs by John Menapace*. Introduction by Donald B. Kuspit. Afterword by Jonathan Williams. Highlands, 1984.

98. Richard C. Notches. *Along the Bible Belt*. Jargon 98 was projected but never published.

99. Thomas Meyer. *Sappho's Raft*. Frontispiece drawing by David Hockney. Designed by Ken Carls. Highlands, 1982.

100. Lorine Niedecker. *From This Condensery: The Complete Writings of Lorine Niedecker*. Edited by Robert J. Bertholf. Highlands, 1985.

101. Ernest Matthew Mickler. *White Trash Cooking*. Photographs by Ernest Matthew Mickler. Highlands, 1986.

102. Thomas Meyer. *At Dusk Iridescent: A Gathering of Poems, 1972–1997*. Photograph by Reuben Cox. Winston-Salem, 1999.

103. Jonathan Williams, editor. *DBA at 70*. Photographs by Jonathan Williams. Design by Jonathan Greene. Winston-Salem, 1989.

104. Mark Steinmetz. *Tuscan Trees: Photographs*. Text by Janet Lembke. Winston-Salem, 2001.

105. Reuben Cox. *The Work of Joe Webb: Appalachian Master of Rustic Architecture*. Text by Reuben Cox. In association with the University of Georgia Press. Highlands and Athens, 2009.

106. Peyton Houston. *The Changes Orders Becomings*. Drawings by James McGarrell. Highlands, 1990.

107. Richard Emil Braun. *Last Man In*. Photograph by Ron Nameth. Highlands, 1990.

108. Williams, Jonathan. *A Hornet's Nest*. Quotes compiled by Jeffery Beam. Drawing by James McGarrell. Frontispiece by Sandra Reese. Photograph by Dobree Adams. Published in association with Green Finch Press. Highlands and Chapel Hill, 2008.

109. Paul C. Metcalf. *Araminta and the Coyotes*. Highlands, 1991.

110. Lou Harrison. *Joys & Perplexities: Selected Poems of Lou Harrison*. Accolade by Ned Rorem. Winston-Salem, 1992.

111. David M. Spear. *The Neugents: "Close to Home."* Afterword by Jonathan Williams. Second edition published by Gnomon Press. Highlands, 1993.

112. Elizabeth Matheson. *Blithe Air: Photographs from England, Wales and Ireland*. Illuminations and pyrotechnic display by Jonathan Williams. Accolade by Thomas Meyer. Winston-Salem, 1995.

113. Jeffery Beam. *Visions of Dame Kind*. Accolade by Thomas Meyer. Winston-Salem, 1995.

114. Phillip March Jones. *Points of Departure: Roadside Memorial Polaroids*. Foreword by Thomas Meyer. Winston-Salem, 2012. [This Jargon published after the death of Jonathan Williams.]

JEFFERY BEAM

BLUE DARTER—A SELECTED CHECKLIST OF JONATHAN WILLIAMS PUBLICATIONS

I have a mind like a blue darter (a kind of Appalachian lizard).
                                                    Jonathan Williams.

This compilation owes much to James Jaffe's *Jonathan Williams: A Biblio-graphical Checklist of His Writings, 1950–1988* (Jaffe, 1989), J. M. Edel-stein's *A Jargon Society Checklist 1951–1979* (Books & Company, NY: 1979), Arthur Uphill's *The Books of Jonathan Williams: Checklist 1952–1979* (Coracle, 1979), and Robert Bertholf's *Jargon at Forty: 1951–1991* (SUNY Buffalo, 1991). All of these sometimes contain more details, if you're interested. I have recently completed a first final draft of a thorough checklist of Williams' work, tentatively entitled *Blue Darter— Jonathan Williams: A Bibliography 1950–2008*, which is intended for a more substantial book publication. For the purposes of this collection I wanted to list the major works for the general reader. My complete check-list will include more descriptive text. For now, the reader can consult the bibliographies listed above, or visit the Jargon archive, Poetry/Rare Books Collection, SUNY at Buffalo.

I've made corrections to previous lists I thought were needed; any mis-takes herein of omission or incorrect refinements, however, are mine. I used items from my personal collection when possible to clarify confusions I had, but I also relied on the cataloging expertise of OCLC and the University of North Carolina North Carolina Collection records.

The terms "major," "minor," "primary" and "secondary" are illusive when it comes to Williams' output. His singular vision and publication aesthetic oftentimes placed as much significance on seemingly ephemeral material as it did on more substantial works. And, of course, tracking down some of the ephemeral is "mite near impossible" as we might say in the South. Thus this list does not necessarily convey the importance that Williams might have placed on a work—although I have striven for a common ground.

The complete *Blue Darter* will name a cosmos: not only larger collections, but also broadsides; postcards; fund-raising "rattling of the begging bowl" letters; introductions and prefaces; jacket blurbs; anthology and magazine contributions; visual contributions; and essays, reviews, and commentaries. In truth, neither Jonathan's commentary on other artists' work, nor his fund-raising missives, for example, were ever secondary; his assessments and perceptions were always as deeply and eccentrically perceptive as his own poems.

In this abbreviated list I have included, besides the expected larger collections, a few of the major works edited by Williams, all the interviews of which I have knowledge, and any major audio and audiovisual recordings I could find. A few smaller broadsides and sheets from early in Williams' career are included because of their historical weight.

I would be grateful for any corrections, revisions, and additions.

Information in square brackets does not appear printed on the publication but is known from other sources or extrapolated from content. Outside of a title, parentheses include editorial or descriptive comment provided by myself or other sources. Whenever possible I have counted the number of actual pages in a work. "Page" means two-sided sheet. A "sheet" usually means a one-sided broadside. The term "leaves" is used mostly for pages printed only on one side, but occasionally is taken from cataloging or other bibliographic records when I did not have the piece before me to confirm whether the count represented one-sided leaves or actual pages.

Garbage Litters the Iron Face of the Sun's Child. Engraving by David Ruff. San Francisco, CA: Jargon Society; *Jargon* 1, 1951, 1 twice folded sheet.

Red/Gray. Drawings by Paul Ellsworth. Black Mountain, NC: [Jargon Society]; *Jargon* 3, 1952, 1 sheet folded to form twelve sides; with envelope.

Four Stoppages: A Configuration. Drawings by Charles Oscar. Highlands, NC: Jargon Society; *Jargon* 5, 1953, 1 thrice-folded sheet to form [8] panels, with envelope.

Jammin' the Greek Scene. Drawings by Fielding Dawson; preface by Charles Olson. Karlsruhe, Germany: Jonathan Williams; *Jargon* 13c, 1956 (sic) [dust jacket states 1959]. (Approximately 4 proof copies produced but the book was never published). From this collection were subsequently published in *Affilati Attrezzi per i Giardini di Catullo* [1967, Italy]/*Sharp Tools for Catullan Gardens* [1968, United States], and in later collections.

The Empire Finals at Verona: Poems 1956–1957. Collage and drawings by Fielding Dawson. Highlands, NC: Jargon Society; *Jargon* 30, 1959 [date stated on colophon but actually published in 1960], 58 pages.

Amen/Huzza/Selah: Poems, Black Mountain, 1956–9. "A Preface?" by Louis Zukofsky; photographs by Williams. [Highlands, NC: Jargon Society]; *Jargon* 13a, 1960, 44 pp.

Elegies and Celebrations. Preface by Robert Duncan; photographs by Aaron Siskind and Williams, Jargon Society; *Jargon* 13b, Highlands, [NC], 1962, [48] pp.

In England's Green & (A Garland & Clyster). Drawings by Philip Van Aver. San Francisco, CA: Auerhahn Press, 1962, [24] pp.

The Macon County North Carolina Meshuga Sound Society: Jonathan Williams, Musical Director, Presents: Lullabies Twisters Gibbers Drags: (Á la Manière de M. Louis Moreau Gottschalk, Late of the City of New Orleans). Covers executed by R. B. Kitaj. Highlands [NC]: Nantahala Foundation; *Jargon* 61, 1963, 20 pp.

Lines about Hills above Lakes (Postals from Williams). Foreword by John Wain; drawings by Barry Hall. Ft. Lauderdale, FL: Roman Books, 1964, 28 pp.

Twelve Jargonelles from the Herbalist's Notebook. Graphic realization by Ann Wilkinson. Bloomington, IN: Department of Fine Arts, Indiana University, 1965, 24 pp.

Petite Country Concrete Suite: Rude Signs & Portents for Col. Al Lingo, Alabama Directory of Public Safety, and custodian of the SBI files on "Civil Rights Advocates" kept quietly near the Holiday Inn in Montgomery. (An undetermined number were published as an insert in the back cover of *Spero Magazine*, 1964; this edition contained 100 numbered copies), [Flint, MI]: Fenian Head Centre Press, [1965], [18] pp.

Paean to Dvorak, Deemer & McClure. San Francisco, CA: Dave Haselwood, 1966, [28] pp.

Ten Jargonelles from the Herbalist's Notebook. Designed by Arthur Korant. Urbana, IN: Design Program of Department of Fine Arts, Indiana University, 1966, [10] leaves.

Affilati attrezzi per i giardini di Catullo (selected poems in English and Italian). Translations by Leda Sartini Mussio; drawings by James McGarrell. Milan, Italy: Roberto Lerici Editori; *Poesia series* 3, 1967 (published in the United States as *Sharp Tools for Catullan Gardens*), 121 pp.

Polycotyledonous Poems. Stuttgart, Germany: edition hansjoerg mayer; *Futura 15*, 1967, single sheet folded to form [8] panels.

Eight Jargonelles from the Herbalist's Notebook. Designed and printed by David Ahlsted under the aegis of George Sadek. Bloomington, IN: Design Department, Indiana University, 1967, [18] pp.

The Macon County North Carolina Meshuga Sound Society: Jonathan Williams, Musical Director, Presents: Lullabies Twisters Gibbers Drags: (À la Manière de M. Louis Moreau Gottschalk, Late of the City of New Orleans). Covers by R. B. Kitaj. (Reprinted with new introduction). Designed and printed by Ira J. Newman. Bloomington, IN: Design Department, Indiana University, 1967, [20] pp.

Fifty Epiphytes (cover title: *50! Epiphytes,-taphs,-tomes,-grams,-thets! 50!*) London, England: Poet & Printer, 1967, 16 pp.

Mahler (a separate pamphlet of poems printed on the occasion of the publication of *Mahler Becomes Politics ... Beisbol*: a suite of screen prints by R. B. Kitaj). London, England: Marlborough Fine Arts, 1967, [44] pp.

The Lucidities: Sixteen in Visionary Company. Drawings by John Furnival. London, England: Turret Books, 1968, [32] pp.

Forty Sporting Questions in Honour of Ian Hamilton Finlay's Fortieth Birthday, October 28, 1965, Asked by Jonathan Williams at Gledfield Farmhouse, Ardgay, Easter Ross, While Piano Music of Erik Satie Trickled Through the Late Afternoon Gloom. Aspen Institute, Aspen, CO: [Jonathan Williams], 1968, [11] leaves.

A *Bestiary for Anti-Laodiceans, Lamed-Vovniks & Lacandons.* Drawings by Aubrey Schwartz. Aspen Institute for Humanistic Studies, Aspen, CO: Jonathan Williams, 1968, [43] pp.

The Plastic Hydrangea People Poems. With glosses by Claes Oldenburg. Aspen, CO: Aspen Institute for Humanistic Studies; *Jargon 69*, 1968, [22] leaves.

Descant on Rawthey's Madrigal: Conversations with Basil Bunting. Lexington, KY: Gnomon Press, 1968, [48] pp.

Sharp Tools for Catullan Gardens. by James McGarrell; introductory note by Guy Davenport. Bloomington, IN: Department of Fine Arts, University of Indiana, 1968, 10 poems/10 lithographs in portfolio, [26] sheets.

Mahler. London, England: Cape Goliard Press (in association with Grossman Publishers, New York), 1969, 60 pp.

An Ear in Bartram's Tree: Selected Poems, 1957–1967. Introduction by Guy Davenport. Chapel Hill, NC: University of North Carolina Press, 1969, [166] pp.

Strung Out With Elgar On A Hill. Drawings by Peter Bodner. Urbana, IL: The Finial Press, 1970, [32] pp.

[Editor and author of preface] *Edward Dahlberg: A Tribute; Essays, Reminiscences, Correspondence, Tributes.* (Prose and poetry collection; festschrift for Dahlberg's seventieth birthday). New York: David Lewis; A *Tri-Quarterly Book,* 1970, 196 pp. First appeared as *Tri-Quarterly* 20 (Fall 1970).

Blues & Roots/Rue & Bluets: A Garland for the Appalachians. Photographs by Nicholas Dean. [New York], NY: Grossman, 1971, [160] pp.

The Loco-Logodaedalist in Situ: Selected Poems, 1968–1970. Embellishments by Joe Tilson. London, England: Cape Goliard Press [in association with Grossman Publishers, New York], 1971, [152] pp. (The Grossman American edition was published in 1972).

An Ear in Bartram's Tree: Selected Poems, 1957–1967. Introduction by Guy Davenport. New York: New Directions, 1972, [160] pp.

Pairidaeza: A Celebration in Lithography & Poetry for the Garden at Levens Hall, Westmoreland. Lithographs by Ian Gardner. Roswell, NM: Donald B. Anderson, 1973, [20] leaves in spiral binder.

[Editor and contributor] *Epitaphs for Lorine,* NC: Jargon Society; *Jargon* 74, 1973, [48] pp.

A Celestial Centennial Reverie for Charles E. Ives: (The Man Who Found Our Music in the Ground). Drawing by Willard Midgette. Roswell, NM: Donald B. Anderson, 1975, 24 pp.

Hot What?: Collages, Texts, Photographs. Dublin, GA: Mole Press, 1975, [36] pp.

Imaginary Postcards (Clints Grikes Gripes Glints). Drawings by Tom Phillips. London, England: Trigram Press, 1975, [48] leaves. (120 copies distributed to friends of the Trigram Press, with the following printed statement inserted: "As a result of a disagreement between the publishers and one of the authors over the design of this book, the publishers have decided not to publish it. Before this decision was reached 120 copies were bound, which are being distributed to friends of Trigram Press.")

Pairidaeza: A Celebration in Lithography & Poetry for the Garden at Levens Hall, Westmoreland. Lithographs by Ian Gardner. Corn Close, Dentdale, Cumbria, England: Jargon Society; *Jargon* 80, 1975, [19] sheets, [13] plates, in portfolio.

gAy BCs. Drawings by Joe Brainard. Champaign, IL: The Finial Press, 1976, [40] pp.

Untinears & Antennae for Maurice Ravel. St. Paul, MN: Truck Press, 1977, 58 pp.

Super-Duper Zuppa Inglese (and Other Trifles from the Land of Stodge). Drawings by Barbara Jones. [Belper, Derbyshire, England]: Aggie Weston's Editions, 1977, [32] pp.

[Editor and contributor] *Madeira and Toasts for Basil Bunting's Seventy-fifth Birthday.* [Corn Close], Dentdale, [Cumbria, England], Jargon Society; *Jargon* 66, 1977, 120 pp.

A Blue Ridge Weather Prophet Makes Twelve Stitches in Time on the Twelfth Day of Christmas. Illustrations by Carolyn Whitesel. Frankfort, KY: Gnomon Press, 1977, [24] pp.

[Editor and author of introduction] *"I Shall Save One Land Unvisited": Eleven Southern Photographers.* Lexington, KY: Gnomon Press, 1978 [95] pp.

Elite/Elate Poems: Selected Poems, 1971–1975. Photographs by Guy Mendes, [Highlands, NC]: The Jargon Society; Jargon 91, 1979, 220 pp.

Portrait Photographs. (Photographs and prose commentary). London, [England]: Coracle Press, 1979, [76] pp.

Portrait Photographs. (Photographs and prose commentary). Frankfort, KY: Gnomon Press, 1979, [75] pp.

Shankum Naggum. Rocky Mount, NC: Friends of the Library, North Carolina Wesleyan College, 1979, [26] pp.

Glees, Swarthy Monotonies, Rince Cochon, and Chozzerai for Simon, Poems 1979. Drawings by John Furnival. Roswell, NM: DBA Editions, 1980, 94 pp.

Homage Umbrage Quibble & Chicane: Poems 1980. Drawings by John Furnival. Roswell, NM: DBA Editions, 1981, 72 pp.

Jonathan Williams—A Poet Collects: February 27–April 30, 1981. Winston-Salem, NC: Southeastern Center for Contemporary Art, 1981, [38] pp.

Ten Photographs. [Belper, Derbyshire, England: Aggie Weston's], *Aggie Weston's* No. 18. 1982, [24] pp.

Get Hot or Get Out: A Selection of Poems, 1957–1981. Metuchen, NJ: Scarecrow Press, Poets Now no. 1, 1982, 175 pp.

Niches Inches: New & Selected Poems 1957–1981. Drawings by Karl Torok and John Furnival. Corn Close, Dentdale, [Cumbria, England]: Jonathan Williams, 1982, [154] pp.

The Delian Seasons: Four Poems. Drawings by Karl Torok. London, Coracle Press, 1982, [21] pp.

The Magpie's Bagpipe: Selected Essays of Jonathan Williams. San Francisco, CA: North Point Press, 1982, 185 pp.

April 19, Lexington Nocturne: A Poem. Illustrated by Keith Smith, [Rochester, NY]: Visual Studies Workshop Press, 1983, [48] pp.

62 Climerikews to Amuse Mr. Lear. Drawing by John Furnival. Roswell, [N.M]; Denver: DBA/JCA Editions, 1983, [50] pp.

The Fifty-two Cleriheus of Clara Hughes. Drawings by Glen Baxter. Atlanta, GA: Pynyon Press, 1983, 54 pp.

In the Azure over the Squalor: Ransackings & Shorings. [New York: NY]: Jordan Davies, 1983, [48] pp.

Letters to the Great Dead. An expansive text/image series in collaboration with visual artist John Furnival, using letterpress, etching, silkscreen, and lithography. [Woodchester, Gloucestershire, England: Openings], 1984-. 23 plates in 2 portfolios. 50 plates were projected to be completed by 1994. 23 were published during Williams' life. The last, *Jonathan's Last Words,* Furnvial published in 2014 and appears reproduced in this volume. Some of these plates have also been sold separately.

Portfolio 1:
Catullus on the Roman wall (Jock Strap Traps Jock)
Frank Cooper's "Oxford" Vintage (Oxford Mallarmé)
Ars longa, vida blue, ave atque vale!
Ite in pace
Wallpaper for a classical passion-pit atop Mount Parnassus (Basho Bonks Sappho)

The feast (Stevie Smith invited Death)
To A.E. Coppard (1/xii/23)
Plink! Plank! real sham Poulenc!
Paintslash for Redon's birthday, May 22 (Odilon Red on)
Du beurre! Donneze-moi du beurre! Toujours du beurre!
Percy Grainger was no stranger to stinging whips or mother's lips

Portfolio 2:
Mr. Lear
Louden lots
Das Lied von der Nerd
Frog pond plop
Monsieur Point
Isolated person in Gloucester, Massachusetts (Charles Olson)
Stevie Smith
Un paisaje para Frederico Mompou
Firbank in fox's furs on Firbank Fell
Ant on Bruckner
Arc en oeil
Bunting at Briggflatts
Jonathan's Last Words

In the Azure over the Squalor: Ransackings & Shorings. Highlands, NC: Otis Editions, 1984, 42 pp.

[Self-interview] *Jonathan C. Williams Interviews J. Chamberlain Williams* in *Dictionary of Literary Biography Yearbook*. Detroit, MI: Gale Research, Vol. 5, 1984: 88–92.

Blues & Roots, Rue & Bluets: A Garland for the Southern Appalachians. Introduction by Herbert Leibowitz. Durham, NC: Duke University Press, 1985, 112 pp.

In the Azure over the Squalor: Ransackings & Shorings. Drawing by James McGarrell. Frankfort, KY: Gnomon Press, 1985, 48 pp.

Lord Stodge's Good Thing Guide to Over 100 English Delights. Cover design by Karl Torok. Roswell, [NM]; Denver [CO]: DBA/JCA Editions, 1985, [100] pp.

Dear World, Forget It! Love, Mnemosyne: A Range of Letters, 1984–85:

Plus a Few Elusive Items. Cover by John Furnival. Roswell [N.M.]: DBA/JCA editions, 1985, [78] pp.

Rivulets & Sibilants of Dent. Illustrations by Karl Torok. [Bradford, England]: Topia Press, 1987, [12] loose sheets and [8] pp book.

The Concise Dentdale Dictionary of English Place Names. Highlands, NC: Otis Edition, 1987, [12] pp.

[Photographer] *St. EOM in the Land of Pasaquan: The Life and Times and Art of Eddie Owens Martin* by Tom Patterson. [Additional photographs by Roger Manley and Guy Mendes; foreword by John Russell]. [Winston-Salem, N.C.]: The Jargon Society; *Jargon* 64, 1987, 260 pp.

Aposiopeses: Odds and Ends. Minneapolis, MN: Granary Books, 1988, [44] pp.

Le Garage Ravi de Rocky Mount: An Essay on Vernon Burwell. Photographs by Roger Manley. [Rocky Mount, NC]: North Carolina Wesleyan College Press, 1988, [8] pp.

Dementations on Shank's Mare: Being "Meta-Fours in Plus-Fours" and a Few "Foundlings" Collected from Rambles (and Drives) in Herefordshire, Gwent, Powys, Avon, Dorset, Gloucestershire, Cumbria and North Yorkshire. New Haven, CT: Truck Press 1988, [48] pp.

Uncle Gus Flaubert Rates the Jargon Society in One Hundred One Laconic Présalé Sage Sentences. 8th Hanes Lecture. Chapel Hill, NC: Hanes Foundation for the Study of the Origin and Development of the Book, Rare Book Collection, University Library, University of North Carolina, 1989, 32 pp.

Quote, Unquote. Berkeley, CA: Ten Speed Press, 1989, 155 pp.

[Editor and contributor] *DBA at 70: A Festschrift.* Winston-Salem, NC: Jargon Society; *Jargon* 103, 1989, [69] pp.

Selected Correspondence; Collected Serendipity. Winston-Salem, NC: Whitney Jones, Mole Press, 1989, [84] leaves.

Metafours for Mysophobes. Twickenham, Middlesex and Wakefield, West Yorkshire [England]: North and South, 1989, 32 pp.

Eight Days in Eire, Or, Nothing So Urgent As Mañana. Photographs by Mike Harding. Rocky Mount, NC: North Carolina Wesleyan College Press, 1990, 24 pp.

[Autobiography] *Cloches a Travers Les Feuilles. Contemporary Authors Autobiography Series.* Detroit, MI: Gale Research. 1990. 12: 339–358.

Quantulumcumque: Sub-Aesthetic Poems. Introduction by Jeffery Beam. Asheville, NC: French Broad Press, 1991, [36] pp.

Polaroids (Liable to Be Anywhere). Draft texts for a proposed book by Coracle of Polaroid photographs with a note by Jonathan Williams, a postface by Simon Cutts, and captions to proposed photos. [This copy inscribed *"for a book to be (maybe) JW for S* [Stanley Finch] *and J* [Jeffery Beam] *2006 Scaly Mtn*]. In an email to Beam November 21, 2016 Cutts explains: "In the early-mid nineties, we had the idea to do a book of Jonathan's Polaroids, parallel to the portraits of *Portrait Photographs*. The book was entirely planned as you can see from the numbers and comments alongside. Don't remember what happened? Money, predictability, something? Anyway, all the photos were mounted in one frame, in the sequence of the listing, and it was around here in Ireland for a few years, then when the photo archive went to the Beinecke, the big mount went too, circa 2007." 1993, [16] pp.

Anathema Maranatha! Drawings by William Anthony. New York, NY: Richard Minsky, 1993, [unpaged].

No-nonse-nse: Limericks (Invented in Ireland c. 1765), Meta-fours (Invented during the Non-Summer of 1985 in Lower Stodgedale) and Clerihews (Invented in 1890 by Edmund Clerihew Bently) 1993 by a Perdurable "True Descendent of Aristophanes and Catullus." Mt. Horeb, WI: Perishable Press, 1993, [39] pp.

Letters to Mencken from the Land of Pink Lichen. New York, NY: Dim Gray Bar Press, 1994, [48] pp.

26 Enlarged, Engorged Polaroids. Corn Close, Dentdale, Cumbria, England: The Press of Otis the Lamed-Vovnik, 1994, [34] pp.

Jonathan Williams' Quote Book, 1992–1993. Drawing by James McGarrell. Highlands, NC: Press of Otis the Lamedvovnik, 1994, 40 pp.

Horny & Ornery: Poems of Solace in Desolate Times by a Gentleman in the South. Drawing by James McGarrell; preface by James Laughlin. Skywinding Farm, Scaly Mountain, NC: Press of Otis the Lamed-Vovnik, 1994, [44] pp.

Long Taters: Jonathan Williams' Quote Book, 1994. Skywinding Farm, Scaly Mountain, NC: Press of Otis the Lamed-Vovnik, 1996, 40 pp.

A Palpable Elysium: Photographs. New York, NY: Dim Gray Bar Press, 1997, ten prints mounted on 4-ply archival mats, in drop-spine box, [13] leaves.

Blackbird Dust: Essays, Poems, and Photographs. [New York: NY]: Turtle Point Press, 2000, 243 pp.

Some Jazz from the Baz: Excerpts from Basil Bunting's Letters to Jonathan Williams, 1963–1985. Skywinding Farm, Scaly Mountain, NC: Press of Otis the Lamed-Vovnik, 2000, [70] pp.

[Compiler] *Poet's Poems* No. 12 (Eight of Williams favorite poems from other poets). Belper, Derbys, [England]: Aggie Weston's Editions, 2002, [9] leaves.

A Palpable Elysium: Portraits of Genius and Solitude (photographs and essays). Boston, MA: David R. Godine, 2002, 174 pp.

A Garden Carried in a Pocket: Letters 1964–1968. Haverford: Green Shade, 2004.

Kinnikinnick Brand Kickapoo Joy-Juice: Meta-fours. Illustrations by John Furnival. Isla Vista, Turkey Press, 2004, [48] pp.

Jubilant Thicket: New & Selected Poems. Port Townsend, WA: Copper Canyon Press, 2005, 296 pp.

A Hornet's Nest compiled by Jeffery Beam (A compilation of Jonathan Williams quotes). Drawing by James McGarrell; frontispiece by Sandra Reese; photograph by Dobree Adams. Highlands, NC; Hillsborough, NC: The Jargon Society; *Jargon* 108; Green Finch Press; *Green Finch Keening* 71, 2008, 30 pp.

Some Meta-fours in Memoriam: Jonathan Williams. Illustrations by John Furnival. 13 drink paperboard coasters in handmade board box, 5 designs, taken from JW's *Kinnikinnick Brand Kickapoo Joy-Juice: Meta-fours.* Isla Vista, Turkey Press, [2009].

Portraits d'Amerique tradiuts et édités par Jacques Demarcq. Introduction de Rachel Stella. Caen, France: Éditions Nous, 2013, 96 pp.

A SELECTED MISCELLANY, INTERVIEWS, AUDIO AND VIDEO RECORDINGS, AND RESEARCH COLLECTIONS

[Jargon Society collection]. Buffalo, NY: State University of New York at Buffalo, 1950–2008. The Jargon Society Collection features an extensive collection of materials relating to the long and influential life of the press, including numerous manuscripts and correspondence from such American and English poets as Charles Olson and Robert Duncan, Irving Layton, Kenneth Patchen, Ian Hamilton Finlay, Robert Creeley, Denise Levertov, Lorine Niedecker, Louis Zukofsky, and many others; production and promotional materials; financial records; photographs as well as the manuscripts and personal papers of Jonathan Williams; and a large number of photographs of Williams and other poets dating back to the 1940s and including scenes from Black Mountain College. The collection is arranged in seven series: Series I. Manuscripts—Jonathan Williams (22 boxes alphabetized); Series II. Manuscripts—other (59 boxes alphabetized); Series III. Business records (17 boxes); Series IV. Letters to Jonathan Williams (487 boxes alphabetized); Series V. Letters from Jonathan Williams (13 boxes alphabetized); Series VI. Art and photographs (51 boxes); Series VII. Peripherals (64 boxes).] http://libweb1.lib.buffalo.edu:8080/findingaids/view?docId=ead/poetry/ubpo_pcms0019.xml&doc.view=content&brand=default&anchor.id=0#node.1.3.1.1

Jonathan Williams at the Electronic Poetry Center, The Poetry Collection of the University Libraries, University at Buffalo, The State University of New York: http://epc.buffalo.edu/authors/williams_jonathan/

[Readings] Vol. 1; Selected readings from *An ear in Bartram's tree*, part 1. —; Vol. 2; Selected readings from *An ear in Bartram's tree*, part 2. —; Vol. 3; Selected readings from *Blues & roots/rue & bluets*; Vol. 4; Selected readings from Elite/elate poems —; Vol. 5; *The loco logaodaedalist in situ; Mahler ; Get hot or get out!* —; . Vol. 6; *Gless—Swarthy monotonies—Rince Cochon —& Chozzerai for Simon ; Supa duper inglaise poems; The fifty-two clerihews of Clara Hughes; Aposiopeses* —; Vol. 7; *Dementations on shank's mare; Delian seasons; No no nonsense ; Quantulumcumque; Ananthema maranatha!* —; Vol. 8; *Horny & ornery; Kinnikinnick brand kickapoo joyjuice; Scumbags from Parnassus; Amuse-gueules for bemused ghouls. Neal Hutcheson Collection of Jonathan Williams Readings* from production of *Talk about Writing: Portraits of North Carolina Writers* [Raleigh, NC]: NCSU (North Carolina State University) Humanities Extension. 8 VHS tapes. (Held at SUNY-Buffalo; originals held at The Southern Historical Collection, University of North Carolina at Chapel Hill) http://findingaids.lib.unc.edu/05074/

Jonathan Williams photographs, (bulk 1950–1990). New Haven, CT: Yale Collection of American Literature, Beinecke Rare Book and Manuscript Library. [The collection consists primarily of Jonathan Williams' por-traits of poets, painters, writers, and artists, as well as photographs of out-sider art. The collection includes transparencies, Polaroid albums, Polaroids, and slides, which largely document Williams' work as a photographer and which relate to his slide show presentations and published books of pho-tography]. [Purchased November 2006 and July 2007.] Finding aid: http://hdl.handle.net/10079/fa/beinecke.williamsj

"Harold Billings: A Preliminary Inventory of His Correspondence from Jonathan Williams," in the Manuscript Collection at the Harry Ran-som Humanities Research Center, University of Texas-Austin. Approxi-mately sixty communications to Harold Billings, a director of the University of Texas Libraries, from Williams. http://norman.hrc.utexas.edu/fasearch/findingAid.cfm?eadid=00388

Jonathan Williams Papers 1962–1967. Special Collections, University of Virginia Library. http://ead.lib.virginia.edu/vivaxtf/view?docId=uva-sc/viu01587.xml

Robert Creeley and Company: home movies by Bobbie Louise Hawkins [filmed from 1962 to 1965]. Williams and Ronald Johnson appear at minute 66:30. http://writing.upenn.edu/pennsound/x/Hawkins-Creeley.html

Jonathan Williams Reading His Poems with Comment in the Record-ing Laboratory, June 18, 1965. (Williams reads selections from his collected volumes: *The Empire Finals at Verona, Amen Huzza Selah, Elegies and Cele-brations, Lullabies Twisters Gibbers Drags, In England's Green &*, and *Fifty Responses to the Symphonies of Gustav Mahler*. In addition, he reads three of his uncollected works). Washington, D.C.: Archive of Recorded Poetry and Literature, Library of Congress, 1965, 1 sound tape reel.

[Interview] *Poet at the Breakfast Table with Leon Rooke*. Durham, NC: *The North Carolina Anvil*, November 4, 1967.

[Interview] *VORT: Fielding Dawson, Jonathan Williams* number includes interview with Barry Alpert as well as critical pieces on Williams' work. [Silver Spring, MD: Barry Alpert] *VORT*, vol. 2 no. 1 (Fall 1973) 112 pp (Interview pp 54–75).

[Interview, March 3, 1976] by William Corbett. (Williams also reads from his work). New York, NY: WBAI Radio, 1976, 1 sound tape reel.

[Reading] University of Warwick. Writers at Warwick Audio Archive. Coventry, England. 76 minutes, 1978. http://www2.warwick.ac.uk/fac

/arts/english/writingprog/archive/writers/williamsjonathan/1978/270.mp3

[Reading] Williams and Thomas Meyer reading. University of Warwick. Writers at Warwick Audio Archive. Coventry, England. 64 minutes, 43 seconds. http://www2.warwick.ac.uk/fac/arts/english/writingprog/archive/writers/williamsjonathan/301079

Jonathan Williams. Interviewed by Tom Pickard. Williams also reads some of his poems. Videocassette, 45 minutes, 1979. http://bufvc.ac.uk/dvdfind/index.php/title/11617

A Quarter Century of the Jargon Society: An Interview with Jonathan Williams [with Susan Howe] in *The Art of Literary Publishing: Editors on Their Craft,* edited by Bill Henderson. Yonkers, NY: Pushcart Press, 1980, 268 pp.

In Marsden Hartley's Hand: A Twittering of Birds. (A poem and an interview with Williams conducted by Tom Patterson). Atlanta: Pynyon Press, *Red Hand Book II,* 1980: 20–30.

[Reading] Baltimore: Maryland Institute College of Art, Mades Audio Cassette Collection, 1981. Two tapes: Tape 1 Side A, 23:01, Side B, 31.11, Tape 2 Side B, 3:59. https://archive.org/details/mma2333-01

[Reading]. London, England: Audio Arts; *Readings at Coracle Press 2,* 1981, 1 sound cassette. [With Glen Baxter, Basil Bunting, Thomas A. Clark, Roy Fisher, and Thomas Meyer] http://www.tate.org.uk/audio-arts/supplements/coracle-press

[Interview with Williams and Thomas Meyer by John Browning] *Gay Sunshine Interviews,* volume 2, edited by Winston Leyland. San Francisco, CA: Gay Sunshine Press, 1982, 288 pp.

Get Hot or Get Out. Washington, D. C.: Watershed Tapes, 1984, 1 cassette, also available online: https://media.sas.upenn.edu/pennsound/authors/Williams-Jonathan/Get-Hot-or-Get-Out/Williams-Jonathan_Get-Hot-or-Get-Out_Watershed-Tapes_1984.mp3

"Mnemonic Wallpaper Pattern," a vocal adaptation of Williams' concrete poem "Mnemonic Wallpaper Pattern for Southern Two-Seaters." Toronto: Sign Language, Cassette Side A, Underwhich Editions, 1985. https://media.sas.upenn.edu/pennsound/groups/Owen-Sound/Sign-Language-A/Sound-Owen_04_Mnemonic-Wallpaper-Pattern_Sign-Language-A_Fat-Alberts_Toronto_2-2-76.mp3

Nearly Twenty Questions. (An interview of and conversation with

Williams by Ronald Johnson). New York, NY: David R. Godine, *Conjunctions* 7 (1985): 224-238.

[Interview] With Robert Dana in *Against the Grain: Interviews with Maverick American Publishers*. Iowa City, IA: University of Iowa Press, 1986, pp. 187–226.

Jonathan Williams: By Eye and By Ear. Directed and Edited by Monty Diamond, 1975. 13 minutes. Made for WUNC-TV, public television. Won best documentary in the North Carolina Film Festival of 1975. https://you tube/H9mvY03A0U0. Also published as Burlington, VT: Monty Diamond Films for South Carolina Educational Television (Columbia, SC), [1989], VHS tape. *Jonathan Williams: By Eye and By Ear*. New York, NY: Mirabell Productions, [1980s], 1 cassette. *Jonathan Williams: By Eye By Ear* by Monty Diamond.

Black Mountain College: A Thumbnail Sketch by Monty Diamond. Burlington, VT: Monty Diamond Films for South Carolina Educational Television (Columbia, SC), [1989], VHS tape.

[Commentary appearance] *Black Mountain College: A Thumbnail Sketch, with Commentary by Jonathan Williams* [wearing his Astrid Furnival knitted "Samuel Palmer" sweater]. 13 minutes. Produced by Monty Diamond and South Carolina ETV. Written and directed by Monty Diamond, 1989. https://youtu.be/G3xSAew7vEU

[Interview] *Jonathan Williams in Prospect into Breath: Interviews with North and South Writers* with Peterjon Skelts. Twickenham, Middlesex and Wakefield, West Yorkshire [England]: North and South, 1991, 189 pp.

High Art & Low Life: An Interview with Jonathan Williams. Minneapolis, MN: *The James White Review*, vol. 11 no. 1 (1992): 1, 3–4, includes six "New Metafours.

Six Writers at the Literary Institute: Erica van Horn, Harry Gilonis, Simon Cutts, Stuart Mills, Thomas Meyer, Jonathan Williams. Muker, Swaledale, Yorkshire, England: [recorded by David Preece], 21 June 1994, cassette recording, and audio CD. Copy held at the Univeristy of North Carolina at Chapel Hill Library: http://search.lib.unc.edu/search?R=UNCb7335868

Twenty-seven Batting-practice Pitches for the John Kruk of American Letters: An Interview with Jonathan Williams with Leverett T. Smith. Greenville, NC: *North Carolina Literary Review*, vol. 2 no. 2 (1995): 98–111; also available online at http://www.jargonbooks.com/jw_smith_interview.html

[Reading] Ear-Inn, New York City. 23 minutes 26 seconds. 1995. https://media.sas.upenn.edu/pennsound/authors/Williams-Jonathan/Williams-Jonathan_Complete-Recording_Ear-Inn_NYC_10-18-95.mp3

Williams reads his 1958 poem "O, For A Muse of Fire!" at the National Portrait Gallery, April 1996, during a symposium and marathon poetry reading held in conjunction with the exhibition "Rebels: Painters and Poets of the 1950s." The video of the entire poetry reading is held in the National Portrait Gallery's audio-visual archive. 1996. http://smithsonianavarchivists.tumblr.com/post/101112983430/the-truffle-hound-of-american-poetry-jonathan

Talk about Writing: Portraits of North Carolina Writers: Jonathan Williams. Produced by Neal Hutcheson. [Raleigh, NC]: NCSU (North Carolina State University) Humanities Extension, 2001, 1 videocassette.

[Commentary appearance] *Mountain Talk: Language & Life in Southern Appalachia,* produced by Neal Hutcheson and Gary Carden. Raleigh, NC: North Carolina State University Humanities Extension, 2003, 1 videodisc.

[Interview] *Tales of a Jargonaut: The Complete "Rain Tax" Interview* with Jonathan Williams with Jeffery Beam. Minneapolis: *Rain Taxi*, Spring 2003: [15] pp. http://www.raintaxi.com/tales-of-a-jargonaut-an-interview-with-jonathan-williams/

[Interview] *Tales of a Jargonaut: Jonathan Williams with Jeffery Beam.* Minneapolis: *Rain Taxi*, 8 no.1 (Spring 2003): 46–48.

[Interview] *Jonathan Williams' Nation of Has, for Those Who Haven't: "A Palpable Elysium: Portraits of Genius and Solitude"* with Jeffery Beam. Unabridged, very lightly edited transcription of the *Rain Taxi* interview with Williams. Highlands, NC: The Jargon Society, 2003, [38] pp. http://www.jargonbooks.com/jw_interview.html

[Interview] Highlands, NC, August 2005, 21 minutes 12 seconds. Produced by Katie Brugger. Appeared on the *Heart of the High Country* TV show, August 29, 2005. https://youtu.be/3QSX2dQfyi0

[Reading] City Lights Bookstore, Sylva, NC, May 27, 2005. https://media.sas.upenn.edu/pennsound/authors/Williams-Jonathan/Williams-Jonathan_Complete-Reading_City-Lights_Sylva-NC_5-27-05.mp3, and Jeff Davis' comments on the recording: http://naturespoetry.blogspot.com/2008/03/jonathan-williams-on-air.html

[Reading and interview] *Jubilant Thicket*. With host Michael Silverblatt. Santa Monica, CA: Bookworm, KCRW Radio, May 12, 2005. http://www.kcrw.com/etc/programs/bw/bw050512jonathan_williams

[Reading and interview] With host Leonard Schwartz. Olympia, WA: *Cross-Cultural Poetics*, Evergreen State College, KAOS-FM Radio, February 25, 2007. https://media.sas.upenn.edu/pennsound/groups/XCP/XCP_131_Williams_2-25-07.mp3

[Commentary appearance] *Fully Awake: Black Mountain College* by Cathryn Davis Zommer and Neeley House. Elon, NC: Elon University, 2007, 1 videodisc.

[Commentary appearance] *Polis is This: Charles Olson and the Persistence of Place*. Gloucester, MA: Ferinni Productions, 2007, 1 videodisc.

Jargon feature, edited by Rachel Stella, with a short essay on JW; photographs; reprint of JW self-interview from the *Dictionary of Literary Biography*; a selection of meta-fours, clerihews, limericks, and other JW poems; poems by Thomas Meyer, Mina Loy, and Lorine Niedecker; a selection of *Palpable Elysium* essays; excerpt from *White Trash Cooking*; and a Jargon bibliography. Auvers-sur-Oise, France: *Fusées*, no. 13 (2008), Éditions Carte Blanche, pp. 51–84.

Jonathan Williams in Conversation with Richard Owens, 1 June 2007. (Phone interview transcribed for online *Jacket* magazine Jonathan Williams feature). Balmain, Australia: *Jacket* magazine, *Jacket* 38, 2009, http://jacketmagazine.com/38/jwd06-iv-jw-ivb-owens.shtml

Kinnikinnick Brand Kickapoo Joy-Juice: Meta-fours, Sueno Road Archive on Vimeo [2009]. Two videos of this limited edition collection of meta-fours from Sandra and Harry Reese's Turkey Press. https://vimeo.com/7808911 and https://vimeo.com/7005874

Jonathan Williams: Lord of Orchards, special memorial festschrift, edited by Jeffery Beam and Richard Owens. Balmain, Australia: *Jacket* magazine, *Jacket* 38, 2009. http://jacketmagazine.com/38/index.shtml#jw

Jonathan Williams in Rochester: Memories of My Days with a Fellow Artist. Keith A. Smith, Book Number 274. Rochester, NY: keith smith books, 2010, [36] pp.

Jonathan Williams, special feature, including reprint of Beam's *Rain Taxi* interview with Williams and a group of last poems, edited by Jeffery Beam and Richard Kitta. Košice, Slovakia: *ENTER* magazine no.4, 2011, pp. 54–60.

https://issuu.com/riskitt/docs/enter4.

Eye/Ojbect: Photographs from the Collection of Jonathan Williams edited by Paul Berlanga. Includes interview with Thomas Meyer, conducted by Phillip March Jones, 121 plates, a few JW poems, and a JW photographic timeline. Chicago, IL: Stephen Daiter Gallery, 2011, 35 pp. Web includes some photos from the collection: http://stephendaitergallery.com/exhibitions/eyeobject-photographs-from-the-collection-of-jonathan-williams/

The following cassettes are held in the Professor Eric Noel William Mottram Collection (1924–1995), Tape recorded material, 1950–1995, College Archives, King's College, London. PLEASE NOTE that this catalogue is unfinished and still in early draft. Many tapes remain to be described and it is likely that there may be revisions or additions to entries.

MOTTRAM: 14/1/175, 1965, Side A. Jonathan Williams reading, no further details, [45] mins.

MOTTRAM: 14/1/67, 1971, Jonathan Williams reading at Polytechnic of Central London, continued from tape MOTTRAM 14/1/29; 60 mins.

MOTTRAM: 14/1/29, 1973 Dec 1, Jonathan Williams reading at Polytechnic of Central London, 1973; 60 mins, continued on 14/1/67.

MOTTRAM: 14/1/33, 13 Jul 1979, Partial Side A. Jonathan Williams reading at Polytechnic of Central London, [30 mins?].

MOTTRAM: 14/1/34. 30 Oct 1980. Side A. Jonathan Williams reading at King's Poetry Series, King's College London, [60] mins.

MOTTRAM: 14/1/53, 1985 Apr 14. Jonathan Williams reading at "UCSD"; 60 mins.

MOTTRAM: 14/1/171, 1993 Oct 4, Side A. Tom Meyer reading at Workfortheeyetodo (London), 1993, Side B. Jonathan Williams reading at the same event; 60 mins.

CONTRIBUTORS

Dobree Adams, fiber artist and photographer, was introduced to JW and Tom Meyer by her husband-to-be Jonathan Greene. In 1974 they honeymooned in England, Scotland, and Wales and slept one night in the sauna at Corn Close on bales of peat moss. Dobree, who was at one time treasurer of the Jargon Society, farms and gardens and makes art on a river bottom of the Kentucky north of Frankfort.

Alex Albright edited the *North Carolina Literary Review* from 1992–96, which published Leverett T. Smith's JW interview in its Black Mountain College issue (1995). Alex and his wife, Elizabeth, live in Fountain, NC, where they operate Fountain General Store. He is the author of *The Forgotten First: B-1 and the Integration of the Modern Navy*, a finalist for the 2014 Montaigne Medal and a silver medalist for "best interior design" from the Independent Booksellers Association. He maintains a webpage that documents African-American Navy bands of World War II: www.rafountain.com/navy/

David Annwn published JW's *Metafours for Mysophobes*, wrote foreword and poems for *Catgut and Blossom: Jonathan Williams in England,* and interviewed JW at length for *Prospect into Breath*. He also published JW's tributes to Zukofsky and Mottram, and convened and introduced filmed readings of JW, Meyer's, and Cutt's readings at the October Gallery, London. A recipient of the Cardiff International Poetry Award and a Ferguson Centre award for African and Asian Studies, his books include *It Means Nothing to Me* and *The Last Hunting of the Lizopard*. His most recent collection of poems, *Disco Occident* (Knives, Forks and Spoons Press), was published in 2013.

Bob Arnold, poet, Longhouse publisher and bookseller, wrote this piece for his *Woodburners We Recommend* column on the Longhouse web site in April 2008. He lives in Vermont.

Michael Basinski, Curator of the Poetry Collection, SUNY-Buffalo and Director of UB Special Collections. He performs his work as a solo poet and in ensemble with the Don Metz Experience (D.M.E.). Among his recent books of poetry are *Poems of a Polish-American Boy Poems*, *Piglittuce*, and *Trailers*. His poems and other works have appeared in many magazines including *Dandelion, BoxKite, Antennae, Open Letter, First Offense, Lungfull, Tinfish, House Organ, Ferrum Wheel, End Note, Ur Vox, Damn the Caesars, Filling Station, fhole, Public Illumination, Eccolinguistics, Yellow Field, Western Humanities Review, Big Bridge, Mimeo Mimeo, Nerve Lantern, Vanitas, Talisman, Steel Bellows, Staging Ground, Lumox, Chiron Review*, and *Poetry*. He lives in Buffalo.

Robert Bertholf served as the Curator of the Poetry and Rare Books Collection at SUNY-Buffalo from 1979 until 2005, when he was named Charles D. Abbott Scholar of Poetry and the Arts. He retired in 2007. His areas of special interest and research included the poetry of Duncan, as well as that of Pound, William Carlos Williams, Stevens, and Olson. He wrote books celebrating and analyzing the work of writers such as Levertov, Duncan, Niedecker, Oppenheimer, and the artist Jess. He published widely in scholarly journals, and served for eight years as editor of the literary journal *Credences*. He also edited *Northwest Review*, and was former American editor of the Australian journal *New Poetry*. He served on the editorial boards of *The Journal of Modern Literature* and the *William Carlos Williams Review*. Bertholf died in February 2016.

Jed Birmingham writes occasional articles on William Burroughs, book collecting, and the Beat Generation for various publications such as *Beat Scene* and *Naked Lunch @ 50: Anniversary Essays* (2009). He is the contributing editor of RealityStudio.org, the premier Web site dedicated to William Burroughs, and was co-editor (with Kyle Schlesinger) of *Mimeo Mimeo*, a magazine and blog about the Mimeograph Revolution.

Victor Brand is a writer and journalist in New York. He has been published in *The Believer* and *Paper* magazines, and is the author of *In Numbers: Serial Publications by Artists Since 1955*. He is currently the standards editor at *The Huffington Post*. This essay was first published in 2006, in a limited edition rare book catalogue by Andrew Roth Inc, New York.

Basil Bunting, one of the most significant Modernist poets and the principle British Modernist poet, is best known for his long autobiographical poem, *Briggflatts*. His mentors included Pound, Yeats, and Zukofsky. For a time in his youth he was an assistant editor at the *Transatlantic Review*. He worked as an interpreter in Persia during World War II where he stayed until being expelled in 1952. Returning to his home in Newcastle he worked in obscurity for the next 12 years until being "rediscovered" by Tom Pickard. Pickard introduced him to the young poets of the avant-garde including JW who became a close friend. He died at the age of 85 after a short illness. There is a memorial to him in the Durham University Botanic Gardens.

Gary Carden is a writer, folklorist, and storyteller from Sylva, North Carolina. Carden has authored a number of collections of Appalachian folktales, and a volume of original stories entitled *Mason Jars in the Flood and Other Stories*. He received the North Carolina Award in Literature in 2012. His piece appeared in the *Smoky Mountain News*, Sylva, North Carolina, in March 2008, a few days after he posted it on the *Netwest Mountain Writers and Poets Blog*.

Poet Thomas A. Clark and artist Laurie Clark run Moschatel Press in Pittenweem, Fife, Scotland, where they publish numerous small books and cards. He has authored numerous works including a 1977 Jargon imprint *A Still Life, The Path to the Sea* (Arc, 2005), *Distance and Proximity* (Edinburgh University Press, 2001), and *The Hundred Thousand Places* (2008) and *Yellow & Blue* (2014) both from Carcanet. Laurie's drawings frequently elaborate Thomas' poems. Laurie illustrated Jargon Society postcard no. 12, *Homage to Barbara Jones*, with text by JW. Moschatel publications investigate "the book as imaginative space, the page as a framing device or as quiet around an image or a phrase, the turning of pages as revelation or delay."

From the window of his 7th floor apartment in downtown Philadelphia, poet Jim Cory enjoys a fine view of the Schuylkill Expressway and points west, where every day a new skyscraper magically appears. In the spring of 1998, he worked with JW to organize and edit the manuscript that became *Jubilant Thicket*, JW's last volume of selected poems, published in 2004 by Copper Canyon Press.

Reuben Cox is a photographer and luthier living in Los Angeles. He was born in Highlands, North Carolina in 1972 and attended The Cooper Union. JW and Tom's "heart-son," his most recent book of photography, *Corn Close, a Cottage in Dentdale*, was published by Green Shade in 2015. He is represented by Blackstone Gallery in New York City. Reuben is the owner of Old Style, a guitar shop in Los Angeles.

Thorns Craven is a native of Concord, NC, and has lived in Winston-Salem since 1969 with his wife Perry. He graduated from Washington & Lee University in 1962, served in the US Army in Germany for three years, and then graduated from the School of Law, University of North Carolina, in 1969. He was director of the Legal Aid Society of Northwest North Carolina for 21 years, became a certified mediator in 1992, and has practiced as a mediator since then. He served as treasurer of the Jargon Society from 1979 until the organization was dissolved in 2013. Upon dissolution the assets of the Jargon Society were transferred to the Black Mountain Museum + Arts Center. Because of his influence, JW became a huge fan of the Tour de France and learned to pronounce "Djamolidine Abdoujaparov."

A long-time friend and JW collaborator, Simon Cutts is a poet, artist, and editor, who has developed Coracle Press over the last forty years in its many publicational forms. His own concern is with the book and its mechanisms as a manifestation of the poem itself. He lives in Ireland with Erica Van Horn.

Richard Deming's collections of poems are *Let's Not Call It Consequence* and *Day for Night*. He is also the author of *Listening on All Sides: Towards an Emersonian Ethics of Reading*. In 2012, he was awarded the Berlin Prize by the American Academy in Berlin. He is currently Director of Creative Writing at Yale University.

Robert Duncan was one of the most important 20th century American poets, a devotee of H.D. and the Western esoteric tradition, and was a key figure in the San Francisco Renaissance. Associated with the poets of the New American Poetry and Black Mountain College, his many books of poetry include *Heavenly City Earthly City* (1947), *The Opening of the Field* (1960), *Roots and Branches* (1964), *A Book of Resemblances* (1966), *Bending the Bow* (1968), *Ground Work I: Before the War* (1984), and *Ground Work II: In the Dark* (1987). In 1944, Duncan wrote the landmark essay *The Homosexual in Society*.

John Furnival's prints and drawings connect his antecedents in the Dada and Surrealist movements to his affinities and associations in the early 1960s with the innovators of Concrete poetry, the Beat poets, and the Fluxus and Mail Art movements. He taught at Bath Academy of Art at Corsham, and latterly at Bath, in its seminal period in the 1960s and '70s. In 1964, he co-founded the press, Openings, with Dom Sylvester Houédard, working with artists and poets in an early move to make art "mailable"—these included Tom Phillips and Edwin Morgan, and also Ian Hamilton Finlay with whom he collaborated for a period for the Wild Hawthorn Press. John and his wife Astrid—famous as an artist-knitter ... see her Samuel Palmer sweater seen in the JW *Life in Pictures* gallery of this book—live in England.

Harry Gilonis is a poet, editor, publisher, and (intermittently) a critic. His piece was first published in *Catgut and Blossom: Jonathan Williams in England* (London: Coracle Press, 1989). His books include *Reliefs* (hard-Pressed Poetry/Pig Press); *Pibroch* (Morning Star); *Reading Hölderlin on Orkney* (Grille/Simple Vice); *walk the line* (Last Adana); and a collaborative renga, *from far away* (Oasis Books), co-written with Tony Baker. He has also published collaborations with visual artists: *Axioms* (Ankle Press) with David Connearn; and *An Envelope Interior History of Art* and *Forty Fungi*, both with Erica van Horn (both Coracle). A poem *i.m. Richard Caddel*, and his obituary of Caddel, appeared in *Jacket* issue 22. He is the only living poet to be published on the lawn of London's Serpentine Gallery.

Jonathan Greene is the author of mostly poetry. He first got in touch with JW in 1963, writing from San Francisco to him in England. That letter eventually led to the Gnomon publication of JW's long interview with Basil Bunting, *Descant on Rawthey's Madrigal*. Gnomon eventually published five more JW titles: *A Blue Ridge Weather Prophet Makes Twelve Stitches in Time on the Twelfth Day of Christmas, "I Shall Save One Land Unvisited": Eleven Southern Photographers, In the Azure over the Squalor: Ransackings & Shorings, Portrait Photographs* (co-published with Simon Cutts at Coracle), and *JW/50* (which Greene edited and co-published with David Wilk's *Truck*). Greene also designed a number of other JW titles: *Blues & Roots/Rue & Bluets* (Duke University Press), and *Jubilant Thicket: New & Selected Poems* (Copper Canyon). Among Jargon titles he designed is the only one to make "real" money, Ernest Mickler's *White Trash Cooking*. Recently he designed *Corn Close: A Cottage in Dentdale* with photographs by Reuben Cox, texts by Thomas Meyer and Anne Midgette, published by Green Shade.

Ross Hair is a lecturer in American Literature at the University of East Anglia. He is the author of *Ronald Johnson's Modernist Collage Poetry* (Palgrave Macmillan, 2010) and *Avant-Folk: Small Press Poetry Networks 1950 to the Present* (Liverpool University Press, 2016). His writings on modern American and British poetry have appeared in, among other publications, the *Journal of Modern Literature, Texas Studies in Literature and Language*, and *Reliquiæ*. His poetry has been published in numerous magazines including *LVNG, Shearsman, The Cultural Society*, and *from a Compost*.

Mike Harding is an English singer, songwriter, comedian, author, poet, folklore enthusiast, dedicated fell-walker, broadcaster, and multi-instrumentalist, and a long-time Corn Close friend of JW and Thomas Meyer. JW's *Eight Days in Eire: Or, Nothing So Urgent as Mañana* includes photographs by Harding. http://www.mikeharding.co.uk/

Neal Hutcheson is an Emmy award-winning documentary filmmaker whose work centers on issues of culture and heritage in transition. Honors include a Midsouth Emmy for *First Language–The Race to Save Cherokee*, a Midsouth Emmy nomination for *Coresounders–Living from the Sea*, a Southeast Emmy for *The Last One*, the Brown-Hudson Folklore award from the NC Folklore Society, the North Carolina Filmmaker Award from the Carolina Film and Video Festival, and an Arts Fellowship from the North

Carolina Arts Council. His work has been featured on PBS, The Documentary Channel, Sundance, and History.

Kenneth Irby was an American poet oftentimes associated with the Black Mountain Poets, particularly Duncan, Dorn, and Creeley. His last book, *The Intent On: Collected Poems, 1962–2006* (North Atlantic Books, 2009) climaxed the over 20 books and chapbooks during his career. In 2010 the Poetry Society of America awarded Irby the prestigious Shelley Memorial Award. Irby died in 2015.

James Jaffe is a bookseller specializing in literature and art, manuscripts, letters, and archives. His Green Shade imprint published *A Garden Carried in a Pocket: The Letters of Jonathan Williams & Guy Davenport, 1964–1968* (2004), and *Corn Close: A Cottage in Dentdale*, with photographs by Reuben Cox, essays by Thomas Meyer and Anne Midgette, and a JW Time-Line (2015). This essay appeared on Jaffe's blog after Jonathan's death. www.jamesjaffe.com

Ronald Johnson and JW were partners for ten years. Ronald Johnson (1935–1998) was the author of the long poem *ARK*, as well as several shorter collections, including *The Book of the Green Man, The Valley of the Many-Colored Grasses, RADI OS*, and *The Shrubberies*. For over a decade, beginning in the late 1950s, he was JW's companion, during which time they hiked together the length of the Appalachian Trail, traveled extensively around the British Isles, and made a Grand Tour of Europe. Born in Kansas, educated at Columbia University, enlisted in the U.S. Army, Johnson lived for over twenty-five years in San Francisco, before returning to Kansas, to Topeka, where he lived with his father for the final four years of his life.

Robert Kelly, currently the first Poet Laureate of Dutchess County, is the author of many books of poetry, fiction, and essays. His most recent publications are *A Voice Full of Cities: Collected Essays, Uncertainties, Opening the Seals, The Hexagon*, and *Heart Thread*. His website is http://rk-ology.com/ and his blog is http://rk-ology.blogspot.com/. He teaches in the Written Arts Program at Bard College, and is married to the translator Charlotte Mandell.

Charles Lambert was born in the United Kingdom but has lived in Italy for most of his adult life. His latest novel, *The Children's Home* (Scribner), is set in neither country. Earlier books include three novels, a collection of prize-winning short stories, and a memoir *With a Zero at its Heart*.

Roger Manley is currently director of the Gregg Museum at North Carolina State University. He co-directed the award-winning film *MANA-beyond belief*, founded the META Conferences at Black Mountain, authored several books for the Weird US series (including *Weird Carolinas*), and guest curated for dozens of institutions, including three blockbuster exhibitions for the American Visionary Art Museum, beginning with its inaugural show, *Tree of Life*. With Tom Patterson, he served on the Jargon Society's Southern Visionary Folk Art Project in the mid-1980s. He traveled the South with JW and Guy Mendes from 1984 to 1991 to help create JW's yet to be published *Walks to the Paradise Garden: Outsiders in the South*. Manley has produced numerous award-winning books, catalogues, videos, and films as well as exhibitions of his own photographs, which are in the collections of a number of internationally recognized institutions.

James Maynard received his PhD in English from the SUNY-Buffalo, where he is the Visiting Assistant Curator of the Poetry Collection. He wrote his dissertation on *Robert Duncan: The Sublime, and Pragmatism/process Philosophy*; and co-edited New Directions' single-volume republication of *Ground Work: Before the War/In the Dark* (2006). His essays and reviews have appeared in such publications as *Mimeo Mimeo*, *Journal of Modern Literature*, and *Process Studies*. He is currently editing a collection of essays on Duncan's late writings and a volume of Duncan's collected critical prose.

A native of Hillsborough, NC, Elizabeth Matheson earned her BA from Sweet Briar College and studied at the Penland School of Crafts with John Menapace. Exhibitions of her work include Hollins University, Virginia Polytechnic Institute, North Carolina Museum of Art, Duke University, National Humanities Center, Craven Allen Gallery, Green Hill Center for North Carolina Art, and Gregg Museum. Her work is in the collections of Duke University, Ackland Museum, and North Carolina Museum of Art, among many others. Her books include *To See: Poems by Michael McFee* (NC Wesleyan Press, 1991), *Blithe Air: Photographs of England, Wales, and Ireland* (Jargon, 1995), and *Shell Castle, Portrait of a North Carolina House* (Safe Harbor Books, 2008). In 2004, she received the North Carolina Award for Excellence in the Fine Arts, an award also received by JW in 1977. Matheson's must recent exhibitions have spotlighted her Italian and Cuban photographs.

Michael McFee has taught poetry writing at UNC-Chapel Hill since 1990. He is the author of ten books of poems—most recently a full-length collection *That Was Oasis* (Carnegie Mellon University Press, 2012), a chapbook of one-line poems *The Smallest Talk* (Bull City Press, 2007)—as well as one collection of prose, *The Napkin Manuscripts: Selected Essays and an Interview* (Tennessee, 2006).

Poet and translator Ann McGarrell, wife of painter James McGarrell, described herself as "internationally unknown." A longtime Jargonaut, her books are *Flora: Poems* (Perishable Press, 1990), *Revenants: A New Orleans Reliquary* with photos by Julie Dermansky (Blurb, 2008), and *Gwen and Other Poems*—based on the life of the Welsh painter Gwen John (Cove House Press, 2012). She won the 1997 PEN/Renato Poggioli Prize for her translation of Vittoria Ronchey's *Il Volto di Iside* (*The Face of Isis*). Other translations include *From Luminous Shade*—Ungaretti's *Il dolore* (Harbor Mountain Press, 2011), Alberto Bevilacqua's *Eros* (Steerforth Press, 1996), and Henri Michaux poems in the anthology *Someone wants to steal my name* edited by Nin Andrews (Cleveland State University Press, 2003). Ann had been currently translating a collection of the painter Balthus' love letters to his first wife, Annette de Watteville; and had recently completed a cycle of hate/love poems, *Reader, I Buried Him*—a commission by a scorned lover which will eventually see publication. Ann died in January 2016.

James McGarrell, husband of the late poet Ann McGarrell, is an American painter and printmaker known for painting lush figurative interiors and landscapes. He began his distinguished academic career at Reed College and then at Indiana University. In 1981 he moved to School of Fine Arts at Washington University—St. Louis, where he remained until his retirement from teaching in 1993. He has been an artist-in-residence most notably at Skowhegan, International School in Umbria, Rice University, University of Utah, Arizona State University, and Dartmouth College. He has exhibited in notable museums, galleries, and exhibitions throughout the world, including five Whitney Annuals and Biennials; the Carnegie International exhibition (1958 and 1983); *New Images of Man* at the MOMA (1960); the Dunn International at the Tate Gallery (1963 and 1964); Documenta III (1964) in Kassel, Germany; and USA Art Vivant at the Musée des Augustins, in Toulouse. McGarrell's paintings are in the permanent collections of MOMA, MET, Whitney, Hirshhorn, Art Institute of Chicago, Pennsylvania Academy of Fine Arts, Portland Museum of Art, St. Louis Art Museum, Santa Barbara Museum of Art, Hamburg Museum of Art, and many other public and private collections. McGarrell is a member of the National Academy and Correspondent Member of the Académie des Beaux-Arts de l'Institut de France. In 1995 he was the recipient of the Jimmy Ernst Lifetime Achievement Award from the American Institute of Arts and Letters. www.jamesmcgarrell.com

After attending Yale University, photographer John Menapace worked at Oxford University Press. In 1956 he became Director of Design and Production at Duke University Press. Although self-taught, he had fruitful exchanges with Ansel Adams, Minor White, and Nathan Lyons. He initiated a studio course at Duke University in 1972, and that same year Penland School of Crafts invited him to teach the first of four summer workshops. Menapace mentored a community of North Carolina photographers, among them Elizabeth Matheson and Caroline Vaughan. In 1984, the North Carolina Museum of Art gave him their first show devoted solely to photography. 2006 saw a one-man show, *With Hidden Noise,* at the Gallery of Art and Design (now the Gregg) at NC State University. The book, includes a poem of tribute to Menapace by this book's editor Jeffery Beam. Jargon published *Letter in a Klein Bottle* (1984). Menapace's work, library, and archives now belong to the Gregg Museum. Since July 2012, scholars have been cataloging and archiving the trove. Never-before-exhibited selections they discovered form the core of *Smokes and Mirrors: Reflections of the Self in Photographs* (2014) an exhibition at the Gregg Museum. He died in 2010.

Guy Mendes, raised in New Orleans, graduated from the University of Kentucky, where he played on the freshman basketball team, worked for *The Kentucky Kernel*, studied creative writing with Wendell Berry, and helped start the underground newspaper *blue-tail fly*. In 1967 he met Ralph Eugene Meatyard, who would become his friend and mentor; in 1969, Jonathan Williams, with whom he would travel on book projects like *Walks to the Paradise Garden: Outsiders in the South*; and in 1970 he spent a year working with writer/photographer James Baker Hall. His books: *Local Light*, an anthology of 100 years of photographs made in Kentucky (1976); *Light At Hand* (1986), a monograph of 45 of Mendes' photographs; and *40/40 Forty Years Forty Portraits* (2010); as well as numerous publications and exhibitions. His work has appeared in magazines such as *Aperture, Newsweek, the Smithsonian, Mother Jones, Playboy,* and *Southern Accents*; and exhibited at International Center for Photography, Aperture Gallery, New Orleans Museum of Art, Ogden Museum of Southern Art, High Museum in Atlanta, and Kentucky Museum of Art and Design, among others. His prints are in numerous collections including Ashley Judd's, Willie Nelson's, Cincinnati Art Museum, New Orleans Museum of Art, University of Kentucky Art Museum, Fidelity Investments national headquarters, and Maker's Mark Distillery. Mendes lives in Lexington with his wife Page. anntowergallery.com and guymendes.com.

Thomas Meyer has always lived where there are rain and cows. Presently with his husband at the foot of the Nantahala mountains in western North Carolina and the Eden Valley in northwest England. Recent books of his include *Porcelain Pillow* (Lunar Chandelier Collective), and *Essay Stanzas* (The Song Cave); and translations *daode jing* (Flood Editions) *Lizard or Easy Answers: They Are None Being a Novel Tracing of the Yi Jing/ I Ching* (BlazeVOX), and *Beowulf* (punctum books). Since publication in the original online *Lord of Orchard, Kintsugi* has appeared in a limited letterpress sewn edition, with the Robert Kelly introduction, and artwork by Erica Van Horn from Punch Press (2009); and a trade paperback from Flood Editions (2011). He was partner to JW for almost 40 years.

Anne Midgette first met JW when she was two through her father, the painter Willard Midgette. Thanks to her stepfather, Donald B. Anderson, who owns Corn Close, she continued to know him all her life. She has been the classical music critic at *The Washington Post* since 2008. She recently contributed an essay to *Corn Close: A Cottage in Dentdale*, a photo book by Reuben Cox documenting JW's and Tom Meyer's part-time home in England. She has also written for the *New York Times*, the *Los Angeles Times*, the *Wall Street Journal*, and various other publications, and is co-author of *The King and I* (about Luciano Pavarotti and his manager) and *My Nine Lives* (the memoir of the pianist Leon Fleisher).

John C. Mitzel devoted his life to securing the civil rights of and promoting the writing of LGBT people. As proprietor of Boston's Calamus Bookstore, he hosted writers and activists from 2000 until his death in 2013. He was a Founder of *Fag Rag* and of Boston's Gay Pride Parade and was voted posthumously as the co-Honoree of the Parade with Massachusetts Governor Deval Patrick in 2014. He wrote articles, columns, books (a biography of John Horne Burns and six novels) and poetry in a career stretching 50 years.

Eric Mottram (1924–1995) was an English poet, critic, and editor associated with Bob Cobbing's Writers Forum and the British Poetry Revival. Retiring from King's College London in 1990 with the title Emeritus Professor of English and American Literature, Mottram served as editor-in-chief of *Poetry Review* (London) from 1971 to 1977. A close friend to JW, Mottram, like JW, took a decidedly transatlantic approach to the study of contemporary Anglophone poetry which exacerbated what Peter Barry and other critics now regard as the Poetry Wars of the 1970s. His archive, catalogued by poet Bill Griffiths, is presently maintained at King's College.

Peter O'Leary is the author of several books of poetry, most recently *The Sampo* (The Cultural Society). He has also edited several collections of Ronald Johnson's poetry, most recently *ARK* (Flood Editions) and *The Book of the Green Man* (Uniformbooks). He teaches at the School of the Art Institute of Chicago, edits Verge Books with John Tipton, and lives in Oak Park, Illinois. His piece is printed with the permission of The Poetry Collection of the University Libraries, SUNY-Buffalo.

Tom Patterson, an independent writer, art critic, and curator, lives in Winston-Salem, NC. Through his apprenticeship with JW, he led Jargon's Southern Visionary Folk Art Project, a three-year effort to document examples of this art in several southern states. This resulted in his first two books, *St. EOM in The Land of Pasaquan* (Jargon Society, 1987), and *Howard Finster: Stranger from Another World*, (Abbeville Press, 1989). His first curatorial project, a 20-artist show titled "Southern Visionary Folk Artists" (co-curated with Roger Manley, 1985) broke new ground in introducing this work to contemporary art audiences. He went on to curate a number of exhibitions at museums and art galleries across the United States. Patterson is also the author of *Contemporary Folk Art: Treasures from the Smithsonian American Art Museum* (Watson-Guptill Publications, 2001) and several exhibition catalogs. Since the early 1980s his writings have appeared in art magazines including *afterimage, American Ceramics, American Craft, Aperture, ARTnews, Art Papers, BOMB, Folk Art, New Art Examiner, Public Art Review*, and *Raw Vision*.

Michael Rumaker is best known for his semi-autobiographical novels that document his life as a gay man in the 1950s and after. He is the author of *Gringos and Other Stories* (Grove Press, NC Wesleyan College Press [new edition]), *Pizza: Selected Poems* (Circumstantial Productions), *Selected Letters of Michael Rumaker* (The CUNY Poetics Document Initiative: Lost & Found), and *Robert Duncan in San Francisco: Expanded Edition* (City Lights). His novel *Pagan Days* (Circumstantial Productions) is told from the perspective of an eight-year-old boy struggling to understand his gay self. *Black Mountain Days* (Black Mountain Press, Spuyten Duyvil [new edition]), a memoir of his time at Black Mountain College, includes many portraits of students and faculty (including Creeley, Olson, and JW) during its last years, 1952–1956. He is a graduate of Black Mountain College and Columbia University and taught at City College of New York and The New School for Social Research.

Kyle Schlesinger is a poet, printer, and teacher living in Austin, Texas.

Poet, teacher, and editor Charley Shively taught at Boston State College and later at University of Massachusetts (Boston). His life's work was as an activist, critic, cultural commentator, and poet. A major force in Gay Liberation in the United States, in the 1970s and early '80s he helped found *Fag Rag* (the first national gay male publication) and *Gay Community News*, the non-profit legal group Gay and Lesbian Advocates and Defenders (GLAD), and the Fenway Community Health Center. His critical literary and political essays—as well as over 500 reviews, columns, and letters— appeared in *Fag Rag*, *Gay Community News*, *Gay Sunshine*, and in a host of other scholarly, literary, and independent journals. He published two groundbreaking works of Walt Whitman scholarship *Calamus Lovers: Walt Whitman's Working-Class Camerados* (1987) and *Drum Beats: Walt Whitman's Civil War Boy Lovers* (1989), and has edited works by the American anarchist Stephen Pearl Andrews, and American political philosopher and anarchist Lysander Spooner. Now living with Alzheimer's, Shively still resides in Cambridge, Mass.

Dale Smith is a poet and critic who lives in Toronto, Ontario, where he teaches at Ryerson University. Recent publications include *Slow Poetry in America* (2014) and *Poets Beyond the Barricade: Rhetoric, Citizenship, and Dissent after 1960* (2012).

Diana C. Stoll is a writer and editor based in Asheville, North Carolina. She writes frequently for arts publications, including *Aperture* magazine, where she served for thirteen years as senior editor. She is the co-author, with Lin Arison, of *Desert and Cities* (Chronicle Books, 2016). This essay was originally published in *Aperture* magazine, number 192, Fall 2008.

Erica Van Horn, artist and writer, was born in New Hampshire, and then lived and worked in a lot of different places in both the United States and Europe. In 1997, she moved to Ireland with Simon Cutts. Together they continue to work on the projects, exhibitions, and publications of Coracle Press. *Living Locally*, published by Uniformbooks in 2014, chronicles the daily detail of her life walking and working in rural Tipperary.

David Wilk is a poet, editor, publisher, and entrepreneur. He was editor and publisher of *Truck* magazine and Truck Press, which issued two books by Jonathan Williams, *Untinears & Antennae for Maurice Ravel* and *Dementations on Shank's Mare*, and co-published *JW/50: A 50th Birthday Celebration for Jonathan Williams* with Gnomon Press.

Wilk was Literature Program Director at the National Endowment for the Arts in the Carter administration, founder of Truck Distribution Service and co-founder of Inland Book Company, which distributed Jargon Society publications for many years. Wilk's poetry and nonfiction have been published in literary magazines and by independent presses, most recently the chapbook, *Lorine Niedecker: The Poet in Her Place*, from Woodland Pattern in Milwaukee.

He is on the boards of the Poetry Project at St. Mark's Church and CLMP (Community of Literary Magazines and Presses), podcasts about books and publishing at *Writerscast.com* and also manages Prospecta Press.

ACKNOWLEDGMENTS

This book would not exist without the cooperation of many individuals, especially the Jargonauts old and new, the Jonathan Williams and Jargon enthusaists, and the critics and scholars all who have contributed to it. Thomas Meyer's support and encouragement for the project was profoundly important, as well as his lending an ear and memory to the process of gathering and refining details. James Maynard (former Assistant Curator; current Curator) and Michael Basinski (outgoing Curator) of the Poetry Collection, State University of New York at Buffalo offered Richard Owens, with Jonathan's blessing, carte blanche in handling the JW/Jargon Society Archive from 2006–2008 for the online feature which was the basis for this book. Both continued to provide support, advice, and clarifications during the production of this manuscript. Our thanks to John Tranter and Al Filreis at *Jacket* magazine for publishing the original *Lord of Orchards* feature and for permission to expand as a print book. The original feature will remain online. Thanks again to Al Filreis, and also to Rachel Blau DuPlessis, Rod Smith, and Steve Clay for assisting with Jeffery Beam's failed attempt to connect with Barry Alpert in hopes of reprinting the *VORT* interview. To Steve Clay again, and Michael Bronski and Bernard Moxham thanks for help locating some other individuals.

Jeffery Beam extends Jonathan's thyrsus to Dobree Adams, Jonathan Greene, Ross Hair, Neal Hutcheson, James Jaffe, Guy Mendes, James McGarrell, the late Ann McGarrell, Ann Midgette, Rich Owens, and Erica Van Horn who served not only as encouraging spirits but delivering angels when he ran into deadends or confusions along the way. He would also like to thank his husband, Stanley Finch, for his patience and understanding during most of 2016 while he struggled with computer problems and spent more time daily with the manuscript than anticipated.

Beam and Owens would also like to express special gratitude to those writers and artists who stepped forward for this expanded edition. And of course, they are deeply grateful to David Wilk for accepting the book with such enthusiasm and making it a reality.

Basil Bunting: *Comment on Jonathan Williams* reproduced from *A Fifti-eth Birthday Celebration for Jonathan Williams* (*Truck* 21, Gnomon Press 1979) and is reproduced here with the kind permission of the Bunting estate.

Since the publication of *À mon cher Stodge*, Ann McGarrell has died and we thank her husband, James McGarrell, for permission to reprint her piece.

Anne Midgette: *On With It*—A version of this piece originally ran in *The Washington Post*. Reprinted with the permission of the author.

Since the publication of *Jonathan Williams: An Appreciation*, author John Mitzel has died and we thank his brother David, for permission to reprint his piece.

Ronald Johnson: *A Microscopic/Telescopic Collage of The Empire Finals at Verona* originally appeared in *VORT* #4 (Fall 1973) and is reproduced here with the permission of the Estate of Ronald Johnson.

Charles Olson: *For a Man Gone to Stuttgart Who Left an Automobile behind Him*. Works by Charles Olson © The Estate of Charles Olson. "For a Man from Stuttgart" is reproduced here with the kind permission of the estate.

Charles Olson: *Nota to Jammin' the Greek Scene* was first published in Jonathan Williams' *Jammin the Greek Scene* (Jargon 1956). Works by Charles Olson © The Estate of Charles Olson.

Robert Duncan: Preface to Jonathan Williams' *Elegies and Celebrations* was first published in Williams' *Elegies and Celebrations* (Jargon 1962) and has since been out of print. It is reproduced here with the kind permission of the Jess Collins Trust and the Estate of Jonathan Williams. All material by Robert Duncan © the Jess Collins Trust.

Ross Hair: *"Hemi-demi-semi barbaric yawps"—Jonathan Williams and Black Mountain*. An earlier version of this article appeared in *Black Mountain College Studies* 3 (2012). Reprinted here with the permission of the author.

Eric Mottram: *An Introduction—"Stay In and Use Both Hands"* was first published as the introduction to Jonathan Williams' *Niches Inches: New and Selected Poems* (Jargon 1982) and is reproduced here with the kind permis-sion of the Eric Mottram estate and Jargon Society.

Kenneth Irby: *"america's largest openair museum"* first appeared as an extended review of Jonathan Williams' *Elite/Elate Poems: Selected Poems 1971–75* and *Portrait Photographs* in *Parnassus: Poetry in Review* 8.2 (1980).

Since the publication of the online feature, Irby has died, but it is reproduced here with his permission for further editions.

Charley Shively: *Toiling in the Bullpen—The Blues of Colonel Williams* first appeared as an extended review of Jonathan Williams' *An Ear in Bartram's Tree: Selected Poems 1957–1967*, *The Loco-Logodaedalist in Situ: Selected Poems 1968–1970*, and *Blue & Roots/Rue & Bluets: A Garland for the Appalachians* in *Gay Sunshine*, Spring 1976, No. 28. It is reproduced here with the kind permission of the author's literary executor, Michael Bronski.

Michael McFee: *"Reckless and Doomed"—Jonathan Williams and Jargon* originally appeared in *Small Press Magazine*, September/October 1985 and is reproduced here with the permission of the author.

Ronald Johnson: *Jonathan (Chamberlain) Williams* originally appeared in 1980 in *American Poets since World War II. Dictionary of Literary Biography* Vol. 5. Donald J. Greiner, ed. (Detroit: Gale Research) and is reproduced here with the permission of the Estate of Ronald Johnson and Cengage Learning/Nelson Education.

Jonathan Williams: Image Gallery: Photographs 4, 11, 16, 17, 18, 20, 22, 23 and 24 are from the former Jargon Society website which is no longer available since Jargon was absorbed into the Black Mountain College Museum and Arts Center in Asheville, North Carolina. It is hoped that the website might be revived by BMCAC eventually as it also contained many other JW and Jargon materials otherwise not readily available. The photographs are reproduced with the kind permission of the Estate of Jonathan Williams. All other photographs, excepting the two listed below, are reproduced from prints held in the Jonathan Williams/Jargon Society Archive at the Poetry and Rare Books Collection, State University of New York at Buffalo and appear here with their generous support and permission, as well as when possible, the direct permission of the photogrpaher. Since the publication of the *Jacket* feature the Jonathan Williams photographic collection has become part of the Beinecke Rare Book and Manuscript Library. Our thanks to Nancy Kuhl, Curator, Poetry, Yale Collection of American Literature for her support of this project. All works by Jonathan Williams are © copyright The Estate of Jonathan Williams with thanks to Thomas Meyer.

The photo by Robert Giard originally published in Particular Voices: Portraits of Gay and Lesbian Writers, © copyright the Estate of Robert

Giard. Reprinted with the permission of Jonathan Silin, executer of the Estate of Robert Giard.

The photo by Ralph Eugene Meatyard *Jonathan Williams with Thrysus* reprinted with the permission of the Fraenkel Gallery and © copyright of the estate of Ralph Eugene Meatyard.

Vic Brand: *Burr, Salvage, Yoke* originally appeared in *Associations*, a limited edition catalog from Andrew Roth's New York photographic gallery, 2006.

Our appreciation to Mary Anne Redding at the Turchin Center for the Visual Arts, Appalachian State University-Boone, North Carolina for her quick assistance with and providing images for Tom Patterson's essay *If You Can Kill a Snake with It, It Ain't Art*. Photos reprinted with the permission of the Turchin Center.

Since the publication of *The Jargon Society and Contemporary Literary History*, author Robert J. Bertholf has died. We appreciate the permission of his wife, Anne, to reprint his piece.

Neal Hutcheson: *Inclemented That Way*. Texts from the documents from the Neal Hutcheson Collection at the Louis Round Wilson Special Collections Library at the University of North Carolina at Chapel Hill transcribed and reprinted with the permission of Neal Hutcheson.

SPECIAL THANKS

The editors and publisher would like to thank book designer Barbara Aronica-Buck for her skillful and excellent work on this project, and proofreader Jeremy Townsend for her dedication to detail at every turn.

Assembling a collection of pieces by many different writers creates special challenges. The editors and publisher are responsible for any and all errors that may be found here, and apologize in advance to our contributors and readers. Blame us, not the proofreader! We hope JW will look kindly on our efforts from on high or wherever his spirit may be watching from.

ABOUT THE EDITORS

Friend of Jonathan Williams and Jargonaut for just shy of three decades, Jeffery Beam's over 20 works include *The Broken Flower* and *Gospel Earth* (Skysill), *The New Beautiful Tendons: Collected Queer Poems 1969–2012* (Spuyten Duyvil), *An Elizabethan Bestiary: Retold* (Horse & Buggy), *Visions of Dame Kind* (Jargon 113), the CD *What We Have Lost* (Green Finch), and the Carnegie Hall premiered (Albany Record *New Growth*) song cycle *Life of the Bee* (with Lee Hoiby). Composers Holt McCarley and Steven Serpa are working on other songs and song cycles. Ceramicist Judith Ernst is creating a series of vessels using his poems. Other JW works include the memorial quote book *A Hornet's Nest*, the *NC Literary Review* essay *A Snowflake Orchard and What I Found There: An Informal History of the Jargon Society*, and the *Rain Taxi* interview *Tales of a Jargonaut*. Forthcoming is *Spectral Pegasus/Dark Movements* (2017), a collaboration with Welsh painter Clive Hicks-Jenkins. He is poetry editor emeritus of *Oyster Boy Review*, a retired UNC-Chapel Hill botanical librarian, and resides in Hillsborough, NC.

Richard Owens is the author of several volumes of poetry, including *Delaware Memoranda* (BlazeVOX, 2008), *Embankments* (Interbirth, 2009), *No Class* (Barque, 2012), *Clutch* (Vigilance Society, 2012) and *Ballads* (Habenicht, 2012; Eth Press, 2015). His poetry has appeared in *Cambridge Literary Review*, *Hi Zero*, *Poetry Wales*, *Shearsman*, and elsewhere; his critical comments and essays have appeared in *Chicago Review*, *Colorado Review*, *Open Letter*, *Paideuma*, and *Poetry Project Newsletter*. Since 2005 Owens has edited *Damn the Caesars*, a journal of contemporary poetry and poetics, and Punch Press—an imprint featuring broadside, chapbook, and book-length works. He currently resides in Southern Maine.